TARDIS Eruditorum
An Unofficial Critical History of Doctor Who

Volume 3: Jon Pertwee

Philip Sandifer

ERUDITORUM
PRESS

Philip Sandifer

Eruditorum Press, 11 Grandview Ave, Danbury, CT, 06810

First published in 2013 using CreateSpace

Copyright 2013, Philip Sandifer

Doctor Who, the TARDIS, and all related concepts are copyright BBC Worldwide, and are used under the principle of Fair Use.

All rights reserved. Don't be a jerk.

TARDIS Eruditorum Volume 3: Jon Pertwee

To Meredith Collins, who I do not think has ever seen a Jon Pertwee episode of Doctor Who, but without whom this book would not exist.

Philip Sandifer

Acknowledgments

The usual suspects – all correctly spelled words and remotely coherent sentences are due to the handiwork of the superlative Millie Hadziomerovic. The gorgeous cover design is the work of James Taylor. No, not that James Taylor. He's even better than that one.

As mentioned in the dedication, large portions of this book exist because of the influence of Meredith Collins, who over the years of our friendship, introduced me to David Bowie, glam rock, dandies, and, really, most good things in life.

I am endlessly grateful for the support and friendship of those around me. Jill Buratto, the love of my life, has put up with far more in the course of my working on thus project than is entirely sane. Anna Wiggins, the interlocutor for most of my thought on this project, not only put up with my rambling but helped explain it.

Thanks are also due to the readers and commenters who have elevated my blog from the ramblings of a pretentious Doctor Who fan into a vibrant community it is my honor to tend to.

Table of Contents

Introduction 1

Pop Between Realities, Home in Time for Tea 1 (*Monty Python's Flying Circus*) 5

I Do Tend to Get Involved (*Spearhead from Space*) 14

Eh? Doctor Who? (*The Silurians*) 27

Where Spacemen Live (The Ambassadors of Death) 38

Go Down Go Down Go Down Go Down (*Inferno*) 48

Time Can Be Rewritten: *The Scales of Injustice* 60

Pop Between Realities, Home in Time for Tea: *Doomwatch* and *The Atrocity Exhibition* 67

He Was a Friend at First (*Terror of the Autons*) 76

Fear Makes Companions (*The Mind of Evil*) 88

This Pretty Little Thing Here (*The Claws of Axos*) 97

The People in Charge of Those Laws (*Colony in Space*) 108

The Evil Has No Name (*The Daemons*) 119

Pop Between Realities, Home in Time for Tea (*The Wicker Man, Chariots of the Gods?, Ace of Wands*) 130

You're Just a Soldier (*Day of the Daleks*) 142

A Life of Ordered Calm (*The Curse of Peladon*) 153

Time Can Be Rewritten (*The Face of the Enemy*) 163

A Finely Tuned Response (*The Sea Devils*) 169

Time Can Be Rewritten Extra: *Who Killed Kennedy* 177

Change, My Dear (*The Mutants*) 183

Prove to Me I Am Not Mistaken (*The Time Monster*) 190

How Does the TARDIS Work? 199

Pop Between Realities, Home in Time for Tea: *The Rise and Fall of Ziggy Stardust and the Spiders from Mars* 205

Time Can Be Rewritten (*Verdigris*) 218

This Point of Singularity (*The Three Doctors*) 226

The Secret of Alchemy ("This Point of Singularity [*The Three Doctors*]") 243

The Outside Universe is Breaking Through (*Carnival of Monsters*) 248

The Sound of Empires Toppling (*Frontier in Space*) 256

A Thousand Years from a Disintegrated Home (*Planet of the Daleks*) 265

Time Can Be Rewritten Extra: *Find and Replace* 272

Tamper with the Forces of Creation (*The Green Death*) 277

Is There Any Way to Reconcile This with *Torchwood*? 290

Pop Between Realities, Home in Time for Tea (*Dad's Army*, the Three-Day Week) 293

Why Not Make Some Coffee? (*The Time Warrior*) 302

Books! The Best Weapons in the World! (*Invasion of the Dinosaurs*) 309

Time Can Be Rewritten Extra: *The Paradise of Death* 318

Pop Between Realities, Home in Time for Tea (*Moonbase 3*). 324

Poor, Pathetic Creatures (*Death to the Daleks*) 332

You Were Expecting Someone Else (*Countdown/TV Action*) 339

Too Narrow, Too Crippled (*The Monster of Peladon*) 346

Time Can Be Rewritten (*Interference*) 356

Be Childish Sometimes (*Planet of the Spiders*) 364

Now My Doctor: Jon Pertwee 376

Introduction

If you are reading this, it is probably because you've bought a copy of my book. Thank you for that. I really appreciate it. But that may not be the only reason you're reading it. Perhaps you're browsing a copy on a friend's bookshelf. Perhaps you found it illicitly on the Internet. Perhaps you're reading the "free sample" of the ebook. That's fine too. That said, I'm a self-employed writer about Doctor Who, and as paths to wealth go that's not a very sane one. The overwhelming majority of this book is already up for free on my blog (Google TARDIS Eruditorum), and these books are how I make my money. Which is to say, please, if you enjoy it, go buy it. I really appreciate it.

In the event you have no idea what book you're holding, let me explain to you, generally speaking, how this book works. First of all, here's what it isn't: a standard issue guidebook to Doctor Who. Those looking for the nitty-gritty facts of Doctor Who can probably get a decent sense of them by inference, but that's not what this book is for. There are no episode descriptions, cast lists, or lengthy discussions of the behind the scenes workings of the show. There are dozens of books that already do that, and a fair number of online sites. Nor is this a book of reviews. For those who want those things, I personally recommend the *Doctor Who Reference Guide*, *Doctor Who Ratings Guide*, and *A Brief History of Time (Travel)* – three superlative websites that were consulted for basically every one of these essays.

What this book *is* is an attempt to tell the story of Doctor Who. Not the story of how it was made, or the overall narrative of the Doctor's life, or anything like that, but the story of the idea that is Doctor Who, in this book from Jon Pertwee's arrival in 1970 to his departure in 1974, but there's more to come. Doctor Who is a rarity in the world – an extremely long-running serialized narrative. Even rarer, it's an extremely long-running serialized narrative that is not in a niche like soap operas or superhero comics – both provinces almost exclusively of die-hard fans. Doctor Who certainly has its die-hard fans (or, as I like to think of you, my target audience), but notably, it's also been, for much of its existence, absolutely mainstream family entertainment for an entire country.

What this means is that the story of Doctor Who is, in one sense, the story of the world from 1963 on. Politics, music, technological and social development, and all manner of other things have crossed paths with Doctor Who over the nearly fifty years of its existence, and by using Doctor Who as a focus, one can tell a story with far wider implications.

The approach I use to do this is one that I've, rather pompously I suppose, dubbed psychochronography. It draws its name from the concept of psychogeography – an artistic movement created by Guy Debord in 1955 and described as "the study of the precise laws and specific effects of the geographical environment, consciously organized or not, on the emotions and behavior of individuals." More contemporarily, the term is associated with writers like Iain Sinclair, who writes books describing lengthy walking tours of London that fuse his experience with the history of the places he walks, weaving them into a narrative that tries to tell the entire story of a place, and Alan Moore, who does the same thing while worshiping a snake.

Psychochronography, then, attempts the same feat by walking through time. Where walking through space involves little more than picking a direction and moving your feet rhythmically, walking through time without the aid of a TARDIS is a dodgier proposition. The easiest way is to take a specific object and trace its development through time, looking, as the psychogeographers do, at history, lived experience, and the odd connections that spring up.

And so this book is the first part of a walk through Doctor Who. The essays within it wear a lot of hats, and switch them rapidly. All involve a measure of critical reading (in the literary theory sense, not in the complaining sense) of Doctor Who stories to figure out what they are about. This generally means trying to peel back the onion skins of fan history that cloud a story with things "everybody knows." But it also involves looking at the legacy of stories, which often means looking at that onion skin and trying to explain how it got there. No effort is made to disguise the fact that the first appearance of the Time Lords is massive for instance, but on the other hand, the book still looks carefully at what their initial impact might have been.

This approach also means looking at how a story would (and could) have been understood by a savvy viewer of the time, and at how the story can be read as responding to the concerns of its time. That means that the essays tend to be long on cultural context. And, in the end, it also means looking at how I personally interact with these stories. This book has no pretense of objectivity. It is about my walking tour of Doctor Who. I try to be accurate, but I also try to be me.

To fully grab the scope of the topic, in addition to the meat of the book – entries covering all of the Doctor Who stories produced with Jon Pertwee as the lead actor – there are four other types of entries. The first are the "Time Can Be Rewritten" entries. One peculiar feature of Doctor Who is that its past is continually revisited. The bulk of these came in the form of novels written in the 90s and early 00s, but there are other examples. At the time of writing, for instance, Big Finish puts out new stories every year featuring the first eight Doctors. These entries cover occasional highlights from these revisitations, using them as clues to how these earlier eras are widely understood.

The second are the "Pop Between Realities, Home in Time for Tea" entries, which look at popular media and culture to build context for understanding Doctor Who. These entries usually crop up prior to the bits of Doctor Who they're most relevant for, and provide background and points of comparison for the show as it wrestles with the issues of its many times.

Third, there are the "You Were Expecting Someone Else" entries, which deal with spinoff material produced concurrently with Doctor Who but that, inevitably, has some significant differences from the approach of the televised material. These exist to give a broader sense of Doctor Who as a cultural object and, perhaps more importantly, because they're kind of fun.

Finally, there are some essays just thrown into the book version as bonuses. These mostly consist of me slogging my way through some established fan debate about Doctor Who and trying, no doubt fruitlessly, to provide the last word on the matter.

It's probably clear by this point that all of these entries began as blog entries on my blog, also called TARDIS Eruditorum. This book version, however, revises and expands every entry, as well as adding several new ones – mostly Time Can Be Rewritten entries, but a few others.

To this end, I should thank the many readers of the blog for their gratifying and edifying comments, which have kept the project going through more than one frustrating stretch. I should also thank the giants upon whose shoulders I stand when analyzing Doctor Who – most obviously Paul Cornell, Martin Day, and Keith Topping for *The Discontinuity Guide*, David J. Howe, Mark Stammers, and Stephen James Walker for the Doctor handbooks, Toby Hadoke and Rob Shearman for *Running Through Corridors*, and Lawrence Miles and Tat Wood for the sublimely brilliant *About Time* series, to which this book is a proud footnote. I'd also like to thank my tireless editor, Millie Hadziomerovic, who made this book better.

A final note – although I have expanded and revised the essays in this book from their original online versions, I have not attempted to smooth out the developing style of the entries. Much like the show it follows, this project has evolved and grown since its beginning, and I did not wish to alter that.

But most of all and most importantly, thank you, all of you. But most of all, thank you, dear reader. I hope you enjoy.

Pop Between Realities, Home in Time for Tea 1 (*Monty Python's Flying Circus*)

Before we start in on the Pertwee era proper, let's take a moment to glance elsewhere in the *Radio Times*, if only to set the scene. After all, it's not like we were going to make it through all of *TARDIS Eruditorum* without dealing with Monty Python. Still, there is something oddly dissonant in the idea that the Pertwee era and Monty Python are part and parcel of the same cultural moment. And yet they were unquestionably part of the same television landscape. The twelfth episode (Season One) of *Monty Python's Flying Circus*, "The Naked Ant," aired the day after the first episode of *Spearhead from Space*. The "Upper Class Twit of the Year" sketch aired the day after Jon Pertwee's debut. The first two episodes of the Jon Pertwee era were followed by the final two episodes of *Monty Python's Flying Circus* (Season One) just over twenty-four hours later – and on the same channel to boot. Those were, it's safe to say, a pretty impressive nine-day stretch of television.

This isn't surprising – the earliest days of colour transmission for the BBC are the sort of period you expect to see some major programs air. But the similarities between Monty Python and Jon Pertwee seem remote. One is explosively subversive; the other is in many ways the most establishment-bound era of its show. Is this, then, just a nifty coincidence? Or is there actually some fundamental understanding about Britain at the dawn of the '70s to be gained from knowing this strange factoid. As it happens, the answer is the latter, but to understand why we're going to have to answer a different question first – why the heck was Monty Python such a big deal?

This requires an overview of British comedy after World War II. As that topic is now two steps removed from what this book is actually about, I'm going to have to overgeneralize. If we leave Monty Python out of the equation for the moment, there are essentially two crucial things to know about British comedy from 1945–1970: Spike Milligan and the Carry On series. Among comedy snobs, there is no ambiguity over which one of these is superior. Spike Milligan is one of the most famed and accomplished comedians in history, and the Carry On films have a reputation round about the Friedberg/Seltzer comedies of the 2000s (*Scary Movie*, *Date Movie*, and the like).

Let's get them over with first, then. Since it's the Carry On film that directly mentions Doctor Who, let's look specifically at 1966's *Carry On Screaming* – a parody of the Hammer horror film line. (Hammer Films is a British production company that focused on gory horror movies, and is more often talked about in relation to the early Tom Baker era of Doctor Who.) *Carry On Screaming* also has, for the discriminating Doctor Who fan, appearances from Peter Butterworth (the Monk from *The Time Meddler* and *The Daleks' Master Plan*), Bernard Bresslaw (several Ice Warriors), and Jon Pertwee (if you don't know, I'm very sorry that you paid money for this book).

The essential premise of a Carry On film is delightfully formulaic. You take a popular genre and do a story in that genre in which every single character is replaced with a blundering idiot. So, for instance, in *Carry On Screaming* there is a sequence that is setup like a familiar horror movie trope. There's a monster kidnapping women, and the police investigate. This is straightforward. But the film takes all the figures this story requires: a girl to kidnap, boyfriend looking for his missing girlfriend, the police, a mad scientist, etc. – and portrays them all as incompetent buffoons. But more importantly, every character is aware of the incompetence of all of the other characters, although not, generally speaking, of their own.

So, for instance, in *Carry On Screaming*, one of the running gags is that Constable Slobotham, played by Peter Butterworth, is continually given the job of taking down testimony, and constantly getting hung up on the wrong details when writing it down instead of getting the important information. So, for instance, in the scene where he encounters a character named Doctor What, Slobotham gets hung up on the question of "what's your name," (which is where the Doctor Who joke comes from) while the other characters all recognize that he is being thick. But in his next scene, Sergeant Bung, one of the characters previously shown berating Slobotham's foolishness, is himself shown as incompetent and unable to function, getting rings run around him by his shrewish wife.

Perhaps more importantly, however, when Bung and Slobotham are confronted with Doctor What, they panic and run away in the same foolish and ill-advised manner. This is the key structure from which *Carry On Screaming's* humor extends: when two characters are in conflict they're aware of each other's incompetence, but if they're on the same page, they will reinforce each other's incompetence. Hilarity, arguably, ensues.

Where the Carry On films are clear examples of lowbrow populism, Spike Milligan is a comedian's comedian. Starting on the radio with *The Goon Show*, he effectively waged a decades-long career in sketch comedy in which he was the defining and most acclaimed comedian of his generation. His reach and untouchability was such that Terry Nation even let him use a Dalek in a sketch, virtually the only break in Nation's otherwise absolute policy of never letting the Daleks be treated as jokes.

In contrast to the fairly rigid Carry On structure, describing how Milligan's comedy works is much harder. Sticking to material from roughly the same period, let's look at the 1961 special *Spike Milligan Offers a Series of Unrelated Incidents at Current Market Value*. The first sketch of this special consists of an orchestra conductor standing in a bathtub conducting a bunch of men with buckets of water who continually drench him. To grab another example, later in the special we get to see coverage of the Australian 440-Yard Standing-Still Race, in which four competitors race 440 yards by standing still, constructed via stop motion animation of people standing but nevertheless steadily advancing around a track as an announcer breathlessly and enthusiastically covers the unfolding events.

What may not be completely apparent from these descriptions is that Milligan and Carry On are both actually doing the same joke, only from different angles. But to understand that, we have to remember that Britain has a hierarchical class system, or, at least, the remnants of one. British humor classically depends on this. The point of a Carry On film is that everybody goes into the film knowing what the correct roles are and how they should be played (since Carry On films are all genre parodies), and then laughs as everyone is too thick to perform their role. The joke, in other words, is that all of these people have social power but they don't actually have any skill. It's the basic overturning of social structures – the people at the top are really daft fools.

Spike Milligan, on the other hand, takes the opposite tack. Consider the sketch about the Standing-Still Race. The humor, as I said, is that the announcer is taking this race completely seriously even though it's absurd. But noticeably, this is the same joke only looked at backwards. If the Carry On films are funny because they tell us that our entire social structure is actually run by raving lunatics, Milligan offers the corollary – that most of us spend a lot of our lives blindly taking raving lunacy seriously. It's the same joke – serious business is secretly ridiculous, and the ridiculous is secretly gravely serious.

It's worth reiterating that Milligan himself was pushing the envelope there in realizing that the joke could be flipped like that, whereas the Carry On films are extremely traditional. The joke that the people in charge are idiots is a long-standing trope in British comedy. The more absurdist bent pursued by Milligan is largely a post-War invention. And Milligan pushed the envelope throughout his career, keeping pace with the people he inspired – Monty Python, for instance. Still, Monty Python evolved his formula significantly. Let's start by looking at the two major proto-Python shows – *At Last the 1948 Show*, featuring John Cleese and Graham Chapman, and *Do Not Adjust Your Set*, featuring Terry Jones, Michael Palin, Eric Idle, and, behind the scenes, Terry Gilliam.

Both are genuinely funny, but for the most part they stick to either the Milligan approach or the Carry On approach. But there are exceptions. For instance, there's a sketch in *At Last the 1948 Show* where the four main cast members, dressed in more or less identical Hawaiian shirts and talking in identical funny accents, discuss their vacation. Over the course of the sketch, it turns out that they are all named Sydney Lotterbie, and all of their mannerisms are identical, even though they insist they are all from different places and play at individuality. This is interesting because it starts to blur the line between the two approaches. Is the joke that the four Sydney Lotterbies are all stupidly failing to appreciate the absurdity of their conformity? Or is the joke that the package tour of Spain has the same rote conformity of the holiday camps (discussed in detail back in the Patrick Troughton volume) it replaced in the popular culture, and that these four men are still taking the holiday in Spain seriously despite the absurdity of it? The sketch doesn't resolve itself between the two points, and this is a large part of why it's so good.

Likewise, in the "Do Not Adjust Your Set" sketch in which a vet is called to make a house call on a hamster, and has a bit of a nervous breakdown upon arrival because he's allergic to and afraid of hamsters. This requires calling a doctor for the vet, who shows up and turns out to be allergic to vets, creating the same problem. Again, it's not quite clear whether the focus of the joke is the people who are supposed to be competent (the vet and the doctor) being idiots, or the woman who is stuck attempting to take care of her hamster in a world run by lunatics.

But it's not until *Monty Python's Flying Circus* that we finally get to the point where the two approaches collapse completely into a single approach. Look at the opening of the first few episodes, in which a man is shown to struggle to cross a considerable distance, only to collapse at the end and utter "It's . . . " before they cut to the theme music. On the one hand, the joke is "man takes the absurd seriously" as he puts considerable personal effort into the trivial and stupid task of saying "It's." On the other hand, the camera in these sequences engages in what can only be called unrepentant sadism. (One of the quieter innovations of *Monty Python's Flying Circus* is its use of the camera and editing as part of the humor.) When the shot begins, the camera tracks the man's motion briefly before zooming out so that he is in the far distance and waiting motionless as he approaches the lens. In other words, the camera is an active participant in the scene. The man can't say "It's" until he reaches his appropriate place in the shot, and the camera deliberately makes him go further than it has to: it could, at any point, zoom in and end his torment. Furthermore, it's the camera that cuts away when he says "It's" instead of letting him finish his announcement, and thus the camera that renders his act pointless.

In other words, you have a psychotic camera torturing someone who is endeavoring to take it all seriously and do what he's supposed to do in an apparently mad world, firmly entangling both approaches in a single sketch. This is characteristic. Consider the most famous Monty Python sketch, the famed "Dead Parrot" sketch. In this sketch there is one character who is either a completely unethical pet salesman who knowingly sold a man a dead parrot and is trying to cover it up, or who is a complete idiot who doesn't recognize a dead parrot when he sees one. And you have another character who is either earnestly trying to correct an absurdly stupid wrong or who is too foolish to realize he's being screwed. But it's never clear which – both parties of the sketch inhabit both roles simultaneously and constantly. And more to the point, both roles are constantly inhabited – if you choose to read the salesman as incompetent then the customer snaps into being earnest, whereas if you read the customer as a foolish dupe the salesman snaps into being a clever sadist.

The joke, in other words, is that the entire system is insane – that it's actually impossible to tell who is sane and who is crazy, and that the terms "sane" and "crazy" don't actually have any meaning anyway. Which brings us to the other piece of true genius of Monty Python: the decision to abandon an actual structure to the sketches and instead thread together a sequence of scenes stitched together out of random transitions and Terry Gilliam's psychedelic collages. In other words – and this is also part of what's going on with the camera in the opening – the entire show is as thoroughly mad as what it depicts. The comedian in Monty Python is not a detached observer who pokes fun at everything else. Instead, the comedian is just as ambiguously sane or mad as everyone else – caught in the same absurd system, and not even able to find a separate vantage point to mock it. (This reaches its zenith in the third season, in which the show has fake BBC continuity announcements and a false ending, solidifying the fact that the show itself – the actual transmission on BBC1 – is in on the joke.)

Now that we've elaborately killed all possible enjoyment anyone might ever take from Monty Python in favor of explaining the jokes, we can ask what this has to do with Doctor Who. The answer comes in the seventh episode of the series, "You're No Fun Anymore." The majority of this episode consists of an extended sketch entitled "Science Fiction Sketch" that is a dead-on, absolutely savage parody of UNIT-era Doctor Who – indeed, several sources refer to it as Monty Python's parody of the Pertwee era.

The sketch has everything, basically. Aliens who are attacking random and pointless locations like New Pudsey by turning Englishmen into Scotsmen via a ray that instantly turns them into redheads wearing kilts who march in unison to bagpipe music that begins as soon as they are turned. This is part of an overly elaborate plot to win Wimbledon, because apparently Scotsmen can't play tennis, which is, I'm sure, news to Andy Murray. And they are opposed by a scientist (specifically an anthropologist, helpfully situated in a room full of microscopes and bubbling beakers) who exposits, often by asking questions and then immediately answering them, while a completely moronic blonde hangs off of his arm and generally annoys him.

It is, through and through, a dead-on parody of UNIT stories. And being Monty Python, it's a brutal parody – one that shows the entire structure to be an absurd farce and sick joke. It's not *Carry On Sergeant Benton*, in which the structures are lovingly parodied with idiots. It's a mockery of the entire logic and approach of the UNIT era that suggests the whole thing is a pointless recitation of formulaic science fiction that makes no actual sense. It's a pretty devastating response to the Pertwee era.

Those who have been paying attention, however, will note the problem. This is the seventh episode of *Monty Python's Flying Circus*. The first episode of *Spearhead from Space* debuted six days after the eleventh episode. In other words, *Monty Python's Flying Circus* let loose a devastating parody of the Pertwee era five weeks prior to the Pertwee era actually beginning. Admittedly this is because the Pertwee era is in part basing itself on earlier modes of science fiction like the Quatermass series, and *Monty Python's Flying Circus* is parodying those modes.

Nevertheless, this poses a real problem, and one I want to frame explicitly before we actually start the Pertwee era, since, after all, the problem predates the Pertwee era by a few weeks. I will admit, up front, that the Pertwee era is far from my favorite era of Doctor Who. And this is not an uncommon opinion in Doctor Who fandom. Though the heyday of Pertwee bashing came in the 1990s, it's notable that when *Time Unincorporated* began collecting major essays from the fanzine scene it devoted an entire chapter to the Pertwee controversy. And while they admit that the controversy had largely dissipated, there is still something about the Pertwee era – something that isn't true of either the Troughton or Hartnell eras – that invites a love-it-or-hate-it debate. It is, in many ways, the first controversial era of Doctor Who.

One of the biggest problems is that the Pertwee era has an at times unbearable level of self-seriousness. More than any other era of Doctor Who, it often has a bewildering lack of self-awareness when it's goes over the top. Doctor Who is frequently over the top, but in most of its history it knows when it goes there, allowing a sort of camp awareness of the whole thing. Whereas it's not always clear (for instance in *Terror of the Autons*) that when the Doctor berates Jo as a "ham-fisted bun vendor" Pertwee realizes it's a joke. And he's not the only actor to frequently find himself on the wrong side of a script's sense of humor.

Another way to put all of this is that the Pertwee era is ridiculously easy to parody in a way that the Hartnell and Troughton eras were not. In fact, it's so easy to parody that the definitive parody predates the Pertwee era. Monty Python's parody, especially given the degree to which their comedic style made it an extremely barbed joke, seems to effectively get the last word in on the UNIT era before it even begins.

This is an important thing to realize about the Pertwee era, and something that is often missing from accounts of it. The default version of the Pertwee era, which we'll talk about more as the book goes on, treats it as an essentially serious action-adventure show. And sometimes that does seem to be all that it aspires towards being. But there is also a counter-narrative to the Pertwee era – one in which the straightforward action-adventure show it is so often read as is recognized as being compromised before the era even starts, and where the era is regularly responding to that. And it is that version of the Pertwee era that, over the course of this book, I want to focus on.

I Do Tend to Get Involved (*Spearhead from Space*)

It's January 3, 1970. Rolf Harris is at number one with "Two Little Boys," a version of a 1902 song about the American Civil War. This is exactly what you would expect to be at number one in the UK, yes? Other artists in the top ten include Kenny Rogers, Glen Campbell, and Elvis Presley. Rolf Harris holds number one for all four weeks this story is going on for. It's not that there aren't other things bubbling under the surface – there are. But apparently January in 1970 was a time for everyone to be mildly obsessed with the idea of American country music.

One aspect of the change to color that happens with this story is that the show reduces its per-season output to roughly twenty-six episodes, as opposed to the forty-plus episode seasons it did for its first six years. This means in turn that the show has much longer summer breaks, having been off the air for six months now. In those six months, the Stonewall riots took place, kicking off the gay rights movement in the US. The Moon Landing actually happened. Ted Kennedy drove his girlfriend off a bridge. That whole Woodstock thing happened, along with the beginning of prosecution for the Mai Lai massacre. Splitting the difference between these was the Altamont Free Concert. The Days of Rage took place in Chicago in a backlash against the trial of demonstrators from the 1968 Democratic Convention. Richard Nixon began winding down the Vietnam War. And, for the tech geeks, the UNIX epoch began, just three days prior to the UNIT one. And that's just the setup before the Doctor crashes into the world. In the four weeks over which this story airs, Biafra finally capitulates, ending the Nigerian Civil War, and the Greater London Council announces the construction of the Thames Barrier to prevent flood damage to London.

While on television we have a very different situation to the last time a new Doctor debuted. Last time we were dealing with a story that nobody could see. *The Power of the Daleks* is a story we peer at, trying to understand this mysterious transition.

Being as its six episodes are episodes two through seven of the second-longest streak of missing episodes in the series, the transition to Troughton is necessarily something we must understand in hindsight.

On the other hand, everybody knows, or at least thinks they know, *Spearhead from Space* – especially since its best-known scene was repurposed as a major set piece in *Rose*, the first episode of the 2005 revival of Doctor Who. As that fact suggests, this is one of the most iconic and classic Doctor Who stories in existence. Under normal circumstances this is actually something of a problem for our approach, as we have to work to escape the received wisdom of fandom. But in this case, if you actually watch the story in sequence, shortly after *The War Games*, what's important about the story becomes much clearer.

Of course, *The War Games* is a whole book away here, so that statement is perhaps less useful than it was on the blog. And anyway, even if the context of transmission is clarifying, some broader perspective on the Pertwee era is in order as well. This is, after all, a very tricky era of Doctor Who to sort out. The next five seasons manage, in popular consensus, the staggering dual feat of being simultaneously one of the most important and iconic eras of Doctor Who and a complete abandonment and selling out of all of the basic principles of the show. Some foresight going in is appropriate.

But not too much. In many ways this is the received wisdom we need to scrape away. The perspective on this story has many of the same problems that *Power of the Daleks* did – the audience knows that the Doctor can change his face, yes, but it's only happened once before. Doing it again is still a huge shift. On top of that the show is now in color – though this isn't something most of the audience noticed at the time, since black-and-white sets were still more common. And it has a completely new earthbound format. Nowadays all of these things are familiar, and so we read *Spearhead from Space* as a classic Pertwee story in the traditional Pertwee mould, forgetting that "the traditional Pertwee mould" didn't exist yet.

If, indeed, "the traditional Pertwee mould" ever existed. Whatever the era may become over the course of five years, it is not as though the Pertwee era can be treated as a homogenous block. Yes, any suitably obsessive Doctor Who fan knows the many tics of the Pertwee era, whether it be the polarity reversals, "Hai!"s, the Pertwee death pose, Pertwee's legendary capacity for facial gurning, car chases, an irrationally incredulous Brigadier, or, really, several other things I could list. But of that list only Pertwee's gurning actually appears anywhere in *Spearhead from Space*, and that only at the very end of the story. The Pertwee era as we know it is hardly present at all here.

Actually, if we take a slightly broader view, the larger issue is that Pertwee himself is hardly present at all here. It's two full episodes before he is actually even vaguely attached to the main plot, and it's not until the fourth episode that he actually gets around to firmly interacting with the plot. On top of that, Robert Holmes, clearly not quite knowing what Pertwee was going to do with the part, clearly wrote most of these scenes with Troughton in mind and figured Pertwee could make it work. (To be fair, there's a long tradition of this, with the early David Tennant stories largely having been written with Eccleston's Doctor in mind.) But more than that, most of what Holmes writes for the Doctor are set pieces. The first two episodes have very little of the Doctor doing anything other than lounging about in a hospital and/or escaping from said hospital. These are good scenes, but they're very self-contained events.

It's not until late into the second episode that the Doctor gets dressed and starts interacting with people in a manner defined by something other than being unconscious and recovering from a regeneration, and even then he starts out strangely, waggling his eyebrows and talking about the planet Delphon. Oh, and he has two hearts now. Again, much of this is standard now. But in its original context it must have been far more striking. Up until *The War Games*, although it had been frequently established that the Doctor was an alien, most of the time the series treated him as a special human. Medical examinations of him were conducted multiple times not only without anyone remarking on his second heart, but also without anyone remarking on his physiology at all. Characters often referred to him as human. He may have canonically been an alien, but this was easy to overlook.

And yet in this story, one of the major plot points is that the Doctor is self-evidently alien. This is a massive shift in the nature of the program. For the bulk of the first six years, the Doctor was presented as, essentially, an idealized human – something to which humanity could aspire. But the events of the previous story changed that, giving him a distinct, non-human identity as a Time Lord. Now he's throwing around knowledge of alien worlds we've never seen and he's manifestly and completely Other. He's gone from being humanity projecting itself forward to being, essentially, a prophet from outer space.

Realistically, part of this probably came from Robert Holmes trying to solve a straightforward scriptwriting problem: how do you get the Brigadier to the Doctor? Answer: have him be a high profile, bizarre alien man, and thus something that would get reported to UNIT. And if we're being honest, Holmes is the sort of writer who would do something like rewriting the series' mythology to deal with a point about character logistics. For all that he's responsible for establishing large swaths of the series' lore, most of those creations were either throwaway jokes or clever solutions to problems like this. All the same, it is a big change to the character, and it stands out in sharp contrast to where the series was when Holmes last wrote for it – which was only nine months ago.

Especially because, as I suggested, alienness is really all the Doctor has to go on in this story. As is the norm for Doctor debuts, the show consciously gives the new guy a way to ease into the series. Troughton got Daleks to overshadow him for six weeks (not that he needed them), Baker would get the entire UNIT crew in a last hurrah, Davison got a reordered production schedule so that he could film other stories before his debut, and so on. In Pertwee's case, he spends most of his first story in the background, and the story instead focuses on establishing the status quo for his new setting, only bringing him on in full force at the end of the fourth episode, where he proceeds to literally chew the scenery as he gurns frantically in the tentacles of the Nestene. From there all he has to do is be a bit impish in a final scene with the Brigadier in which he agrees to work for him, about which more later.

So for the most part this isn't even a story about introducing the Pertwee era. It's a story about introducing the UNIT era, which is not quite the same thing. This is, to be sure, a tall order. Holmes has four episodes in which to set up a military organization empowered to investigate the inexplicable, give us a sense of how they operate, introduce a new enemy, and then have the Doctor team up with the military organization to defeat the enemy. Thankfully not all of the standard tropes of UNIT are introduced here. Instead Holmes only has to introduce two new characters. The first is Liz Shaw. It's tempting to call Liz the new companion – and the official list of companions does just that. Certainly she's more like a companion than she is like any other regular role in the show. But that doesn't mean it's quite what she is, and her presence there has more to do with the fact that she's the female lead of the show than that she's a "companion" as the term is understood.

Traditionally the job of the companion is to provide a character who requires the Doctor to explain things for them so that the audience hears them too. Sometimes this is crassly simplified to saying that the companion is an "audience identification figure," but that's not quite right. Yes, some of the companions have been overtly similar to either prospective audience members or people like them – most obviously Ian and Barbara. But it's not fair to say that they're audience identification figures. It's more accurate to say that they're known quantities – types of characters the audience recognizes – who are then put into stories that are highly abnormal for that sort of character. But this isn't based on the fact that Ian and Barbara are similar to the audience – it's based on the fact that they're people the audience understands. The same thing is accomplished with Jamie and Victoria, who are both stock fictional characters constantly thrust into the types of stories they don't belong in. What's key is not the companion's similarity to the audience, but their familiarity. The companion is someone whose thought processes the audience is supposed to understand who is then turned loose in a type of story they don't understand, thus forcing exposition. (From there, of course, they fulfill important narrative roles in a given plot, but these aren't the purpose of the companion any more than they're the purpose of any other fictional character.)

Liz, however, is something different. She's the Doctor's partner. The setup is not the explainer/explainee dynamic, but something much closer to a buddy cop show with scientists here. In modern terms, we'd call it the Mulder/Scully setup, with the Doctor being Mulder and Liz being the skeptical Scully. The Doctor and Liz work together to solve mysteries, and both of them are capable of figuring out the major leaps of logic.

The job of asking what the heck is going on actually falls to Brigadier Lethbridge-Stewart, back now for his third appearance. He is, from this point, ensconced as a series regular, appearing in sixteen of the twenty-four Pertwee stories. He's clearly intended to serve double duty. On the one hand, he's the guy in charge to whom the Doctor (nominally) reports. On the other, he's the person to whom the Doctor explains things, usually in the name of getting him to do something like make the army attack something. And the basic shape of this setup is established in the first episode. The Brigadier is in charge. Liz is supposed to investigate weird things for him. When she finds something out she's supposed to tell the Brigadier so he can do something about it. And then, after that's set up for an episode, the Doctor gets dropped in as the unpredictable element that shakes things up.

From there, Robert Holmes dutifully shows how this is all supposed to work with a very straightforward, effective adventure. There's a whole school of thought about Doctor Who – a school defined by Jon Pertwee's recitation of the claim that the scariness of a Zog from the Planet Zog is far less than that of a Yeti in your loo in Tooting Bec. (Actually, half of that is from Russell T Davies, but the two maxims I stuck together there are basically the same thing.) I talk about it more back in the essay on *The Web of Fear* in the Troughton book, but the basic idea behind this is that that Doctor Who should work in the register of the everyday becoming a source of fear.

If you take that seriously – and there are good reasons to, even if I'm a bit skeptical, then Holmes provides an absolute master class here. *Spearhead from Space* is about finding a potentially cool threat – evil plastic people is an excellent choice – and then exploring its consequences. Most of the attention in this regard goes to the iconic sequence in the fourth episode where the mannequins attack, and that sequence is extraordinary, but overt focus on it leaves us to ignore the delicious creepiness of the sequence in the second episode where characters are walking through a doll factory. The doll parts are never made overt objects of horror, but the camera gleefully lingers on the production as we watch plastic representations of fragmented human bodies – of babies, specifically – produced in industrial bulk. And it's utterly disturbing. This is a better representation of the point of Yeti-in-the-loo theory than anything actually involving monsters. As I said way back the first time we came anywhere near Yeti-in-the-loo, the point of all of this isn't to make the monsters scary. The idea is to make the everyday surroundings into which the monster is injected scary. Anyone can make a giant furry death beast scary. Making a toilet scary, apparently, requires Jon Pertwee. And so this story is about making an everyday object like plastic children's dolls strange. Not strange because they might suddenly kill you – that's the next Auton story – but strange on their own merits.

Having come up with a suitably strange core for the series, Holmes builds outwards, creating an assemblage of people who are impacted by the plot. And here we really start to see the questions raised by *The War Games* addressed. If the point of *The War Games* was that the Doctor needed to engage with people instead of just monsters, it's hard to imagine a better story than this one, which features characters from walks of life we simply haven't seen on Doctor Who before. The story, clearly taking its cues from *Quatermass II* (as about eighty percent of the plot here is), opens with a man in rural Britain stumbling upon a meteor. Throughout the story we see him hiding the meteor from his wife, adding a second working class, rural character to the mix. Yes, both turn out to be an example of the obnoxious stock character of the Pertwee era – the comedy yokel – but on the first appearance of this trope the remarkable thing is not that rural Britain is played for laughs; it's that it's played at all.

More interesting, perhaps, is Ransome, whose entire motivations in the story come down to being upset over an unjust firing and concerned about his friend and former partner who is acting a bit strangely. This is a character that there's no obvious analogue for in any of the stories set on Earth from the Hartnell or Troughton eras – one who is thoroughly involved in an alien invasion plot for reasons that have nothing to do with wanting to fight or help the aliens, but who is instead motivated by mundane human concerns in a way that heavily impacts the alien fighting. It's a brilliant addition to Doctor Who's box of tricks. Holmes has, in the first outing, thoroughly nailed the new direction in the way that counts – he's shown what it can do that other forms of Doctor Who couldn't. By starting in a world known to the audience, the show can go into depth showing the sorts of people you can't show when you have to introduce the rules of a world in order to do anything.

Except for one tiny thing. This isn't our world. It can't be. Even with the slightly deferred "near future" lens the UNIT stories ostensibly had, our world isn't just one where the evacuation of London due to evil cobwebs, the possession of the entire planet by Cybermen, and now the unleashing of homicidal mannequins has ever happened. And more to the point, if they had happened it's difficult to believe that they'd be covered up in the way that the Brigadier asserts the Cybermen incident was. Yes, cover-ups happen, including of mass deaths, but this seems a bit extreme.

But beyond that, as we already suggested back in the Troughton volume, it's tough to treat this as the near future given that all of the aesthetics of these stories are firmly rooted in the early 1970s. In terms of someone actually sitting down and watching the UNIT stories, as opposed to someone who is carefully analyzing lines of dialogue from stories across multiple seasons in an attempt to determine a firm UNIT chronology, the UNIT era is pretty clearly set around the time of transmission. The episodes say nothing about their dating, and everything looks like 1970s Britain. (A fuller version of this argument is provided in the previous volume of this series.)

This is crucial, given the obsession people have with the UNIT era and its supposed "realism." The UNIT stories – especially if we start counting from *The War Machines*, which is a UNIT story in approach if not in its actual references to UNIT – are remarkable in part because they are the first stories to establish that Doctor Who is not in our world. Ian and Barbara fell out of what we (naturally) assumed to be basically our world. Liz and the Brigadier are walking around a world that looks like ours, but isn't quite.

Which brings us back around to the Brigadier and Nicholas Courtney, and, in a larger sense, to what we talked about last essay – the UNIT era coming pre-parodied. Much of Monty Python's parody comes from the fact that the UNIT stories, especially in Season Seven, are fairly close remakes of the Quatermass serials, and are thus a known quantity. Courtney is thus cast in the unfortunate role of having to be in charge of a situation that is obviously out of control. His role is written straight, but it's written as a character who is calm, collected, and in control. Fine – a military leader character is easy enough to play. But Courtney has to play him in a world that is insane, albeit ostensibly in a paranoid manner instead of a comedic one. But once the Doctor shows up and starts throwing a spanner in the works the paranoid/comedic line becomes a thin tightrope at best.

Nicholas Courtney was, through his life, rightly considered something of a treasure by Doctor Who fans. And yet if you asked most of them what it was about the Brigadier that was so amazing, I suspect most would give an answer along the lines of his steadfast loyalty and friendship with the Doctor. Which, while possibly true, has next to nothing to do with why he's so memorable a character. No, what makes the Brigadier so memorable is that he's played in such a way as to split the difference between two distinctly comic roles in a way that is not quite a comic turn in and of itself.

Put another way, the Brigadier feels like a character in a Spike Milligan sketch, and, to a lesser extent, in a Monty Python sketch. He's got to play the usual part of taking absurdity very seriously. Except that once the Doctor shows up, he's got the opposite part – the Carry On problem, where he has to be the not-entirely-capable leader who couldn't get by without their nutty and eccentric scientific advisor. In other words, Courtney has the job of playing two distinct but related comic parts. And in response to this, he turns in what is probably the only acting performance in Doctor Who thus far to rival Patrick Troughton's.

The best way to understand how Nicholas Courtney plays the Brigadier is as follows. Imagine a show set in a mental institution. Then take one of the stock characters of a mental institution – the guy who believes he is a historical figure. (I believe the traditional delusion is the belief that one is Napoleon Bonaparte.) Think about how someone would play that part. The usual approach would be to project an exaggerated straight-faced persona with a focus on showing the audience that this person has fully inhabited the role of Napoleon. But crucially, that part is also played with a sort of continual awareness that the person is not Napoleon. They take their role completely straightforwardly, but play only what people expect Napoleon to be like as opposed to actually playing the part of Napoleon.

Now imagine that instead of Napoleon, you have Brigadier Alistair Gordon Lethbridge-Stewart, head of UNIT, dedicated to protecting Britain from alien threats. That is how Courtney ends up playing the Brigadier – he plays the part like someone playing at being the noble heroic soldier, despite the part being written as someone who straightforwardly is that. The effect is remarkably subtle. One gets the sense that the Brigadier is not so much a capable soldier as a man playing at being a soldier. But he's playing at it with such all-encompassing totality that he is effective in ways that the more straightforward soldiers around him can never manage.

The result is that the ambiguity intrinsic to most Monty Python sketches is at play with the Brigadier as well. He takes the "sane man in a mad world" stock character of British comedy and then plays him without ever seeming overly phased by how mad the world around him is. As a result, one is never entirely sure, watching the Brigadier, whether the character is the bumbling straight man for the Doctor's wit or whether he's the one rolling his eyes knowingly at the insanity of the world.

This turns out to be exactly what the program needs. For one thing, as Pertwee grows more comfortable with the part and begins playing the Doctor with a confident larger-than-life quality, the Brigadier becomes the person in the story who can stand up to the Doctor simply by treating him as just another completely insane thing not to react to. When you have a character who is utterly unphased by all manner of alien threats there's not a lot that Pertwee can do to throw him off his game. No matter how far the story stretches to insanity or the people around him act like lunatics, the Brigadier remains an anchor of sanity. And the show repeatedly takes it well past the point where sanity is a remotely reasonable reaction.

In this regard it's fitting that the story ends with the Brigadier finally pinning the Doctor down and forcing him to do something he'd never really done before: have an official name. Yes, the name the Doctor throws back is obviously fake and a joke. But the Brigadier knows that as well as the audience.

The point isn't to get the Doctor's name. It's to establish that the Brigadier is a powerful enough figure in the story to make the Doctor have a name in the first place. We still have to get around to establishing who this new Doctor is, but we'll get there.

To some extent, equal credit here is due to Robert Holmes, who writes the part in a way that is dead-on perfect for Courtney's approach. And there is a sense that the presence of someone like the Brigadier has freed Holmes up in the scripting. As good as *The Krotons* and *The Space Pirates* were – and both were quite good scripts – *Spearhead from Space* represents a major step up for Holmes. And a lot of that is that Holmes has a newfound confidence in ambiguity.

This lets him get away with things like the story's main set piece, the mannequin attack in London. There's a lot in that set piece. It's a massive Yeti-in-the-loo climax, yes. But it's a joyfully low-rent one. After sequences of Cybermen, Yeti, Daleks, and giant robots marauding London, we get one in which London is under attack from something as mediocre and unheralded as mannequins. This is not some great, gleaming alien invasion. This is homicidal clothing stores. Yes, that makes the threat more immediate and scarier, but it also makes it more ridiculous, and thus plays up what Nicholas Courtney is so good at.

On top of that, embedded in all of this is a snide consumerist backlash. One thing we did not note about this story is the establishing shot of a picture of Earth from space. Throughout the Troughton era we looked up at space from the Earth. Now we look down from space at the Earth. This is one of the major shifts to take place in the nine months the series was off the air. When we ended the last book we were at the height of the Space Age. Now we're at the dawn of the environmental age. Embedded in any story about plastic people and evil mannequins is a critique of consumerism. And that critique's high point comes in the most consumerist, superficial, and spectacle-oriented scene in the story. For all that the Troughton era was allied with the radical politics of the

Situationists and their technique of détournement, this is by far the most effective détourning the series has offered to date.

But note that the ambiguity inherent in this approach is the same ambiguity that Courtney is bringing to the Brigadier. This is a world that is, on some level, aware of its own foolishness, but not aware in a way that lets it offer any external comment on the foolishness. This is, of course, exactly how détournement works, but it's also how Monty Python works, suggesting that the two aren't as distantly related as one might think.

Eh? Doctor Who? (*The Silurians*)

It's January 31, 1970. Edison Lighthouse has been so kind as to depose Rolf Harris, reaching number one with "Love Grows (Where My Rosemary Goes)." It holds number one for five weeks before being unseated by Lee Marvin's "Wand'rin Star." Peter, Paul, and Mary, Jethro Tull, the Jackson 5, Simon and Garfunkel, and Chicago are also in the charts, but perhaps the most interesting thing is the Beatles "Let it Be" debuting at its chart peak position of number two in the last week of this story. Also in music news, Black Sabbath releases their first album, effectively establishing heavy metal music.

Elsewhere, avalanches and train crashes give everything a nice disastrous feel. But here's perhaps the more interesting thing. Something we have to remember about 1970 was that what we now call "the sixties" was not entirely and firmly tied to the calendar decade. What I mean by this is that hippies and the like did not simply roll over and die at the strike of midnight on January 1. Case in point, Jeffrey R. MacDonald, a US Army officer, murdered his entire family and then claimed "drugged out hippies" had done it. This, however, is really just a reference to the Manson murders, another story that unwound over the six months between seasons. The significant thing about the Manson murders is not the murders themselves, which are just a slightly more homicidal version of Jim Jones, David Koresh, or the Heaven's Gate cult. No, what's significant about the Manson killings is the fact that they fed a story that hippies were dangerous. Note that the prosecution in the Manson murders stuck closely to arguing the connection between the Beatles and hippie culture. The central idea of the Manson murders and the reason they grabbed the popular imagination was because they featured the real fear of evil hippies. This, again, shows us how quickly things were collapsing and changing.

Other news involves the Weathermen, America's most hilariously toothless domestic terrorist organization, inadvertently blowing three of their own members up (two more than the death toll of non-members across their bombing campaigns). The Poseidon bubble, a bizarre speculative bubble involving Australian nickel mining, bursts. Rhodesia fully separates from the UK, and still nobody supports its existence. And the Chicago Seven are acquitted.

Interesting times in other words. On television it's interesting as well, with *The Silurians*, mistakenly broadcast under the title *Doctor Who and the Silurians*, airing (I'll go ahead and use its intended title). *The Silurians* is interesting for a couple of reasons. It's a story that all but went out without a producer, with Peter Bryant and Derek Sherwin, who had been tag-team running the program since late in Season Five, departing and Barry Letts entering. But Letts had other commitments keeping him from having much to do with the story until the end, which we'll talk about in a bit. It's also the first solo script of Malcolm Hulke, who has previously co-authored for both Season Four and Season Six, and who will have a story every season of the Pertwee era. But this is perhaps less interesting than the fact that it's the first Pertwee script by an avowed skeptic of the Pertwee era. This is ironic given that of the eight scripts Hulke was involved in for Doctor Who, six are in the Pertwee era. And yet he was the most vocal critic of the earthbound idea.

Even more ironic is that, given all of that, Hulke gets only three non-earthbound stories in his entire tenure, and one of those is *The War Games*, which is pretty earthy in its own right. This isn't a tragedy for the viewer, at least: Hulke is very, very good at the thriller subgenre and puts out many of the best earthbound Doctor Who stories. But good as he was at earthbound stories, he viewed the move to Earth as extremely limiting for the series. Legend goes (although legend, in this case, is told by Terrance Dicks, and thus, as is common in series lore as told by Terrance Dicks, features him as the hero) that after Hulke criticized the idea of an earthbound Doctor Who as being good only for alien invasions and mad scientists, Dicks shot back with the premise of this story.

Whoever came up with it, it's a fantastic premise and one of the best in Doctor Who. One of four televised Doctor Who stories to date featuring some version of these antagonists, *The Silurians* features one of the more interesting setups for an alien invasion in Doctor Who. The aliens are actually the former dominant species on the planet, forced into hibernation for vaguely defined reasons. The plot generally involves them waking up and wanting their planet back. Obviously what's interesting about this is that they're not entirely unsympathetic. The setup is an obvious analogue for the politics of indigenous peoples (a slight parallel, then, to the Rhodesia situation), with the Silurians being the put upon indigenous people who just want a place to live and are being mistreated by their invaders, the humans.

This puts *The Silurians* in an odd position. On the one hand, its concept is actually just a warmed over base under siege. In this regard it is like much of Season Seven: a period in which the show hasn't quite figured out what it's doing. This is perfectly reasonable – Season Seven was a one-off gamble in which the show tried to reinvent itself following the plummeting ratings of Troughton's final season. In that regard it was an experiment, and like all experiments of this sort, was simultaneously bold and tentative. With the producers changing over as well the situation was such that not only did nobody quite know what Doctor Who was in 1970, nobody had actually had any time to think about it either. And so many parts of *The Silurians* just reach back to the old standards of the series even as it seems to throw its past away by not even mentioning the TARDIS.

On the other hand, *The Silurians* is striking in just how prescient it is about the latter parts of the Pertwee era. This is, if we're being honest, where a lot of its compelling concept comes from. Two of the major thematic concerns of the Pertwee era are the early '70s fad of ancient scientific mysteries and the growing cultural awareness that the British Empire had some serious ethical deficiencies. And here, in the second story of the era, Hulke hits them both, and furthermore hits them in a way that combines brilliantly. The Silurians are both an ancient secret history of the world come back to play and an indigenous population fighting back against their colonial masters.

This latter point allows Hulke to continue the détournement of the base under siege that he previously enacted in *The War Games* by having the Doctor flit between the two sides. In the classic Troughton base under siege the Doctor is concerned with maintaining the absolute sanctity of the boundary between "inside" and "outside," putting him in a continually and awkwardly xenophobic position. But here the Doctor's relationship between humanity and the Other is more complex – as is appropriate for this new "man who fell to Earth" concept, allowing Hulke to continue the series' newfound commitment to a more social-justice sort of storytelling.

There are a few problems here. First of all, for all the purity of his moral commitment (and I think Hulke is easily the most steadfastly moral writer of the Pertwee era), he's not as good at dealing with human beings as, well, Robert Holmes. Last time the thing we praised Holmes for just about the most ardently was that he does an incredibly good job of bringing in characters who had an involvement in proceedings beyond an immediate investment in the alien invasion. That's mostly lacking in this story, where every character of any note is either working on the base somewhere or a Silurian. (There's a brief farmer who gets killed by a Silurian, but he's largely decoration.)

This limits the degree to which Hulke can subvert the base under siege story, and in practice the tinkering doesn't extend beyond the moral logic. It means that the fact that this story is set on Earth is largely inessential – a colonized planet would do just as well for this story. Hulke pierces the barrier between "us" and the Other, but he doesn't really sell the "us" part of it. This shouldn't be the case. It should be the case that it matters that these events take place on Earth – that it be recognizable human beings that are tasked with understanding and accepting the legitimacy of the Silurians' claim to the planet. But Hulke never quite gets there. His idea is more interesting than his execution, and that hampers this story. (And, to be fair, every other story in which the Silurians have ever appeared.)

That's not to say, though, that the execution is bad so much as it is not good enough for the idea. As I said, Hulke is very good at this type of story. The popular critique is that *The Silurians* is overlong. Tat Wood makes the sensible argument that one ought watch *The Silurians* not as a seven-part single story but as a seven-episode experiment in crashing Doctor Who into an imaginary TV program about the Silurians. It's mostly a fair argument. (A brief moment of pedantry: the third volume of *About Time* is, in its second edition version, which is the one I own, credited purely to Tat Wood. In fact it's a revised version of the Wood/Miles-penned first edition and still has large chunks of Lawrence Miles in it, but the book credits just Wood and I'll reflect that throughout this volume.) I'm not entirely convinced that Season Seven is the right place to advance an argument that is so dependent on the idea of the show as a continual serial, simply because at twenty-five episodes and only four stories it moves dramatically away from the ongoing, ever-changing serial that Doctor Who had been. On the other hand, the propensity of Season Seven to engage in long seven-part epics does give this season a sort of long-form feel that is itself kind of lost until 2005 and the introduction of coherent season-long plot arcs. Certainly Wood is correct that the story, week to week, moves to new places and works well serialized – which is, as I often point out, exactly how these stories were meant to be watched. It all comes to a bit of an abrupt conclusion, sure, but it's tough to treat that as the biggest problem its ending has, as we'll get to.

No, the problem with *The Silurians* isn't its length. It's that it ends up wasting most of its characters. Hulke may have found a way to make Doctor Who work as an Earth-based thriller, but he's clearly got massive problems with the cast he's given here. This is still at its heart a base under siege, and that structure requires an authority figure who stonewalls the good guys at every turn. Unfortunately, Hulke is now stuck with the Brigadier, who is an authority figure and who is by definition sympathetic to the Doctor. This means that Hulke has to find ways of sidelining the Brigadier so he doesn't fulfill his basic plot function of calling in a lot of soldiers to shoot things. Which means the Brigadier is left angrily pouting about how he's going to say very mean things to some civil servants while not actually doing anything. Likewise, Hulke seems not quite sure what to do with Liz, leaving her never quite on anybody's side and, with irritating frequency, standing around with nothing to do.

Of course, this does have the side effect of actually giving Jon Pertwee's Doctor his debut. Pertwee himself, of course, debuted last story, and was solid enough, but was basically given entirely lines and scenes written for Troughton. Whereas in this story (at the start of the fourth episode) Pertwee gets his first truly distinctive scene as the Doctor when confronted with the monster. The third episode ends with one of the standard issue Doctor Who cliffhangers – the Doctor is confronted with the monster for the first time, the music swells intensely, and we get a series of close-ups of the monster and the Doctor's alarmed face. Then, in the fourth episode, after the recap, the music cuts back and the Doctor simply extends his hand and happily says, "Hello, are you a Silurian?" This is probably the best moment of the story. By and large, the distinctive thing about Pertwee's Doctor is his unflappable confidence. Where Troughton's Doctor was always scheming, reacting, and planning, Pertwee's Doctor maintains an implacable calm over all proceedings, and this is the first time that is used consciously, with the Doctor confidently subverting expectations of a cliffhanger resolution, resolving it not by sorting out the danger but by showing us that the Doctor being confronted by an angry lizard person simply isn't a danger in the first place.

All told, a story that actually gave Pertwee some chances to shine was probably what the series needed for these seven weeks, having barely introduced him in the first story.

Especially because the freed up time lets Hulke accomplish the other thing this story really needs to work – extended amounts of time with the Silurians . . . whom we should probably talk about in more detail at this point.

One of the most interesting things about the Silurians is how ahead of their time they are. Given that the BBC costuming department was nowhere near able to produce decent Silurian costumes that would allow for expressive acting, the entire production has a bit of a problem with these guys. They're supposed to be aliens that have actual personalities and individual motivations – something the series regularly failed to do, instead treating alien cultures as a monstrous and monolithic "Other." Unfortunately, much as Hulke may have intended this, the practical limitations of the production limit him: the Silurians have identical costumes that are incapable of facial expressions, and one actor, Peter Halliday does all the voices. Which means that much of what people respond to here is more the idea of the Silurians.

What's odd, then, is how limited people's understanding of this idea is. *The Silurians* introduces a significant theme in the Pertwee era – one that gets revisited in significant ways at least twice more. On the surface, the plot of this is a clone of *Quatermass and the Pit*, except the aliens are also natives of Earth. But as I said, this is also the first time the series played into the "secret ancient histories" fad of the early 1970s. What's particularly interesting in this case is this story's explanation of how the Silurians were driven underground. (The explanation changes almost every time they appear.)

This time, the claim is the implausible idea that a giant asteroid strike was predicted, but that the asteroid instead got pulled into orbit and became the Moon. Any attempt to retcon this and say that actually they correctly foresaw the asteroid that formed the Chicxulub crater runs into the larger problem that they're firmly established as having co-existed with apes. The long and short of this is that there is no remotely plausible way to reconcile the Silurians as a race with established human science – in no small part because of their name, the Silurians, which makes no sense from a paleographic perspective.

But even if the science is preposterous, we can see what's going on from the shape of the claim. The Silurians are intended, in part, as a secret origin of the Moon. Similarly, look at how the race memory/fear idea is actually handled. Initially it's one of the mysteries: why is everyone afraid of something in the caves? The explanation – that there's a primal memory of fear of the Silurians who once hunted man – puts this story firmly in the tradition of "the secret explanation for X is Y," where Y is a fairly paranormal event usually involving aliens. As I said, this sort of thing was huge in the 1970s – we'll see it in Doctor Who in one form or another throughout the next decade. But it does form a significant difference between this story and *Quatermass and the Pit*. Where *Quatermass and the Pit* was about the novel radicalness of the idea, this story is very much about taking the by-then familiar idea and using it to tell a story about the sufferings of indigenous people.

Which is an immensely appealing idea, but relatively ill-served in this particular script. For one thing, the Silurians have exactly one sympathetic character in their number, and they kill him off when he starts to get in the way of them being over the top villains. Yes, excepting Hulke's own work, this is more dissent than we've seen among aliens since *The Ark*, but it's still pretty feeble. The idea of the Silurians is done a lot better elsewhere – including, for all of its faults, in the Matt Smith Silurian two-parter, in which you can practically see Chibnall ticking off the boxes of problems with this story and fixing them as he writes it. The result is a deeply clumsy 2010 story, and I think *The Silurians* is a much better 1970 story than Chibnall's version is a 2010 story. But as a Silurian story, Chibnall's is by miles the superior take. Put another way, try explaining to someone who has just watched this why it's inferior to a remake in which the Silurians have faces, the characters have motivations other than how they respond to alien invasions, and the tragic ending actually extends from a character trait.

Which brings us to the other big obsession with this story, the tragic ending. This requires that we go back to production details. Let's start at the very beginning, which is actually, as it happens, *The Celestial Toymaker*: the first story produced by Innes Lloyd following the brief and apparently (in the BBC's eyes) unhappy tenure of John Wiles. Given the brevity of Wiles's tenure, we can basically treat Innes Lloyd as inaugurating the second coherent era of Doctor Who following Verity Lambert's initial run. Lloyd was followed by Peter Bryant, who was script editor under Lloyd and whom Lloyd actively tried out as producer on *Tomb of the Cybermen*. Bryant was, at least in terms of the credits, followed by Derek Sherwin, who produced *The War Games* and *Spearhead from Space*. But in practice, Sherwin and Bryant were effectively co-producers for the end of Troughton's run and the start of Pertwee's. Which means that not only does this story exist in a gap between producers, it marks the end of an extremely long-running form of thought about what the show is.

With this story, however, Sherwin and Bryant left for another project and the BBC put Barry Letts, who had previously directed *The Enemy of the World*, in as producer, thus inaugurating the third creative era of the show. As mentioned, however, Letts had to finish a commitment to another show, and so only came in towards the end of production on this. And his first act as producer was thus to rejig the final episode to focus more on the moral outrage of the destruction of the Silurians, including the addition of the final scene, in which the Doctor expresses his horror at the Brigadier's decision to blow up the base.

Barry Letts is an interesting figure. Much like Hulke, he's one of the primary forces for overtly progressive politics in the show. He's also, uniquely among producers, both a writer and director, and he wore those hats at times during his tenure as well. This means that he has a measure of deep influence on the show that we've never really seen before, and never will again. (Eventually Letts will end up writing, directing, and producing Pertwee's swansong.) Much of this influence is good. Some of it is bad. And then there's this, his first and most strangely ambiguous act.

Basically, the issue is this. After the Doctor tricks the Silurians back into hibernation, he wants to pry them out one by one to negotiate peace. The Brigadier, apparently acting on orders from above, blows up their base without telling the Doctor. Staring in horror at the exploding base, the Doctor declares, "That's murder. They were intelligent alien beings, a whole race of them, and he's just wiped them out." I give the quote because there are people who try to underplay the apparent intent of this moment, particularly based on later stories that establish that there are scads of Silurians about. But the quote is unambiguous in the context of this episode, and on transmission there was only one way to read it. The Brigadier has wiped out an entire race of alien beings, and the Doctor views it as murder. This is unambiguously an accusation that the Brigadier has committed genocide.

Watching *The Silurians* in sequence, it's difficult to imagine how any viewer seeing this wouldn't assume that the Doctor and UNIT were simply not going to be working together anymore. That is, after all, surely the only thing that can possibly follow this. The alternative is for the Doctor to accept genocide – to say that, sometimes, intelligent species that have brilliant scientists and civilization get exterminated, and that's OK. If the Doctor shows up next episode, he effectively undermines the entire point of this story.

And of course, he does, and it does. If it were just Hulke that was responsible for this I would assume that it was a deliberate attack on the new premise of the show; that, given his distaste for this new direction, he was simply demonstrating conclusively, in one shot, why it couldn't possibly work. That this was an overt effort to force a change of direction in the show. But it appears that it wasn't just Hulke. That it was actually Barry Letts who set up this ridiculous undermining of the show's premise, knowing full well that he wasn't going to carry through on its consequences.

It's bewildering. It's a massive blunder for Letts to do it, creatively speaking. And yet it's widely cited as the best part of the story. Ironically, this isn't even entirely wrong. It's admirable that the show is willing to follow the premise of a story so thoroughly and to that kind of a consequence. And if you take this story in isolation – if you don't treat it as something that has to segue into another story next week, it even works and is as brilliant as people want it to be.

And given the fact that the classic series is usually consumed as discrete stories instead of as a serial, this almost makes sense. But just as it doesn't make sense to complain about the pacing because it doesn't work when you watch it all in one chunk, it doesn't make sense to praise the ending because you don't have to tune in next week. As an end to a story, it's great. As something that sets up the next one, it damn near destroys the series.

Philip Sandifer

Where Spacemen Live (The Ambassadors of Death)

It's March 21, 1970. Lee Marvin continues the apparent obsession with country and western in UK music with "Wand'rin Star," unseated after only one more week by Simon and Garfunkel's "Bridge Over Troubled Water," which lasts until mid-April before being unseated by Dana's "All Kinds of Everything," the 1970 Eurovision winner. This is actually mildly controversial, given that Dana herself is from Northern Ireland, but represented the Republic of Ireland in Eurovision. (As you will recall, The Troubles, the lengthy period of unrest between the UK and Ireland, were getting into full force here.) Dana is in turn unseated by Norman Greenbaum's "Spirit in the Sky." "Spirit in the Sky" is an interesting piece. Looking at its single cover, in 2011, it looks, frankly, redneck – a bright red cover featuring a photo of a long-haired man in front of an American flag. However in practice, the song is a vaguely psychedelic piece about the afterlife that is treated as a precursor for a lot of glam rock. Andy Williams, Kenny Rogers, Stevie Wonder, and Steam also make appearances.

In other news, the Concorde makes its first flight, and the first Earth Day proclamation is made. Ian Paisley wins a by-election to the House of Commons. But more importantly, the seven weeks of these stories surround Apollo 13's launch, catastrophic malfunctions, and eventual (and damn near miraculous) safe landing – this is essentially the last time that the public followed the space story as an ongoing matter instead of in the aftermath of a fatal catastrophe. But perhaps the most important news story is one of music. This is also the story that was on when The Beatles, who had provided, in many ways, the nearest analogue for the artistic movements of Doctor Who throughout the 1960s, announced their imminent breakup.

Every once in a while we reach a point in Doctor Who that is just too metaphorically perfect to believe. It would be uncanny enough for Doctor Who to be doing a story about troubled space launches during Apollo 13. But this story goes further, marking the end of the Space Age for Doctor Who at the same time that the general public has its last mass fascination with space travel. On top of that, we have the first stirrings of glam rock in the charts while Doctor Who does a story that seems to take much of its imagery and tone from David Bowie's "Space Oddity." And yet Bowie's first glam record, *The Man Who Sold the World*, is still some eight months away, and has barely begun being recorded. And this transition coincides with the breakup of The Beatles, previously the musical act with which Doctor Who seemed most in sync. Their departure from the scene comes alongside the departure of David Whitaker, the writer who most thoroughly defined the series in the 1960s.

This is, of course, the most pressing thing about the story. The bulk of Whitaker's influence is tracked over the first two volumes of this series, with his most prominent contributions coming in the Troughton era, but the short form is this: David Whitaker is largely responsible for building an explicitly alchemical metaphor for who the Doctor is that treats him as an avatar of Mercury: a brilliant, clever, chaotic, anarchic, and transformative force. From the perspective of 2013 this seems like an almost banal thing to say, since that's become the default way of thinking about the Doctor, but that is, in a large number of ways, down to just how well Whitaker established that concept.

And so while there's a lot going on in this story, nothing beats the fact that this is Whitaker's departure. Nothing possibly could. Mind you, this is not quite a David Whitaker story, whatever the credits might say. Indeed, the last solo story by Whitaker was the sublimely good *The Enemy of the World*, with his prior story to this, *The Wheel in Space*, being a not-entirely-smooth joint venture with Kit Pedler. With this story, Whitaker apparently had trouble working in the new format for Doctor Who. This is not surprising – everybody else was having trouble working with it too, as the bewildering ending of the previous story demonstrates. And with chaos behind the scenes there weren't a lot of people around with a clear vision of what the new format was who could provide Whitaker with helpful notes. On top of that, Whitaker was busily moving to Australia as this story was being written. As a result, Whitaker only completed the first three scripts of this, with Malcolm Hulke working (uncredited) from Whitaker's outline on the fourth through seventh episodes, and then doing a rewrite on the first through third episodes to make the story match up better (with, apparently, an additional rewrite by Trevor Ray on the first episode).

It's tempting, based on this, to assume that Whitaker was responsible for the basic idea, but that Hulke did the work to turn it into a gripping thriller. But that ignores the fact that Whitaker had written a contemporary thriller for Doctor Who before with *The Enemy of the World*, which was basically Doctor Who does James Bond. Similarly, while it's tempting to give credit for the critique of reductionist views of alienness to Whitaker, if we're being fair that's the exact same point that Hulke was making last story. The point here is that the two writers of this story were always relatively in sync and compatible, and the details of the collaboration are difficult to parse.

This is especially true given the visible extent to which Hulke works to preserve Whitaker's approach. (It's telling that the story of how much Whitaker had been rewritten here was held back until after Whitaker's death – a further testament to the regard held for Whitaker despite the problems with this script.) In rewriting the first three episodes, for instance, he made no effort to tone down the sense of whimsy that Whitaker brought to the proceedings. Within them, the TARDIS console makes its return with a strange little sequence in which the Doctor and Liz shuffle around in time, the Doctor has apparently gained the ability to spontaneously teleport objects through time, and Bessie has an anti-theft system, presumably based on static electricity, which glues people to the car. There's an odd dissonance to all of this – a sense that it's far too silly for the Pertwee era. But there's also a charm to that silliness – a sense that a few small changes that led Pertwee to be more grandfatherly wizard than swashbuckling dandy could have led to a whole wonderful era unto itself. It's oddly beautiful and innocent in a way the show doesn't quite see again until Amelia Pond and fish custard. None of this is Hulke's default style, but there is no sense that Hulke is fighting against the script's impulses here.

If anything, Whitaker seems to be upping Hulke's game, so to speak. The eventual revelation of Carrington's villainy is very much a Whitakerian move, paralleling similar revelations in *The Rescue* and *The Enemy of the World*, and, more broadly, both *Power of the Daleks* and *Evil of the Daleks*, which feature similarly delusional and obsessed villains. But Carrington's actual motivations, stemming from a misguided sense of honor, are pure Hulke. As a character, he's certainly helped by the fact that John Abineri is a quite solid actor, but the peculiar collaboration of Hulke and Whitaker also serves to make him one of the best villains of the Pertwee era. He's both ruthless and crafty enough to be effective and visibly driven by human concerns. As with any decent villain, including several from both Whitaker and Hulke, he's convinced that he's doing the right thing. But the fusion of the two means that, unlike a lot of their other villains, the audience can see his point, making him chillingly compelling. He becomes exactly what *The Silurians* so lacked: a well-developed human character within whom the story's central moral debate plays out on terms other than a strict parable. And the collaboration clearly had a long-term effect on Hulke. After this story he does much better with these sorts of characters, but he never manages to do it quite as well as he could working from Whitaker.

Whitaker's influence improves Hulke in other ways. Even once the story reaches the Hulke-written episodes there's something odd and charming in the way it seems to unfold. It is strange and fascinating in a way that Doctor Who isn't always. It's a story that transfixes you as much as it excites you. It continually fails to quite make logical sense, but equally constantly makes a perfect sense of its own. The story jumps tone freely (and credit is due to director Michael Ferguson for following the jumps with appropriate changes to visual style), but never loses its way. There's something to its narrative structure that one is never quite sure whether is elegance or just plain oddness.

Of course, reducing David Whitaker to his copious oddness is a mug's game. He's far, far more than just that. One of the things we've seen Whitaker to be best at is colliding Doctor Who with other narratives – whether it be Shakespeare, *The Forsyte Saga*, James Bond, or Kit Pedler. This time, he's merging Doctor Who with conspiracy thrillers of the *Manchurian Candidate* style. This means that the first three episodes (and the back four, though Hulke isn't quite as methodical about it as Whitaker) all feature huge action set pieces. And generally they're really quite well-done action set pieces – the gunfight in the warehouse during the first episode is extraordinary, and the action sequence in the second episode has a truly heart-in-throat moment as the Brigadier is apparently shot down halfway through it. Brilliantly, the sequence doesn't even emphasize this, letting the possible death of a major character get swallowed up in the chaos of the scene. This story also features the last of the Doctor-as-astronaut set pieces, which had previously been central features of both *The Seeds of Death* and *The Space Pirates*.

The other thing Whitaker has long been brilliant at is having Doctor Who subvert the genre it seems to be playing with. This was the true genius of *The Enemy of the World* – the way that it continually played with our expectations of what a Doctor Who/James Bond story should be, finally subverting it by becoming something entirely different in the end. *The Ambassadors of Death* is similarly structured, with its last two episodes undermining the conspiracy plot and, indeed, the entire ethical basis of the conspiracy genre. This, again, appears to be something that is definitely Whitaker's handiwork, with Hulke doing a very capable job of executing it.

There is an obvious reason, however, why Hulke and Whitaker work so well together. They are both cut from the same cloth in terms of an interest in ethical science fiction. For all the quality of Whitaker's Dalek stories, it's notable that, when left to his own devices, he never wrote a monster story. His first contribution hinged on the discovery that the supposed alien presence invading the TARDIS was in fact the ship itself; his second on the fact that the monster isn't actually a monster at all. He wrote the only story devoid of monsters in Season Five. So pairing him with the guy who just did a story about subverting the idea of "monsters" is eminently sensible. Likewise, for all the developing genius of Robert Holmes, Hulke is still the writer most invested in the human dimensions of science fiction. Griffin the Chef in *The Enemy of the World* is, in his own way, more of a prototype for Earth-based adventures than *The Web of Fear* ever could be, even if his conspicuous normality was never as frequently chosen a direction as it could be.

Furthermore, their strengths are oddly complimentary. Only David Whitaker could come up with the idea of black box communications with aliens, where communication can only take place via a set of pre-selected messages. But only Hulke could make that black box into an elaborate game of diplomatic chess. Similarly, both are good at their set pieces, and so their collaboration leads to wonderful things like the "Space Oddity" flavored rocket sequence, a key moment in Doctor Who moving from the NASA dream of moon landings on to a far more vexed and unusual view of space. The sequence in which Pertwee's face appears slightly distorted on a monitor, cast entirely in blue light, being deformed as he's assaulted by a high powered fan to mirror the effects of G-Force is stunning. It's a sort of agony we've never seen the Doctor in – one that's made all the more powerful by the fact that it's not just the silly gurning that the audience has already become used to Pertwee delivering, but is actually a real, direct assault on the character and, indeed, the actor himself. With that single shot Doctor Who makes its first steps into treating space less as a realm of infinite possibility and more as one of uncertainty, mystery, and danger.

And more importantly, it makes steps into a realm of magic. The Ambassadors are oddly magical figures, which is part of why the gorgeous sequence of them walking slowly towards the Space Center, framed by the sunlight, is, by all accounts, the second most memorable sequence of Season Seven, at least to people who actually watched it on television. Indeed, the sense of the uncanny that the Ambassadors generate – a sense no alien since the original Cybermen has really offered – is such that Steven Moffat visibly borrowed the iconography of this episode in *The Impossible Astronaut*. Their entire effect hinges on the fact that human beings in space suits themselves look alien and foreign. The idea that we become alien by going into space is an old one in science fiction: it forms the basic core of *The Quatermass Experiment*. But it's one that's often overlooked, and Whitaker picks up on it deftly here.

All of this leads inexorably to the story's final sequence, in which Whitaker and Hulke demonstrate, almost effortlessly, what the UNIT era should look like. The Doctor ends up resolving the situation by laying a non-violent siege to the Space Center using only some UNIT guards and the Ambassadors. That is to say, the Doctor, the military, and the aliens team up to non-violently take over a secure government facility and stop the bad guys. It's beautiful, and exactly what the Doctor working with the military should look like, and nothing like what we've seen before this season, or, for that matter, will see again for some time. It's extraordinary. It's thrilling. And it's a beautiful passing of the torch. Just as the Beatles give way to glam rock and David Bowie here as the most visible cultural parallel to Doctor Who, so does the role of the ethical heart of the series (or as Tat Wood puts it, the series' conscience) pass on from Whitaker to Hulke in this moment.

So let's end with that: our farewell to the mad and magical David Whitaker. The question of who created Doctor Who is historically, and wrongly, considered complicated. Certainly the question of who thought up the idea of doing an ongoing series about a time traveler is a complex matter with many players. But a man with a time machine could be any number of shows. When it comes to creating Doctor Who – the show we know and love today – there is only one answer: David Whitaker created it.

This is the man who script-edited the creation of the Daleks, who wrote the story that introduced the TARDIS as a living, conscious character, who supervised the first regeneration and the first companion change, who wrote the two best Dalek stories of the 1960s (and arguably the best Dalek story ever in *Power of the Daleks*), and who had a hand in nearly every formative decision of the show. More to the point, this is the man who treated the Doctor as more than just another sci-fi hero, whose odd obsession with alchemical symbolism helped establish the character as the transformative, chaotically brilliant man we know him as.

On top of that, Whitaker managed the incredible feat of both being unmistakably brilliant in his time and unmistakably brilliant in hindsight. Things like *Power of the Daleks* and *Evil of the Daleks* were recognized as landmarks when they aired, but looking at the ways in which his oddly alchemical approach influenced the structure of his narrative, one sees ideas and structures that were years and decades ahead of their time in mass entertainment. Almost every time we see a truly great writer stride onto the series from here on out, one of the first things I'm going to say about all of them is that their ideas are unmistakably derived from David Whitaker. This is a man who Neil Gaiman cites as the first author he learned to look for by name, and who handled the only era of Doctor Who that Alan Moore likes. Heck, we're talking about the man who invented the Doctor Who novel, one of the most important aspects of the series.

He's the best writer we've seen so far on the series. For my money, he's one of the three best writers in the classic series, and maybe one of the three best writers ever on the series. Actually, if I'm being honest, I think he was one of the great science fiction writers ever and one of the greatest television writers ever. He deserves to be mentioned in the same breath as Isaac Asimov, Gene Roddenberry, and Joss Whedon. That he's not is an absolute tragedy.

And with this story, as the series found itself nearly pulled apart by the consequences of its new direction, he made his last and in some ways greatest gift to the series – showing it yet another way forward. As though the half-dozen ways forward he'd already figured out for it weren't enough. For all that Whitaker is said not to have "gotten" the new format, the fact that *The Silurians* ended the way it did shows that Letts and Dicks didn't get the format yet either. They're hardly the ones to be judging Whitaker for it. The sense of this story is far more one of Whitaker and Hulke schooling them on how to make their premise work than it is of Whitaker having trouble. This story consists of one of the most fundamental figures in the series' creation stopping by on his way to Australia in order to scribble off a few notes about how to make the new premise of the show work with its history and ideology. Not nearly enough of his suggestions were taken, but enough were that, in his final moments with the show, he provided one last burst of direction and vision in a way only he could have, and at the moment when the show needed it most.

Looking at the story, we have a man who brings wonder and magic into the world set loose into a plot that is brilliant, multi-layered, and that ultimately subverts the inside/outside paradigm of invasion and base under siege stories more thoroughly and completely than the much more lauded *The Silurians*. We have a story that shows how you can have the Doctor and the military work together in a way that doesn't lose the essential Doctorness of the story. We have the best UNIT story to date, and very possibly the best one ever. One that is almost good enough to fully heal the almost irreparable damage done the week before. And although, as we'll see in the next few stories, the darker sides of the UNIT idea still rear their heads regularly, we have something that, once again, feels like it might be able to go on forever, especially if the Doctor finishes the repairs to the TARDIS. (It's a nice touch that it's under Whitaker's pen that the first steps towards restoring the TARDIS are made.)

After this story, David Whitaker spent nearly a decade teaching in Australia. He returned to the UK and began work on the novelization of *The Enemy of the World* before dying of cancer at the tragically young age of fifty-one. There are no biographies of him, nor much in the way of interviews. I have a sad feeling his life is about as well documented as it will ever get, though I, at least, would love to write a definitive biography. He, like much of his work, is something of a mystery, and over far too soon. But if you take fifty-one years that include "I am single-handedly responsible for the heart and soul of Doctor Who," and stack them against the lifetime of almost anyone else it becomes hard to see David Whitaker as anything other than what he was: a genuine wizard.

Philip Sandifer

Go Down Go Down Go Down Go Down (*Inferno*)

It's May 9, 1970. Norman Greenbaum continues to be at number one. A week later, and far more alarmingly, it's the England World Cup Squad with "Back Home," the first of many post-1966 humiliations England's national football team would suffer. They stay there for three weeks, which is almost as many weeks as games they lasted in during the World Cup itself. They're unseated by Christie's "Yellow River," a song in the classic "soldier returning home" subgenre. This lasts a week before Mungo Jerry's "In the Summertime" plays us out of Season Seven. The Hollies, Creedence Clearwater Revival, Tom Jones, The Moody Blues, Fleetwood Mac, and The Supremes also chart.

Since *The Ambassadors of Death* wrapped, the most obvious news story is the Kent State Massacre. Most obvious, however, is not a synonym for most interesting; all Kent State amounts to is a confirmation that the hippie/anti-war movement was successfully so marginalized that affixing bayonets, advancing towards them, and shooting them dead is not entirely outside of the mainstream. More interesting for us is actually something like Thor Heyerdahl setting sail with a papyrus boat called Ra II to try to prove that it was theoretically possible for the ancient Egyptians to have influenced the design sensibilities of South American civilizations. This is proper 1970s stuff – bewilderingly overreaching theories of human development held together by sticky tape and charisma.

But perhaps most interesting for our purposes, two days before the final episode of this story aired, the UK held a general election in which, in a shock result, Harold Wilson's Labour government fell and Tory Edward Heath became Prime Minister. Exactly why Wilson went down is a matter of debate, with theories ranging from the fairly improbable (that England did poorly in the World Cup) to the quite likely (a raft of poor economic data doing in the not actively unpopular but not particularly popular Labour government), to the marginal and frankly disturbing (Tories were fired up following Enoch

Powell's River of Blood speech). We'll track the consequences of this through most of the Pertwee era, but in a lot of ways this is Britain's 1968 moment, setting off a chain of political events that will take us through to 1997.

While on television we have *Inferno*. On the blog, at least, this was one of my more controversial posts. See, the *Doctor Who Magazine* "Mighty 200" poll ranks this as the best Pertwee story, and it's terribly popular. And I . . . just don't like it all that much. This begins to point towards a larger problem that lurks around the edges of this book in particular: if I'm being perfectly honest, the Pertwee era is just about my least favorite period of the classic series, with only the Colin Baker era contending with it. And while I'm a firm believer in redemptive readings and trying to argue for the best possible vision of a text, the fact of the matter is that I'm not the only one who dislikes the Pertwee era. It's the first era of Doctor Who that can be described as "controversial."

And while I can readily see what everybody likes about *Inferno*, I think it also serves very well as exhibit A for those who want to argue that the Pertwee era is fundamentally flawed. Because on the whole, *Inferno* is a script with massive flaws and visible acts of desperation undertaken to rescue itself from those flaws that is redeemed primarily by the quality of its actors and direction. Give this to actors less skilled than Nicholas Courtney, Caroline John, and, for all the stick I'll give him throughout this volume, Jon Pertwee and to directors less skilled than Douglas Camfield and Barry Letts (who stepped in after Camfield had a health crisis on set) and you'd have a work of mediocrity at best. Even with those advantages, though, I admit to finding something puzzling about this story's reputation. I can't even see how one would argue it as the best story of Season Seven (both *Spearhead from Space* and *The Ambassadors of Death* seem straightforwardly preferable). Tat Wood suggests that people are more enamored with the idea of *Inferno* than they are with the actual episodes, and I suspect this is more or less on target.

The biggest problem that *Inferno* appears to have when you start watching it is a crushing sense that we've seen this before. Here we are after two seven-part adventures set in scientific installations where mysterious things were afoot, and what do we get? Another scientific installation with mysterious deaths and monsters. Another idiotic leader who will insist on ignoring the Doctor until it's too late. In other words, we have, at the start, seemingly the exact same setup as what we've been watching, at this point, for fourteen weeks. It's been over three months since we've seen anything on Doctor Who besides mysterious deaths and monsters around a scientific installation. That's longer than the entire run of a season of the BBC Wales version. Unsympathetic as I may be to the claim that the seven-parters of Season Seven are padded, the fact remains that this is a bit exhausting.

This would be one thing if Doctor Who had a deep reserve of interesting ideas to match up with its scientific installations. After all, even in the depths of Troughton-era base under siege mania, the show had more variety in location. Season Five had the decency to set the exact same story in a frozen tomb, a monastery, a scientific installation, the London Underground, an offshore drilling platform, and a space station. And that was draining even with *The Enemy of the World* in the middle to break things up. Now, however, it seems like an entertaining bit of variety to be longed for.

Perhaps most alarmingly, the first three stories of Season Seven each nearly exactly tracked one of the three Quatermass serials. *Spearhead from Space* was visibly modeled on *Quatermass II*, *The Silurians* is a dead-ringer for *Quatermass and the Pit*, and *The Ambassadors of Death* is a revamp of the original *Quatermass Experiment*. And as *Inferno* opens there's a sort of awkward moment of "oh dear, we're out of Nigel Kneale serials to rip off, we're going to have to start ripping off ourselves instead."

Of course, both of the previous efforts in Season Seven have had some real depth to the idea. *The Silurians* was a story where the monsters were plausibly right. *The Ambassadors of Death* was a story where the monsters weren't actually monsters at all. Both of these are interesting ideas that can just about sustain seven episode explorations on their own merits, and the fact that both are set at a scientific base is beside the point: *The Silurians* didn't have to be, and *The Ambassadors of Death* didn't need a scientific installation so much as it specifically needed a space launch. The judgment of how good *Inferno* is, ultimately, hinges on whether or not you think *Inferno* has a deep and interesting twist on its base under siege as well.

Here's what it has: at the start of the third episode the Doctor is shunted into a parallel universe where everyone is fascist, and stays there until the end of the sixth episode. In these episodes he faces the same crisis that was happening in the first and second episodes, only in the fascist universe the crisis starts at a more advanced stage. And those who love this story think that this is absolute genius. They think that seeing the story unfold with alternate universe versions of the same characters and then seeing this alternate world actually and cataclysmically end before the Doctor gets back to the real world to try to save the crisis builds suspense, and that it's a brilliant way to get the show to push to bigger stakes than it should be able to by actually destroying the planet and killing everyone.

And described like that, you can see it. But what, exactly, are you seeing? That is to say, why is it compelling to put the Doctor opposite a fascist alternate universe version of UNIT? Phrased like that, the answer seems obvious – the reason you do that is to play off exaggerated versions of the existing tensions between the Doctor and UNIT. Since the problem the Doctor normally has with UNIT is that he's an iconoclast and UNIT is the military, an even more militaristic version of UNIT gives the Doctor a problem with strong resonances with the rest of the series. In theory it should answer the problem left to us by the end of *The Silurians* – why the hell does the Doctor work with these people?

There are two problems here, however. The first is that the "alternate versions of the main characters" trick is one of the standard tricks of television. It works well enough, sure, but it's also one of the stock things that TV shows reach for when they're getting desperate. It's not as though Doctor Who is overusing the trope or anything, but I admit that I'm at a loss for why falling back on one of the most cliché tricks in television is considered an inherent virtue.

But more to the point, I just don't think *Inferno* succeeds at doing anything more than having a superficial spectacle. The parallel universe is little more than a way of stretching the story by four episodes and finding a way to get a "the end of the world" sequence in that doesn't actually oblige them to end the world. There's not actually a point to the two universes idea beyond the basic eye candy implicit in it.

In order to get the two universes thing to work on a meaningful level, the story would have to hinge on the difference between the two worlds. If the story is going to have the Doctor fail to save the fascist world then save the real world, there has to be a reason why the fascist world can't be saved — one that presumably sheds light on what it is about UNIT that can and should be saved. Which is to say, as Chekov pointed out, if you have a set of fascist doppelgangers in the first act, you need their fascism to be central to the resolution in the third. If you're going to go through with the massive set piece of making all the regular characters fascist, that should probably matter.

So, let's ask at what points the Doctor could possibly have saved the alternate universe. The main one — about the only one, actually, where the Doctor seems to be approaching a convincing account of why they should stop drilling — is when the Doctor exposes the fact that Stahlman has an injured hand because he's slowly mutating into a Primord. Except that nobody in the alternate universe has any idea what's going on with the Primords, so they don't care about this evidence.

In other words, the reason the alternate world gets destroyed is purely down to the fact that they don't know about the Primords and thus don't go "Ooh, you're right, our chief scientist is turning into a monster, maybe we should stop listening to him." You can argue that this means that the real world is saved because it had the Doctor investigating earlier and figuring out the Primords. But this does little to rescue the middle four episodes, as the Doctor doesn't have to go to the fascist world to figure that out. All the Doctor has to do is get back and everything will be fine – the entire trip sideways was just a stalling tactic – a slightly spruced up version of "the Doctor gets captured for four episodes."

But, the *Inferno* defender retorts, that's not the only difference. In the fascist world, Sir Keith gets murdered whereas in the real world he survives, and the seventh episode makes it clear that this is central to why there's hope for the real world. The story becomes about a noble secondary character. OK. That works. The only problem is that while the script may assert that Sir Keith's survival matters, Sir Keith has nothing to contribute to the actual resolution of the story. His presence is irrelevant to the climactic scene. So while we may be told he's vital, the script does nothing to back that up.

Perhaps most bewilderingly, though, the fact that the Doctor knows Stahlman is infected proves irrelevant as well. Part of this is that despite spending four episodes avoiding letting the Doctor anywhere near the actual plot the script is stuck with an episode to kill in which the Doctor still can't do anything until the end. So upon returning to the real world, the Doctor's course of action is to run around acting like such a lunatic that even the Brigaider thinks he's lost it. As opposed to, for instance, explaining to anyone what's going on or, perhaps most obviously, revealing Stahlman's infection, since now he's on a world where people know about Primords and are reasonably likely to appreciate that the man whose hand is turning bright green might be a problem. Instead the resolution has barely anything to do with him. Instead it's Stahlman, post-Primord transformation, who defeats himself. At one point Stahlman is locked into a room, the drill is set so that nobody can stop it, and Stahlman has turned into a Primord and so can't be reasoned with. And so, quite helpfully, he walks out of the room and reveals himself to be a monster, allowing everyone to start disregarding his orders and save the day.

Put another way, nothing whatsoever that the Doctor learns in the course of the four episodes spent in the alternate universe matters in the slightest when it comes to saving the real world. The four episodes dealing with the fascist alternate Earth only pad out the story. They have no consequences. All they do is redo the plot of the other three episodes, this time with fascists. It's possibly the most cynical piece of padding we've seen yet in Doctor Who – an excuse to interrupt one story by telling the exact same story in the middle.

The closest thing there is to a point is the Doctor's declaration that "free will is not an illusion after all," but like the survival of Sir Keith this is a declaration without content. Nobody's free will seems to actually affect anything. The only action that clearly matters is Stahlman's, and it takes place after he's possessed and not really having free will anymore. If anything the story seems to cut against free will mattering: given that the most visible difference between the worlds is that one is full of evil fascists and the other isn't, it doesn't seem like individual choices matter nearly as much as broad social circumstances. At best it's an interesting point that is simply made as an abstract statement with nothing in the script to back it up: another case where *Inferno* has good ideas that it's just not that interested in executing.

Except it's actually even worse than that, because for the second time in four stories we have an ending that sells out the show. The Doctor declares that the Brigadier sometimes reminds him of his other self – i.e. accuses the Brigadier of being in some sense implicitly a fascist. It's a stinging critique, in part because it gets at what should have been the point of the story – what is or isn't the difference between a fascist UNIT and the real one. Except that moments after it's made the Doctor slinks back into the hanger having inadvertently teleported the TARDIS console to a trash heap, and does a sort of "aw shucks of course we're still friends" routine with the Brigadier, with the joke being how quickly the Doctor sold out his indignant critique of the Brigadier when it was convenient to him. So the Doctor's a hypocrite and it's silly to ask whether the parallels between the military and fascism amount to anything. This is not what one hoped for when the anarchist Doctor was sent to Earth. And it's certainly not what one hoped for when the idea of a fascist version of UNIT was raised. Instead it's exactly what the worst case scenario for a parallel universe story was at the start: an excuse to get away with blowing up the world without having to clean up afterwards.

The only thing saving these episodes, effectively, is the fact that the actors are having a blast. Not just the supporting cast, though they are excellent. Derek Newark and Sheila Dunn get their teeth into a romantic subplot, with Newark doing a wonderful job of throwing his testosterone around. Olaf Pooley is a more mixed bag as Stahlman, though this may be down to the fact that the script requires Stahlman to be a barely motivated psychopath through the entire story and to never do anything but complain until he turns into a Primord. And, of course, mention has to go to John Levene, reprising the role of Benton for the third time, although his role in *The Ambassadors of Death* was minor. Still, the show has enough confidence in his recognition to give him an extended Primord transformation scene, and John Levene (who, we should remember, started as an actor in a Yeti costume) clearly gets a kick out of getting to do what's basically a werewolf scene.

No, the real acting prizes in this one go to Nicholas Courtney, Caroline John, and Jon Pertwee, who more or less singlehandedly keep the story afloat for the four parallel universe episodes. Courtney is sublime as Brigade Leader Lethbridge-Stewart, switching the confident and slightly caricatural understatement of the Brigadier out for an overconfident, slightly caricatural overstatement and playing, essentially, the Nazi soldier Brigadier instead of the British one. Hints of the hilarious military bravado of Bret Vyon pop up again here.

Caroline John, on the other hand, enjoys the fact that the writer appears to have understood her character (so there's at least one thing Houghton does better than Hulke), playing

Section Leader Elizabeth Shaw with an appealing humanism. She starts the part as far to the villainous side as Courtney, but slowly brings flickers of her normal character back into the role until her final act of shooting Lethbridge-Stewart (so the Doctor can escape) pays off. Unfortunately, the fact that Houghton is the first person to manage to write Liz the same way Holmes did means that it's too little too late – John is effective here, but a season in there's nothing to grab onto with Liz. The slow transformation back into "our" Liz carries no impact if we haven't been sold on our Liz. John does brilliantly, but as turns out to be the effective epitaph for her character, she was wasted on the part.

And then there's Pertwee, who, forced onto the back foot and made, for the first time, to be in a situation where he doesn't understand what's going on, sparkles. But as with John, this starts to shed light on a problem developing with his take on the character. An interesting aspect of Pertwee's Doctor is that it is the first time the character of the Doctor was modeled directly on the actor. This is a bit surprising. Pertwee's reputation prior to Doctor Who was as a funny voice character actor. Usually hiding behind glasses, props, and/or wigs, Pertwee would take on a voice and disappear into a character part. The appeal of him was how many character parts he could do.

As was the case with Troughton, initially much of the thought went in directions that were too over the top. Just as Troughton was going to be a windjammer captain or (allegedly) going to be blacked up, apparently one of the original plans for Pertwee was that he was going to be a relaxed, suave sort who played flamenco guitar. But eventually the idea was hit upon that playing the Doctor as Jon Pertwee might work. (Pertwee, by all accounts, found this to be a tremendous acting challenge.)

The consequences of this are wide-ranging. A fair case can be made that part of the dip in reputation the Pertwee era suffered in the '90s came down to Pertwee's somewhat stiff and rehearsed manner at conventions as he appeared "in character" as the Doctor. Certainly the degree to which Pertwee simply handled almost all interviews with a set of rehearsed lines ("Yeti-in-the-loo" and all) and vaguely in character is somewhat oddly alienating to watch, even decades later. But another, and for our purposes here more significant consequence came up in terms of the writing.

See, Pertwee was effectively playing himself. But he was also the star. I don't mean to paint him as a prima donna (although there are certainly some problematic stories about him), because the obvious consequence of this would likely have happened to any star in that circumstance. The inherent egoism of being the star is going to bleed into the part. And with Pertwee it rapidly did.

Look at the opening of *Inferno*, as he drives along in Bessie singing. It's a scene that assumes, unhesitatingly, that the viewer just likes watching Jon Pertwee as the Doctor for the sake of watching Jon Pertwee as the Doctor, doing Doctory things. And again, this isn't a problem either. Central to any love of Pertwee's Doctor is a love of his defiant, flamboyant self-confidence, and that comes right out of Pertwee's leading-man charm. Pertwee's relish of being the leading man is poured into the part in the dashing action hero elements of the character.

And to be fair, Houghton puts that to good use – only Pertwee's unflappable Doctor could calmly debut his skill in Venusian karate with a sort of idle sense of "well of course you've never seen me use it before. It never came up." But on the whole, the problem with a Doctor defined by pure confidence is that you can't knock him off his game. As a result, Pertwee's Doctor is kept safe to a degree unseen in previous versions. Which is what's so nice about Houghton's setup – it's the first time we've really seen this Doctor off his guard and afraid. And it reveals something interesting about Pertwee as an actor.

For all that the heart of his performance of the Doctor is him finding a way to confidently project himself in front of a camera and read someone else's lines, Pertwee is reliably at his best when his Doctor is knocked off his game. Pertwee generally seems to want to play the part confident and in control. But when the script doesn't let him, the challenge pushes him to a new level. From here on out, one thing you'll notice throughout the Pertwee years is that when Pertwee is knocked off his game or given a problem to deal with, he does better than when he's left to his own devices.

But all of this should just show the root problem. It's not that the show needs to be carried by the actors. That happened in both the Hartnell and Troughton eras at times. But when it happened there, it happened towards the ends of their runs. The fourth story into a bold new direction for the show shouldn't be relying on the fact that its actors happen to really get their teeth into the conceit of part of the script to paper over the fact that the script has no ideas and minimal logic. Yes, they're up to the task, and the result is a compelling story, but it's hardly a good omen.

What we have here is an era gasping for breath and visibly out of ideas that's already had to have its blushes saved by the actors bootstrapping the story into watchability. However good the story is, it's also a clear sign that something has to change. This has been a good twenty-five episodes of television, but unlike Doctor Who, the show we have here isn't one that can run forever. Thankfully, the general consensus of the viewing public was that whatever this was, it was indeed quite watchable. Ratings are up, and the series, to many people's mild surprise, gets picked up for another year. Which, we should remember, was something that very nearly didn't happen towards the end of the Lloyd/Bryant/Sherwin era. The fact of the matter is, the Season Seven team saved the show from cancellation. This new idea may not be fully formed, but then, twenty-six episodes into Doctor Who's first season the show was just through with *The Keys of Marinus*. Given time, it figured itself out. Barry Letts, the newly installed producer, had to hit the ground running. At this point he hasn't had time to stop and think about what he wants the program to be. What he has had time to do is put out a bevy of fires and ensure that some pretty good television made it to screen. Now he gets a chance to pause, take a deep breath, and work on making Doctor Who great again.

Time Can Be Rewritten: *The Scales of Injustice*

There is a concept within the novel era of Doctor Who called "fanwank." What this rather aggressively memorable term means is the profusion of continuity references for the sake of it. The term is, obviously, at least a bit disdainful, although as with most masturbation it's a sort of disdain expressed primarily by practitioners. And of the writers from this era, one of the ones with the biggest reputation for fanwank is Gary Russell.

But the supposed disdain of fanwank is a complex thing. Ostensibly one of the differences between the novel era and the revived series is that the revived series is for the general public and doesn't do fanwank. This raises the question of why there's a difference between fanwank and, for instance, having the Macra pop up for a cameo forty years after their last appearance. And *The Scales of Injustice*, deliberately or not, explores the nature of that line thoroughly.

This book is not so much continuity heavy as it is capable of producing continuity gravity. Direct references exist not only to the four Pertwee stories preceding it but also to *Time-Flight*, *Remembrance of the Daleks*, *The War Machines*, *The Invasion*, *The Web of Fear*, *The Sea Devils*, *Warriors of the Deep*, and probably a fair swath more that I didn't even notice. One thing you may notice about that list is that not all of the stories are even ones that we've covered by this point in the project. This book features continuity from ahead of its supposed era of television.

Which means we're in the wild and wonderful world of future continuity, a topic we've picked up in a couple of the "Time Can Be Rewritten" entries in the first few books, perhaps most obviously *The Dark Path* back in the Troughton volume. But more even than *The Dark Path*, this is a book about reconciling Doctor Who stories and squaring away continuity errors. It tackles not only the nature of the Brigadier's love life (glimpsed in *Planet of the Spiders* and *Battlefield*), Mike Yates's assignment to UNIT and promotion to Captain (complete with a gratuitous scene to explain why

Benton didn't get the promotion), Liz Shaw's departure (about which more later), but also, for the horde of people who were concerned about it, the question of why the Doctor claimed to have twice negotiated with the Silurians for peace in *Warriors of the Deep* when in fact he only did so once.

Let's pause here for a moment and look at that. I don't want to get too far into *Warriors of the Deep* some thirteen seasons too early (actually, I'd have preferred to never get too far into it at all), but accounting for this supposed continuity error is trivial. First, a bit of context for anyone who is actually trying to use this blog to learn about early Doctor Who. *Warriors of the Deep* is a 1984 story in which the Fifth Doctor faces both the Silurians and the Sea Devils, the latter being cousins of the Silurians introduced in Season Nine. It's fairly obvious that Johnny Byrne, the writer of that story, was intending the line to refer to the events of *The Silurians* and *The Sea Devils*. The mistake is not in the number, but in whether or not *The Sea Devils* counted as extending the hand of friendship or not. This is admittedly debatable, but there's at least a case that can be made for *The Sea Devils*.

In other words, despite it not even being clear that there's a continuity error to fix here, Gary Russell has written an entire book to try to fix one. Which is, roughly speaking, where fanwank goes problematic. Because there is something a bit weird about the series continuity for the purposes of resolving and explaining arcane points within said continuity. It is more, well, masturbatory. It's not entirely clear that this is a solid reason to write an entire novel. Indeed, I think it's probably a fair bit easier to argue the other side of that debate.

I'm not going to say that fanwank is a bad thing. Far from it, I enjoy a meticulous bit of continuity wrangling as much as the next mildly antisocial anorak. But there's something necessarily odd about these attempts to stitch continuity together. The results by necessity do not quite fit with the stories they're assembling, reading as a strange awkward midpoint between being a story about the familiar characters from Doctor Who and an abstract intellectual exercise that's been written up in narrative form.

Within *The Scales of Injustice*, for instance, Department C19, a concept invented in *Time-Flight*, is revealed as a secretive organization that controls UNIT's funding, setting off a somewhat messy bit of conspiracy wrangling involving The Glasshouse, a mental institution basically for people who snapped seeing top secret alien stuff, and the Vault, a massive collection of alien memorabilia salvaged from the various Earth-based stories. These are cool ideas, undoubtedly, but it's tough to see how they fit in around the UNIT era as we've seen it thus far. It's not that it contradicts anything. It doesn't quite (although the book does contain a massive retcon to *The Silurians* in which the Doctor's accusation of murder turns out to be totally false). But equally important, it doesn't quite fit either. There's nothing within the UNIT era that is made clearer or more sensible by the introduction of the Glasshouse and the Vault, and there's a fair amount that would need to be re-explained. It's not, if you will, terribly useful.

But there's a larger problem with this book's efforts at continuity. This book came out in July of 1996, which was a particularly bleak historical moment for Doctor Who. The TV Movie had just aired, and it was already clear that it was not going to lead to a larger revival of Doctor Who. What it was going to lead to, however, was the novel rights being taken away from Virgin so that the BBC could do books in house at a greater profit. So this book came out at a moment when Doctor Who's future prospects seemed bleak, as part of a novel line that had one foot in the grave already. Doctor Who looked like a finished thing that could be safely made the subject of a forensic effort to tie up all its supposed loose threads.

Now, however, it's 2013, Doctor Who is alive and well, and there's been a pretty major thread introduced to Doctor Who that's in hindsight visibly absent from *The Scales of Injustice*. Looking at the descriptions of C19 and the Vault, it's inconceivable how these things could exist and function without any reference to *Torchwood*.

Ah, yes, *Torchwood*. The hot new pet game for Pertwee-era watchers – how the hell does any of what we see within the Pertwee era reconcile with *Torchwood*? I have an entire essay on this later in the book, but the short form is that there's not a lot of good ways to do it. Then again, it's no harder to work *Torchwood* into the Pertwee era than Department C19 or *Remembrance of the Daleks* are, and the book does that. So why doesn't *The Scales of Injustice* deal with *Torchwood*?

Well, because *Torchwood* was still a decade out in 1996, obviously. And OK, that's probably fair. Except that *The Scales of Injustice* is already holding the Pertwee era accountable for things from its future, and so there's something about this defense that doesn't quite hold up. Once the door is opened to the sort of ludicrous retconning this book embraces, it's tough to draw a line on something as arbitrary as historical possibility. Especially because the book as it stands feels . . . obsolete. Certainly it's nearly impossible to imagine that Russell would approach it the same way today as he did in 1996. That's the problem: anyone writing this book in 2013 would include *Torchwood*. Russell included. Heck, Russell especially. And so this book can only hope to capture its author's intentions with relation to an already lost historical moment of Doctor Who.

Which is something that the fanwank genre, love it as I do, can never quite account for. All attempts to cobble together pet theories out of existing evidence are as much a product of their own eras as the "errors" that they attempt to correct. The idea of seamlessly fitting a big continuity fix into the era whose errors were never realized at the time (and often couldn't be realized at the time) is inherently absurd. This is what's so intensely masturbatory about fanwank – its only pleasure is in its own creation, and not in any legacy.

All of which said, this book has the marginal advantage that at least some of the problems it tries to correct were visible in 1970/'71. The big three are the introduction of Mike Yates, the departure of Liz, and the question of the Brigadier's personal life. The first of these is easy to account for – Yates appears in *Terror of the Autons* fully formed, with everyone treating him as an established part of UNIT, despite that being his debut. There's no effort to do anything more than treat him as a character who's been around but off-screen and never mentioned. This story's attempt to deal with Yates as a Sergeant and to show his promotion to Captain fills what is at least a visible gap on the screen, if not one that necessarily counted as a problem, and is unobjectionable.

The second is downright welcome. The fact that Liz was abruptly written out between seasons without significant explanation is really comparable only to the writing out of Dodo, Ben, and Polly in its sheer callousness. Much like having a major character commit genocide with no consequences, dropping a major character abruptly and without expectations does damage to the show, making it harder to invest in new characters. When characters are treated as disposable by the show itself, why should we invest in them? And this is a larger problem in the UNIT era than it ever had been before because the UNIT era is based around the presence of a larger regular supporting cast than the series has ever had before. The damage had, of course, been done and healed from by 1996, but there's something understandable about filling in such a visible gap even after the fact.

Finally there's the Brigadier's personal life, in which we discover that his wife, Fiona, and he have a fractious marriage because of the Brigadier's having to be called off to work constantly. Over the course of the book, his marriage dissolves utterly. This is the most bizarre portion of the book, tying in barely at all with anything we see over the course of the actual UNIT era. In fact, it's actively dissonant with the UNIT era, in which the Brigadier is defined precisely by his slightly over the top detachment and calm. Adding a breaking marriage actually undermines the character as we see him and as he functions on the screen. The fact that the Doctor has the ludicrous line "I am truly sorry about Fiona and Kate. I hope you find some amicable way to get on with your respective lives without too much pain" doesn't help. (Go ahead. Try to imagine Pertwee delivering that line.) This entire thread is weirdly dissonant.

It's not, mind you, that the story it offers is a bad one. Rather, it's that everything about it jars with the point of the rest of the book. Everything else in this book is about reconciling the Pertwee era with other bits of Doctor Who. This, on the other hand, is about telling a story that is actively irreconcilable with the Pertwee era. A book that treats all the programmatic UNIT characters as real people with lives outside of UNIT would be a fascinating alternate take on the Pertwee era. But to do it inside a book that's otherwise obsessed with making the series consistent just doesn't work. Fanwank and making the characters richer and more lively than they were in the original are crossed purposes.

But that this is a problem in the first place points to a larger issue with the Pertwee era. As we saw with *Inferno*, the show is getting to a point where it's a character drama. It's starting to rely on audience investment in characters as part of what makes the show work. This is why Liz's non-send-off is such a problem in the first place. With Jo, the Master, and Yates all arriving in the next story, we have a fixed recurring cast that's going to stick around for three seasons in its entirety, and, for many of the characters, for four seasons. That Letts immediately made such an investment in the supporting cast suggests he was very much aware of the problems caused by writing Liz out the way they did, and it shows how what Russell tries to do with the Brigadier is still fundamentally compatible with what the series was trying to do in 1970 – '71. Even if Russell overshoots the mark with the Brigadier, there is a sense in which this dimension of the book is a case of making the UNIT era – both up to this point and beyond – live up to what it tries to be better than the show does.

But in the end *The Scales of Injustice* is still a bit of a mess. The depth of retcons and the degree to which they jar with the actual era on television muddy the waters to the point where it feels like you're reading about Doctor Who impersonators rather than the characters. It feels, in effect, like fanfiction instead of like Doctor Who. But on the other hand, there's something intriguing here. It may be fanfiction, but it's got some interesting ideas. It doesn't fit seamlessly into its gap, but no "Time Can Be Rewritten" story has ever (or will ever) fit seamlessly into its gap. The dissonance is the point – the reason to revisit the past. This is 1970 avec 1996. Now that it too is a historical object, it has become, in an odd way, more interesting for it. In a topic as vast as Doctor Who, the opportunity to see vividly a 1996 take on what Doctor Who is in 1970 is an oddly compelling signpost in the show's evolution. That nobody but a die-hard fan would care seems, if not beside the point, like no more of an issue than the fact that nobody but a die-hard fan would have cared about *The Scales of Injustice* in the first place.

Pop Between Realities, Home in Time for Tea: *Doomwatch* and *The Atrocity Exhibition*

As we watch the generally compelling, if occasionally kind of sad spectacle of Doctor Who frantically trying to reinvent itself on a brand new formula and premise, it may be worth looking at other contemporaneous British attempts at Earth-based science fiction to get some idea of what exactly Doctor Who is aspiring towards. It's not, of course, as if Doctor Who has never morphed itself into other genres before. But those usually amount to a well-defined thing called Doctor Who crashing headlong into some other genre. For instance the historicals, especially in their latter days, were all about genre crossing. But note the specific wording – a story like *The Gunfighters* was about taking Doctor Who and crashing it into the Western, then filming the explosion. With the UNIT stories we are by and large seeing something different: a fair swath of the production team does not seem to be trying to cross Doctor Who into another genre. They're trying to make Doctor Who as an example of another genre. Until we understand what that genre is, it's going to be difficult to say what can be accomplished by turning Doctor Who into that genre.

To some extent we've already seen what that genre is via Monty Python. Or, more to the point, we've seen that whatever Doctor Who is trying to do, it's so flamingly obvious within the context of British culture that it can be parodied prior to Doctor Who doing it. Of course, if we re-watch the Science Fiction sketch, we can see that it's just as much a parody of the old Quatermass formula. In other words, there's an established sort of science fiction here that Nigel Kneale invented with Quatermass that Doctor Who, under UNIT, comes perilously close to faithfully and blindly discharging. Indeed, three of the four stories in Season Seven owe obvious debts to Quatermass, by which I mean they flagrantly borrow the basic plot or key scenes. And *Inferno* would frankly have made a better fourth Quatermass serial than Quatermass. (Of course, we've also seen with the Brigadier the beginnings of a response to this sort of obviousness, which we'll see expanded on when we get to *Terror of the Autons*.)

But Doctor Who wasn't even the only contemporary sci-fi thriller airing on BBC1, little yet the only one being made in Britain at the turn of the decade. In 1970, at least, the most prominent and respectable show along those lines was *Doomwatch*, created by Gerry Davis and Kit Pedler. Like *Adam Adamant Lives!*, *Doomwatch* is a case of "what Doctor Who people did next." And like *Adam Adamant Lives!*, the answer is "something that is almost, but not quite, what Doctor Who did next." Just as *Adam Adamant Lives!* prefigured the charismatic lead model of the Troughton years, *Doomwatch* was an attempt by Davis and Pedler to work through their issues (well, Pedler's issues mainly) regarding contemporary science via contemporary Earth-based sci-fi that featured maverick government employees patrolling the frontiers of science, led by Spencer Quist, a Nobel Prize-winning scientist haunted by his guilt over the Manhattan Project, and played superbly by John Paul.

Perhaps the most surprising thing about *Doomwatch* is that it's actually quite good. (This is alarming because the creative talent on it was, as I mentioned, Kit Pedler and Gerry Davis.) The bulk of their contributions are covered in the previous two volumes, but neither came out of our analysis looking very good. Kit Pedler is generally capable of coming up with neat ideas, but showed little inclination to do anything with them. Gerry Davis, on the other hand, is responsible for *The Celestial Toymaker*, and *The Tomb of the Cybermen* – two of the most offensively frustrating stories in Doctor Who's history. (Although, to be fair, he's also responsible for *The Tenth Planet*.) But *Doomwatch* is far better than anything they did for Doctor Who, and suggests strongly that Doctor Who might just have not been the right show for their genuinely prodigious talents.

Part of this may be that *Doomwatch*, with its single episode stories, enjoys some pacing advantages over the serialized Doctor Who. More broadly, it's just a more normal way of writing television: the serialized story model is unusual outside of children's television. And while it's not clear that Doctor Who is outside of children's television as such, it drew plenty of writers from other science fiction shows, which made for a strange transition. *Doomwatch*, with its relatively lean forty-five-minute stories, tends to be much more of a taut thriller. It seems, in many ways, like Davis has a certain quantity of ideas per story, and that number is better suited to a single forty-five-minute story than it is to stories made up of four or, more often, six twenty-five-minute episodes.

In a forty-five-minute container, Davis's considerable talent for set pieces absolutely sings (I am assuming, based on the fact that Pedler's role on Doctor Who was largely as an idea man, that he played a similar role on *Doomwatch* and that Davis did most of the scripting as such). The cold open of the first episode, "The Plastic Eaters," which ends with a plane falling out of the sky as all its plastic components melt in front of its crew, is a thing of wonder, and a highlight of the sort of horror that *Doomwatch* is good at. *Doomwatch* hinges on the idea that the scientific advancement of the world could be a source of terror instead of a good thing. So what was, in 1970, a familiar but still relatively shiny and new piece of technology, the airplane, is ripe for this. And Davis plays deftly off of the basic terror of an airplane: the fact that one is trapped in it, and that if anything goes wrong with it one is almost certainly doomed. The image of the plane melting, thus keeping its basic form and shape even as everything becomes useless, captures this horror perfectly, and the BBC proves surprisingly good at making it happen.

If anything, Davis benefits from having a container that is slightly too small for his stories, in that it requires him to actually be deft in his plotting and structuring. *Doomwatch* is a piece of television that actually requires its audience's attention – I failed several times at watching it while doing other things. While this isn't unheard of for television in 1970, it suggests a savvy use of the medium. Certainly Doctor Who has never required its audience's complete attention by this point in its life. But *Doomwatch* is quite clever, and avoids overstressing its points with dramatic "look at me" pacing and incidental music in favor of a subtler, more detached presentation.

"The Plastic Eaters" itself, of course, is a bit silly. But even in it there's a sense that this is a more mature and interesting depiction of contemporary science than we've gotten elsewhere. It gives a strong sense of how much things have changed in the seven years since Doctor Who showed up. It is worth recalling how in the early days of Doctor Who whenever the Doctor met another scientist there was a ton of chinwagging about how they were both scientists, and thus part of some elite and enlightened order of rationality. The clear ethical assumption was that scientists were special people we should all listen to by virtue of the fact that they're scientists.

Doomwatch, on the other hand, displayed a far more pessimistic view of scientists, viewing them largely as amoral obsessives playing with fire and underestimating the dangers of doing so. The scientists at fault for the plastic-melting virus, for instance, are not lunatics bent on power. Rather, they're driven by the amount of money on offer if they can figure out how to make it work, and willing to cut corners on safety to get there faster and cheaper. The Doomwatch team exists to protect the general public from the consequences of this recklessness. The opposition they face isn't from people who want power at any cost – people like Stahlman, for instance – but from bureaucrats loathe to cut a promising and prestigious project who are willing to blind themselves to evidence that it threatens the public. In other words, *Doomwatch* essentially tracks a civil war among scientists between those who work for their funders and benefactors and those who work for the people.

Let's look at another, and even more extraordinary episode: "Re-Entry is Forbidden" – an episode of particular interest to Doctor Who because the space capsule set it uses was also used in *The Ambassadors of Death*, having been built as a co-financed item between the two shows. Furthermore, it's an absolutely extraordinary piece of television. The conflict in this one stems over an experimental nuclear rocket that has a fault during re-entry and nearly risks exploding and spraying nuclear fallout over half of Britain. The rocket, launched by NASA, turns out to have one of Spencer Quist's former students on it, and speculation arises that human error on his part is the cause of the near-disaster.

First we should acknowledge the degree to which this episode has a firm confidence in its mastery of television. In a characteristic moment of *Doomwatch* subtlety, we see the mistake on camera as Larch, the astronaut in question, makes an error in punching in some numbers. The error is never commented upon explicitly, or even acknowledged – it's down entirely to the viewer to notice that he gets a number wrong when pushing buttons. Similarly, when the rocket starts to take flight at the end of the cold open, the camera begins cutting to test patterns and static, with the soundtrack from the space launch carrying over for a few seconds, thus blurring the line between the cold open and the credits sequence, which also begins with a chaotic series of images. It's remarkably savvy, and a case of the medium of television becoming a part of the storytelling itself.

But what's really fascinating about "Re-Entry is Forbidden" is the way in which it handles the space program. As the investigation into what went wrong on the rocket continues, it becomes increasingly clear that the problem is that Larch is suffering from severe mental illness, specifically intense paranoia. The seeming reason for this paranoia is the fact that his wife is cheating on him, a fact subtly but repeatedly stressed throughout the episode. (In one of the better lines, a member of the Doomwatch team observes that behind every jealous husband is an unsatisfied wife.)

It's worth comparing this to the equivalent Doctor Who episode. As good as *The Ambassadors of Death* was – and I think it's one of the highlights of the Pertwee era – "Re-Entry is Forbidden" beats it in a significant regard in that the motivating factors are so intensely human. Carrington has human motivations, but they're nothing as everyday and pedestrian as Larch's jealousy. It's extremely gutsy for a science fiction program to engage in a plot that hinges on human concerns like mental illness (in a genuine sense, as opposed to a pantomime Stahlman sense) and marital infidelity. It's a far more interesting, human take on science fiction, and it does a better job of answering the challenge of *The War Games* than anything Doctor Who manages in the whole of the Pertwee era. And perhaps more to the point, it does a better job of living up to the broad purpose of science fiction. The merging of everyday concerns with technological ones is what science fiction should do. Watching *Doomwatch*, the sense is as much "yes, of course this is how it should be done" as it is "wow, that's really impressive." It is in other words, a damn fine television show that does the same general sorts of stories that Doctor Who does, albeit with fewer aliens. But frankly, it upstages Doctor Who by a considerable margin, at least at this point.

Even more extraordinary is JG Ballard's 1970 novel *The Atrocity Exhibition*. I will freely admit that there is a certain madness to citing Ballard in relation to Doctor Who, at least at this stage. Come the Sylvester McCoy era we'll get to a story that is overtly and consciously based on Ballard's work, but in 1970 Ballard is so far outside of the mainstream that the idea of it directly influencing Doctor Who is almost farcical. Even *Doomwatch*, although radical in some key regards, was nowhere near experimental enough to borrow from Ballard, and it's downright absurd to imagine Doctor Who coming anywhere near an episode title like "The Assassination of John Fitzgerald Kennedy Considered as a Downhill Motor Race," little yet the (absolutely brilliant) "Why I Want to Fuck Ronald Reagan."

On the other hand, it's important to look at the fringes of the culture in understanding its progression. Doctor Who may not usually be overtly influenced by radical counterculture, but the two have never been complete strangers.

All of which said, the suggestion that *The Atrocity Exhibition* belongs to the counterculture undersells it a bit. The book is absolutely staggering, and feels radical even today. Part of this is its sheer obscenity. Its basic premise is that each chapter follows a different facet of the same protagonist (whose name changes among similar names – Travis, Talbot, etc.). This protagonist has suffered a sort of psychotic break, and is obsessed with, as the novel puts it, causing World War III, though not in a conventional sense, given that World War III will apparently take place entirely inside his own head.

The result is a novel that detonates the boundaries between sex, celebrity, violence, technology, and the human body. No. Not plays with. Detonates. Take, for instance, a more or less randomly chosen passage (the list structure it uses is common in the novel):

> (1) The flesh impact: Karen Novotny's beckoning figure in the shower stall, open thighs and exposed pubis – traffic fatalities screamed in this soft collision. (2) The overpasses below the apartment: the angles between the concrete buttresses contained for Talbot an immense anguish. (3) The crushed fender: in its broken geometry Talbot saw the dismembered body of Karen Novotny, the alternate death of Ralph Nader.

What is interesting here is twofold. First, of course, is the extremity of Ballard's writing – the fact that he's pushing the limits of taste and sense to paint a disturbing picture. This is, of course, something the BBC would (one assumes) have trouble doing. But the second and frankly more interesting thing he's doing comes in the way in which his book uses the visual thought processes of film and television. Look at the first numbered item – the description of the naked body of Karen Novotny, which asserts traffic accidents are screaming in her pubic area. Clearly we are not meant to believe that there are cars literally driving around her vulva. Instead this line works along a logic of actualized metaphor – some visual similarity between her public region and traffic fatalities (other sections of the book elaborate on these similarities in disturbing detail) that gets turned into an actual equivalence within Talbot's mental landscape.

But this is exactly what cinema and film do via cuts all the time. *Spearhead from Space* did it repeatedly with a trick where someone would ask a question and then the camera would cut forward in time, but the first line of the new scene would also serve as an answer to the previously asked question, thus collapsing time via camera work. This is what editing is for. The human mind makes a link between two consecutive shots, and if that link is not immediately literally obvious, instead metaphoric links get made. All Ballard is doing is reappropriating this logic into prose and exploring its implications there. And while that logic doesn't extend out of prose's technological features in the same way it does from television's, it still works in that context.

What Ballard does in the novel that's so incredible, then, is to engage in a massive project of suturing that conflates wildly disparate objects into a semi-coherent whole. These objects are picked from the mundanity of everyday life – sex, celebrities, car crashes, war, etc. But Ballard builds them into a collaged edifice that is striking and horrific. And, notably, he binds the process by which this edifice is built into the edifice. At one point it is commented that "for Traven science is the ultimate pornography, analytic activity whose main aim is to isolate objects or events from their contexts in time and space." Science is explicitly granted a power equivalent to film editing. The scientist is not a detached figure in a lab coat, but a figure who wields the power of television over reality itself.

This, in theory, is something Doctor Who could do – use its structure to expose and comment upon the parallels between the military, science, everyday life, the alien, and the flashy dandy aesthetics of Jon Pertwee. The result would not need to be car crash pornography (although there will always be a part of me that wants to see a Doctor Who story entitled "Mae West's Reduction Mammoplasty"). But like *Doomwatch*, it would be compelling and challenging in a way Doctor Who in the Pertwee era has yet to be.

But the truth is that at the end Season Seven the *Doomwatch* approach is starting to feel increasingly limited and played out. Whereas the other idea of the Pertwee era, the one implicit in *Spearhead from Space* – has not really been thoroughly explored since that story. And the ideas implicit in that – big, programmatic characters who sit on the edge of parody and drama – come close to those of *The Atrocity Exhibition*, fitting comfortably with a logic of spectacle and media. It's not coincidental that these ideas are coming up in the culture at the same time as glam rock is making its first forays into the mainstream. The approach taken by *Doomwatch* and Season Seven is compelling, but also just about the most obvious thing for contemporary Earth-based sci-fi in 1970. There is another option, and it's altogether stranger and more wonderful.

He Was a Friend at First (*Terror of the Autons*)

It's January 2, 1971. Dave Edmunds is at number one with "I Hear You Knocking." That's unseated the next week by Clive Dunn's "Granddad," a piece of Victorian nostalgia by one of the stars of the sitcom *Dad's Army*, which holds number two for the next three weeks. Lower in the charts are the Jackson 5, Neil Diamond, Glen Campbell, and Andy Williams. But the real action is T. Rex's chart debut with "Ride a White Swan," which starts at number ten in the first week, and rises to a peak position of number two at the end of this story. The success of "Ride the White Swan" is generally recognized as the real start of glam rock as a cultural phenomenon. And glam will serve as the primary musical accompaniment to the Pertwee era from here on out.

In other news, we've jumped ahead a few months, and they were relatively eventful. The US withdrew from Cambodia. Thor Heyerdahl's Ra II expedition was completed successfully. The Aswan High Dam opened in Egypt. The largest rock festival of all time happened on the Isle of Wight, while both Jimi Hendrix and Janis Joplin died of drug overdoses. The US's ridiculously meager and pathetic version of the BBC, PBS, begins broadcasting, which will turn out to have profound ramifications for Doctor Who as, with minimal budget, importing BBC shows proves to be a cost-effective policy for them, resulting in Doctor Who's US debut in 1972. The October Crisis begins in Canada when, in a series of events that seems deeply bemusing given Canada's current stereotypical reputation, Quebecois separatist terrorists kidnapped the British Trade Commissioner and held him hostage for sixty days.

Which catches us up to this story. During the month this is on the air, a stairway crush at a Scottish football match between the Old Firm results in sixty-six deaths. (For those playing along at home, the Old Firm refers to Celtic and Rangers, two Glaswegian football teams whose sporting rivalry serves as a proxy rivalry for Catholic/Protestant sectarian disputes and thus, by extension, for the Troubles that continued to calmly rear their heads.) Harold Wilson's flagship venture, the Open University, begins. And the world's first ODI cricket match is played between Australia and the UK.

Which finally brings us to Doctor Who. On the one hand, *Terror of the Autons* is one of the most beloved Pertwee stories, full of classic moments, fantastic scary bits, and, furthermore, the debut of three classic characters in Jo Grant, Mike Yates, and the Master. And this is its general reputation. But there's another aspect of this story that's worth noting.

I've talked before about a general downturn in the reputation of the Pertwee era that took place in the 1990s. One of the most significant artifacts of this downturn was a review by Paul Cornell in the magazine *DWB*. This may require some context. Paul Cornell is, of course, familiar as the writer of two television stories during the Russell T Davies years. But his career began in the 1990s as one of the primary writers of the Virgin Books line. A peculiarity of the early 1990s, though, is that the major writers of the time were also active in fandom at large. (Paul Cornell even edited an anthology of fan writing in the mid-'90s called *License Denied*.)

Which brings us to *DWB*. Starting in the late 1970s there were several major Doctor Who publications, most notably *Doctor Who Magazine* and *The Celestial Toyroom*. But these represented a very orthodox view of fandom. *Doctor Who Magazine* was an official publication that served primarily as a mouthpiece for the production team, while *The Celestial Toyroom* was the publication of the quasi-authorized Doctor Who Appreciation Society. So in 1983 Gary Leigh started *DWB*, short for *Doctor Who Bulletin*, as a fanzine that rapidly became quasi-professional and, eventually, relaunched as *Dreamwatch*, a perfectly mainstream general sci-fi magazine that survived into 2007.

But during its fanzine days, *DWB* became, essentially, the major dissident Doctor Who publication. It was notorious for its hatred of John Nathan-Turner, the producer at the time, but it was also just the major place in general where contrarian commentary on Doctor Who could be published. And in 1993 Paul Cornell published his review of *Terror of the Autons*. The text of the review is easily Googled ("Paul Cornell Terror of the Autons" brings it up), and I recommend going and having a look. Spoiler: he's not very fond of it.

The crux of Cornell's objection is something we talked about last week with *Inferno* – the way in which the conflation of Pertwee and the Doctor has given the character an egotism he previously lacked. But Cornell's real bitter swipe comes at the end of the review, where he dryly declares that "they exiled the Doctor to Earth and made him a Tory." Here there is some complexity to sort out. The Tories are the colloquial name for the Conservative Party in the UK – the party that was in power in 1970, and also in power in 1993, having won their fourth and final consecutive election the year before. But by 1993 they were most associated with Margaret Thatcher, who led the party and served as Prime Minister from 1979 to 1990 before being ousted and replaced by John Major. Thatcher is largely a subject for another book, but it's important to realize the degree to which she was vilified by a particular sort of liberal counterculturalism – specifically the sort that characterized Doctor Who from 1987 on, and that Paul Cornell was unabashedly sympathetic to, making his line particularly cutting.

The crux of Cornell's objection is that Pertwee's Doctor is portrayed as an upper class elitist. This is, by and large, a fair cop. Even Pertwee's visual appearance, with the velvet smoking jacket and frills, speaks to an old-fashioned sort of wealth that is inexorably linked to the Tories. But the problems also extend to the dialogue. Cornell highlights moments like the Doctor speaking confidently and off-handedly about how gentlemen only talk about money, or his downright nasty attack on Jo after she innocently tries to help him when he apparently sets his lab on fire, "You ham-fisted bun vendor!" It's worth looking at the nature of this attack in particular, as he specifically attacks her based on her perceived (working class) job. That's the thing that Cornell finds problematic, and honestly, he's right to.

There is something deeply uncomfortable about the continual smug superiority of the Doctor in this era.

But Cornell's review, insightful as it was, was also terribly controversial. This is, as I said, largely a beloved story, and that's understandable; there's a lot to like. One thing of note is that the core cast as it exists in this story – the Doctor, Jo, the Brigadier, Benton, Yates, and the Master – remain intact basically for the next three seasons. That's not as many episodes as Hartnell or Troughton got, but it's as many years as either of them got, and something we've never seen Doctor Who do before: take a production team and just continue with one approach over three years. The only problem is that at the moment there doesn't seem to be a consensus as to what the approach they're continuing with actually is.

One way we've started to look at the Pertwee era is in terms of the Brigadier as an almost Pythonesque (and for once we're using that term to mean something other than "stupidly zany") character who continually highlights the absurdity of the situation. This was Robert Holmes's invention back in *Spearhead from Space*, and served to give Pertwee's Doctor an immediately necessary object – a foil. What Holmes does in *Terror of the Autons*, then, is to expand on this technique by introducing two new characters who work the same way the Brigadier does.

The first of these characters in Jo Grant. Jo is a hilariously brilliant companion. But to understand why what Holmes does with her is so brilliant, you have to understand the counter-narrative – the person who manifestly isn't on the same page as Holmes here, Terrance Dicks. See, it was Dicks who decided that Liz Shaw had to go (though the pregnant Caroline Johns probably would not have returned anyway) because she wasn't working as a Doctor Who companion, and who designed Jo as her replacement.

Dicks is a puzzling figure, as I may have alluded previously. On the one hand, he is unquestionably one of the most skilled writers in Doctor Who. On the other, he falls somewhat short of the legacy one might expect him to have given that for several reasons. First, absence makes the heart grow fonder, and Terrance Dicks's Doctor Who writing career spans the years from 1968 to 2008, leaving little room for absence. Second, a forty-year career is going to have a lot of turkeys no matter who is doing the writing, and many of those turkeys were centered in his latter years writing novels for the program, which disproportionately impact his reputation.

But third, and perhaps most significant, Dicks's long-term association with the show and frequent appearances at conventions and on DVD documentaries mean that his accounts of the behind-the-scenes aspects of the show are frequently disseminated. And they're . . . well, aside from the fact that Dicks has as much of a gift for a memorable phrase in his storytelling as he does in his writing, and as much of a willingness to use that phrase over and over again (a neither cruel nor cowardly sound, for instance, or the fact that the Doctor never wheezes or groans), Dicks is, when telling stories about the series, not always the most sympathetic figure.

There's a fair case to be made that this is just another facet of Dicks's skills as a raconteur: that he quietly and self-deprecatingly sends himself up with stories he knows don't make him look too good because they're better stories. Certainly fact-checking Dicks's accounts often turns up some problems. But he's prone to doing things like publicly identifying himself as a supporter of the British Empire. Or, more relevant for this story, saying point blank that he thinks the only real job of a Doctor Who companion is to ask the Doctor to explain the plot and to get kidnapped. Accordingly, he claims, with a pride that is thoroughly irksome, that he ditched Liz in favor of Jo because Liz was too smart and what the show really needed was an unintelligent ditz. Which more or less confirms every single one of the worst suspicions the Pertwee era raises.

On paper, Jo looks like exactly what Dicks claims she is. She's designed as an unintelligent blonde bimbo with no demonstrable skills who got assigned to UNIT because of her powerful uncle and who the Brigadier has decided to foist off on the Doctor because he's a raging egoist who isn't going to listen to a scientist like Liz anyway and, as the Brigadier puts it, just needs someone to hand him test tubes. But watching *Terror of the Autons* one gets the distinct feeling that Robert Holmes reacted with a deep horror at this idea and, in characteristic Holmesian style, proceeded to mock it ruthlessly without anybody noticing. (This is neither the first nor the last Robert Holmes script that makes the most sense if you read it as deliberately insulting or taunting the people running the program. See also *The Space Pirates* from the preceding volume.)

So what we get is Jo Grant as a parallel to the Brigadier: another character who is far too sane for the world she's in. But where the Brigadier is a sane, levelheaded military type in a world in which that makes no sense as a reaction, Jo is a plucky, well-meaning ditz who's in a world full of complicated science, thrilling adventure, and mortal peril. And so she approaches it, basically, by unceasingly being plucky and ditzy no matter how convoluted or dangerous things get around her. Holmes establishes this beautifully in the first episode of *Terror of the Autons*, where Jo is found by the Master and sheepishly rises from her hiding place and calmly says "Oh. Hello!" It's perfect – the companion walks into her first moment of mortal danger and is utterly unfazed by it.

The effect is to take the character Terrance Dicks designed to be a useless bimbo and make her into yet another subversion of the entire structure of the show. And Katy Manning is more than game for it, proving every bit as capable as Nicholas Courtney in selling illogical reactions based on character integrity. The two of them are both essentially ontological forces in the narrative; you can do anything you want in a Doctor Who story featuring Jo or the Brigadier so long as Jo is still a ditz and the Brigadier is still completely and utterly composed. They become hard limits of how the narrative can be stretched, and because they're absolutely ridiculous characters, the narrative delightfully skews around them.

The other character Holmes does this with, as Cornell notes, is a bit more of a mixed bag. The Master is, to say the least, a vexed Doctor Who character. It is certainly possible to write a very good Master story, and it is possible to play the part of the Master very well. But for some reason these two things hardly ever happen in the same story. Usually with Delgado it's the acting that's solid, but in this story he's still finding his feet in the role, and is hobbled by the fact that Barry Letts, as director, is working at cross purposes with Holmes as a writer. Letts wants the Master to be all sneering menace. Holmes wants the Master to be hilarious.

Let's note that the Master's plan makes no sense. No. Not only no sense. A sort of sprawling anti-sense that makes Cybermen schemes look efficient. In this case his overt plan appears to focus primarily on messing with the Doctor – indeed, he admits that he's in this more to play with the Doctor than for any particular goal. Reading the script, the Master is clearly meant to get many – indeed most of the good lines, including some fantastically bleak jokes.

Given that Holmes has already created two characters in the programmatic mould of the Brigadier, it makes sense to assume that the Master is meant to be a third. But he is, perhaps, the funniest of the lot. If Jo is defined by always being ditzy and the Brigadier by always being levelheaded, the Master is defined as a character who is always, in any circumstance, hatching elaborate schemes. In any scene that the Master appears in here, he is busily coming up with an evil plan. As a result, the Master becomes a preposterously baroque trickster figure – one who simply keeps the plot going via utterly insane twists and ideas. No matter what, he has to complicate the plot via insane schemes.

This makes his role in the script genuinely compelling, because he's combined here with the Autons, who are able to produce a delightful stream of weird and creepy ideas on their own. The result is that the Master has, in his first story, many of the best schemes and tricks he'll ever have, making use of deadly chairs, killer plastic daffodils, plastic impersonators of everyday figures like policemen, homicidal toy dolls and a lethal phone cord.

Look at that list for a moment, and one of the things you'll notice is that we're in the version of Yeti-in-the-loo that actually works here. This story hinges on the subversion of expected objects into uncanny ones. But Holmes, gifted with both the Autons and the Master, has thrown the process into overdrive. Instead of taking a single object and making it uncanny and scary, he's gone ahead and made everything scary. And more to the point, he changes what's scary over and over again throughout the story. Once the good guys encounter a given horror, that's it for that horror. He doesn't try to milk it. Instead he just moves onto the next big idea. So this story is not about taking an individual object and making it scary; it's about making it so that any object is potentially an object of horror. This is what the uproar over this story, which focused mostly on whether it was acceptable to make policemen scary, missed: it didn't make policemen scary. It made the entire world scary.

This is helped tremendously by Barry Letts's direction. Although Holmes and Letts failed to see eye to eye on the role of the Master, when it comes to this broad set of fantastic terrors Letts is exactly on target, using cuts and editing to make the random objects seem genuinely uncanny and disturbing. So, for instance, when the Master impersonates a telephone repairman to install a deadly plastic phone cord, we know something is wrong not because the plot has explicitly told us anything but because the tone and pacing of the scene is telling us we're seeing something important happen as it's installed. And since we know anything can be scary, we read the phone wire as scary before we have any overt reason to know that it is scary or how it might be dangerous. The result is that any time a character goes near the phone it's scary even though we can't quite articulate what's wrong beyond the knowledge that there's something wrong with the phone.

Letts inadvertently (or perhaps deliberately) increases this sense further via what is usually taken as a flaw in this story: the gratuitous overuse of CSO. CSO, short for Colour Separation Overlay, is an early version of what we usually call blue screen, although Doctor Who actually used green so as not to conflict with the TARDIS. It's also the default special effect of 1970s Doctor Who, and quickly becomes part of the basic vocabulary of the show. But although it allows a bunch of new tricks and conventions, CSO shots are always ever so slightly off. They require a fixed camera, as the camera can't synchronize movement of the background with movement of the foreground. On top of that, there's always a halo of black lines surrounding objects that makes them feel slightly unreal. Letts, as it happens, is absolutely wild about the technology. Elsewhere in the Pertwee era the effect is deeply unfortunate, but here its gratuitous overuse is strangely wonderful, making even more objects feel uncanny and strange.

The end result is a lurid collage of objects that flicker between representations of real things and terrors. Tonally and structurally, it's far closer to *The Atrocity Exhibition* than *Doomwatch*. It's a glitzy, madcap story with a delightful subtext about consumerism. And Holmes uses his unparalleled skill at writing ordinary people to give this lurid festival a sense of grounding in the real world. So we get intersections of media, consumerism, adventure narratives, and the everyday all feuding and overlapping.

But none of this quite erases Cornell's critique. The heart of the problem is something Cornell identifies spot on, and that I alluded to already: Letts and Holmes are, in some key ways, working at cross purposes, as are Holmes and Dicks. The result is that there's a sense of dissonance to this story — a sense that not everybody is on the same page.

But perhaps the biggest problem is that with three creative visions for the story, the leading man, Jon Pertwee, doesn't seem to share any of them. As I said with *Inferno,* Pertwee is at his best when he's pushed out of his comfort zone with the material. But with three distinct artistic visions the story doesn't have the coherence to push him, which means he gets to simply strut about at the center of the production, a sort of unceasing stretch of egotism in the middle of all the interesting bits. Worse, he at no point seems to understand the show around him, a point shown by his bizarre attempt to bully Mr. Brownrose. There's a line in which the Doctor makes reference to talking to his boss "in the club the other day" to try to put him in his place after he's rude to the Brigadier and the Doctor.

As scripted, the line is clearly intended as a bit of Troughtonesque bluster and fakery. With Brownstone making snooty assumptions about the Doctor, the Doctor bluffs his way to an authority he doesn't have. One can imagine Troughton delivering the line, visibly pausing to try to remember the name he wants to throw around, changing his demeanor slightly to stress the fakery of it, etc. But Pertwee just delivers the line like he means it: as if the Doctor really does hang about bridge clubs talking to the nobility and joshingly calling them things like Tubby Rowlands. Which isn't right for the Doctor at all.

Of course, all of this presumes Pertwee even cares about the show around him enough to misunderstand it. And it's not always clear that he does. Case in point, his flagrant stealing of Richard Franklin's lines in the second episode. It's in the scene in which the Doctor is working on deconditioning Jo from the Master's hypnosis. Mike begins to deliver a line in which he trots out the old "but you can't hypnotize someone to do something they don't want to do" line and Pertwee interrupts him to steal the line, a move that's made both worse and more obvious by the fact that he then has to pause in order to try to remember the line he just stole. This is a deeply nasty move on Pertwee's part, and shows shocking contempt for his newest costar.

But even if Pertwee weren't missing the intended tone of his lines and bullying his costars, there'd be something wrong here. When left to his own devices Pertwee tends to play his role with the same flat programmatic nature that characterizes the Brigadier, Jo, and the Master. But the only reason those characters work is because they're in orbit around the Doctor. For six years, that's what the Doctor was: the mercurial figure who would flit around and do whatever the narrative required.

The programmatic characters work because they're responding absurdly to the chaos introduced by the Doctor.

But when the Doctor is just as programmatic as they are, there's suddenly no center to the narrative. The Doctor becomes a brilliant man surrounded by stupid apes that he grudgingly saves. And that's just not who he is. And it's certainly not a usable response to the challenge laid down by *The War Games* to invest more meaningfully in the lives of people.

That said, the tendency doesn't get completely out of control here for several reasons. First, Katy Manning and Jon Pertwee got along extremely well from day one, with Pertwee being extremely protective of Manning. As one would expect, this gets reflected onscreen, with the Doctor being exceedingly warm and friendly with Jo. Since Jo is by any rational standard the least competent person around the Doctor, the fact that he is so warm with her mitigates helpfully against his disdain for everybody else. And Jo quickly manages to inherit some of the anarchic charm of the Doctor through things like her nonplussed reaction to being captured by the Master, which lends useful balance to proceedings.

The second thing that balances Pertwee is Roger Delgado, who, in the fourth episode, strides into UNIT headquarters and immediately commences being more decadent and pompous than the Doctor (including having the gumption to step on one of Pertwee's lines) while simultaneously beautifully underplaying everything. Delgado is amazing in this scene, managing to turn every moment of calm understatement into a mockery of the Doctor. And Pertwee, who was supposedly a bit sensitive about Delgado getting better billing in the promotional material for the season than he did, rises to it, finally finding himself on the back foot and losing control of a scene for almost the first time since he took the part. Which, as ever, means that he's absolutely on fire.

And so while the central concept is still in some peril, having not quite found its way out of the quagmire of Season Seven, there's also the beginnings of a way forward emerging.

The broad, slightly over the top characterizations that are becoming prevalent in this story and the kaleidoscope of strange images point to a different way of doing things that's also emerging in the music charts in the form of Marc Bolan and T. Rex. Over the next two stories the series will further develop this idea, and the series as it exists in *The Claws of Axos* is almost unrecognizable when compared to the one from *Inferno*. But right now it's caught in between in an odd and stuttering transition between a limited approach that it had learned to do well and one with much more potential that the series, and indeed the culture, still doesn't quite understand.

Fear Makes Companions (*The Mind of Evil*)

It's January 30, 1971. George Harrison is at number one with "My Sweet Lord," having unseated Mr. Dunn. He enjoys a five-week run before Mungo Jerry's "Baby Jump" unseats him. Lower on the charts, T. Rex still stalks about upon a "White Swan." The Supremes are on the charts with "Stoned Love," a song that is actually probably not about sex while smoking cannabis, not that that has any real relevance to its interpretation. Judy Collins, Paul McCartney, Neil Diamond, and Elton John also chart.

In other news, Idi Amin, or as he'll eventually become known, His Excellency, President for Life, Field Marshal Al Hadji Doctor Idi Amin Dada, VC, DSO, MC, Lord of All the Beasts of the Earth and Fishes of the Seas and Conqueror of the British Empire in Africa in General and Uganda in Particular, deposes Milton Obote in Uganda. Charles Manson is convicted. The Apollo 14 mission takes place to the rapidly diminishing interest of the public. Rolls-Royce, one of the great symbols of luxury, goes bankrupt and is nationalized by the Heath government. The Seabed Treaty, outlawing nuclear weapons on the ocean floor, is signed by the major countries that should sign something like that. The Weather Underground, in a rare stab at effectiveness, manages to bomb a bathroom in the US Capitol building. The UN formally establishes Earth Day, signaling that the environmental movement has thoroughly gotten underway, and also manages the Convention on Psychotropic Substances, formalizing an international effort to crack down on psychedelics. But perhaps most importantly, it's Decimalization Day! One of the things that most firmly sticks the UNIT era in the 1970s was the fact that back in Season Seven, it visibly used pre-decimal currency. All that comes to an end and we finally learn that Susan was right way back in *An Unearthly Child* as, on February 15, the UK adopts decimal currency.

While on television, it's *The Mind of Evil*. Back when I first wrote this essay it was one of the last "missing stories," in that it existed only in black-and-white then despite having originally been transmitted in color. As of when I'm revising the essay, however, it's due out on DVD in a colorized version. This poses an interesting problem for this story, since one of the pieces of received wisdom about it is that the lack of color is a blessing in disguise, giving the story a dark, noir tone that is appropriate for its content and was probably lacking in color. On the other hand, the black-and-white format of the story did no favors for its basic popularity – it's one of the least reviewed and discussed Pertwee stories, and a high profile color release is likely to lead to a reappraisal in general. In any case, hello, people from the future. This essay was written about the black-and-white version.

As we saw in *Terror of the Autons* at the start of Season Eight, the Pertwee era was profoundly schizoid. On the one hand you had the default approach of Season Seven, where the series was a *Doomwatch*-inspired, straightforward action show. Thus far the story to most purely exemplify this approach is *Inferno*, and indeed, in many ways it's the single purest example of this approach at all. Let us call this approach Action Pertwee.

On the other hand you have a much stranger, almost postmodern show that repeatedly highlights the absurdity of its own premises or deconstructs them to reveal their inadequacies. This is the one characterized by juxtaposing standard sci-fi tropes with characters who operate by their own system of rules that is slightly different from the rules of the story they're in. It's closer to *The Atrocity Exhibition*, but eventually we're going to tie it very closely to the glam rock era, so let's just call it Glam Pertwee. Thus far the story to exemplify it best is *Terror of the Autons*, although more glam stories will follow.

There are two big observations to make here. The first is that even though the glam style is far less developed at this moment in time, it mostly came first. It's the style that has the firmest historical roots in the Troughton and Hartnell eras, and it's very clearly being set up by Robert Holmes as of *Spearhead from Space*. Even *The Silurians* and *The Ambassadors of Death* have numerous and profound glam touches, and there will be plenty of Pertwee stories that are as pure glam as *Inferno* is pure action, whereas *Inferno* really is the sole representative of the pure action model.

Which brings us to the second observation, which is that almost no single creator ever decisively fits into one school or the other. The era isn't switching back and forth between action and glam stories; it's being pulled in each direction every single episode. Some creative forces are more inclined towards one than the other – Robert Holmes, Katy Manning, and, as a director at least, Barry Letts all tend to push towards the glam. Terrance Dicks, Jon Pertwee, and, to a lesser degree, Malcolm Hulke push towards the action.

For the most part *The Mind of Evil* is very Action Pertwee, as one would expect from the writer of *Inferno*. In many ways, in fact, this is just *Inferno* done with a bit more polish. In *Inferno* Don Houghton figured out how to write for Pertwee better than anyone else has to date, and he puts that to good use here. He keeps the Doctor on the back foot through large swaths of the story, having him be assaulted by the Keller Machine and terrorized into submission multiple times. The result is at times genuinely scary. Pertwee is so often an almost invulnerable charismatic leading man, and so when he's genuinely harmed by the machine and broken down into a barely-able-to-stand exhaustion it's chilling and unnerving. This is similar to what Houghton did in *Inferno*, but he takes it much further here.

The other thing that was quite good about *Inferno* was its sense of scale and atmosphere. Again, Houghton excels here. The peace conference, for all its faults, gives the story a tangibly global scale instead of the implied global scale of most stories. Even if we only see people from the UK, US, and China in the course of the conference, the fact that the Doctor is involved in a global affair like this instead of just showing up somewhere else within the home countries and stopping a quaintly local invasion gives this story a new impact. Similarly, putting the Doctor in the midst of a prison riot is a case of using the earthbound setting to put the Doctor into a situation that it's genuinely difficult to imagine past incarnations appearing in. This story is using the opportunities given by the setting in a way the show hasn't yet. (It's ironic that the Earth setting should finally be used this well on the story where the Doctor flashes back to his many alien encounters.)

And on top of that, there are a multitude of little touches that work here. Having the first of the Doctor's nightmares be a post-traumatic flashback to *Inferno* where he watches a world being destroyed is a moment more powerful than anything in the ill-paced and sloppily plotted conclusion to that story. Having the Master attacked by the Keller Machine so that we see our villain writhing in pain and scared is a brilliant way to ratchet the stakes up higher and make the machine look really scary (which it risks not being in a story that already has the Master and a nerve gas nuclear missile), and having his worst fear be the Doctor standing over him and laughing at him is a moment that awards him more mythic status than the Troughton era ever managed to give the Cybermen.

There's also an absolutely gorgeous sequence in the fifth episode where the action cuts back and forth between the Doctor and UNIT as the Doctor attempts to escape the prison and UNIT readies a helicopter to fly over the prison. The action switches back and forth repeatedly over several minutes until finally the two sequences converge into one as the Doctor tries to signal the helicopter. Then the helicopter flies off and, instead of returning to an intercut narrative, the camera stays with the Doctor. This is terribly clever, since in order to know if the Doctor is going to be OK we have to know whether the people in the UNIT helicopter saw him, but that's the part of the narrative we don't get to see. It's the sharpest use of editing that Doctor Who has done to date.

This is, in other words, very well made television. There's a reason the show was so popular through these years, and one of them is that it did things like this effectively. Despite my misgivings about *Inferno*, I have no trouble understanding why the stories more in tune with Action Pertwee are beloved to so many people.

But here I have to finally just go ahead and tip my hand. As mentioned, this is one of my least favorite eras of Doctor Who, and a large part of my distaste for it is the Action Pertwee model. However well-made it is, stories like this are just very, very far from anything else in Doctor Who. This is not a show about a man with a magic box who can go anywhere and meet anyone, and does. It's a show about a smug man with a big nose who saves the world from bad guys and is sometimes kind of a bully. It's a very, very good show about a smug man with a big nose. But it has minimal ambition beyond competence. For all its faults (and they are more considerable than those of *The Mind of Evil*) *Terror of the Autons* had a mad and challenging ambition.

And *The Mind of Evil*, in this regard, suffers not because of any particularly grating flaws but because it advances many of these aspects just a little bit further than they had been advanced before. For instance, UNIT is as far as they've ever been from their "investigators of the unexplained" brief, somehow being responsible for running security at a peace conference. There's nothing wrong with running security at a peace conference – a plot point along those lines forms the series finale of *The Sandbaggers*, one of my favorite TV series ever. It's just that it's yet another step towards the Doctor working for a generic military operation instead of one defined by its relationship to the unusual.

On top of that, you've got the Brigadier casually calling a D-Notice on a news story, which is one of the more chilling moments of the series ever not to be intended as one. (A D-Notice, for American readers, is a quasi-voluntary system by which the British government can spike news stories for endangering national security. In 1971 one was filed relating to a bank robbery that is widely regarded as actually having been filed to protect a member of the royal family from embarrassment. So, you know. That kind of national security.) The Master, who on his first appearance was at least an entertaining villain, is wheeled on in order to give the story a black hat character and is stuck being a generic Bond villain with generic criminal henchmen. Jo, charming in her first appearance, is shoved to the sidelines here, though she's still the best part of the story, as we'll see shortly.

Then there's the casual racism. And it is intensely casual. I'm not going to go all *Celestial Toymaker* here, but really? The stereotypical Chinese woman turns into dragons? In fact, the Chinese are the villains in the first place, being run and manipulated by the Master, himself the very image of the vaguely foreign Svengali from Shiftystan? The horrid theme when Chin Lee makes her first appearance? The Doctor concluding that because a Chinese woman was involved in installing the Keller Machine, there must be a link between it and Chin Lee, despite there being no other evidence than the fact that apparently one of the half-billion Chinese women in the world was involved in both? It's nothing major. It's just a smattering of a little obnoxiousness someone should have known better than.

But the real problem here, for me, is the central premise: a machine that drains the evil out of people. It's not that this is a poor idea dramatically. No. A machine that turns aggressive, violent people into docile, compliant people is a great idea for an interesting, gripping *1984*-inflected thriller. The problem is that this isn't what *The Mind of Evil* has. It has a machine that works on the principle that there is a tangible quality of evil that some people inherently have. That's not interesting. That's just horrible and lends itself to all sorts of entrenched patterns of discrimination.

And make no mistake, this script is firmly in favor of the Keller Machine. The only problems the Doctor ever raises about it are the short-term cruelty to its subjects and the fact that the machine is actually a dangerous alien that will destroy everyone. Notably missing from the list is the idea that forcible mind control to ensure compliance with social norms is morally revolting. And worse, the Keller Machine works. Barnham, who we see undergo the process at the beginning, is treated as an innocent child thereafter, with his death in the climax clearly meant to be the noble sacrifice of a simple, good man. So the problem is that the Keller machine hurts people (who then forget about the experience) and is dangerous. The actual process of forcible brain damage to cure criminal impulses is fine.

And this isn't, to my mind, just a dissonant note. This seems to me emblematic of everything that has been so frustrating in the Pertwee era to begin with. Bad people are inherently bad. Good people are justified in what it takes to stop bad people. And it's that simple. The world divides into good people, who are either smart (i.e. agree with the Doctor) or foolish (i.e. don't agree with the Doctor), and bad people, who all work for the Master. And that's just how people are. Bad people want to hurt us. And we have to stop them.

In the end, though, given that I view the entire point of *The War Games* as being that the Doctor has to take a more complex view of the world than "there are monsters and we need to stop them," seeing a story where the concept amounts to treating humans with the same moral seriousness usually reserved for rubber suits is dismaying. But here's the thing – the flaws I find in this story's ethical approach are fundamentally intertwined with the stuff that makes the story so good. The simplistic worldview is in part a consequence of making the Keller Machine truly terrifying. The reason the clever editing is so effective is that it amps up the pace and thrill of the story at the expense of slower and more contemplative bits.

And herein lies the rub. For me, there is an irreconcilable gap between these aspects of the Pertwee era and the bulk of what Doctor Who does. And the gap is not incidental to the Pertwee era – it's part and parcel of what the era does and what it is. Fans, by and large, can bridge this gap, and many do. Those that also enjoy Action Pertwee simply enjoy this era as a bit of a different flavor of the show, and treat it as an odd little dalliance with a different approach. And that's a completely valid approach. I'm more than capable of it. The Pertwee era may be my least favorite of the classic series eras, but I still named my first car Bessie and enjoy these stories tremendously.

But at the end of the day there is still something profoundly dissonant about this and so much of what the series stands for elsewhere in its history. The critique of the show's morality in *The War Games* applies better to this story than it did to most of Season Six. And even though this is an excellent story – one I recommend as one of the highest quality pieces of Doctor Who to date, and one I think that a lot of fans badly underrate in that it doesn't get credit for being better than things like *Inferno* or, frankly, *The Silurians* – I don't feel like I can come down in its corner. In terms of what I'm trying to track in this project, this story is frankly almost as much of a mess as *The Dominators*.

All of which said, the seeds of the glam approach are still clearly maturing throughout this story. This is the first time since the Doctor was exiled to Earth that we've seen a clear reference to anything pre-Pertwee besides the Brigadier and UNIT. Not only do we see a montage of the Doctor's past enemies, we see such an utterly strange one –including the Daleks as well as out-of-left-field choices like a Zarbi and Koquillion. But these are oddly charming choices, harkening back to one of the eras where Doctor Who was at its most gloriously strange. These days the oddity of the choices is widely panned by boring people who would prefer to see a standard set of recurring monsters (no doubt a Dalek, a Cyberman, a Yeti, an Auton, and an Ice Warrior), but the fact that the series is not only calling back to its strange past but calling back to such bizarre gems as *The Rescue* and *The Web Planet* is a firm assertion that the weirdness of Doctor Who is still alive. And sure enough, for all that it's a grim-faced action serial about prisons, this is also a story where the machine that eats people's evil is actually a really silly-looking alien. Whatever else might be said about this story, it is, in that regard, unmistakably Doctor Who.

There's also Jo, who on the one hand is largely marginalized in the story, but who also gets the story's best moment in a charming little scene in which she beats the Doctor in Checkers, to his utter puzzlement. What's charming here is that there's no way in which Jo beating the Doctor in Checkers makes sense, and the Doctor knows it. More to the point, Jo knows it, and Katy Manning simply plays it off with a cheeky smile. As I said in *Terror of the Autons*, much of Pertwee's problematically domineering nature is helpfully countered by the impish glee that Katy Manning brings to her part, and scenes like this do a lot of the heavy lifting. Pertwee is in many ways the least mercurial Doctor, but he has one of the most mercurial companions. It's clear, in other words, that the wave has broken and begun to roll back on Action Pertwee. Now all that needs to happen is that Glam Pertwee needs to have its day in the sun.

This Pretty Little Thing Here (*The Claws of Axos*)

It's March 13, 1971. Mungo Jerry is at number one still, followed by dueling ex-Beatles as both McCartney and Harrison jostle for chart position. Elsewhere in the charts are Deep Purple and John Lennon and the Plastic Ono Band. But it's week two of the story where it finally happens. T. Rex hits number one with "Hot Love," establishing glam rock as no longer the next big thing but simply as the big thing. We deal with glam in detail in a "Pop Between Realities" essay further in the book, and if you need a primer on it you can just flip ahead. But it's also worth, if you never have, going and looking up some T. Rex appearances on *Top of the Pops* to get a sense of it. Or, alternatively, early David Bowie stuff like "Starman," or things by Slade, The Move, Sweet, or Gary Glitter. What you'll notice immediately is that there's clearly a shared visual aesthetic between glam and Doctor Who.

In real news, Bangladesh splits off from Pakistan, William Calley is found guilty of the Mai Lai massacre, *The Ed Sullivan Show* airs its final in the US, and the fourty-seven-day British postal workers strike ends. There's going to be a lot of strikes over the next few years, so keep your eyes on that.

But let's get back to T. Rex. T. Rex is one of those bands that really consist of a single creative force – Mark Bolan. This was, to be fair, not always true. In the late '60s, under the fuller name of Tyrannosaurus Rex, Bolan and Steve Peregrin Took brought psychedelic folk to what were almost, but not quite, the masses before Bolan sacked the hobbit and created glam rock. The nature of this transition is a watershed moment in popular culture, and gets at a point I made last volume: the crash-and-burn of '60s counterculture that occurred in France and the US simply didn't happen in the UK. Instead, after a bit of fussing about, its psychedelic and countercultural aspects made a coherent and traceable transition into glam.

And as a cursory examination of the visual record shows, there's an intuitive connection between glam rock and Doctor Who. Tat Wood argues for it at length in *About Time*, and it's something we'll explore throughout this volume. All of which is an extremely lengthy way of circling around to the fact that *The Claws of Axos* is the point where Doctor Who finally and unequivocally embraces the Glam Pertwee approach. Indeed, it's arguable that this is the single most glam story in Doctor Who, although unlike the Action Pertwee approach glam doesn't find itself receding until the very tail end of the Pertwee era. Tat Wood refers to this story as the moment when Doctor Who was more glam than glam rock. Which means that it's finally possible to explore in detail how the glam approach to the show works in the first place.

We should start, perhaps, with the writing. This is the debut of Bob Baker and David Martin, who will go on to write eight stories over eight years, with Baker writing one last one on his own in 1979. Along with Robert Holmes they are the defining writers of the 1970s. Unlike Robert Holmes, however, the Bristol Boys, as they were known, are not regular mainstays on people's "best writers of Doctor Who" lists. Admittedly, none of their stories are obvious shoo-ins for classic status save perhaps *The Three Doctors*. But on the other hand, Bob Baker is the writer of several Wallace & Gromit cartoons, including *Curse of the Were-Rabbit*, which means that Bob Baker is the only writer of Doctor Who to have won a film BAFTA or to have written for an Academy Award-winning film. Which is to say that the evidence is reasonably strong that Baker knows what he's doing as a writer, and that Martin presumably does as well.

There's a degree, however, to which one must cling to this assumption like a warm blanket while watching *The Claws of Axos*, because it is very easy to lose faith and conclude that the show has no idea what the heck it's doing here. At first glance the logic in this story seems all over the map. For all of its flaws something like *The Mind of Evil* is broadly defensible on the grounds that it's very well made television. This, on the other hand, seems shockingly amateurish in places. Plot logic is more or less an afterthought. Characters are introduced without meaningful explanation and behave in seemingly insane ways. And the plot is bursting at the seams with an excess of ideas.

Many of them are quite cool, but there's a shockingly large number of them, and they just barely hang together as long as you don't do anything like think too hard about them.

But for the most part, the absurdities of the plot are simply extensions of things that Robert Holmes was already doing in both of his Pertwee scripts so far in his development of overtly programmatic characters such as Jo, the Brigadier, and the Master. All of those characters are defined by the absolute and slightly absurd. The Brigadier is so steadfast that he remains resolutely calm even in situations where freaking out is probably the sane thing to do. The Master is a character who develops elaborately villainous schemes regardless of the sensibility of doing so, and often at the expense of actually realizing any of them. Jo is a plucky ditz who remains plucky and slightly naive no matter how horrible a situation she's put into. All of these characters are not just consistent but overly consistent, holding steadfastly to a logic that is just slightly off-kilter for the world of Doctor Who.

The Claws of Axos takes this approach to its inevitable conclusion. In it, nobody behaves in any way like a person in a recognizable or understandable world. Instead, every character is a programmatic high-concept character in the Holmesian mould. This has its plusses and minuses. Its most obvious minus is that all notion of human storytelling goes out the window. There are no people in this story. There are just plot roles interacting. This can be exhausting to watch – this story borders on actively tedious if one attempts to watch it with the assumption that it works anything like *The Mind of Evil*. The tone shift here is as stark as anything from the Hartnell era, but it's easy to miss because both stories share most of their supporting cast and their setting.

But that problem only arises if you try to watch *The Claws of Axos* as though it's the same sort of television that the story before it is. It's true – it's a deeply flawed piece of character drama. But its biggest flaw in this regard is that it's simply not actually a piece of character drama. The question, then, is what it's trying to be instead.

Thankfully, for our purposes at least, the story is not particularly subtle about what it is trying to be. The story works much better if you take it on its own terms, and its own terms are pretty clear. It's very clear that what this story is interested in is throwing as many wild and interesting ideas together as it can possibly fit. This is characteristic of Baker/Martin scripts, which tend to be distilled down and simplified from far more elaborate and over-the-top plots. *The Claws of Axos* originally involved a gigantic skull spaceship landing in Hyde Park and dispensing wishes, for instance. Later, a giant carrot crashes into the Earth.

It's really only in comparison to something like that, however, that *The Claws of Axos* can possibly be considered low key. And unlike skull spaceships in Hyde Park and flaming death carrots, the spectacle that *The Claws of Axos* offers is, at least, actually accomplishable on a BBC budget. Indeed, *The Claws of Axos* in its final form is perfectly suited to the BBC in 1991. More than any story to date, this one takes advantage of the fact that it's made in color. The Axons are a blur of colors not usually associated with aliens. Contrary to Terrance Dicks's maxim that the color of monsters is green, the Axons, in their monstrous form, are an intensely memorable seething mass of orange tentacles. Their spaceship is a garish yellow, which makes for a wonderfully incongruous shot as we see it, on film, in a drizzly English countryside. The inside of it is similarly all yellows and oranges marked by pulsating lights.

What's key about this is not just that the color palate is so lush, but that it's so unnatural: the oranges and yellows are like nothing on Earth, and by extension, like nothing that is familiar to the audience. Although we usually think of the switch to color as a move to greater realism in television, this moves in the opposite direction, using color to present a world that's even more extreme and unusual. Similar touches of overt strangeness abound – the collage of gold-faced Axon heads and evil, tentacled Axons swirling as the Doctor and Jo stagger through a pulsing, strobing Axon spaceship is an amazing visual sequence that is notable in how unlike anything else in

Doctor Who before or really since it is. (Indeed, the only point of comparison is the visual effects of glam rock performances on *Top of the Pops*.)

It's clear that this is where the effort in this story went. And lest there be some confusion, note that I'm not suggesting that this is a poorly written story rescued by good special effects. This is a story carefully and deliberately crafted to provide a foundation for alluring, fascinating visuals. The entire point of this story is to swirl previously unimagined sights in front of the audience for twenty-five minutes at a time. It is, in other words, *The Web Planet* for the 1970s.

Except that *The Web Planet* was about showing strange and unimagined things to the audience. The point wasn't that the Zarbi or the Menoptra looked strange. It's that Vortis as a whole was a strange place full of strange creatures. The entire setting and logic of the place is supposed to be alien. That's not true of *The Claws of Axos*. *The Claws of Axos* is still a UNIT story set during the Doctor's exile, and is thus ostensibly meant to be based in our world. In *The Web Planet* the central question is "what is this place," but there's no such mystery to *The Claws of Axos*. The nature of its world, and by extension its logic, is basically familiar. This is where the programmatic characters come in – all of the characters are recognizable in an archetypal sense. We know everything they're going to do. Even the aliens aren't, conceptually, that strange. The basic plot is just the Trojan Horse from Troy's perspective.

Instead, *The Claws of Axos* has a sense of strangeness based on the visual and on the incongruous. Yes, it has swirling and bewildering visuals, but it also creates unusual conceptual spectacles. This is again a factor of the programmatic characters. By boiling the characters down to broad types, the story can begin offering compelling and strange combinations of characters. Usually it accomplishes this by taking two characters that are a reasonably interesting pairing to begin with – the Doctor and the American action hero – and throwing them with a third item that is thoroughly strange – floppy orange Axon monsters. The result is a plot comprised, much like *Terror of the Autons*, out of a series of strange and fascinating set pieces, all surrounded by a bewildering and amazing visual aesthetic.

It's tempting to simply be snooty and suggest that there's some falling off involved in moving from presenting strange things to presenting strange images. That, in other words, the show has become superficial. But this is where we really turn to glam and to Ballard, both of which provide compelling, intelligent takes on the interplay of images. *The Atrocity Exhibition* was all about the deep power of superficial images. Glam rock, similarly, is in part about taking the opulence of conspicuous consumption and rearranging it into the wrong aesthetic. Its most famous figure is David Bowie during his Ziggy Stardust phase, a phase defined by the character of an alien would-be rock star who gets it ever so slightly wrong. The result has all of the over-the-top excess of the luxury associated with power and authority, except it's all put together pointlessly and haphazardly. It revels in decadence and consumption while denying the systems that ostensibly justify that behavior in society.

And this approach largely describes how *The Claws of Axos* works. On the one level, its central pleasure is a revelry in spectacle and glitz. We are meant to enjoy its images for their own sake. On the other hand, its plot is a straightforward anti-consumerist parable. The Axons are beautiful creatures of gold who offer untold wealth and then drain the world of its resources. And there's a fundamental tension between these two goals. The story is simultaneously reveling in superficial images and warning of their malign influence.

But this isn't a contradiction or a case of sloppy and incoherent execution. This is what concern about the rise of a purely image-based culture of spectacle (which was one of the major concerns of the Situationist International in France in '68) looked like in 1971. The critique of images was phrased in an image-based, superficial form. *The Claws of Axos* is designed to make the viewer feel uncomfortable about the pleasure they are taking in the object. It's constantly reveling in images that are lurid and unnerving instead of being "fun" as such – ones that are over the top and unlike what things should look like – while simultaneously cautioning us about the very pleasure it is taking.

Which, at long last, brings us around to the Master. One of the standard critiques of Season Eight is that the decision to use the Master in every story robs him of the element of surprise. But this complaint presupposes that the Master is supposed to be a surprise. In future seasons, admittedly, he will be. Once he starts appearing only occasionally the series does settle into a rut of having his revelation as the villain be a surprise. But we shouldn't use the future of the series to judge what it's doing in 1971. Only *The Mind of Evil* actually uses the Master's involvement as a twist revelation any later than the first episode, and even it doesn't make a cliffhanger out of his involvement. And by *The Claws of Axos* it's clear that the audience is supposed to have figured out that the Master is going to be in every story for a while. They take great pains to have everyone be concerned about what the Master might be up to in the first episode well before he actually appears. So his involvement isn't supposed to be a surprise any more than stories taking place on Earth are supposed to be a surprise. That's how the show works now. Consistent setting, consistent antagonist.

Given this, then, Baker and Martin delight in playing with the audience's expectations. Because the Master is supposed to be the villain behind everything – what, post-*Buffy*, we call the Big Bad – Baker and Martin do everything they can to keep him from actually playing that role. So his first appearance here is structured visually as if it's supposed to be a big surprising reveal in classic "Oh look, the story that says it has Daleks in it has Daleks in it" fashion. Except the shot that reveals him also reveals that he's chained up in the Axons' prison. Eventually he manages to sneak out, but then he has to slum it in a team-up with UNIT, spending an episode basically playing the Doctor's role while the Doctor goes and does more important things. He never manages to be in control of this story. It's a little too early in the Master's time on the program to suggest that he's descending into self-parody here, although it's also telling that the idea that the Master is fundamentally inadequate and that his schemes all kind of suck eventually becomes an implicit part of the character. But *The Claws of Axos* clearly is playing with our expectations of the character and refusing to quite give us what we want – an approach that is a clear cousin of the lurid-not-fun sense of the visual.

This also shows an interesting, new approach to Pertwee. Simply put, they've built a story where his charismatic leading-man confidence is pointless. Since Pertwee is prone to playing the part as a set of tics and catchphrases for the audience to delight in, Baker and Martin write a script that's nothing but tics and catchphrases. Since the story is all artifice and image, Pertwee's performance of the part no longer stands out. Pertwee is just another generator of spectacle in a world that consists of nothing but spectacle. His spectacle happens to be "leading man," just like Jo's is ditz and the Axons' is pulsating orange hues. But in a world where everything is spectacle, "leading man" becomes a flavor, not a role that gives the text a center of gravity.

The result can be read in two ways. In one, it's a continuation of what we saw in *Terror of the Autons*, where this version of the Pertwee years functions by critiquing the Doctor from within his own narrative. Here the critique comes by making an entire world that looks like the Doctor and then taunting the audience for enjoying it. It's effective and it's interesting, and finds a new and challenging take on the era. You couldn't do every story like this, but the point of Doctor Who in the past was to always do something new, so the fact that the idea would be tedious much past four episodes is hardly a fault in a four episode story. And more to the point, the approach provides a crucial breaking point for itself. This story makes it much easier to see Pertwee's Doctor as just another absurd character in the set. That his absurd character is the leading man is not irrelevant, but it's also not something that makes him the center of the show's universe anymore.

But there's another possibility that's even more interesting. The leading man role is, in many ways, the most superficial role available in the story. The traditional leading man is a part defined by the social structures of male privilege and a particularly charismatic figure. It's a role that by its nature demands that everything else cater to it. The leading man is, in other words, fundamentally decadent; he's someone who is the center of attention because of his charm and sex appeal rather than his competence. And it is a part of pure consumption. The leading man exists to be pleasurable for the audience, and he functions by demanding the adoration of the world. He is both the ultimate consumer in his own world and a commodity to be consumed in ours.

But that's not what the role of the Doctor has historically been. Under Hartnell, the Doctor was manifestly not the leading man. Instead he regularly vanished off to the sidelines of stories, and was often removed entirely and put in a coma or otherwise incapacitated. He relied upon being underestimated so that he could then roar up and take control. Troughton introduced leading man charisma to the role, making the Doctor someone we liked and wanted more of – a consumable product. But as we discussed, he used that charisma to constantly take a surprising position within a scene or in the narrative. This is what made him mercurial and fascinating. He was defined by the way he always slipped out of your grasp even as he charismatically drew you in. Troughton took the leading man role, but then never quite gave you the moment of pleasure as you get to watch him vamp around. (Indeed, the only times he vamps in his tenure are at the very beginning in *The Highlanders* when he's taunting the audience with not being William Hartnell, and in *The Dominators* when he finally gets to the point of just giving up on the part.) He made himself into a consumable product, but then never allowed himself to be consumed.

But Pertwee, thus far, is playing the part as a pure leading man in the traditional sense. This fundamentally alters the structure of the show, and not necessarily in good ways.

Indeed, it's quite off-putting in parts of this story. The Doctor is basically not nice to anyone at all until the second episode of the story, and spends the entire first episode marching about and rudely shouting at people. This is something we've never really seen in the Doctor before, not even with Hartnell's grumpy version. There, at least, the character was explicitly unsympathetic and a threat to the show's real stars, Ian and Barbara. Pertwee's Doctor, though, is similarly irritable, but is positioned as the leading man such that every other character must either respect him or eat crow.

But by shifting the entire show in a direction that weakens the leading man's hold on proceedings the leading man stops having that absolute power and starts being a more, well, mercurial character. And the way that this switch works is fundamentally glam. Although Pertwee does not dress in a glam manner as such, his fashion sense provides essentially the same effect we ascribed to glam. He is clearly a luxury-loving aristocrat, but he's the wrong sort of aristocrat. He's part of the establishment, but getting it slightly wrong and turning it into a mockery of it.

Likewise, although he's playing the leading man, the world he's playing it in isn't quite letting him have the part. He's the dashing hero who fixes the problem by fiddling with a control panel somewhere. He may run around and have action scenes and car chases, but at the end of the day he's just going to reverse the polarity of something. The story doesn't need his charisma. It has enough swirling and superficial images to stare at. And when every character operates by an unchanging logic, so that the Brigadier will always be calm, the Master will always be scheming, and Jo will always be plucky, his charisma becomes wholly impotent. A story like *The Claws of Axos* doesn't need a leading man simply because every other character in the story is functionally a leading man in that they have a sort of absolute control over the narrative. And yet there's the Doctor, pointlessly being a leading man even though that's not his job in the story.

But since the Doctor is the clever one who figures out

what's going on this becomes self-aware, especially because he's slightly different from the other programmatic characters in the story. The Brigadier, the Master, and Jo are all too good at their roles – capable of maintaining their roles even when circumstances say they should change. The Doctor, on the other hand, is getting his role slightly wrong. In a world where everyone's mask is too big, his is just a bit too small. This makes him the one person who gets to break the rules of the world. And so he plays the glam rock hero in his own era, mocking the job of UNIT's dashing scientific advisor even as he performs it.

The effect, if you will, is a variation of *The Emperor's New Clothes*. Nobody is allowed to say that the emperor is naked. Except here, the emperor knows full well that he's naked. He's enjoying the power of making everyone allow him to strut around naked without being allowed to comment on it. Everybody knows that Pertwee's Doctor is a ridiculous joke. But because he's the leading man they have to take the joke seriously no matter how many ridiculous things he tries to get away with. And thus by seemingly abandoning his mercurial nature for crass consumerism, he gains an even more powerful version of that nature.

It's a very fresh and new take on the character. It's not the only one going on in the Pertwee era; the fundamentally schizoid nature of the era means that other takes still play in. But it's perhaps the defining one – the one that is unique to the era and could only happen in the early '70s while glam rock was blazing its brief trail across the culture. And now, at least, it's firmly established within the series. Seven stories in, Doctor Who has finally found a way to be like no other show on television again.

The People in Charge of Those Laws (*Colony in Space*)

It's April 10, 1971. T. Rex is still at number one, and remains so for three more weeks for a total of a six-week run at the top. He's finally unseated by Dave and Ansel Collins's "Double Barrel," a reggae track that survives for two weeks before Tony Orlando and Dawn take over with "Knock Three Times." The charts also see Ringo Starr follow his three former bandmates into the top ten, and The Rolling Stones hit number two with "Brown Sugar/Bitch/Let it Rock." Andy Williams, Olivia Newton-John, and Waldo de los Rios also make the top ten, the latter with a recording of Mozart's Symphony No. 40. And lower down, The Sweet are at number thirteen with "Funny Funny," another visible sign of glam's reign.

The news is mostly incremental progress on various fronts. Charles Manson and his followers are sentenced to death, Bangladesh formally comes into being, and, perhaps most significantly, several of the events that will eventually bring down the Bretton Woods system kick up as central banks in several European countries halt currency trading due to an excess of US dollars flooding their markets.

While on television we have *Colony in Space*. I've been saying that the Pertwee era is schizoid for a while now, but there is perhaps no point where it becomes more so than here. In *Colony in Space* the show we've been getting used to over the course of the last sixteen months or so, one about an eccentric scientist helping a military operation fend off alien invasions, suddenly vanishes to be replaced by some other show. The setup we've become used to over the past seven stories make a token appearance in the first episode in the form of the Brigadier, but the bulk of the start of this story is concerned seemingly with completely dismantling the premise of Doctor Who: the main character runs off in that Police Box he's been fiddling with, which, improbably, turns out to be a time machine that can take him to other worlds.

This is, of course, being a bit facetious. The TARDIS has never been entirely absent from the series: it played a major role in the resolution of both *The Claws of Axos* and *Inferno*. The idea that the Doctor would stay on Earth forever was looking increasingly strained as of *The Mind of Evil*. But on the other hand, it's been two years almost exactly since the Doctor had a working TARDIS. The last time the Doctor visited an alien world was in *The Krotons*. By any reasonable standards this comes out of left field within the context of the preceding years of stories.

The result is a strange position. The show is not doing something unexpected in heading out into space. It's an event, yes, but not as big of one as something like the revelation of the Doctor's people or the introduction of his opposite number. This is still familiar as "the sort of thing Doctor Who does," or at least, as a familiar older version of the program. Much like Troughton and Hartnell showing up again in a season and a half, the connection with the past is visible. But it's still been so long since the show has done something like this that this is still, in a real sense, a relaunching of the series. Everyone knows Doctor Who is a show that can go to other worlds, but it's been long enough that the exact mechanics of how that works are forgotten. And the show has been inventive since *The War Games* – simply returning to the old Troughton base under siege format isn't really an option.

Not that Malcolm Hulke, the writer tapped to execute this, would have gone for it anyway. Hulke, after all, was around on the program for the Troughton era – he co-wrote both *The Faceless Ones* and *The War Games*, both explicit critiques of the base under siege structure and of the blithe xenophobia it implies. Along with Robert Holmes, Hulke is the veteran contingent of the series' writers at this point. Nobody is more acutely aware of the flaws of the old model than he is.

But on the other hand, Hulke was also the most vocal critic of the earthbound format. On the one hand, this means that it's wholly fitting that he should get the honor of relaunching this aspect of the series. But given that he viewed many of the fundamental concepts of the Pertwee era as ill-conceived mistakes (even as he helped set them up, writing over half of

Season Seven and helping write *The War Games*), his take to the stars was always going to have a heavy retro streak to it. He, after all, wanted to show that the turn to the earthbound format was ill-advised.

The result is that *Colony in Space* is pulled in two different directions. On the one hand, Hulke wants to reinvent the alien planet for the 1970s to show that it still has legs. But he also wants to defend its past so as to critique the turn towards the earthbound format. He's trying to show that the existing approach perfected in the Hartnell and Troughton years is more interesting and mature than what the '70s were doing. And so the story largely embodies C.S. Lewis's observation that the person who reverses course first after a wrong turn is being the most progressive. Hulke is trying to drive the program forward by going back as decisively as possible. You can see that from the way the story starts – with the single oldest form of alien world story the program has: the exploration based story. After it gets around to easing us into the idea of the Doctor traveling again, his approach to the planet is the old classic Hartnell approach – wander around until someone captures him and Jo. The entire structure of this story is based on the Doctor steadily understanding the rules of the world he's landed on – figuring out whom he can trust and who has what secrets. This isn't just nostalgic, this is nostalgic for Season One.

Yes, as Tat Wood complains in *About Time*, there are some real clichés here. But there are also subversions of the clichés, which Wood largely overlooks. The major one that Wood misses is that he accuses the story of wheeling on the Master to stretch the story out. This is a completely fair and accurate assessment of the story only if you've started watching from when the TARDIS dematerializes. If, however, you actually watch the entire first episode in which the Time Lords tell us that the Master is pursuing a doomsday weapon of some sort and then the Brigadier helpfully reminds us that the Master is still out there, the idea that the Master is "wheeled on" in the fourth episode becomes ridiculous. This story, like every other story this season, is built around the assumption that the Master is involved somehow.

This is not an incidental detail. Rather, it's key to how Hulke is structuring this story. At two key points in the story Hulke uses a very savvy trick in which he reveals something to the audience and then trusts the audience to forget about it by the time the revelation matters. This means that when the revelation eventually comes into play it's simultaneously a surprise and a satisfying moment of everything clicking into place. (This is still a sound tactic: the climax of *The End of Time* depends on the fact that the audience has completely forgotten about Wilf in all the confusion.) The first one of these is that the audience is trusted to forget that the Master is going to be involved by the time he actually appears. Hulke actually handles this pretty deftly; a viewer looking for the Master but not knowing in advance where he'll be is almost certain to assume that the Master will turn out to be behind the lizard attacks directly. So when we discover that IMC is behind it, we are meant to immediately assume that the Master will turn out to be in charge of IMC.

In other words, Hulke sets us up to make a wrong guess, and then trusts that when we find out that guess is wrong we'll be so caught up in the implications of what's actually happening that we'll forget to make another guess. As a result, when the Adjudicator strides on in the fourth episode, arriving in what appears to be a normal spaceship, we aren't looking for the Master anymore. But when he arrives it's still not the revelation we're used to in later Master stories. The revelation isn't "Oh no, it's been the Master all along." It's "Ahhh, so that's where he was hiding. It all makes sense now."

The other hidden twist comes in the handling of the city of the indigenous Uxariens. The Doctor spends a good portion of the fourth episode in the city trying to rescue Jo as the Master steadily ingratiates himself with both the colonists and the IMC. The result is a fairly normal tension for Doctor Who – bad things are happening at point A while the Doctor is stuck at point B. The show uses this trick almost every story. But here there's another subversion. Not long after the Doctor catches up with the Master we discover that the real action was back at point A in the Primitive's city all along. But again, Hulke trusts that we will be so eager to see the Doctor get to where the Master is that we won't stop to think about why nearly a full episode was spent dealing with the indigenous Uxariens when there's no obvious relevance to the larger plot.

The result is a plot that manages, particularly when taken in discrete chunks (which is, after all, how the classic series is designed to be taken), to remain surprising and interesting. Hulke keeps us from understanding the world we're looking at until the absolute end. And he does so by presenting a genuinely complex world. There are some severe plot holes, as ever: it's never quite explained why the Master was looking for planets high in the same mineral IMC is looking for. Presumably there's some connection between that mineral and the Uxariens, but the nature of it is obscure. And the question of why mining and agriculture are an either/or proposition on a planetary scale is a mystery throughout the story. But this is a world with multiple moving parts: the colony, IMC, the Uxariens, the Master, and the Doctor. And they interact in surprising ways whereby whenever we think we have a handle on it the plot swerves and shows us that there's more to this world than we assumed.

Whether the characters live up to this is somewhat more ambiguous. There are, in essence, three levels to which characters in a Doctor Who story can be developed. The first is in terms of competence. This is the sort of characterization we got through most of the Troughton bases under siege, and it's where a lot of the more programmatic characterization ends up in stories like *The Claws of Axos*. In it, the characters all have essentially two traits: goodness and competence. They are either good or bad, and are either competent or incompetent at doing their good or bad things. It works to tell exciting adventure stories, but really not for much else.

The second level, which is where Hulke ends up, expands on the sense of morality. Instead of simply being good or evil, characters have a somewhat nuanced moral worldview. So, for instance, Ashe believes in using the existing structures of government and power to protect the colony, whereas Winston believes in the use of violent revolution. Dent believes in doing what is necessary to crush the colonists while Caldwell is willing to exploit but not actively harm the colonists. The ways in which this is more interesting than the first level should be clear: it allows you to have scenes and events that turn on something other than the mere competence of the characters.

It's tempting to criticize Hulke for failing to make it to the third level, which is characteristic of the new series. A contemporary story like *The Rebel Flesh/The Almost People*, for instance, is a base under siege in the classic Troughton mold, but it hinges not only on the ethics and ideologies of characters, but on specific and seemingly arbitrary characters traits. For instance, the fact that one is a father, or that one imagined a stronger, better version of herself when growing up matters tremendously to the plot resolution. This is the most mature and interesting level of characterization. But it's difficult to criticize Hulke for not reaching it given that Robert Holmes, who has gone the furthest in this direction, has still just begun to scratch the surface of this approach. Faulting Hulke for not going further than any writer has ever gone before in Doctor Who seems unfair. Especially because the second level of characterization is already well ahead of what almost any other writer in this era is capable of.

By using this sort of characterization, Hulke manages to lend an ethical weight to this story that has been lacking from other stories. The result is a story that doesn't fit well into the glam or action tendencies of the Pertwee years. It's not a story about exciting things happening, nor is it a story about unusual images happening. It's a moral parable, about people with differing world-views and the consequences of those world-views.

The schizoid nature of the Pertwee era makes it difficult to make general case statements about its world-view. But discussing Hulke's world view is relatively easy, and, given that

Hulke is one of the major architects of the Pertwee era, in particular responsible for many of the best-remembered early novelizations, it's worth doing as well. Hulke was an active communist. Unfortunately, being a member of the Communist Party of Great Britain in the 1970s isn't as great a clue as one might hope, because the CPGB was ludicrously factionalized. The main two factions were the traditional trade-union based faction and a newer faction inspired by Italian Marxist Antonio Gramsci. Unfortunately, no source I can find actually says definitively which camp he belongs to, so there's some guesswork required here.

That said, *Colony in Space* strongly suggests that Hulke is a Gramscian. I should pause here and explain something basic about Marxism in the twentieth century. I've talked about this a bit before, but basically, after its early phase concerned primarily with "how do we go about staging an effective revolution," Marxism turned to the somewhat more interesting question of why it's been failing to successfully have a revolution. Gramsci's answer to this is that the bourgeois, to survive, cannot simply pursue their economic interests, but must instead create intellectual and moral justifications for its sustenance. This larger system, in which economic and social forces work together to sustain capitalism, is called hegemony, and it's one of the central concepts for Gramsci and Marxists that follow in his footsteps.

It also almost perfectly describes how IMC functions, complete with Hulke appropriating Charles Erwin Wilson's famous (albeit misquoted) claim about General Motors and having a character declare that what's good for IMC is good for Earth. IMC, in other words, has become a moral force unto itself, required to function not just for its own profit but because Earth needs it. What is so toxic about IMC is that it has integrated itself into the political system, finding gaps in the law and enforcement that allow it to function in a corrupt fashion without fear of reprisal. In other words, it is not merely an evil corporation, it's part of a deeply interconnected system that enables evil.

Opposed to this hegemony are two forces. The first are the colonists. A lot of commenters get it a bit wrong in terms of how the colonists work, assuming *Colony in Space* to be a Western of some sort. It's not, and really it would be a bit odd if it were, since it's not like Hulke lacked a British-based reference point for issues of colonialism. The Western is defined by an ethos of rugged individualism, which simply isn't what we have here. No, these colonists, if they're anything related to America, are Puritans. Again, we probably need to pause and point a few things out, particularly for those whose primary associations with the word "Puritan" are the Salem Witch Trials or something like that. Although it was Puritans doing the nasty things there, the Salem Witch Trials are not your average Puritans.

For the most part, the Puritans were an intellectual movement committed to religious reform. Those that colonized America (which was in no way all of them) did so because it became increasingly clear that it was easier to go set up a utopian community on the other side of the Atlantic Ocean than it was to reform existing structures. In *Colony in Space*, this is made particularly clear when the colonists talk of returning to Earth and of the problems with Earth. The colonists mostly want to be left alone to build the world they want to build. The only major difference is that instead of being motivated by religious ideology, the colonists appear to be pragmatic scientist sorts.

Remember, though, that in the '60s and '70s there was a sense of scientists as a privileged class who should be looked to for leadership. They were, in other words, a new sort of clergy, and lab coats were the new collars. The turn of things like *Doomwatch* towards a more skeptical and suspicious view of science was a recent phenomenon and a reaction against the deification of scientists characteristic of the relatively technocratic impulses of the '50s, '60s, and, to a lesser extent, the '70s. We talked about the Bretton Woods system starting to come apart at the seams, but what's perhaps more interesting is the fact that there was such a thing as the Bretton Woods system — an agreed upon top-down management of global economics. These were the dying days of technocracy, but the underlying imagery still worked. And so the colonists are portrayed as, in effect, Science Puritans. Which is where the Doctor fits into this worldview; even though he is superficially a member of the bourgeois (albeit filtered through a glam performance), the Doctor is perfectly suited to the role of science vicar.

Note also that the role of science vicar is not one where the authority is inherent. The Doctor's authority does not stem from the fact that he is the Doctor, but rather from the fact that he is clever and right. This is the central difference between him and the Master, who outfoxes him in the fourth episode by rubbing the Doctor's face in the fact that he isn't as good as the Master at manipulating identity papers and systems of government. The Master's authority comes from his ability to work within existing systems of power and claim roles and identities that have power. The Doctor, on the other hand, takes no special identity and instead gains power through his actions and their supposed inherent goodness.

The final piece of this moral puzzle, of course, comes from the indigenous Uxariens. Or, as they're called throughout the story, the Primitives. It's tempting to read them as a parable about the oppression of indigenous people, especially since the word "colony" is involved here and these days that usually means that we're doing a story about colonialism and its oppressive nature. But to do so is to confuse our morality with the script's. The script clearly does not much care about them – the Doctor is downright blasé about killing them, and doesn't seem worried at all when they all die in an explosive inferno at the end. The point of the script is not that IMC or the colonists mistreat them. So clearly some other explanation is needed.

The key thing about the Uxariens is in fact that they are a fallen civilization. Or, more to the point, that they are a civilization that fell because they created a doomsday weapon. Here Hulke is reverting to a more traditional mode of Communism – one that believes in a historically inevitable progression that will eventually bring down capitalist systems. The Uxariens fell because creating a doomsday weapon is something that destroys worlds – a fact that, for Hulke, is simply a historical inevitability.

It is also worth looking at their leader. He is the leader for the simple reason that he retained the ability to talk and other advanced functions – like the Doctor, he's the leader for what he does, not who he is. And so, being a science vicar type himself, he has an understanding of the necessary progression of history. He understands that destructive hegemonies must be avoided and that the Doomsday Weapon is a curse. This isn't because he has a particular set of values, but because he's the one Uxarien with the capacity for speech and reason, and reason leads inexorably to this view of history.

By taking this approach, Hulke becomes the first writer to fully answer the challenge he set out at the end of *The War Games*. Here the Doctor comes upon a situation and has to disentangle it not by fighting monsters but by sorting through ideologies. The climax is an argument over the inevitable arc of history and about how civilization works. Stopping the bad guys isn't sufficient in this world. The Doctor has to go further and find a way to make society work. This is everything that was lacking in the Troughton era – a sense of morality where good is not just fighting monsters and opposing evil, but a positive action – something that has to be worked towards. Other writers will take differing views of what that positive action is, but Hulke has made major progress in the ethics of the series by demanding that positive action exist in the first place.

And in this regard the most interesting thing about *Colony in Space* is the character of Caldwell, the IMC employee who eventually defects and joins the colonists. The fact that such a large part of the story is taken up by the evolving moral principles of an ordinary person caught in events is a significant development in the series. Ironically, the first time the series has really fully responded to the challenge set by *The War Games* to engage with the human element of its stories is also the one where it turns back the clock and returns to the space-bound format it abandoned in the same story.

The Evil Has No Name (*The Daemons*)

It's May 22, 1971. Tony Orlando and Dawn are still at number one with "Knock Three Times," and hold it for four more weeks before giving way to Middle of the Road's "Chirpy Chirpy Cheep Cheep," which is just one of those things that happens on the British charts. The lower reaches of the charts are downright inscrutable: John Kongos, Tami Lynn, Blue Mink, East of Eden, R. Dean Taylor, and the Elgins were also in the top ten, and if you've heard of any of them I congratulate you.

In other news, a massive earthquake levels Bingöl, Turkey. Neville Bonner becomes the first indigenous Australian to sit on the Australian Parliament. But the big stories are the US dropping its trade embargo with China, which we'll talk more about in the entry on *Day of the Daleks*, as well as the beginning of publication of the Pentagon Papers.

While on television: one of the landmarks of the Pertwee era, which means that we should slow down and look at this thoroughly. We've been playing of late with the idea that there are two completely distinct modes of thought operating in the Pertwee era at any given time: Glam Pertwee, a style based on the interplay and juxtaposition of images and Action Pertwee, a style based on telling tense techno-political thrillers. Thus far virtually every Pertwee story can be understood reasonably well as a combination of influences from the glam and action styles. *Colony in Space* started to challenge this by restoring the "travel in time and space" aspect of the story, but that aspect of the Pertwee era remains vestigial, and will, eventually, get caught up in the glam/action divide.

The Daemons does not shatter that dichotomy, but more than any story to date it does manage to embody both halves of the divide, which makes it an unusually complex story. So to some extent we have two essays on this, with the "Pop Between Realities" essay following this serving as a sequel to this post that tries to make sense of the larger cultural signifiers going on here, whereas in this essay we'll focus primarily on how the story fits into the evolving nature of the Pertwee era.

The Daemons is, by any measure, one of the major Pertwee stories. It's well remembered both by everyone who worked on it and by audiences at the time, and Pertwee rates it as his favorite story of his time on the program. It also marks the introduction of one of the major writers of the Pertwee era as Barry Letts puts on his third hat, already being the producer and occasional director of Doctor Who. Here he and his soon-to-be-usual Robert Sloman collaborate under the pseudonym Guy Leopold, but the season finales for the next three seasons, all credited to Sloman, are similarly co-scripted.

This is also significant, of course, because it's the first time where we have to assume we are getting a more or less untempered look at what the producer wants the show to be. It is not the story where Letts has the most control – he simultaneously writes, produces, and directs Pertwee's final story, *Planet of the Spiders*. But that story is self-consciously a retrospective of the entire era. This and *Terror of the Autons* are the first two times he has such a direct hand in the series, and so give us the perhaps more important spectacle of seeing Barry Letts try to demonstrate what he wants the program to be, as opposed to reflecting on what it has been. Watching it, then, two things become immediately clear. The first is that Barry Letts is a visionary with a genuinely interesting take on what Doctor Who should be. The second is that Barry Letts very often has not got the first clue how to go about making the show he wants it to be.

On the basic level of plotting, *The Daemons* is puzzling at best. It's one of those stories whose premise essentially promises what its ending is going to be. If you have the Master in a small English village trying to summon the Devil in the first act then you have to have a three-way showdown among the Master, the Doctor, and the Devil in the third. This sort of setup has pros and cons, but the biggest problem it has is that the bulk of what's in between the setup and finale is necessarily a matter of working actively to prevent the ending from happening too soon. Instinctively, then, this should explain why Devil's End gets surrounded by a force field. The obvious reason to do that is to have the Doctor trapped outside the village having to give advice to the Brigadier, who is trapped inside the village, but being unable to actually do anything. Except that, inexplicably, the force field gets set up backwards from how it should be: the Doctor is trapped inside the village and the Brigadier is left to stand around outside it.

This means that the story is left with few good ways to avert the ending while simultaneously having to avert it for four-and-a-half whole episodes. The kindest thing to say about this is perhaps "at least it wasn't a six-parter." The fourth episode is particularly egregious. Starting from the cliffhanger of the Master successfully summoning Azal and a massive earthquake seeming to hit, the episode has everyone not immediately around the Master calmly go back to what they were doing without worrying much about the earthquake and the Master sending Azal back to sleep for a bit. Then the story wanders off and squares away some other plot points it had introduced to delay things, and ends with a cliffhanger of . . . the Master summoning Azal. In other words, the fourth episode opens with a big cliffhanger, resolves everything it can possibly resolve without addressing that cliffhanger, and then simply repeats the cliffhanger.

Even stranger, despite these delaying tactics, when Letts and Sloman actually reach the final confrontation they're so pressed for time that they have to have Jo suddenly pipe up to save the Doctor and have Azal explode for reasons that had no setup whatsoever prior to this scene. It's genuinely difficult to account for what happened here. On the one hand, this story is a four parter that has been tediously stretched out an episode, as evidenced by the fourth episode's stalling. On the other hand, the climax is rushed in a way to suggest they were simply out of time. Not since *The Enemy of the World* (covered in the previous volume and directed by Letts) have we seen this strange mixture of delaying tactics and a hurried ending, and there, at least, the delaying tactics were the point – Whitaker systematically moved through all possible configurations of

"Doctor Who meets James Bond" before getting to the one everyone wanted to see. *The Enemy of the World*, at least, clearly just needed one more episode to get through all the setups Whitaker wanted. *The Daemons* manages to be both an episode too long and an episode too short. When combined with some of the strange ineptness of certain aspects of *Terror of the Autons* (the excessive reliance on CSO in particular) the strong sense is that for all of Barry Letts's vision of what the show should be he had some serious deficiencies in the basic visual storytelling department.

But comparisons to *The Enemy of the World* raise an alternate possibility: what if, as with *The Enemy of the World*, the point isn't the final confrontation but the journey? OK. But what is the supposed value of that? I mean, if we treat this not as a story that builds towards a climactic three-way showdown but rather as one where the things seen along the way are the fun, what is it that we see instead? This is, after all, more in line with the glam approach where the images and spectacle of the thing are at least as important as what actually happens.

Unfortunately, the answer is just as confused as the other option. If this is the point of the story, the decisions taken are deeply inscrutable. The show has, in this season, a staggeringly large six-person regular cast – by some margin the largest it ever has had and probably ever will have. On the one hand this enables the glam tendency – a lot of characters means a lot of different things to look at. But there's a real challenge in finding things for them all to do. The Doctor is mostly used up solving problems, which is wholly proper. The Master is mostly used for towering over people and manipulating them, which is also a sound choice. After that, however, we have some problems. If the process of exploring the world is the point of Doctor Who, the truth is that it's not entirely clear this is the right supporting cast for that. There are four remaining regulars on the show after Pertwee and Delgado: Manning, Courtney, Franklin, and Levene. And the truth is that two of those are very good actors, one of them is a fantastic utility player, and one of them was an abject failure of casting. And, more to the point, the story sidelines the stronger two while relying too heavily on the weaker.

Manning and Courtney, as we've discussed previously, are both absolutely fabulous because they play their characters with illogical consistency. Because Courtney and Manning are both, in their own ways, utterly unflappable and at ease, it's consistently a hoot to put them in a scene with someone. Think for a moment about how much more fun this script would be if the Brigadier got to share a major scene with Miss Hawthorne. Instead, however, he spends most of the story staring at an invisible wall waiting to get into the town and deliver his immortal "chap with the wings there" line (which is, admittedly, pure genius). Manning, on the other hand, enjoys her fourth consecutive story as a vapid peril monkey as the writers continue to not quite be certain what to do with her. (Thankfully in her second two seasons this stops as people realize how to write a good Jo Grant scene, whereas previously only Robert Holmes and whichever of Houghton or Dicks wrote the chess scene in *The Mind of Evil* seemed to have a clue.)

Instead, it's Richard Franklin and John Levene who get put in the village to interact with people. Which is just a staggering mismanagement of your cast. Levene is a fine utility actor who showed back in *Inferno* that he both has range and has the good sense of when not to use it. He understands that Benton's role is a simple action man and infuses the part with a genuine working-class charm here, but the character is limited by design. His scenes with Miss Hawthorne are admittedly great, but his character is consciously designed not to have as much to do with her as others. Benton is mostly there to provide a sort of everyman charm, and while Levene is excellent at it there are limitations.

As for Richard Franklin . . . he's just not very good. He imbues almost all of his scenes with an awkward and artificial stiffness that makes it nearly impossible to effectively hang a scene on him. Again, I'm more than capable of loving Mike Yates, but I'm hard-pressed to argue seriously that my love is based on anything that can reasonably be construed as actual quality. So having him be one of the major contributors to all the local color scenes is . . . a mistake.

But there's a larger problem here. One gets the sense that we're supposed to care about Benton and Yates hanging around the village primarily because they're Benton and Yates. This isn't completely out of line; one thing that does steadily happen over the course of the Pertwee era is that a style of plotting heavily influenced by soap operas begins to take hold. In contrast to the disposability of companions that has infected the series in the past (most obviously under Innes Lloyd), the soap opera style requires an intense commitment to characters, because that commitment is what generates long-term viewership. (Soaps, like cult science fiction shows, depend not on gaining new viewers but on holding onto the ones it has forever. They are actually among the closest cousins on television. Not that Doctor Who in this phase is cult sci-fi, but it does at least explain how the large supporting cast is supposed to work.) So according to that logic it's reasonable to expect us to be interested in Benton and Yates for the simple reason that they are regulars on the show. But soap characters generate viewer interest in characters by giving them plot arcs and doing things with them. Let's pause here to think about Benton and Yates's plot arcs in stories past, then.

Except there aren't any. Benton got turned into a werewolf once in an alternate universe, and Yates was kidnapped once by the Master. That's really all we have to hang our commitment to the characters on. The only way they're distinct from the mass of replaceable UNIT figures is that they appear in multiple stories. And in Benton's case, that's purely down to Douglas Camfield's directorial style relying on actors he can trust, and thus his decision to bring John Levene back in *Inferno*, at which point it was decided that he should just be the same character he played in *The Invasion*. Recall that this is also how Nicholas Courtney became the Brigadier – Camfield wanted the actor, so they recycled his character from *The Web of Fear*.

Which is all well and good, and the characters – especially

Benton – are beloved for it. But there's a difference between loving a bit character and being able to hang an episode on them. Shows have managed this before, perhaps most obviously the *Buffy* episode "Superstar," in which a beloved bit character suddenly takes over the show, including the opening credits. But the whole point of that episode is that there's something wrong with the world where the bit player has taken over. The point is that we actually don't want to watch *Jonathan the Vampire Slayer*. To inflate a bit character, you have to actually do something with them. (And, of course, once Jonathan was inflated by "Superstar" and the earlier "Earshot," he could be used as the basis for episodes after that.) Without that, the characters fall flat. And so just because we love to watch Benton tell the Doctor that he still doesn't understand doesn't mean it's inherently fun to watch him hang out with the local color. It could be, but there needs to have been more in the past of the character to get that to work.

Of course, you'll note also that the only bit of local color we've mentioned thus far is Miss Hawthorne. There is a reason for this, which is that Miss Hawthorne is the only actual character in the village. The rest are just stooges that get dominated by the Master. This has been a recurring problem in the series since *Spearhead from Space*: rural Britain has been repeatedly depicted as nothing more than a stable of comedy yokels. But here we run into real trouble because the entire story depends on a rural village. Unlike *The Silurians* or *The Claws of Axos* where there are lots of other people running around, virtually everybody in this story is either a regular or a villager. Admittedly the villagers clear the incredibly low bar set by *The Claws of Axos* in terms of nuanced portrayals of rural life, but this is hardly an accomplishment given that *The Claws of Axos* is the worst offender of the season.

Which is where the "it's about exploring the setting" theory fails. Because Letts and Sloman don't let anyone interesting explore the setting, nor do they make the setting interesting. The result is that one of the key scenes of the story is the Doctor being burnt at the stake in broad daylight by a bored crowd. There's a good idea here: a crowd of angry people who won't listen to the Doctor burning him at the stake. In fact, for Pertwee, it's a great idea, since his character is defined by his casual insistence on respect from the social order, and having that social order turn on him as an angry, unthinking mob is an interesting case of giving the Doctor the exact sort of problem he's ill-suited to solving. But the execution is painfully flat, in no small part because Letts and Sloman decide to collapse their evil Morris dancer set piece and their angry mob set piece into one event. Ultimately, it just doesn't seem like Letts and Sloman are that interested in their set pieces beyond those involving Azal or Bok.

Which brings us back to our first theory – that the point of the story is the three-way confrontation. This is actually fortunate. For the most part, "The Doctor, the Master, and the Devil face off" is a considerably more interesting idea than "Mike Yates chats up a witch" anyway. Indeed, whatever the story's flaws, its premise is fantastic in general, and this alone is sufficient to explain the story's popularity. As we've pointed out before, in a world where there's no way to revisit a past Doctor Who story, flawed plotting is forgettable. But iconic images are eternal. For all its flaws, *The Daemons* features the Doctor arguing with Satan, and that's enough to make it a landmark transformative story – especially because this is the first story to ever play with the mixture of fantasy and science fiction that it does, and is thus all the more memorable for it.

But it's worth noting exactly why it's interesting, which is that it is a premise that seems impossible to fulfill. The Devil exists outside of Doctor Who's paradigm – so much so that Russell T Davies was able to recycle this exact same trick thirty-five years later for *The Impossible Planet/The Satan Pit*. The premise isn't just that it's fun to see the Doctor and the Devil face off, it's that the Devil is something that shouldn't exist inside Doctor Who's premise in the first place. That's why the intrusion of fantasy into Doctor Who is so interesting in the first place.

And so for all the missteps in execution we still have to

admit, Letts has hit on something brilliant here. The evidence is how much of a standard Doctor Who concept this has become since *The Daemons*. Part of why it's so hard to see why *The Daemons* is beloved is because everything it does has been repeated with better execution. But given how original it was at the time, imitation is quite a form of flattery indeed. And the ideas that are being imitated are all Letts's. He's figured out that when the premise of the show is that anything can happen – and now that the Doctor is partially restored to time travel, that's back to being the premise of the show (note that next season the Doctor travels away from contemporary Earth in four of the five stories, with two having no Earth segments to speak of) the trick is to come up with ideas that the audience would never have thought of when they imagined what stories might be showing up in Doctor Who. And fantasy, in what is assumed to be a sci-fi show, is certainly one of them.

And notably, Letts goes to great lengths to have it both ways in this story, avoiding subsuming the fantasy into the science fiction. Yes, there's a scientific explanation for the Devil and he's really just an alien. But, equally crucially, Miss Hawthorne ends up winning her debate with the Doctor over science and magic by saying that the Doctor's account of what the Master is doing is wholly consistent with her claim that magic works. This is a story that revels in the gap introduced by the observation that any sufficiently advanced technology is indistinguishable from magic, using this to assert that traditional occultism is in fact extremely advanced technology. This means that the creature the Doctor meets may just be a powerful alien, but he's also genuinely and truly the Devil, with all of the power that concept implies retained. The fact that he's actually an alien like most Doctor Who enemies doesn't actually reduce that.

This is a new approach – find something that on paper sounds like you can't do it in Doctor Who and then find a way to make it work. And what's so interesting about the approach is that it restores a lot of the original point to Doctor Who: taking things that shouldn't go together and putting them together. It's just that it moves the game to a higher level. Instead of just creating a collage of dissonant images, the show now takes things that shouldn't go together even in Doctor Who and puts them together. It's the sort of clever advancement of the premise that a show — even one as flexible as Doctor Who — needs going into its ninth season. And it's a refinement and expansion of the glam approach that has been steadily developing over the course of Season Eight.

The only real downside is that this effectively ends the Master as an interesting character. Once you've summoned the Devil in Doctor Who, you've kind of peaked. The remaining room for the character to come up with a mad scheme is vanishingly small, and arguably nobody manages it until Russell T Davies. Arresting him at the end of the story not only brings to a close an entire season's plot arc, it's a fitting tying off for a character that has, at this point, seemingly run his course. (Not that there won't be any good Master stories to come, but he doesn't have nearly as high a success rate after this season.)

But the upsides are massive. Doctor Who has, with this move, opened an entire new bag of tricks. Suddenly myth and legend are as much a part of its repertoire as science or history. We've seen glimpses of this — *The Myth Makers*, most obviously, carried with it a hint of the supernatural. But we've never seen something like this, which establishes that magic, in the general case, is real. And it's done so aggressively. The bulk of the first two episodes consists of the Doctor behaving seemingly entirely out of character, siding with mystics and New Agers through and through. It's delightfully shocking, and while no attempt to merge science and fantasy will ever generate quite so much frisson the basic idea of finding premises that challenge our assumptions about what Doctor Who can be about in the first place is rock solid.

And this is what is so good about *The Daemons* and why it is such a landmark despite its flaws. Letts and Sloman are dragging the show from its comfort zone into completely new territory. Simply quietly doing a story in which something that seems to be the Devil is really an alien wouldn't work. That, after all, is the usual trick: the giant lizard is really a mining robot, the Yeti are really robots, and the man in a rubber suit is secretly a man in a rubber suit. The clever thing here isn't that the Devil is really an alien; it's that he actually is the Devil. It's that the Doctor is completely correct to believe in magic. This is the ultimate trick of the story. We spend the first two episodes expecting to find the scientific explanation behind it all. But there isn't one. The Doctor may have an explanation . . . but it's still magic.

Which might be worth looking at as well.

Pop Between Realities, Home in Time for Tea (*The Wicker Man, Chariots of the Gods?, Ace of Wands*)

And now, then, for the other part of the argument. *The Daemons* was, as we saw, revolutionary in terms of how it expands the domain of what Doctor Who can do. But why is juxtaposing fantasy with the show so strange? This is, after all, a show that only two-and-a-half years ago was exploring the Land of Fiction, and where one of its most iconic stories is about Yeti attacking a Buddhist monastery. It's a show where one of its dominant creative forces over the first five years was obsessed with alchemy. There's always been something a bit fantastic about the series.

And yet on the other hand the show has always praised science over superstition, promoted the idea that there is a rational explanation behind everything, and treated scientists as enlightened men of peace who can bring about positive social change. So to some extent, what's happening in *The Daemons* is the resolution of a fundamental tension that has been in place in Doctor Who ever since the Doctor equated the TARDIS with television in the first episode, making it simultaneously a scientific marvel and something that is primarily understood in terms of more wooly notions like "the power of stories." It's not accidental that this resolution happened in 1971. But understanding why 1971 was the time for it requires some explanation. Which is what this essay is.

Let's start with Jo's first line in *The Daemons*, invoking the Age of Aquarius. The most obvious cultural association with that phrase comes from the 1967 musical *Hair*, which memorably began by proclaiming "this is the dawning of the Age of Aquarius." The idea is that the world is passing out of one era and into another, and that this new era will be one of peace and harmony. But this is just a utopian version of eschatology. Every generation is convinced the world is going to end on their watch because they were dealt such a lousy hand by their parents' generation. And then they narrowly survive and deal a lousy hand to their kids, and the cycle cheerily repeats itself. Eschatology is just a way of being; the end of the world is a lifestyle choice.

More interesting than the idea that we're at the dawning of some new aeon of possibility – or than the idea that we're all going to die of some terrible misfortune – is what sort of apocalypse we imagine (remembering that the apocalypse can be positive or negative). And so what's most interesting about the Age of Aquarius is not that everyone believed an egalitarian society based on peace and love was inevitable – the 1960s were hardly the world's first bit of utopian eschatology. It's that they believed it to be inevitable because of astrology.

I mean, pause for a moment and look at the essential idea of the Age of Aquarius. Basically, over time the direction that the North Pole is pointing changes, moving backwards through the zodiac (itself being the set of constellations through which the sun moves over the course of a year). Each change takes a bit over two millennia. The core idea of the Age of Aquarius is that when these changes take place, it maps to massive social change on Earth. And, in at least some accounts of astrology, one of those changes takes place somewhere in the twentieth century as the North Pole moves into Aquarius. (Or the fifteenth. Or possibly the thirty-sixth. Astrology isn't really big on precision.) The opportune question isn't why everyone believed a utopian society was going to dawn – that happens all the time. The question is why people were basing this belief on what stars the North Pole was pointing at.

But let's back up and look at what astrology is. The bulk of it is a pre-modern version of astronomy: an observation-based practice of cataloguing celestial phenomena. Onto this is grafted an elaborate system of symbols that ostensibly explain aspects of day-to-day life. But think about how this system worked. Most people were not astrologers. So a farmer would ask an astrologer "Hey, Astrologer, why are my crops failing this year?" and the astrologer would consult a bunch of charts and data and say that it had something to do with the influence of Saturn in Aries. This is, of course, very silly to a contemporary science-minded ear, and obviously inferior to the vast systems of empiricism that we have. But from the farmer's perspective it is not actually a substantially different process from asking a climatologist and getting an answer about how El Niño has changed the course of the jet stream. They're both a chain of explanatory jargon involving things the farmer has no direct interaction with. The end-user experience is more or less identical.

The thing to recognize here is something we discussed in the *Colony in Space* essay: there are some key ways in which scientists serve a function otherwise most analogous to the priesthood. Science is, in terms of its social role (as opposed to its intellectual foundation), a modern-day religion. Which is why, throughout the Hartnell era, you saw characters appealing to the Doctor by saying "we're both scientists, we're reasonable men, we can surely work this out." Because science is not just an empirical process as theorized by Karl Popper or someone. It's also a social phenomenon. And for a significant time period, it was a social phenomenon given a tremendous amount of credence. Scientists were, broadly speaking, the people we turned to in order to design the world in the aftermath of World War II, and in 1971 that period was just starting to draw to a close.

Exhibit A is, of course, still *Doomwatch*. The entire point of that show was that scientists, if left unchecked, would kill us all. That this was mainstream entertainment shows a pretty clear change in how scientists were culturally viewed. And it's not hard to see the immediate causes for that. First and most obviously is the prospect of nuclear war. Consider the social position around the late '60s and early '70s. Massive global conflict was still something that happened. It had, after all, happened twice in the first half of the century. It was, each time, absolutely horrible in terms of its human cost. But now, if it happened again, it would be apocalyptic. And the reason this was true was because of how science changed war from something that was nasty but basically survivable to something that would outright end all life on the planet. So when, in the late '60s/early '70s, it started to feel like it might be time for

World War III, science was to blame for the fact that this meant a looming apocalypse, and not one of the good ones.

Second is the rise of the environmental movement, which we've talked about a bit before. There was, in this period, a growing awareness that there were unintended and dangerous side effects to an industrialized and technological world, namely that it might eventually kill us all just as an incidental byproduct. This was the era of *Silent Spring* and *Unsafe at Any Speed* – books that focused intently on the way in which scientific and industrial progress were dangerous precisely because of their unchecked prevalence.

So, of course, when the Science Priests began to look like they were leading people off a cliff, people reversed course, building a utopian vision out of the debris of the past. Because that's what you do. And since they were trying to get out from under the dangerous yoke of science, they turned to pre-scientific concepts like astrology and, as *The Daemons* picked up heavily on, the pagan traditions that were still very much visible and prevalent in rural Britain. All the bits about Beltane and maypoles and Morris dancing in *The Daemons* are there because there was a growing interest in the pagan roots of these archaic practices. (We saw the earliest roots of this way back in the first volume when we looked briefly at the underground magazine *Gandalf's Garden*, which embraced the various connections between Tolkien's work and the mystical tradition of rural Britain.) There is, of course, a lot of very dodgy history and heritage involved in this pagan/druidic revival, but there's also a lot of long-standing cultural artifacts to draw on.

And on a basic level this is what *The Daemons* was playing on. The most obvious thing to compare it to is *The Wicker Man*, a film which it is blatantly a rip-off of. *The Wicker Man*, which if you've not seen you should really just put this book down and go watch, concerns a police officer investigating a creepy but seemingly fluffy and harmless island full of pagan types that, at the end, turn on him and burn him alive as a sacrifice. The use of the seemingly silly rural traditions of maypoles and Morris dancing as a source of horror, along with the overt contrast between the "civilized" police officer and the pagan traditions of the isle, are so obviously the inspiration for *The Daemons* that it borders on the irrelevant that *The Wicker Man* wasn't actually released until almost two years after *The Daemons* aired. Which is to say that *The Daemons* really was picking up on some visible and big cultural trends. Britain in 1971 was simultaneously experiencing a surge of skepticism towards science as an ideology and a revival of the role of the magical in popular consciousness. What's so striking about *The Wicker Man* is the way in which Sergeant Howie dismisses the island's pagan culture until it is far too late for him to do anything about it. He, being a representative of the modern world (here framed in Christian terms instead of scientific ones, but this is largely incidental), is blind to the power within the discarded symbols of paganism, just as *The Daemons* hinges primarily on the fact that skeptical science-minded folks underestimate the threat that the pagan imagery of Azal represents.

But just because science and magic were intensely antagonistic does not mean that they're utter polar opposites, nor that the entire world was faithfully divided into one camp or the other. Instead you had a weird, schizoid state in which magical thinking and scientific thinking butted up against each other in the popular consciousness. Exhibit A here, of course, is Erich von Däniken.

On one level, von Däniken is a textbook New-Age nut job. His major contention – that in ancient human history Earth was visited by aliens who guided its technological progress – is, of course, utter lunacy, full of downright hilarious moments like the assertion that numbers with fifteen digits are evidence of alien intervention because they're so big not even computers can handle them. He is easily and not entirely inaccurately readable as nothing more than a period-specific crank.

But underneath the nuttery is a fundamentally interesting approach. The entire second chapter of *Chariots of the Gods?* is concerned with imagining the space-based future of Earth so that it can demonstrate just how plausible it is that aliens showed up in our ancient history. In other words, von Däniken isn't just spinning any old ludicrous New Age theory, he's spinning one that adopts much of the iconography and logic of science. He has a foot in both worlds, which was enough to make him exceedingly trendy in 1971.

We can see the von Däniken approach reflected several times in the Pertwee era, and not just at its most obvious in *The Daemons*. The idea in *Colony in Space* that the Crab Nebula is a result of the test firing of an ancient alien weapon is distinctly Däniken-esque, and the entire plot of *The Silurians* is based on Däniken-style ideas. Coming up we have *The Time Monster* and *Death to the Daleks*, and that's just in the Pertwee era – the approach becomes bog standard Doctor Who after this, cropping up several times in the Tom Baker era (*Pyramids of Mars*, *Image of the Fendahl*), the Davison era (*The Awakening*, *Four to Doomsday*), and all the way into the Sylvester McCoy era (*Ghost Light*, *Battlefield*). Even the new series has played with it in *The Impossible Astronaut/The Day of the Moon*.

But *The Daemons* went further than von Däniken. Remember, the key point of *The Daemons* isn't that the Devil is secretly an alien. It's that the Devil is real, and black magic actually works to summon him. This isn't just "aliens built the pyramids." It's not even von Däniken's idea that biblical and mythic stories make an equal amount of sense if reskinned as science fiction stories. The idea is that black magic and the occult are accurately preserved guides for summoning Azal – that the occult is actually the completely accurate secret record of the alien astronauts, not just a misunderstood representation of them.

Of course, the sort of black magic we see in *The Daemons* is one very small portion of the New Age pool. Unsurprisingly, when interest in everything old and mystical ramped up, one beneficiary was anyone who happened to have some useful legal rights to the last big mystical revival, which started up in the Victorian age and wound down in the early twentieth century. One effect of this was Kenneth Grant, whom we talked about in the context of *The Tenth Planet* back in our first volume. Grant, though, was really just a bit of a second rate follower of one of the more prominent figures of the Victorian/Edwardian magical revival: Aleister Crowley.

The relevance of Crowley to *The Daemons* is obvious to anyone familiar with both subjects. The Master in *The Daemons* is blatantly a Crowley reference. For all that his incantations are made up and, in some spots, apparently just "Mary Had a Little Lamb" read backwards, in other spots they demonstrate that either Letts or Sloman (probably Letts, if we're being realistic) had at least a passing familiarity with Crowley. The Master repeatedly invokes the Tetragrammaton, a mainstay of Crowley and hermetic mysticism, and twice delivers variations of Crowley's famous "do as thou wilt shall be the whole of the law," including the truly clever galactic conqueror subversion of it, "do my will shall be the whole of the law." (Also, at some point one must acknowledge the cross-story parallelism here. In *Colony in Space*, I described the Doctor as playing the role of science vicar. Not only does he repeat the performance here, quite literally turning the ethos of science into a form of spiritual gospel that he preaches to a congregation, but his explicit double is playing a literal vicar in this story.)

Here's where things get just a little bit odd. Invoking Crowley for this sort of thing is a no-brainer. Crowley was a decadent attention whore who liked talking about how he was the Great Beast and talking about lengthy sex magick rituals with the Scarlet Woman Babalon. He proudly played the role of the wickedest man in the world, and as such spent the remainder of his life typecast as an over-the-top villain. But the thing is, in practice, he was a fairly garden-variety occultist of his time, albeit one with quite a flair for self-promotion.

And garden-variety occultists of his time were common. The big thing to talk about here is the Hermetic Order of the Golden Dawn – the occult secret society from which Crowley split. The Golden Dawn is a surprisingly big deal, at least as occult secret societies go; among its members were such relative luminaries as Algernon Blackwood, Arthur Machen, Bram Stoker, and William Butler Yeats. More to the point, though, it proves to be a kind of common ancestor to virtually any British-based magical tradition going. Both of the major British Wiccan traditions owe major debt to the Golden Dawn for the ways in which they patched together the scattered fragments of pagan lore.

The thing about the Golden Dawn is that it was much closer to an aesthetic movement than it was to a religio-scientific movement. Britain's current greatest living occultist, Alan Moore, makes the most extended version of this argument, claiming that the optimal way to think of magic in general is as an art. (His extended essay on the matter, "Fossil Angels," can be found straightforwardly with Google). We're a ways from where it's quite fair play to actually use Moore as our interpretive lens for Doctor Who, but here his basic point stands: magic is an aesthetic movement as much as anything. The logic of occultism is primarily narrative. And here comes the shoe anyone who's read the previous two volumes could see waiting to drop from the start of this essay.

The thing about Doctor Who that made it uniquely poised to do something like *The Daemons* is that this aesthetic occultism has been a part of the show from day one. And that's mostly down, as ever, to David Whitaker. It is, after all, Whitaker who repeatedly wrote Doctor Who by taking the iconography of science fiction and wrapping it around a plot structured on an occult aesthetic – *The Evil of the Daleks* being only the most blatant example. Doctor Who has existed in the gap between science and magic from day one. And so when that gap became trendy it was able to do far better stuff with it than anyone else around.

To get a sense of how important this is to how a story like *The Daemons* comes off, it's helpful to compare to another show that was the nearest equivalent to Doctor Who on television in 1971: ITV's *Ace of Wands*. Unfortunately, both of the first two seasons of *Ace of Wands* are lost, so the only window we have on the series is from further ahead than 1971. But let's look at a fairly representative example: *The Power of Atep* by Victor Pemberton.

Ace of Wands is basically a younger, hipper, more Age of Aquarius take on Doctor Who. To imagine it, take Doctor Who, then remove the Doctor and replace him with Tarot, a stage magician with real powers. Give him a pair of sidekicks: a female who's basically Polly only psychic, and a male who's . . . well, basically Ben, actually. And then have him fight crime and/or evil magicians. *The Power of Atep* falls into the latter category, featuring a former friend of Tarot's who is now going by the name John Pentacle and serving the ancient Egyptian magician Atep, whose power cowed even the Pharaoh and can still be accessed today.

Quality-wise *Ace of Wands* is nondescript; it's a perfectly serviceable children's adventure show for the early '70s, but it's difficult to mistake it for a classic. Like Doctor Who, it has some real skill at iconic set pieces. And also like Doctor Who, the acting is sometimes cringeworthy. It's one of many attempts by ITV to create a rival for Doctor Who, and not inherently one of the more interesting ones. But *The Power of Atep* is interesting in how it attempts to balance rationality and the occult, and provides a useful counterpoint to *The Daemons*. See, it turns out that Atep was actually a fraud in his own time with no great power. But the strange thing is, the ancient evil merely lacks the great power John Pentacle ascribes to it. It still has some power, as we spend four episodes watching Atep and his followers wage various psychic attacks on Tarot and his friends.

There's a really strange vacilation here. On the one hand, this is a skeptic plot. Ancient evil turns out not to be all that. The popularity of the New Age was as much a boon to people with a flair for debunking, and the plot fits firmly in that tradition. On the other, it's a straight supernatural/New-Age plot. Magic works, psychic attacks happen, there are ancient Egyptian tombs with dead mystics that can pose a problem for people. The story, in other words, is simultaneously confirming and denying magic, and ends up feeling a bit like a cheap copout as a result. And it particularly pales when compared to the delicious strangeness of magic and science both being right in

Doctor Who. As ancient evils go, Azal is far more interesting than Atep simply because one is actually the Devil and the other is a dead Egyptian confidence man.

But why is Doctor Who able to bridge that gap? I mean, yes, Whitaker had been doing it since day one, but what was he actually doing? What makes Doctor Who better at sitting in the gap between magic and science? Because it is. Its two closest cousins on television right now are *Doomwatch* and *Ace of Wands*, but nobody would suggest *Doomwatch* and *Ace of Wands* of being very similar to each other, which makes it difficult to explain what it means to sit at the midpoint between them.

The answer comes if we look closely at the Victorian/Edwardian magical revival that the Hermetic Order of the Golden Dawn was a part of. Victorian England, we should note, was absolutely gaga for spiritualism. In the UK, at least, the New Age movement is really just a repeat of the Victorian craze for the mystical. And remember, it's Whitaker's Victorian story – *The Evil of the Daleks* – where his occult and mystical themes come most to the forefront. These aspects of Doctor Who have always had an antiquarian flare to them, which is why *The Mind Robber*'s hat tip to Victorian children's literature was so inevitable and necessary.

But that's not the only Victorian tradition Doctor Who belongs to. William Hartnell's version of the Doctor was also always in the mould of the Victorian inventor. Remember, in the early days the strong implication was that the Doctor had built the TARDIS himself. In the Peter Cushing films, this is explicit and the Doctor simply is a human inventor with a distinctly Victorian flare. There's a particular British image, tied firmly to the Victorian era, of the lone eccentric who, through plucky cleverness, figures something out that had eluded the more mainstream thinkers. In the late '60s and early '70s, this figure was a sort of yearned for prophet in the UK – the Science Priest who would finally show up and, through good old fashioned British cleverness, suddenly put the UK back on top of the world through some brilliant method of generating energy or flying or something. Hence the variety of promising new energy installations that the Doctor shows up to save through this era.

And one way of understanding Pertwee's take on the Doctor is that he takes the charismatic leading-man aspects of Troughton's performance and weds them to the Victorian inventor flare of Hartnell's performance. Which is to say, this Victorian tradition was alive and well in Doctor Who at this point. Just as the Victorian spiritualist tradition was still knocking around in there. In fact, the two were never entirely separate in British culture. The first great occultist in England was John Dee, spymaster, occultist, and mathematician for Queen Elizabeth. Dee invented the idea of the British Empire, was a major mathematician of his era, and, almost incidentally, regularly spoke with Enochian Angels by scrying through crystal balls at his magical table and engaging in complex numerologically derived rituals with his assistant Edward Kelly.

Which is to say that there has always been, in British culture, the possibility of this odd fusion of the wizard and the scientist. And that Doctor Who, given that it was heavily indebted to both magic and science from the last era where both were intensely dominant in British culture, is connected with this merged figure more than virtually anything else in the culture in 1971. So *The Daemons* marks a significant change and advancement in the relationship between these two aspects of Doctor Who more than it marks a new idea as such. Key to this is its decision to pretend to break the rules in its first three episodes by having the Doctor appear to be on the wrong side of the science/magic debate, only for it to turn out not only that the Doctor is on the right side after all, but that the whole debate is wrong and there aren't actually sides in the first place. Instead of tacitly balancing two creative traditions, *The Daemons* finally goes ahead and openly, actively unites them.

It is, in effect, a brilliant conjuring trick. The audience, forgetting that both elements exist in Doctor Who's cultural DNA, assumes that the current feuds between science and spirituality in the culture are in play in Doctor Who. When in fact, Doctor Who is far smarter and more interesting than that.

And now that the moment is right in the culture, Doctor Who is able to do more than exist within the gap between science fiction and fantasy – it's able to fill the space of the gap, embodying not only its very nature but also the connections that make the gap sensible in the first place. By letting the relevant two elements of its past seem to be pulled apart and made irreconcilable before quietly showing that not only are they reconcilable, they aren't actually two different elements at all, Doctor Who manages to find an approach that isn't between science fiction and fantasy, but rather a pure example of both at once.

You're Just a Soldier (*Day of the Daleks*)

It's January 1, 1972. Little Jimmy Osmond is at number one with "Long Haired Lover From Liverpool," for which the UK continues to seek a formal apology. We regret to inform you that the number one does not change over the time this story is running. More alarming, the Osmonds at large are also in the top ten. Also in the charts, however, are David Bowie, Slade, Elton John, The Sweet and T. Rex, along with Carly Simon's "You're So Vain." So it's not all bad.

Since *The Daemons* the UK has begun negotiations to join the EEC now that Charles de Gaulle isn't there to block them, continuing a process you may remember from way back in *The Faceless Ones*. Jim Morrison has died. The UK has abandoned its Black Arrow space program, formally consigning *The Ambassadors of Death* to a future that never happened. Tensions in Northern Ireland ratcheted up, with the UK sending more troops and with UK security forces beginning Operation Demetrius, i.e. the long-term internment without trial of suspected paramilitary rebels. To say that this went over poorly with large numbers of people would be an understatement. Richard Nixon formally took the Bretton-Woods economic system out back and shots it by decoupling the dollar from the gold standard. The result, termed Nixon Shock, is a great way to make obsessive Tea Party/Ayn Rand devotees rant for a long time, but it also, as we've noted previously, marks a fundamental shift in the nature of technocratic authority. The UN swapped out the People's Republic of China for Taiwan, which we'll unpack a little in the paragraph after next, and Ian Paisley founded the Democratic Unionist Party in Northern Ireland. India and Pakistan had another quick spot of war, and both Qatar and the United Arab Emirates were formed.

While during this story, Kurt Waldheim becomes Secretary General of the UN, while Nixon begins development on the Space Shuttle, a decision that will turn out to be a deathblow to the Space Age. And the planned libertarian utopia Minerva declares independence before being annexed and successfully invaded by Tonga, which has to go down as one of libertarianism's more hilariously ignoble defeats.

While on television we have the second story in two years to spend time being paranoid about China and nuclear war, which we should maybe look at for a moment. To recap, back in 1949 Mao Zedong and his forces successfully took over China. This was followed by some awkward moments like the Great Leap Forward, which proved fatal to forty-five million people, and the Cultural Revolution, which managed to go even worse. But what's really important is how all of this went over with the USSR. Initially, at least the USSR was more or less in favor of China. Yes, each country viewed the other with some suspicion, but that was due as much to the fact that each of them was very big as to the fact that they had markedly different takes on Marxism.

The US, meanwhile, was none too pleased with any of these developments, fighting the Korean War as a proxy war against Sino-Soviet influence. Then came the Cultural Revolution, and China and the USSR definitively split and discarded almost any pretext of getting along. In fact, they kind of started shooting each other, resulting in a situation where the US was stuck in a proxy war with China and the USSR in Vietnam while China and the USSR were themselves having a bit of a war. All three countries, of course, were nuclear powers, so this all looked very bad from the perspective of anyone who didn't want to explode. (This also ties back to the previous essay about the New Age movement.)

But in 1971, following Nixon's winning election in the US on a platform that included "maybe we should chat up China," and, in August of 1971, his sending of Henry Kissinger with a secret delegation to China to try to negotiate, things began to calm down. Following a failed coup in China in September of 1971, in February of 1972 Nixon himself went to China, effectively normalizing relations there and defusing the colossal global instability that had previously looked to be headed to World War III. All of which is valuable context for *Day of the Daleks*, which features as its central plot point yet another peace conference in which the Chinese are the sticky wicket.

The most obvious thing to say about *Day of the Daleks* might be that we were just able to go 750 words without mentioning it. This has never been true about past Dalek stories, where we have usually just dived in and dealt with the epic connotations of the Daleks. But there's something . . . odd about this round of Daleks.

Behind the scenes, the reasons are clear enough. Louis Marks, who wrote the script, had an idea for a story about time travelers trying to change the past. In parallel, Robert Sloman was working on a Dalek story as the season finale. But Barry Letts decided he needed something bigger for the season launch, and decided to take the Daleks from Sloman (offering him the Master in compensation, which we'll talk about at the other end of Season Nine) and tell Marks to use them. The result is that the Daleks got shoehorned into this script where they didn't really belong, leading to a Dalek story that isn't quite a Dalek story.

But on the other hand, this is the return of the Daleks for the first time in over four years. The time between their first appearance and the end of *The Evil of the Daleks* is actually shorter than the time from that story to this one. Even if they're barely here, there's simply no way to escape the gravity of this as an event story. But with the Daleks appearing in an average of two-and-a-half minutes per episode and the Doctor never actually getting a confrontation with them as such, as an event the story is, frankly, frustrating. Not that the show needs to be about Daleks instead of time travel intrigue – indeed, there's a fair case to be made that the latter is preferable. But if you're going to bring the Daleks back, you might want to use them.

But in an odd sense the story seems almost, if not quite, aware of its ambiguous nature. On the one hand, the first episode behaves like a normal first episode of a Dalek story, which is to say that it builds relentlessly towards a cliffhanger that reveals the presence of the Daleks in a story we knew was about the Daleks from the moment the words "of the Daleks" appeared in the opening credits. As cynical as this sounds, we should probably admit that it is not an entirely unreasonable use of audience time. The use of the end-of-first-episode reveal is still a major part of the show's DNA, and holding off on the Daleks until then makes sense and builds anticipation. Except that about halfway through the episode, the camera zooms back and reveals, for a half second, a Dalek shouting "REPORT!"

It's difficult to understand how and why this happened. For all the sloppiness in the series to date, it has never really made a mistake like this one. The closest equivalent is probably the odd reveal of the Master in *The Claws of Axos*, but that can at least be read plausibly as deliberate subversion, and the Master, by that time, was already defined as a transgressive trickster figure who could do things like that. The Daleks don't have that kind of definition, and the unimpressive half shot of a Dalek seems inexplicable. Perhaps the idea was supposed to be that an extremely quick cut of a Dalek would build anticipation for the proper reveal later in the story? If so, someone probably should have put some effort into the proper reveal, which features the most lackluster Daleks ever, talking in a flat monotone. When it comes time for their big chorus of "Exterminate" at the end they sound almost bored, as if they're tired of chanting about extermination and just want to go have a cup of tea.

In fact, all three of the cliffhangers are oddly lacking. The second two are at least played well, but are also classic cases of cliffhangers of future potential – that is, a cliffhanger where the point is not the danger one of the regulars is in but rather the establishment of a situation that is going to change how the plot proceeds. The delayed revelation of the Daleks is certainly an example of this; it pays off the audience's expectations and desires just in time to cut to the closing credits and leave them wanting more next week. Similarly, the second episode's cliffhanger is a Dalek materializing in some tunnels to chase the Doctor. The point of a cliffhanger like this is not that the Doctor is in immediate danger of extermination. It's that the episode stops just before we see what we want to see: a confrontation between the Doctor and a Dalek.

The problem comes with the resolution in the third episode. So when the third episode starts up (and this happens within a minute of the credits) the Doctor escapes by getting dragged into the future by the guerrillas he's with. All the build-up turns out to lead to nothing in particular. Likewise, when the Doctor is strapped to a table and the Daleks confirm that he really is the Doctor, it appears to be leading towards the same thing: a scene where the Doctor faces down some Daleks. Instead, after a brief exchange, they release him to let a human interrogate him. Indeed, in the whole story there's never actually a proper confrontation between Pertwee and the Daleks.

This is less of a problem than it might be by virtue of the fact that the plot that the story spends time on instead of the Daleks is actually very good. The story Marks actually wants to be telling, about time travelers from the future trying to change the present, is great. It moves beautifully from seeming like a ghost story in the first to being about soldiers from another time to being about the Doctor trying to bring down a corrupt society in the future, with each stage of the shift being a distinct and interesting type of story. When bits don't work, it's mostly down to the fact that pretending to be a ghost story when the audience knows full well there are Daleks to be had doesn't work as well as what one assumes was Marks's original plan of simply pretending to be a ghost story. Which is to say, it's an easy enough flaw to forgive once you know that this story was never supposed to have Daleks in the first place.

That said, Marks does do something very interesting with the structure here. There's an old maxim about how to tell stories that divides them into open and closed structures. Basically, in an open structure the audience gets to see everything that's going on, while in a closed structure their knowledge is made to stay equivalent to the main characters' knowledge. But in this story Marks manages to have his cake and eat it too. For most of the first two episodes he writes in an open structure. The audience knows considerably more about what is going on than the Doctor does, and we watch the Doctor catching up with what we already know. In these episodes the main figure who knows stuff is the Daleks' main human lackey, the Controller. This is all very normal for Doctor Who; we frequently get to know more about the villain's plans than the Doctor does. So there's nothing particularly amiss.

But then Marks does something clever. He slowly stops giving the audience new information at the exact point where he has the Controller begin to play both sides of the Doctor/Daleks conflict. The character who previously had been the major source of information in the story becomes opaque, and Marks refrains from telling the audience what his real plan is. And eventually, in the third episode, the Doctor meets the Controller. But by that point, the narrative has switched to a closed one: now we know what the Doctor is doing and don't know what the Controller is doing. The effect is to make the Controller a considerably more effective villain. He started in a position where we knew what to expect of him and where he appeared to be like a normal Doctor Who villain, and suddenly occupies a different role in the narrative. Normally it's the Doctor who can abruptly change the rules of the story to his advantage, and to see that ability end up in the hands of the bad guy is disturbing. Indeed, in a small way it echoes the narrative collapses familiar from past Dalek stories like *The Chase* and *The Evil of the Daleks*.

Equally interesting is the decision to have the Doctor object to the state of the world primarily because of its labor conditions. Look at this bit of dialogue:

DOCTOR: Well, better than jumping from the crack of a whip from some security guard. Do you run all your factories like that, Controller?
CONTROLLER: That was not a factory, Doctor.
DOCTOR: Oh? Then what was it?
CONTROLLER: A rehabilitation centre. A rehabilitation centre for hardened criminals.

DOCTOR: Including old men and women, even children?
CONTROLLER: There will always be people who need discipline, Doctor.
DOCTOR: Now that's an old fashioned point of view, even from my standards.
CONTROLLER: I can assure you that this planet has never been more efficiently, more economically run. People have never been happier or more prosperous.
DOCTOR: Then why do you need so many people to keep them under control? Don't they like being happy and prosperous?

And shortly thereafter:

DOCTOR: When I meet a regime that needs to import savage alien life forms as security guards, I begin to wonder who the real criminals are.
JO: Those creatures aren't really savage.
CONTROLLER: Exactly. They are simply guard dogs. They just do what I tell them.
DOCTOR: You mean there aren't enough humans around that will follow your orders so blindly?
CONTROLLER: That is not what I was saying.
DOCTOR: Isn't it? Then what you're saying is that the entire human population of this planet, apart from a few remarkable exceptions like yourself, are really only fit to lead the life of a dog. Why?

What's interesting about this is that the Doctor is objecting primarily to the way in which the masses are treated. He repeatedly phrases his objection in the general case. In fact, we never even meet any of the oppressed workers. The Doctor objects to the general condition of cruelty – the way in which the workers are treated as a class. He even, in the final line quoted, phrases it in an almost overtly Marxist way, dividing the population of the planet into the few who get a good life and the massive working class that gets abused.

But this is very different from the Doctor's usual views, which are at once more philosophical and more personal. In

Colony in Space – the other story thus far where Pertwee has taken a view like this – he may talk about how people need a world where they're not treated like battery hens, but this has impact largely because we are by that point familiar with the people he is defending as characters. Here we see him make a purely class-based argument, which seems, in its way, like further progress towards considering the impact of his adventuring on ordinary people. He's learned to think of ordinary people not just as the one or two exceptions that he notices but as a broad group that is impacted systemically.

The other thing to note about these scenes is that Pertwee is on fire in them. Outside his comfort zone in the same ways he was in *Inferno* and *The Mind of Evil*, he's sublimely good at playing anger and fear. And having those scenes nearby adds interesting nuances to his performance elsewhere. In particular, when faced with that most Doctor Who-ish of circumstances – sitting around discussing philosophy with the human villain instead of doing anything that costs money – he comes out swinging.

But what's interesting is how he plays the scene, reclining on one elbow while dining on good food and throwing out bon mots about social justice. It's exactly the sort of scene that has been frustrating about Pertwee in the past, and yet here, couched among scenes where we see him in real danger and peril, it works, coming off in a beautiful space between the Doctor putting on an unflappable front to put the Controller off his game and the Doctor genuinely enjoying himself in the moment. It invokes an earlier moment in the story, in which the Doctor "Hails" his way through a few people without spilling his glass of wine, then calmly sips from it. When that moment happens, it falls right on the edge of being a genuinely fun, clever bit and being another example of Pertwee's vanity. But by establishing that aspect of the Doctor so memorably when he's in genuine control of the situation, the later scenes where he isn't in control seem all the better.

Also great in this story is Katy Manning, who finally has a script that treats her with some respect and so gets to return firmly to the potential she showed in her first two stories. She does delightfully in her scenes with the Controller as she tries and fails to work out what's going on, and her scene with Pertwee in which they're both tied up in Sir Reginald's basement is a thing of real beauty, their easy familiarity and sense of fun working in a delightful contrast to the danger of their circumstances. After five stories worth of promise, this is the story where it becomes clear that we have a classic companion on our hands.

But all of this seems beside the point, which inevitably has to be the Daleks and their strange non-return to the series. In the past, the Doctor's confrontations with the Daleks have seemed definitive – asking questions with deep ramifications about who the Doctor is and who the Daleks are. Only one scene of this story seems to deal with that, namely the cliffhanger/resolution forming the end of the third episode and the start of fourth. In it, the Daleks (not the mind) probe the Doctor to see if he really is the Doctor. The most obvious thing to say about this is that it compares strangely to *The Power of the Daleks*, where the Daleks' recognition of the Doctor is one of the absolute key scenes of the whole story and the thing that cements Troughton as the Doctor.

Here, however, the Daleks are unable to recognize the Doctor without considerable effort – so much so that the Controller comments that they've nearly killed the Doctor trying. Never before have the Daleks shown this kind of failure to recognize the Doctor, and there are only two more instances in the entire rest of the series where it happens again. What, then, are we to make of this?

The most obvious answer would seem to be that the Doctor is in some sense unrecognizable in this form. I actually don't mean this as an attack on Pertwee or the Pertwee era in general. Remember that the means by which the Time Lords restricted the Doctor to Earth is in part by damaging his TARDIS and in part by altering his knowledge of time travel. These are both key parts of who he is, though. A madman without a box is just a madman. A Time Lord without knowledge of time is just someone calling themselves Lord. The Doctor's punishment was, in one sense, the stripping away of who he is. Until he reaches the point where the Time Lords deem him worthy of being the Doctor again, why should the Daleks recognize him? How would you bring back the Daleks, the vast, ontological threats to the very nature of Doctor Who, when the show hasn't yet returned to being the show they threaten?

To be fair, the general progress of the Pertwee era has been towards that point. All parts of the era are working more and more like Doctor Who. Letts and Dicks, starting with *The Silurians*, gave us the Doctor with every part of what had defined the character in the past taken away, and slowly have allowed him to reclaim pieces of who he was by adjusting them to fit his new circumstances, steadily reinventing him for the 1970s. The show that is emerging is certainly not the show that existed in the 1960s, but in a way that couldn't be said of Season Seven, it's at least becoming an heir to that show in more than just name and some continuity points. But the reinvention isn't quite there yet. And in many ways, *Day of the Daleks* serves as a preview of what will come when it is there. It's deferred and incomplete – still emerging just as the show itself is at the start of Season Nine. This is, in many ways, the season where the show earns the right to be Doctor Who again, building inexorably towards not only the full return of the TARDIS in *The Three Doctors* but the glory days of Season Ten in general.

Another way to look at this story, then, is as the intersection of two familiar but not-yet-reconcilable worlds. The first is the world of UNIT, and the second is the world of the Daleks. Note that both worlds are, on their own merits, well established. The Daleks are particularly interesting in this regard; we're told they have a massive empire that Earth is only a part of. But the stakes of this story are limited purely to Earth. There's not the sense that changing history and stopping the Daleks from taking over Earth will disrupt their larger empire. This story is small potatoes to them, which oddly reinforces their peripheral role in it. One small part of the Daleks' vast empire and one small part of our world briefly touch.

It's notable, then, that the Doctor's end solution is not to defeat the Daleks, but essentially to separate the two worlds again. He gets the Daleks to go into the house, gets UNIT to run out of it, blows up the house, and calls it a day. There are a few action scenes between UNIT and the Daleks, but nothing too climactic. The end point is that these worlds need to, for a little while longer, remain separate. The Daleks' Empire lives on as someone else's problem; someone who isn't quite the Doctor of their nightmares, and, more to the point, someone that the Doctor isn't quite yet.

Yet.

A Life of Ordered Calm (*The Curse of Peladon*)

It's January 29, 1972. The New Seekers, with no trace of irony whatsoever, would like to teach the world to sing, and are going to have to insist that the harmonies be perfect. T. Rex mercifully puts this out of its misery quickly with "Telegram Sam," which, as with most glam acts, really needs to be seen as well as heard. This spares us for two weeks before Chicory Tip have their one hit with "Son of My Father," a song that is actually marginally fitting for this story. America (with "Horse with No Name," of course), Cat Stevens, Melanie (with "Brand New Key"), Sonny and Cher, and Don McLean (with "American Pie") all also make it into the top ten.

While in news without power chords, the famed Bloody Sunday massacre of U2 fame takes place as the British army opens fire on unarmed civil rights protesters in Northern Ireland. So still power chords, actually, but let's pause and look at this one. One of the things that really is worth stressing is that Northern Ireland is part of the UK. So when I say that the British army shot and killed fourteen unarmed protesters, what needs to be stressed is that this is a military deployment inside the UK shooting its own citizens. Reports exist of soldiers prior to the massacre actively declaring "we want some kills" going into the day, and the overwhelming reports from anyone other than the military itself is that those shot were unarmed and fleeing for their lives. It is, in short, a dark and genuinely horrific atrocity. So when, in a few paragraphs, we get to talking about a sci-fi show with an inadvertent giant green penis alien, remember the context is that this story is going out in times of egregious, serious unrest in the country.

In any case, now well and truly power chord free, in what Phil Ochs dryly referred to as the State of Richard Nixon, Billy Graham visits the White House and implores Nixon to break the stranglehold of the Jews on the media. This takes place one day after mandatory searches and screenings are instituted for all air passengers. Returning to the UK, we should also note that *The Curse of Peladon* was transmitted during the first of the three big miners strikes – one that set off rolling power cuts that meant that large swaths of the country missed parts of this story and it was shown with helpful "here's what you missed" recaps. Although the miners' strikes are going to become an increasingly fascinating microcosm of issues in British society, at this point they're fairly simple strikes for increased wages that have broad support. No, you want the next Peladon story for that one.

The other thing going on is something we began talking about way back in *The Faceless Ones*: UK membership in the European Economic Community – a sort of proto-European Union. This is a monstrously complex event that the jury is still out on, but it basically amounted to an effort to leverage the multiple strong economies in (Western) Europe into a coherent power, which would then presumably offer those charming economic development packages that were rapidly emerging as colonialism's tasty new flavor. ("Here, have a big pile of money. All you have to do is let us restructure your economy and possibly your government so you can become more like us, by which we really mean give us all your money.")

So it's against the backdrop of all of that that we find ourselves watching *The Curse of Peladon*. There's something genuinely strange about this one. On the one hand, it's difficult to think of anything less obviously suited to the mood of strikes, power cuts, and brutal massacres than a sudden return to space for a pseudo-medieval adventure with the aforementioned giant green penis monster. (I should probably go ahead and explain this – the two Peladon stories feature the alien Alpha Centauri, played by Stuart Fell in an astonishingly naughty-looking costume. Upon noticing the problem director Lennie Mayne hastily arranged to have Alpha Centauri wear a cape, which ended up just looking like a split condom.) On the other hand, this is an overtly and consciously political story that is specifically talking about the EEC. The plot – a controversy over admitting the planet of Peladon into the Galactic Federation – is blatantly a reference to those political events. Which makes this one of the most overtly timely stories of the

Pertwee era.

The thing is, once you establish that a story is political, most people (in trying to explain the politics as an allegory) tend to try to get everything precisely and definitely refer to specific political events. Apparently efforts to hammer *The Curse of Peladon* into that format have gone so far as to take hairstyles as evidence for the allegory, so let's just back away slowly from that approach. Especially because *The Curse of Peladon*, although certainly timely, is very much the story that illustrates why reading Doctor Who as allegory tends to be the wrong approach.

The main issue we run into is the fact that King Peladon insists on the importance of helping Peladon "raise [itself] from the Dark Ages" and of discarding religious superstition. Whatever can be said of Euroskepticism and the debate over joining the EEC, it's a challenge to convincingly argue that the central issue in the UK's joining is that the UK was stuck in the Dark Ages. It's important to make a distinction here. There was certainly the widespread accusation that Euroskepticism was an outdated idea, and the fact that Euroskeptics talked about the need to preserve "a thousand years of history" didn't help with the accusation that they were stuck in the past.

But the "thousand years of history" argument is Hepesh's. What's going on here is stranger: King Peladon views his own civilization as hopelessly outdated, and he believes that it is necessary to have outside help in uplifting it. Which, if nothing else, has to be taken as a very extreme position that would fly poorly if Edward Heath had ever said anything like it. So it suggests strongly that what we are looking at is not an allegory for the UK's accession into the EEC as such. And yet the parallels are unmistakable. So how ought we describe this story's relationship with contemporary Earth?

Actually, when you put it that way, this is a question that's been looming over the Pertwee era. In Season Seven, Doctor Who was a show about a scientist who went to various installations and solved problems, generally ones involving alien life forms. The season after that, it was a show about hunting an evil counterpart to the Doctor that went to various places, including, in a one-off, another planet. In both cases the UNIT supporting cast is omnipresent – this is the first Pertwee story not to feature the Brigadier at all.

But what is it now? The season opener started as a UNIT story in the Season Seven vein, only with an English country house and a peace conference instead of a scientific installation. But it morphed into something jumping between two worlds, with UNIT in present day Earth backing up the Doctor as he fought the real threat in the future. And now we have a story that was blatantly written as a straight space story for a Doctor with a functional TARDIS, which Terrance Dicks had to tack on a bit at the end in order to fit it into Doctor Who's continuity in general. On the one hand, they're clearly moving away from the UNIT paradigm.

In other words, we have Doctor Who in a place where it's accepting scripts in the pre-Pertwee format, even though its format is still something related to the UNIT-based style. So it's not the format of either of those seasons, but it's also not actually a return to the old format. The result is that show lacks any mission statement or clear declaration that this is the sort of show it is now. The audience goes four weeks thinking it's a show about other worlds only to find out it's still the UNIT show. (Though actually, UNIT doesn't show up in the next story either, meaning that Season Nine, despite ostensibly still having the earthbound format of Seasons Seven and Eight, actually has fewer UNIT stories than Season Eleven, which ostensibly has a fully functional TARDIS.)

On top of that we have Peladon. Peladon is, let's be clear, a great planet – very possibly the best one Doctor Who has done to date. But it's like nothing we've seen on Doctor Who in recent memory. With *Colony in Space*, yes, the story started with a traditional bit of exploration, but the overall planet was extremely sensible and easy to grasp, fitting firmly in familiar sci-fi traditions. But fire up *The Curse of Peladon* and imagine what its opening scenes of a stormy pseudo-medieval castle and men in purple making speeches about galactic federations must have looked like to someone who had started watching Doctor Who with *Spearhead from Space*. It had been three years since Doctor Who last tried to define an alien planet by its strangeness, and suddenly *The Curse of Peladon* jumped in with no attempt to ease the viewer into it. *Colony in Space* went to great lengths to justify its breaking of the rules. This just assumes the rules don't apply.

And on top of that, Peladon is weird even by Doctor Who standards. The medieval alien planet is not unprecedented in science fiction, but it's an odd concept. On top of it, this is a particularly visually striking story, which does play up the strangeness. It's not just the reams of purple or the frequent statues of a strange pig/bear creature called "Aggedor" (which turn out to be hilariously accurate representations when we actually meet Aggedor). Nor is it the Ice Warriors, who we've met before, after all. It's not even Arcturus, upon whom the Face of Boe was obviously modeled – a floating head in a vat who rolls around and gratuitously vaporizes things to show his strength.

No. It's the thing we've already alluded to. Alpha Centauri. An apparently hermaphroditic character, referred to (and the Doctor corrects Jo on this, so we can assume he's accurately reflecting convention on what is, I believe, Doctor Who's first firmly genderqueer character) by the male pronoun, and voiced by the (female and reasonably famous for playing Grace Archer, who was spectacularly killed off on the radio soap *The Archers* the day that ITV launched) Ysanne Churchman, who, as we discussed, is strikingly rude looking. There's really nothing in the preceding eight years of Doctor Who that quite prepares the viewer for a strangely high-pitched giant green penis in a cape. It's one of the most bewildering sights in Doctor Who history.

The result is that, in a way we have not seen Doctor Who do in ages, Peladon feels like a strange place where interesting things happen. This is, in other words, a sudden return to *The Web Planet*'s style of showing a strange place as opposed to strange things (which the show can do quite well on Earth). For all that the climax of *Colony in Space* was strange, on the whole that was a planet defined precisely by its familiarity. This is a planet made to be weird, executed with few concessions to the viewer to get them used to the idea that this is something Doctor Who does. We start on Peladon, and only then cut to the TARDIS where the Doctor says he's got it working again while an improbably prudishly dressed Jo Grant insists that she has a date with Mike Yates.

So what we get is a story that is simultaneously pushing in two very different directions – on the one hand towards a striking depiction of strangeness, on the other towards an equally striking depiction of the real world. The place to start untangling this, ironically, is the bit that Brian Hayles didn't write – the decision to declare this a mission for the Time Lords. We haven't really talked about them much in this book so let's break this out again in detail. When they first appeared in *The War Games*, we observed that the role of the Time Lords appears to be the maintenance of the proper order of time. But since then, there seems to be a somewhat stranger game in play.

Even if we ignore the Master as a wholesale renegade – though we can't, quite, for reasons we'll see shortly – the Time Lords since their first appearance have seemed odd. *Colony in Space* can be accounted for fairly straightforwardly, as at least the Master stole information from them and they had to stop him. But *Terror of the Autons*, with its Magritte-inspired Time Lord, is far more puzzling. Here the Time Lords send a clearly mischievous agent to talk to the Doctor and warn him about the Master. Clearly, then, they know exactly where the Master is. And yet they are content to let this meddling renegade run around freely with only the Doctor to oppose him. And now we have them sending the Doctor seemingly to clear up a small political disruption on a relatively backwater planet. Is there anything we can possibly do to have this look like something other than just shoehorning the Time Lords into whatever plot contrivance is needed?

Yes, actually, we can. But it requires some thought about what we mean by "time." Specifically, it means sidestepping the question of time as a scientific phenomenon – the question of how time works in a physics sense. Let us remember, after all, that the Time Lords are, as originally debuted, apparently counterparts to other conceptual lords such as the War Lords. This is something that's been largely dropped from their conception over time, but in the pre-*Deadly Assassin* Pertwee era, and indeed, the pre-*Three Doctors* Pertwee era, it remains one of the few things we can firmly understand about the Time Lords. The order in which they were introduced in *The War Games* was that we met the War Lords first, and then the Time Lords. The one is defined in terms of the other. War is not a phenomenon of physics – it's a social phenomenon. And if we want to go further, we should remember that there is still that implied connection between the Doctor and the Land of Fiction from *The Mind Robber*. Treating the Time Lords as the detached technocrats that they become is, in other words, a mistake at this stage.

In this context, then, it makes the most sense to treat time as a synonym for history. But even here, this clearly does not mean "making sure everything that has happened in the past remains consistent," since the Time Lords have here seen fit to send the Doctor to deal with something that is not visibly in danger from any anachronistic elements. The Time Lords of Season Nine are simply not primarily about time paradoxes and the physics of time. If any species is linked with that at this point it's the Daleks, who just appeared in a very time-paradox heavy story, and who have previous schemes along those lines.

But what if we took history in a more Marxist, dialectical sense? That is, what if we took the view that history trends inevitably towards certain outcomes? For our purposes, they need not be overtly Marxist outcomes – one can imagine that the dialectic of history proceeds towards anarcho-capitalism or pastafarianism just as easily. But what if the Time Lords are meant to preserve and maintain this sense of progress for all intelligent life in the universe?

In this view, we would maintain that the ideology offered by the Doctor – which is basically, at this point in the show, somewhere in the vicinity of *Colony in Space*'s Science Puritanism – is historically inevitable (since he is working for the Time Lords). Which means that organizations like the Federation which promote compatible ideologies will, over time, win out over backwards, superstitious, or un-scientific attitudes such as Hepesh's, as well as the destructive greed of Arcturus. And that in this case, the Time Lords for whatever reason decided to send the Doctor to make sure this process worked correctly.

Thus the way to look at Peladon is not as an allegory, but rather as a story in which the same historical processes at work in Britain in 1972 are shown in another context. The alienness is there to stress the inevitability of these processes – to show that superstition succumbs to reason in all cases. The Federation and Peladon are clearly a similar situation to the EEC and the UK, but the similarity is based on nothing except for the necessary arc of history. It's not an allegory, but it's also not a mere parable about alienness. Rather, it's a story that attempts to illustrate a relevant moral force – a story that tries to argue what the zeitgeist (a word I use in its fullest meaning) is and what its implications are.

The biggest piece of evidence for this reading of the story being about the inevitability of progress, of course, is the *Ice Warriors*. The big trick of this story, after all, is that the Doctor and the audience wrongly suspect the Ice Warriors of villainy when in fact they're among the good guys, having renounced their former ways. But remember exactly what this means – that they have gone from monsters to people. They are, in other words, walking illustrations of the fact that progress exists. This is something we've never seen before in Doctor Who, and now that we have it seems so utterly obvious and necessary. Of course monsters get reformed – they'd have to for progress to be meaningful.

This also goes a long way towards explaining the Time Lords' objection to the Doctor in *The War Games*. In the Troughton era he spent much of his time slaughtering monsters (and remember the willingness he had to kill the Ice Warriors on their last appearance) when monsters, in at least some cases, are just people who haven't engaged in their full historical development yet. Remember how the Time Lords accept his claim that there is evil to be fought, but exile him anyway. This, at last, explains that decision: while there may be evil in the universe, the Doctor's old declaration that it must be fought specifically is inadequate. Other alternatives exist. And so he was sent to Earth until he could learn to do better, and here he shows that he can.

Indeed, perhaps this is why the Time Lords sent the Doctor to Peladon. Later fan speculation, based largely on the same logic that brought us Season Six-B, has the use of the Doctor for missions like this down to a need to maintain plausible deniability for the Time Lords. But there's no real evidence for that reading of the Time Lords at this point in the series. Whereas there is, as we've discussed at length, evidence for a reading that the Doctor is stuck on Earth to learn a lesson. More likely than not, this is simply a test to see if the Doctor is ready to have his TARDIS back. The Time Lords picked something they wanted to nudge, and instead of using whatever their normal means are, decided to send the Doctor. And as an added bonus, there was a species around that the Doctor had recently casually slaughtered that was now at a much more civilized point in their history than when he'd met them. So that would be a good way of testing him. And it's a mixed bag – he jumps to conclusions, and never apologizes for it. So perhaps a little more time cooling his heels is in order after all.

There are, of course, issues left to deal with. The puzzling policies of the Time Lords towards the Master, for instance, still fail to make sense even with what we understand from this story. And the fact that the embrace of historical inevitability has more than a whiff of imperialism to it disturbs. (Here come the nice enlightened people to do the dirty work of uplifting you savages.) But notably, we still have three stories to go before the original premise of the show is restored properly.

But the nature of Season Nine is rapidly shaping up. These are stories in which the Doctor and, to an extent, the show itself demonstrate that they're ready to be Doctor Who again. The show is rapidly developing more and more tools to deal with the world, and finding better and better ways to take a nuanced view of the world. And perhaps more importantly, this isn't just a matter of undoing the Pertwee era and returning to the way the show was. This isn't the show slowly undoing the mistake of tying itself to Earth. Rather, this season is the show demonstrating what it's learned by doing two seasons in a primarily earthbound format, and showing that it's a far stronger series for having done so.

Time Can Be Rewritten (*The Face of the Enemy*)

The Face of the Enemy is an oddity in the Doctor Who novels range. It's one of two books from the Missing/Past Doctor Adventures lines to focus entirely on characters other than the Doctor. The first of these – Virgin's *Downtime* – is just the novelization of a Marc Platt-penned direct to video story with the Yeti in it, and we'll deal with the video version in Volume Six. But this one is a different beast – a story of what UNIT gets up to while the Doctor is on one of his periodic jaunts off-world – in this case, during *The Curse of Peladon*.

The result is a story that goes a long way towards disentangling some of the issues and juxtapositions of the Pertwee era. Because we've only really seen, at this point, two Pertwee stories that work much like traditional Doctor Who: *Colony in Space* and *The Curse of Peladon*. Other than that, Pertwee has been paired up with the Brigadier and, in most of the stories, Yates and Benton. *The Curse of Peladon*, in fact, was the first story in the Pertwee era not to feature the Brigadier. So thus far, there's been no way to meaningfully tell the difference between a Pertwee-era Doctor Who story and a UNIT story. And as I've already suggested, this is perhaps at the root cause of some of the tensions we've found so far in the Pertwee era. On the one hand you have the era's glam tendencies, which, while not antithetical to UNIT, at least have an uneasy relationship with it. On the other you have its action tendencies, which UNIT is perfect for.

On the one hand the result is almost classically Doctor Who: the show tends to charge off in a given direction, and then, in the next story, charge off in a different direction with minimal heed paid to its compatibility with the last direction. This is what it always did. But there are enough markers that suggest a level of intended consistency that this is, at times, jarring in a way it isn't normally. Simply put, the presence of UNIT cuts against the rapid changes in tone that the series is going for, making it seem like a series that doesn't know what it wants. I mean, that's really the only way to describe a show that went from the social realist thriller approach of *The Mind of Evil* to the glam mania of *The Claws of Axos* while maintaining the same supporting cast and setting. It's one thing to go from the tone of *The Web Planet* to the tone of *The Crusade* with a time machine. It's quite another to do it while remaining on Earth.

But that's changing. UNIT stories, in Season Nine, become one format among many. In fact, there are only two of them all season, leading into Season Ten, which restores the original premise of the show properly in its first story. And if Doctor Who no longer has to mean UNIT, why should UNIT continue having to mean that the weird dude with the frilly shirts shows up? And that, in essence, is what this book is – an exploration of this strange obverse of the Pertwee era. Since Pertwee gets a show without UNIT, here we give UNIT a show without Pertwee.

Obviously some adjustments need to be made. Just as Jo finds herself taking on new roles in space stories compared to earthbound ones in order to fill out some of the plot roles vacated by other characters, so is some effort needed to fulfill the Doctor's plot functions. McIntee seems to largely identify two major roles the Doctor plays: the genius who can figure things out that humans can't, and the moral conscience of the story. And the choices he makes to fulfill these roles in the Doctor's absence are both fascinating and, ultimately, the heart and soul of the book.

The science genius role mostly ends up going to the Master in a bit of a *Silence of the Lambs* inspired "deal with the devil" storytelling. This makes sense – McIntee's fondness for the character is well established, after all. And in many ways this book is a sequel to *The Dark Path*. McIntee maintains his portrayal of the Master as a hero gone wrong. And unlike in his previous Master story, this focuses on the Master when he has well and truly gone wrong, which has advantages over "the story of how the Master became a villain," which was inevitably going to be an anti-climax. Instead we get scenes like the Master admitting that scientific curiosity is his "one uncorrupted vice," a line that is delightful in its implications about the Master's psyche.

As for the moral conscience of the book, McIntee manages a truly brilliant move. Actually, to be fair, he manages it on both fronts. The obvious solution to both problems is just to call Liz Shaw in for this story and have her provide the science and conscience for the book. But the less obvious solution of using the Master is self-evidently more interesting, and McIntee is savvy to keep Liz out of this book. (Indeed, she's virtually the only UNIT character kept out – even Harry Sullivan is in there.) The only problem is that you then need a second character for the moral duties. And as I said, McIntee manages a belter here: Ian and Barbara.

It's genuinely tough to overstate the sheer cleverness of this. I am admittedly a massive Ian and Barbara cheerleader, but I think this book mostly just shows why fawning adoration is the sensible approach to Ian and Barbara. Of course, much of that is also down to McIntee: the roles he finds for them within the narrative are absolutely perfect.

Essentially what he plays on is the seniority of Ian and Barbara – the fact that they are, in terms of the Doctor and his world, genuinely the people who have known and dealt with that world for the longest. And as a result, and this is the key part, they display genuine and earned misgivings about that world. And, freed by the twenty-five years of social liberalization between 1972 and 1997, McIntee is able to put some powerful depth to those misgivings, most notably when Barbara reflects that, "It was as if the Doctor had left a shadow on her and Ian, just waiting to darken their lives. Like the one the Daleks' poisoned atmosphere had left on them. But that was a shadow they had cheated through treatment, and John was living proof of that."

There's a lot to like about those lines. Obviously they're a case of darkening and maturing Ian and Barbara as characters. But this isn't done crassly or exploitatively – the lines are discrete, and it's not like it's an Ian/Barbara sex scene. The real cleverness is that they add a depth to their adventures that wasn't there in the original episodes, but that is wholly compatible with them. In fact, these lines might be more compatible with the basic spirit of *The Daleks* than any of the subsequent Dalek stories ever were. After all, Doctor Who in its first season was about the juxtapositons of the mundane (Ian and Barbara) and the fantastic (the Daleks). By running that process in reverse and having Skaro intrude on the ordinary domestic lives of Ian and Barbara in such a starkly painful way, and long after they'd seemingly extricated themselves from that world, is a case of the books doing exactly what the show itself is supposed to do, only in ways the show never could.

Given this, it's not a surprise that the book is clearly having the most fun in the scenes where it gets to have the Master interact with Ian or Barbara. The high point, of course, is the Master manipulating Ian out of committing suicide following Barbara's apparent death, and then deciding to conceal from Ian the fact that she's still alive so he remains angry and effective. But other smaller moments like the Master being surprised that Barbara thinks to ask why he hates the Doctor instead of blindly siding with the Doctor, or Ian surmising the Master's motivations and history in a way we've never seen anyone do (and never really see again) are equally lovely. The characters play off of each other very well, and for subtle reasons. If the Master is the clever science person for this story, and he is, it's key that the moral conscience of the story remains sympathetic to him in some way. This is difficult, given that he's a horrible villain, but the use of Ian and Barbara, who have a more complex relationship with the Doctor, is enormously clever.

Not that the focus on McIntee's characterization of the Master, Ian, and Barbara should detract from his excellent handling of the UNIT regulars. All of them – particularly the Brigadier, who benefits from McIntee doing a much defter job of exploring his personal life than Gary Russell earlier managed while still picking up Russell's threads – are well handled, with the same deftness that Ian and Barbara get. In other words, these are small moments in which the broad strokes of character traits we see on the show get used to show new depths of the characters. Without the Doctor to charismatically anchor things the characters have room to breathe and be a bit more nuanced.

All of this is slotted into an effective conspiracy thriller plot, but that's beside the point in many ways. It's a straightforward Doctor Who plot, and a sequel to *Inferno*. But that's how it should be. The point of this book is to show the way in which the UNIT era could have forked off of Doctor Who as easily as Doctor Who forked off of the UNIT era. That means remaining adjacent to what Doctor Who was at the time, and the plot is just about the last thing to futz with. Much like *The Power of the Daleks* used the Daleks to ease a big transition, this book uses *Inferno* to do the same, even if its transition is more of a glance down a historical blind alley.

Which is, of course, what's interesting about books like this in the first place. It's an effective study of aspects of the Pertwee era that weren't adequately explored over its five years. It does things that couldn't have been done on television, but that were still worth doing. It expands on our understanding of characters, and throws up juxtapositions we haven't seen before. It's one of the rare retro stories where one feels as though the era is enriched by its presence. Having this in continuity gives reason for the UNIT era to come to a close. It shows that they don't need the Doctor. In fact, strictly in terms of UNIT, it's a better story than anything the Pertwee era actually gave them. Without the Doctor to fix them all in their predictable orbits, all seven familiar characters in this book shine in ways they never could in Doctor Who.

The result is to show us a sort of inversion of the Pertwee era. If becoming the glam spectacle that the show does in the latter part of Season Nine and in most of Season Ten required distancing itself from the earthbound action format of UNIT then perhaps becoming the action thriller that it attempted to be in Season Seven required distancing itself from the Doctor. And what's so impressive and extraordinary about *The Face of the Enemy* is that it shows how this can be done without distancing the series from Doctor Who. This is unmistakably a Doctor Who story that owes considerable debt to the legacy and heritage of Doctor Who in the forms of the Master, Ian, and Barbara. But it's also something new that can only exist if the series decides to stick with the earthbound format and explore its implications.

It doesn't, of course, and it was never going to. When the Doctor and Earth finally decide they should see other people the series is obviously going to follow the Doctor. But there was another way, and, perhaps more importantly, it could have been an interesting other way.

A Finely Tuned Response (*The Sea Devils*)

It's February 26, 1972. Chicory Tip is still at number one. Two weeks later, it's Nilsson with "Without You," which holds the title for the remainder of the story. Michael Jackson, T. Rex, Paul Simon, Slade, and, regrettably, Chelsea FC also chart.

In other news, Nixon concludes his visit to China. He follows this by attempting to get John Lennon to conclude his visit to the United States, using the somewhat novel method of deporting him as a "strategic counter-measure" to his anti-war beliefs. (The phrase is not Nixon's but Strom Thurmond's. Not that that's an improvement.) Two days thereafter, he passes an executive order setting standards for classified information, allowing the US to engage in a thirty-year campaign to cover up the FBI surveillance of John Lennon. Also in the US, demolition begins on the infamous Pruitt-Igoe housing complex, a disastrous public housing project that was a marvel of architecture, and a travesty of virtually everything else including "remembering to think about the tenants when doing architecture."

While in the country I'm actually supposed to be writing about, Edward Heath renounces the use of the "five techniques," a set of approaches used widely by the UK in Northern Ireland for what I believe the current euphemism declares to be "enhanced interrogation," but those of us not seeking to excuse our own monstrosity just call torture. He follows this by proclaiming direct rule over Northern Ireland, dissolving the Northern Ireland Parliament and administering the country from London.

While on television we have *The Sea Devils*. On the surface, this is as straightforward a piece as we could have. It's vintage Action-style Pertwee (which to be fair we haven't really seen since *The Mind of Evil*), and a flat-out attempt to remake *The Silurians* with the Master and some impressive naval footage. It's also Malcolm Hulke stuck on a script that in no way flatters his strengths. All of this points towards an essay in which I find some bright spots to emphasize amidst the general sense that there's just something crushingly lackluster about this approach to Doctor Who when compared to the manic inventiveness of the glam style. It should be straightforward: wrap it all up in just over two thousand words, declare it a short one, and actually have some free time to do something besides write today.

Except that the convergences of circumstance and the fact that the show is moving successfully away from the Season Seven mould (which, while fascinating, was at its best when Whitaker and Hulke tried to break it) and toward a new approach mean that, under the patois of earthbound-by-numbers storytelling there's something altogether stranger here.

First of all, let's talk about the big weirdness in *The Sea Devils*: this is the only earthbound Pertwee story to feature no appearances by the Brigadier or any other UNIT characters. Watched on its own, as a stand-alone movie, this doesn't jump out, but watched as part of a lengthy run of Pertwee stories the odd structure of this is extremely visible. And, of course, Doctor Who's proper form is as a lengthy run and not as a disordered anthology of DVD releases.

Much as it pains me to say, given how extraordinarily good Nicholas Courtney is, pushing UNIT out of the picture for this is a good idea. I've commented before that Pertwee's Doctor thrives when forced onto his back foot. This story, however, cinches it. Putting Pertwee in an environment where he doesn't have the Brigadier to smooth things over or provide him cover from people in charge makes the story far more interesting.

For one thing, it means that the Master is actually in a position to have allies in positions of power, which is largely prevented in the UNIT stories. The sequence where the Master manipulates Trenchard into arresting the Doctor (while setting the Master free) is fantastic, because it presents the Doctor with an earthbound situation in which things are far more out of his control than usual. It's one thing to have the Doctor imperiled by angry villagers, or to have a stupid but powerful government figure slowing things down. It's quite another to have an active alliance between the structures of military power and the

Master. In the past creating that sort of situation has required shunting him off to alien planets, alternate universes, or the future. As fun as the familiar UNIT acting pieces are, one thing *The Sea Devils* really calls into question is whether those characters actually add new storytelling options for the show, and especially whether whatever options they add outnumber the ones they close off.

To some extent the same can be said of the Master, who here serves in part to cause the major alterations in the plot between *The Sea Devils* and *The Silurians*. Where *The Silurians* spent the bulk of its time fretting with the possibility that peace could be negotiated between the Silurians and humans, *The Sea Devils* spends only five or ten minutes on this before the Master manages to exploit a human attack on the base to foreclose all possibility of peace. While he adds some variety so that this story isn't a straight remake of the original, the fact is that it's been two years since the original version of the story. Compared to the non-existent gaps between reiterated bases under siege in the Troughton years, the gap here is an eternity. It's tough to argue that the need to create variety between the two stories was a solid reason to swap out moral complexity for Delgado showpieces. There's a strong case to be made that the presence of the Master dumbs down this story to a deeply unfortunate extent.

But on the other hand, it's not like the moral ambiguity of *The Silurians* worked. Instead it led to an ending that, by all rights, should have derailed the entirety of what the series was attempting. Having the Master win out over the Doctor in persuading the Sea Devils at least makes the resolution of blowing them up be something other than a series-derailer. The real problem is that the absence of UNIT makes this the story where the moral ambiguity could have worked. Had the Master shown up in *The Silurians* he would have provided moral cover for the Brigadier blowing up the Silurian base. Whereas here we finally have characters who can commit an atrocity and not have to be seen next week and a story that can't get away with the moral ambiguity necessary to pull it off.

But this story also ends up starting to show some of the weaknesses of the Master as a character. Because the problems he introduces to this story are problems for any story he appears in: he's incompatible with moral ambiguity. This isn't surprising: he's defined as "the evil one." That fundamentally cuts against the notion of moral ambiguity. In some stories, that works – in something like *The Daemons* or *The Claws of Axos* where all of the characters are overtly either good or bad guys, having the Master on there as the ultimate bad guy ups the stakes effectively. But in a story with actual moral issues, putting him in distorts the gravity. The irony, of course, is that Hulke is the one who figured out in *Colony in Space* how to use the Master in a story with moral ambiguity – have him loom over it in the background for two-thirds of the story, then bring him on once tensions are already ratcheted up. But that's not an option here because we've moved out of the season where the Master is a regular whose involvement can be assumed to haunt a story. Now his appearance is a to-be-hyped event, requiring that he be in the thick of things early on.

The thing is, for all the apparent simplicity, this story is, as Tat Wood argues in *About Time*, trying to do something far more interesting. Wood draws a distinction between two modes of Pertwee stories. They roughly correspond to the glam/action division I've already articulated, though Wood focuses it differently . . . identifying stories where we're presented with the Doctor's world and stories in which we're presented with our world plus the Doctor. The former roughly maps to the glam stories, while the latter maps with the action stories. But the thing is, as Wood points out, this story finds a third option. This isn't the Doctor's world, hence him being on the back foot, but it's also not our world. Instead it's the world of the Sea Devils.

Wood comes up with a host of details supporting this claim – the strange focus on the way in which the human characters eat, for instance, and the odd music (a last hurrah of the "let's just make this show seem really weird" style). But, of course, as Wood admits, this side of the story is drowned out by the desire to make a big showpiece about the Navy starring Jon Pertwee, a Navy veteran himself. Which is a pity. The central idea, in which humans are cast as creatures of raw consumption and opposed by the original inhabitants of the Earth who want it back because humans keep screwing it up – is brilliant. But it's drowned out by the need to do a big runaround with expensive props and the Master.

But at that point, why bother with the earthly setting? If all you want is spectacle, why limit yourself to the spectacles of the home countries? There's not really a good answer for that, and *The Sea Devils* is in many ways the last hurrah of the earthbound format. It's the last story in which the TARDIS is not mentioned at all, and the last one before the Doctor gets a functioning TARDIS back to be set entirely on contemporary Earth. And given that it demonstrates the ways in which the earthbound format is its own worst enemy, it's tempting to call it the story that shows conclusively why that format doesn't work. The only problem is that it does work, as the series' future demonstrates. After all, *Torchwood* exists and is functional.

Here's the thing about *Torchwood*. At this point, as I said last entry, Doctor Who and UNIT are going in two separate directions. Doctor Who is returning to its space and time-traveling roots, and in two years will embrace the eccentric wanderer through space and time approach in a deeper way than ever before. UNIT, on the other hand, basically winds down, although as David McIntee showed, it didn't really have to. But imagine an alternate universe – one in which the format of Season Seven reigned supreme and the Doctor never used the TARDIS again.

Furthermore, however, let's assume that this is all that changes. The show abandons time travel, but it doesn't abandon its history in an attempt to just become *Doomwatch* for kids. The show never integrates the Doctor fully on Earth, leaving him as an eccentric ex-time traveler now trapped on Earth. And the show still keeps regeneration, such that it can run as long as there are interesting ideas. It's just that instead of going to Tom Baker and the bohemian traveler, it continues on variations of Jon Pertwee – Action Man heroes. Now I'll admit, I don't think the show could have reached 1989 like that, little yet been the subject of a massive and unprecedentedly successful revival.

But if it had, would it, in 2011, actually look any different from *Torchwood*? I would propose that it would not, and that Captain Jack is a dead ringer for what the Eleventh Doctor would look like if Jon Pertwee were the dominant model for the part. A socially transgressive Action Man who is slightly out of place and old-fashioned, seeming like the leading man from another era. Or, to put it another way, a sort of drag leading man – exaggerated characteristics of the leading man that aren't quite played right. (After all, the glam aesthetic that's so influential on the Pertwee era was always sexually ambiguous.)

Indeed, the entire plot of *Torchwood*'s fourth season could just as easily work with the Doctor becoming mortal and everyone else getting eternal life. And *Torchwood* goes out of its way to remind us once an episode that Jack is a former immortal time traveler. Crucially, the similarities are not simply between the shows' main characters. They are present in their whole structures; *Torchwood* still depends on the sort of gonzo plot logic of *Inferno* or *The Claws of Axos*. That's the entire point of the fourth season, as it steadily changes right before our eyes from a straightforward American show in the model of *Heroes* or *Flashforward* to a much stranger and more ridiculous show. The central concept of *Torchwood* remains that it works along Doctor Who logic. It's just that instead of being the natural extension thirty-nine years later of *The Curse of Peladon*, it's the natural extension of *The Sea Devils*.

And, of course, watching the brutal dramatics of *Torchwood*, it's easy to see the logic of something like *The Sea Devils*, with its not-quite-working attempt to be an earthbound story written from the monster's point of view, as something that would fit in. Indeed, with *Torchwood* seemingly over, the idea of a story from the perspective of the aliens seems like one of the niggling things that would have been wonderful to see.

But what's most visible about this what-if scenario is that this road wasn't taken. This is actually a bit strange. By all reasonable standards Pertwee and Tom Baker are the two classic series Doctors that are the most ingrained in cultural memory. The show may have run for a quarter century, but its reputation and legacy rests primarily on the 1970s. Tat Wood, in fact, makes a compelling case that 1973 was the absolute peak of the series' influence in the culture. And we mustn't forget that when Russell T Davies relaunched the series, it was *Spearhead from Space* he took the iconography from.

And yet despite all of this it's difficult to come up with any compelling account that suggests that Pertwee's Doctor was particularly influential. None of the new ideas he brought to play in his Doctor seem to have been borrowed particularly by his successors. One could argue that the idea that the Doctor travels the universe for the love of it comes from Pertwee, but that requires us to take a very blinkered reading of the Troughton and Hartnell eras.

Instead the series' virtues are largely in its production. The Letts era contains some of the most rapid development of televisual storytelling that Doctor Who ever saw. This era pioneered editing techniques, introduced CSO (which is still used, albeit in different and more technologically advanced forms), reformed production so that stories could be shot out of order (*The Sea Devils* was actually shot prior to *The Curse of Peladon*, a fact that is amazing when one considers that the Troughton era at one point got to where episodes were being aired a week after they were shot), and generally tightened the ship. On top of that, in working through and, ultimately, out of the earthbound format the series had to reinvent the component parts of itself consciously, in a way that prevented it from simply resting on its laurels. The Pertwee era, at this point, is combining James Bond, *Doomwatch*, glam rock, *Ace of Wands*, and Doctor Who as we knew it in the '60s into a coherent collage.

This is deeply, idiosyncratically tied to 1972, and the specifics of it thus translate poorly to other eras. But by doing it the series acquired a new vocabulary to take back to its former structure. The specifics of the era didn't translate to that former structure very well, and have mostly fallen away. But it's impossible to argue that the experience did not improve the program tremendously. And, perhaps more importantly, it's difficult, in hindsight, to argue that the particular details of the era didn't make good television. They still do some forty years later. It's just that the show is almost, but not quite, Doctor Who.

Time Can Be Rewritten Extra: *Who Killed Kennedy*

One of the animating tensions of the Pertwee era is the question of whether or not the world depicted is our world or not. Certain facts resist it – the reference to a Prime Minister named "Jeremy" in *The Green Death* is clearly meant to be a joke about Jeremy Thorpe, then-leader of the Liberal party, or the fact that the British never had a serious space program. Plus, you know, there's the fact that it does not appear that the Earth was subject to a large wave of alien invasion attempts in the 1970s.

All of this would seem to push definitively towards "this is not our world." And yet the central premise of the Pertwee era is the "Yeti-in-the-loo" theory that depends on the degree to which the world depicted in Doctor Who is intended to be our world. If *Terror of the Autons* and its evil plastic daisies are terrifying they're terrifying precisely because of the familiarity of the world they're in.

At the time, at least, the theory that navigated this was that the UNIT era happened in a nebulously defined "near future," with the actual nearness of that future advancing or receding depending on the whims of the production team. So when it implies a future election won by Jeremy Thorpe it's moved out a bit further, but for the most part it exists in the "one minute in the future" style. And as we discussed back in Volume Two, for the most part this is where to put it, since the production and aesthetic of UNIT stories is for the most part grounded in the time they were produced.

But while this approach works on a story-to-story basis, it poses something of a problem when the Pertwee era is taken as a whole. Any given UNIT story can be safely treated as taking place one minute into the future of whenever it was made, but once you get to a few of them you run back into the problem that eventually the accumulation of supposed alien invasions becomes difficult to sustain. It's not just that you have to be rather more than a few minutes into the future before you get to *Invasion of the Dinosaurs*, though. Quite frankly, the Pertwee era is often difficult to square away with itself. Not only does our world not really resemble one with a large swath of alien invasions here and there, neither does the world of Doctor Who.

This is a significant hole in the Pertwee era. Because the Pertwee era was so invested in portraying itself as essentially our world it never stops to look at the ways in which the constant parade of alien invasions actually impacts the world. *Who Killed Kennedy*, then, is the response to this: a book that imagines the Pertwee era from the perspective of ordinary people. There are, of course, many ways that this could be done. But *Who Killed Kennedy*, published in 1996, only really had one way that it could approach this. 1996, after all, was the high-water mark of *The X-Files*, which meant that the only way that a look at the "real-world" version of the Pertwee era could possibly proceed was to treat it as a conspiracy thriller full of shadowy government agencies.

There are two problems here. First is some of the added implications of conspiracy thriller Doctor Who. As the title would suggest, *Who Killed Kennedy* links up with the Kennedy assassination. This is inevitable – given that Doctor Who's debut was the first non-news program the BBC aired after the Kennedy assassination, there's an inevitable connection between the two. (Indeed, the book originated from Bishop looking at the simultaneous waves of Kennedy and Doctor Who thirtieth anniversary material in 1993.) But this has, by Bishop's own admission, unfortunate knock-on effects for the plot.

The core of it is that, being set mostly in the Pertwee era, everything within the story happens well after the Kennedy assassination. Which makes it tough to build well to a denouement about the Kennedy assassination, and sure enough that material feels awkwardly grafted on, distending the shape of the book. This is unfortunate, blunting the impact of the book. In effect, two thirds of the way through the narrator realizes that all the conspiracies he's been uncovering about UNIT are wrong and that UNIT are the good guys. Then the

Doctor asks him to go stop a plot by the Master, and so he does, and that's that.

Which brings us to the second problem with the book, which is that it ultimately can't bring itself to carry through with its conspiracy theory plot. This is, within Doctor Who, understandable. Not even the Virgin line, for all its vaunted darkness and cynicism, was going to publish a book that wholly rejected the Pertwee era as morally bankrupt. That's not actually a path open to Doctor Who.

This doesn't just mean that the book is irritatingly half-hearted in its central idea, however. The problem is larger than that: *Who Killed Kennedy* is more persuasive than it wants to be. Its eventual disclaiming of the idea that UNIT is anything other than a bunch of noble heroes may be necessary within Doctor Who, but it comes after so much genuinely interesting stuff about UNIT as an unsettling source of paranoia that it feels lackluster. In a fundamental sense the version of UNIT that *Who Kills Kennedy* presents for most of the book is more interesting than what it settles on – an organization whose secrets are necessary and that provides a vital line of protection for the poor helpless people of the world.

At the heart of this is an unsettling realization: there are real problems with the basic ethics of UNIT. A reasonable person could object to the basic decision to keep the existence of aliens a secret from the general public, or to cover up incidents like UNIT does. There's a fundamental rejection of the value of transparency implicit in UNIT – a tacit belief that democracy is simply unsuited to dealing with some problems and that heavily armed technocrats without meaningful oversight are necessary to protect us. This is a deeply troubling ethical position that deserves to be pushed back against. And for most of its length *Who Killed Kennedy* does that, albeit without understanding the real nature of what UNIT does. And then, once we find out that the enemies really are aliens, all sense of the value of transparency vanishes and the book simply decides that, yes, sometimes the government does have to keep secrets from its citizens.

It is not that this position is prima facie unreasonable. But *Who Killed Kennedy* frames this argument entirely in terms of the Doctor's innate heroism. A complete lack of transparency and an essentially unaccountable military force with broad powers operating within the UK are perfectly OK because the Doctor is the good guy. Which isn't just ethically horrifying, it's naive in a way that clashes badly with the grey-area-filled complexity of the conspiracy thriller.

At the heart of this is a mildly uncomfortable fact about the Pertwee era: it can't actually sustain this sort of approach. The show is genuinely, actively, and consciously uninterested in the larger effects of what happens in it. This is unsurprising. There is a real sense in which you can either be fascinated by the Axons or fascinated by the geopolitical effects of their arrival, but not both. The gaudy superficiality of the Axons precludes getting too far into the question of the government response, which in that story consists only of broad caricatures.

There are several angles to take here. The most basic is an ethical one – the elephant in the room about the entire Pertwee era, which is that, given the generally leftist and anti-authority bent of Doctor Who, putting the Doctor as the assistant to a military outfit is uncomfortable. For all that it is both easy and essentially required to adore Nicholas Courtney and the Brigadier and for all that he developed over the decades into "the Doctor's best friend," there's something jarring about the idea that the Doctor is so attached to such a standard authority figure, and, more to the point, to such a violent sort of authority. The Doctor working with the military is understandable in specific contexts, but there's a difference between him helping the military with a specific threat and then leaving (as in *The Web of Fear* and *The Invasion*) and him repeatedly returning to work with them even after he's gained his freedom.

The Pertwee era gets away with it, of course, by being a glam spectacle, not a sincere effort at a show about the military. UNIT isn't the military so much as it's a prop – the vague outline of a military over which the spectacle of the Pertwee era sashays. Because the alternative reading – treating UNIT as in any way a serious attempt at portraying the military – leads inexorably towards a frankly horrifying authoritarianism. To treat UNIT as a dramatic portrayal of the military responding to alien threats requires an outright endorsement of an essentially unchecked military with the ability to engage in domestic law enforcement all in complete secrecy, with the sole justification for why it's all right being that the Brigadier and the Doctor are both decent chaps who won't do anything wrong.

It's hardly a surprise that *Who Killed Kennedy* stops short of that conclusion – it's a series-destroying one. But in doing so it illustrates the larger problem with its own premise. I don't quite intend this as a criticism of the book. It's largely a case of something that had to be done in order to show why it shouldn't be done. But it doesn't work and can't work. An effort to treat the Pertwee era and UNIT as a show about the government, the military, and the continual threat of alien invasion is doomed to failure.

That there remains a significant number of people who want the Pertwee era to be a straightforward military action thriller is thus unfortunate. But it just doesn't support it. Not just on the ethical level, but on a creative one: it does a rubbish job of it. It doesn't think through the implications or consequences of its ideas at all. It's simply not trying to do any of the things a serious attempt at a military action thriller would do, a fact that has been obvious since we compared it to *Doomwatch*, i.e. a show that actually is about the relationship between science and politics. It's been clear since the end of *The Silurians*, where by far the most interesting aspect of it, the fact that the Doctor's allies commit genocide, is completely ignored forevermore. It's not just the moral trainwreck implicit in this that's bad; it's the aesthetic one. It's the fact that a show that's tackling concepts like "what if the original inhabitants of Earth woke up and exposed us all as colonists" should probably care a bit about the implications of genocide as a solution, and it just doesn't.

Who Killed Kennedy, on the other hand, is a book that tries to go down that route. And in the end it discovers what should have been clear from the start: that route and Doctor Who are mutually exclusive, and attempting that route within the context of Doctor Who is an absolutely miserable experience, no matter how many people think they want it. In this regard its status as a not-quite-Missing-Adventure novel is perfect. It fits into the Pertwee era precisely because of the way in which it is not a part of it, and can never be a part of it.

Change, My Dear (*The Mutants*)

It's April 8, 1972. Nilsson is still at number one. After one week, however, they are stunningly unseated by, and this is one of those moments where I love following the British charts, Pipes and Drums and the Military Band of the Royal Scots Dragoon Guard, with "Amazing Grace" which further impresses by staying there for five weeks. Also in the charts are Lindisfarne, Ringo Starr, Tom Jones, Neil Young, and T. Rex.

The IRA sets off a wave of fourteen bombs in Belfast in response to the Bloody Sunday Massacre. In a show of all being friends now, China gifts two giant pandas to the National Zoo. More bits of Pruitt-Igoe gets blown up, the Paris Peace Talks to try to end the Vietnam War derail spectacularly, and Nixon announces that the US will be mining North Vietnam's harbors. And J. Edgar Hoover finally displays an ounce of taste and dies.

On television, meanwhile, it's *The Mutants*, the second outing by the madmen behind *The Claws of Axos* and, for my money, the best Pertwee story since *The Ambassadors of Death*. Which, puzzlingly, does not seem to be what you'd call the consensus view of this one. So that's probably a good place to start.

The thing about Baker and Martin is that, more than any other Pertwee-era writers, they are a pile of strange tics. Going into one of their stories it is necessary to simply accept that the characters are going to be intensely programmatic, the narrative aimed primarily at spectacle, and that the whole thing is going to be completely and utterly gonzo. But it's not as though, on their own, any of these things are unique to Baker and Martin. The programmatic character was invented by Robert Holmes, nobody out-gonzos a Robert Sloman script (Or *The Curse of Peladon* for that matter), and those inclined to complain about a spectacle-based story should probably take a long, hard look at exactly what all those shots of impressive ships cutting through the ocean are doing in *The Sea Devils*.

Rather, it's that Baker and Martin have shown more willingness than almost anyone save perhaps the Sloman/Letts team to push all of these to their max. But unlike the Sloman/Letts team, who contributed four of the great curate's eggs of Doctor Who history, Baker and Martin offer a sort of ruthless consistency to their stories. Indeed, if there's a criticism to be made of Baker and Martin it's that when we get to the end of their tenure on Doctor Who in the next volume they'll still be churning out stories largely indistinguishable in quality and tone from their first few. These are writers who have their style and are unashamed to stick with it.

The thing about Baker and Martin is that they're not just impressive at coming up with spectacle (in fact, most of the really top notch spectacle in *The Mutants* comes from the effects department anyway). They're damned good at using spectacle for other purposes, instead of just setting spectacles up and going "ooh, shiny." This may seem like a strange claim, given that we usually treat spectacle as just about the lowest of the low in terms of artistic goals. And there's something to be said for that as a critique of pure spectacle. The problem is that those of us with "proper" taste tend instinctively to confuse creating a spectacle with creating nothing but a spectacle, and thus tend to treat spectacle as a bad thing in and of itself.

If you'll forgive the lapse into theory, think about how the traditional narrative works for a moment. Compared to real life, narrative is strangely lo-fi. By which I mean, we get a lot less information in a movie or television episode than we do in real life. But this information is bizarrely efficient. We can make judgments about fictional characters based on five minutes of screen time that would take hours to learn by actually talking to a real person.

The reason for this is that narrative is structured according to its own logic. And familiarity with that logic makes it easy to fill in gaps. And there are multiple options for what that logic is. There's realism, for instance, in which we understand how something works because it resembles how a real thing works. We don't need to be told the meticulous details of the governmental structure of the Solos colony because we're (or, at least, British audiences of the early 1970s were) familiar with the real structure of colonial government, and can just assume it's similar on Solos. There's also Aristotelean logic, summed up best by Chekov's maxim about the gun on the mantle. This is just the assumption that things we're shown in a story are inherently significant details. This one is particularly important in terms of how we sketch in details. The reason we're able to judge a fictional character more accurately and quickly than a real person is that we know there is little to no noise in the depiction – everything we learn about the character is an important detail about understanding them.

Spectacle is another one of these logics, and it's a very straightforward one. In the logic of spectacle, one accepts whatever it is that creates the biggest spectacle. It's a logic where we accept that characters, when given a range of options, will pick the one that leads to the most interesting results even if it is not strictly speaking the most sensible one according to other logics. The big visual moments are what provides the logic and justification for the rest of the material, which is just filler to link them up.

The thing about the logic of spectacle is that it allows for some really strange linking material. You can put all sorts of weird stuff in the spaces between big set pieces and it will hold together because the logic of the spectacle means that as long as we get to another cool sequence of flashy lights and swirling colors, we don't care too much about how we got there. And what Baker and Martin do with *The Mutants* is that they pack the filler stuff full to the brim with images and concepts, then trust the spectacle to tie it all together somehow.

To wit, let's ask what should be a fairly simple question. What exactly are the humans in this story supposed to be representing? On one level, the answer seems like it should be obvious. They're explicitly colonialist, a declining empire, and giving some of the last of their colonies independence. That's self-evidently a metaphor for the British Empire. On the other hand, the German rocket scientist OK with exterminating a species and the use of gas to kill the Mutants in the cave is blatantly a Nazi reference. Then there's the inclusion of Cotton and the presence of an Afrikaans accent, suggesting South Africa and apartheid. But of course the teleporters are segregated in a blatantly American South sort of way.

Note that the problem here is not, as it seemed to be in *The Curse of Peladon*, a case of unclear reference points. Rather, what we have here is an excess of reference points – four separate overarching metaphors, each of which is clearly signified. It's not that the metaphors are contradictory as such, but on the other hand it's tough to argue that they go together straightforwardly. But none of this renders the story nonsensical because it's clear that the real point of the story is glittering caves of shifting lights, weird looking mutants, and strange ideas. With those to anchor the narrative, the linking material can become safely oversaturated with signifiers.

Where it all gets very interesting, at least for my money, is in the fact that the ideas, much as they may not go together straightforwardly, do at least exist in the same general orbit. Effectively, the spectacle allows these disparate metaphors to fuse together into a functional overall whole that, while gratuitously an overdetermined signifier, nevertheless hangs together, and that thus creates a massive web of strange juxtapositions and equations. Although its basic approach to political metaphor is very different from that of *The Curse of Peladon*, the result is similar – the smorgasbord of metaphors turns the story into a general case commentary on the nature of a dominant culture oppressing a minority one.

The focus on spectacle also allows the story to do something interesting with the Solonians, which is to create an indigenous culture on a planet that has its own value. And more to the point, that value is neither instrumental (as was ultimately the case with the Primitives in *Colony in Space*) nor based purely on abstracted ethical principles (as is ultimately the case in *The Silurians*). Rather, the Solonians are valued aesthetically – not even because they produce spectacle, but because they are simply interesting and fascinating.

A fair part of this is down to Barry Letts, who apparently originated the idea for the Solonians. And it is a good idea – one that feels like it must be a nick from *Star Trek* or some other science fiction show, but isn't. Solos turns out to be a planet with a two-millennia-long year, and five-hundred-year seasons, whose people engage in a sort of chrysalis-like evolution as the seasons change, presumably with no individual generation ever encompassing more than one phase. The monsters, in other words, aren't monsters at all, but are simply an intelligent species in an intermediate stage of evolution. It's a brilliant sci-fi idea, and for once Doctor Who got there first without having to rip anyone else off.

The other thing that this story does, though, is to find a new way of making the Doctor vulnerable – one that provides an interesting wrinkle to our understanding of the Time Lords. In *The Curse of Peladon* essay, I suggested that the easiest way to understand the Time Lords in this phase of the program is as enforcers of the arc of history; they're the regulators of a natural tendency in the history of rational species towards certain outcomes. Nothing in *The Mutants* contradicts that as such, but their actions here are nevertheless somewhat puzzling.

Simply put, their method of getting the Doctor involved in this one is nuts. They give him a package that he has to deliver to someone, but don't tell him whom to deliver it to. When the package is opened, it contains stone tablets unreadable by the recipient, and once those stone tablets are deciphered they just reveal a helpful historical tidbit about the nature of Solos. As attempts to intervene and help an oppressed indigenous population go, this has to be considered something of a debacle.

But more broadly, it makes sense. One thing to note is that the humans have no place whatsoever on Solos. The overwhelming message of the story is that they should simply get out. And because the question of what the humans represent is so over-signified, this ends up having a pretty wide-ranging effect as a moral consequence. Effectively, it appears that white, Western European culture has nothing of value whatsoever that it can contribute to the indigenous culture. The only thing it can possibly do is cause problems.

And this ends up applying even to the Doctor and the Time Lords. The Time Lords try to help and end up doing so in appallingly stupid and ham-handed manner. The Doctor tries to help, and mostly manages, but is actually absent from the main moment of resolution for the Solonians (about which more in a moment). The polite but mildly patronizing paternal tone that Pertwee takes has always borne a slightly uncomfortable resemblance to the patronizing "it's for their own good" ethos with which the British treated colonial subjects, and which justified so many atrocities. This is a critique of degrees – it's unquestionably the case that the Doctor is a good guy, especially when compared to the deliciously over the top lunacy of Paul Whitsun-Jones's Marshall. But crucially, the Doctor is allowed to be imperfect in this story in a way that strengthens the story's ethics – something that the show hasn't really managed since the very earliest days of William Hartnell.

Let's talk about that final resolution of the Solonian plot. Ky eventually succumbs to the same mutation affecting the rest of the Solonians. But because the characters have figured out what the mutation really is, they're able to help him by giving him a crystal that allows him to make the next evolutionary step as well. This allows him to turn into a transcendent energy creature who then goes and wraps up the rest of the plot, largely without, as I said, the Doctor having to do anything.

What's really interesting, however, is who's in the room with Ky when his ascension happens. You've got Cotton, Sondergaard, and Jo. That is to say, you've got one non-European character, the white guy who has forsaken his culture and effectively joined the Solonians, Cotton, and Jo. One of these things is not like the others. Leaving Jo aside for a moment, notably this salvation of the Solonians happens with the only two human supporting characters who do not straightforwardly display the white European ideologies that are portrayed as problematic. And when the newly ascended Ky arrives to vaporize the Marshall, the Doctor is uncharacteristically silent, not even offering any condemnation of Ky for murdering a man, as if to finally admit that this just is not a world in which he has any right whatsoever to comment.

The sticky wicket, of course, is Jo. But Jo has, all season, been a fascinatingly transgressive character. Look at the way in which she first responds to the mysterious box appearing, asking the Doctor if it's lunch, and when he says no asking, with equal calm, whether it's a bomb. Jo has taken the programmatic character to new levels by this point, remaining completely separate from the narrative logic of the story, and combining this with plucky determination that means that she has an enormous ability to transgress against the actual logic of the story. Thus it's not inappropriate for her to be the lone "pure European" in the room when Ky ascends, because her character is defined precisely by the ability to simply walk across lines like that and stray into unlikely roles.

The result is a story that combines the social relevance pursued by Holmes and Letts with the glam spectacle pursued by Holmes and Sloman, all the while beginning to push towards some genuinely interesting critiques of both the Doctor and the Time Lords. It's a startlingly ambitious story, but unlike the ambitions of *The Sea Devils*, it's also a story that is completely in command of the capabilities of television in 1972. And more than that, it's tough to think of a story that feels more like we expect the Pertwee era to feel than this one. If we take this story as a test of whether the Doctor is ready to leave Earth, it's tough to come up with any answer other than "Yes, absolutely."

Prove to Me I Am Not Mistaken (*The Time Monster*)

It's May 20, 1972. T. Rex is back on top with "Metal Guru," which, continuing our rule that glam songs should be seen as well as heard, is linked. It holds number one for four weeks before finally yielding to Don McLean's "Vincent," Elton John, Johnny Cash, David Cassidy, The Rolling Stones, and Wings also chart. But perhaps the most remarkable moment, chart-wise, is the final week of this story, where T. Rex, Slade, The Move, Sweet, and Gary Glitter are all in the top ten. This period, with David Bowie's *The Rise and Fall of Ziggy Stardust and the Spiders from Mars* entering the charts (with its lead single, "Starman," entering the singles chart at number forty-nine the same week that five glam acts are in the top ten). In fact, if you want an experience that is aesthetically indistinguishable from *The Time Monster*, has far better acting, and is viewable in less than one sixth of the time, I recommend just tracking down the Top of the Pops videos for the songs in question ("Metal Guru," "Take Me Bak 'Ome," "California Man," "Little Willy," and "Rock and Roll Part 2"), all of which are easily found on YouTube. Grab the Bowie "Starman" performance too, actually. You'll want it next essay.

While in the news, Nixon becomes the first US president since World War II to visit Russia, a trip during which the Apollo-Soyuz mission is agreed upon. While he's out, the first Watergate break-ins happen, and the first Ford Pinto explosion happens, beginning one of the most horrifying episodes in the history of corporate capitalism as it eventually becomes clear that Ford knew full well that the car was dangerous, but determined that the cost of settling lawsuits from exploded drivers and their families was lower than the cost of performing a recall. Then, in the tail end of the story, comes the big Watergate break-in, as Nixon campaign operatives are arrested following a botched attempt to bug the offices of the DNC. Nixon quickly moves to squash the FBI investigation of the break-in, a move that will bring down his presidency when it's finally uncovered. In Europe, Andreas Baader of the Red Army

Faction is arrested, with Ulrike Meinhoff following two weeks later. And finally, British European Airways Flight 548 crashes into Staines shortly after takeoff in the worst airplane crash in British history until Lockerbie.

While on television, we have something we haven't seen in a while. I mean, we've had bad stories before, but the last few times we've had an unmitigated disaster of a story it's been because the entire thing was misconceived – that is, stories that never should have been attempted in the first place done badly. That's harder to say of *The Time Monster*, where the basic ideas seem remarkably solid but the actual execution is an absurd train wreck. The last time we've really seen something like this, where a solid idea on paper just goes terribly wrong, is probably actually *The Chase* way back in Volume One.

I'd list the problems in *The Time Monster*, but the easiest thing to do is frankly just pull up the end credits, which list them effectively. The acting is some of the worst in Doctor Who's history. The guest stars are nearly universally disasters, and even the regulars at times seemingly decide to phone it in with party piece-laden showboating. Add in absurd padding and the questionable decision to make Kronos obviously be a man in a sheet wearing a glorified lampshade on his head and you have a story that is genuinely hard to find a way to enjoy.

But again, the problems here are firmly with the execution. I referred to the Sloman/Letts scripts as among the great curate's eggs of Doctor Who, and it's thoroughly true. Parts of this abomination are excellent. The basic idea of this story seems rock solid, with an interesting and successful escalation from what looks like a routine scheme of the Master meddling with a scientific project to a universe-threatening danger, followed by a surprise trip back to ancient Greece, all with lots of cool set pieces and ideas, plus a conclusion in which the Doctor's triumph is as much a moral one as a practical one. So since this is *The Chase* of the Pertwee era, let's do what we did with that story and stitch together the sympathetic reading of this story whereby it's a brilliant tour de force decades ahead of its time, and ignore the fact that nobody involved in this preposterous exercise demonstrates anything remotely resembling the skill needed to be intending that reading. Those wanting a thorough denunciation of this story's myriad of excruciating flaws can easily find one online. Consider this my penance for slagging off *Inferno*: I will try to say only (OK, mostly) good things about *The Time Monster*.

There's a broader issue at play here, which is the quartet of Sloman/Letts scripts in general. Given the fact that they're all season finales, the heavy involvement of the producer and the fact that among the four are: Pertwee's favorite story, one of the most memorable images of the era (the maggots in *The Green Death*), and Pertwee's regeneration scene, these stories have to be taken seriously. But the fact of the matter is, all four of them have egregious flaws. All the same, they also stand out for having a completely different tone and ethos from almost everything else in the Pertwee era, if not from almost everything else in Doctor Who period. Much of this comes from the fact that Barry Letts kept shoehorning in Buddhist imagery and metaphors that nobody else in the Pertwee era was trying to reflect.

It's not that they're the only overtly Buddhist pieces in Doctor Who – that trend starts back in *The Abominable Snowmen*, and continues through to at least 1983's *Snakedance*. Rather, it's the degree to which the Doctor is an overtly Buddhist hero in these scripts. And more broadly, it's the degree to which it's clear that Letts and Sloman have thought very hard about the philosophical and spiritual foundations of the show. (Indeed, they've clearly thought harder about that than they have about the actual storytelling foundations of the show.) There's a reason it took us an entire entry to sort out what the heck was going on with *The Daemons*, and it wasn't that it was incoherent – it's that there was actually a lot going on there.

In this regard, any discussion of *The Time Monster* has to begin with its sixth episode, in which the Doctor reassures Jo by relating a story from his childhood. The story, about looking at a daisy on the "blackest day" of his life and seeing that "it was simply glowing with life, like a perfectly cut jewel, and the colours! Well, the colours were deeper and richer than you could possibly imagine. Yes, it was the daisiest daisy I'd ever seen." The story evokes the Zen parable of the Flower Sermon, in which the Buddha holds up a flower, and his disciple Mahākāśyapa smiles, resulting in his being selected as the Buddha's successor. There's a strange ambiguity to the story as told here, however. The Doctor tells it in the first person, as something that happened to him, suggesting that it is merely an adaptation of the Flower Sermon. But later he admits that he laughed the first time he heard the story, as if he's simply recounting someone else's anecdote.

But regardless of the story's literal accuracy (and it is hard to square away with most other revelations about the Doctor's past: this apparently major figure in his life, who is presumably K'anpo from *Planet of the Spiders*, is never mentioned again in any televised story after that), this is a major theme through the story, with an earlier sequence allowing Jo to hear the Doctor's thoughts, including faint incoherent echoes of his subconscious thoughts, which he admits he's not proud of. This is an overt effort to recast the Doctor as an actively flawed hero, and it's like nothing we've seen before. (And Pertwee, as he usually does when the Doctor gets wrong-footed somehow, shines with it.)

But where this story gets strange is when this Buddhism is juxtaposed with overtly Platonic philosophy. Which brings us to this story's engagement with Ancient Greece. In *About Time* Tat Wood describes how Greece was going through a trendy patch in Britain at this point due to a large number of expats fleeing the military coup that took place in Greece. But regardless of why this story goes Greece-happy, it does, and it does so in a peculiar way. King Dalios, the most enlightened figure in Atlantis (and played by the same actor who will play K'anpo in *Planet of the Spiders*, creating an interesting thematic link between the two characters) refers to the Doctor as a "true philosopher," seemingly viewing this as the reason why the Doctor has some chance of stopping the Master. There are of course any number of Greek philosophers, but in practical terms if we're talking about Greek philosophy in popular culture we're probably doing either Plato or Aristotle.

In this case, the strong sense is Plato. I base this mostly on the Crystal of Kronos, which is said to exist in a pure and absolute form outside of time, with the shards existing in the present day and Atlantis both being fundamentally connected parts of the true extra-temporal object. By far the easiest way to translate this into Greek philosophical terms – as it seems we have to given the setting and King Dalios's admonitions – are that the crystal is a Platonic Form that is manifesting imperfect echoes into reality, and that these echoes are still genuinely and directly linked to the supposed whole.

This has the most obvious implications for the TARDIS, or, in this story, TARDISes. Every decade or so someone gets it in their head that they should do a story about the nature of the TARDIS. David Whitaker started it off with *The Edge of Destruction*, the 1980s have *Castrovalva*, and the wilderness years have a couple. And *The Time Monster* is the nature of the TARDIS story of the 1970s. Perhaps surprisingly, these nature-of-the-TARDIS stories actually vary considerably less than one would expect from the decades. Admittedly they are not straightforwardly compatible; everyone who does one tends to reinvent the wheel. But nobody ever ends up too far from what everyone else has done.

In this story, at least, the most obvious feature is that we have more than one TARDIS involved, which means that we get an insight into TARDISes instead of into the TARDIS. And the strong implication from how they work, particularly when the Doctor's TARDIS and the Master's become nested inside one another, is that they fundamentally resemble the Crystal of Kronos. (Indeed, the Doctor equates the two directly when talking to Dalios.) Specifically, the interiors of both ships appear to exist outside of time, but are said to have their appearances in the world, thus making the outer police box form of the TARDIS a version of the smaller Crystal of Kronos – a shard of the ideal form.

But it's striking how far this is from anything we've seen before. The TARDIS, in this model, is an unbreachable, essential thing existing outside of reality. It is, in other words, truly immutable and eternal. But this is the antithesis of the chaotic alchemical mercury that was the dominant metaphor for how the TARDIS worked. Instead of being the formless, protean, raw energy of creation that can be morphed into anything, the TARDIS is the exact opposite – absolute, fixed Newtonian certainty.

But, of course, the story has another major concept – interstitial time. Kronos, we are told, exists within this concept, which Sergeant Benton of all people (both he and Jo get a surprisingly verbose amount of exposition in this story) ends up explaining as the space between two instants. This points towards a third concept, also rooted in Greek thought, this time in Zeno's Paradox – the old canard about how if you conceptualize motion in terms of closing half of the distance between two points, then half again, and so on, motion becomes impossible. This time the answer comes from Aristotle, who rejected the notion that time can be divided into discrete and atomic units. Which is a solid enough defense as such things go, but one that is tacitly rejected in this particular conception of things – interstitial time is clearly explained in terms of indivisible units of time.

The implications of this are significant – in particular when, in the sixth episode, we are told that Kronos, apparently because she is within interstitial time, is "beyond good and evil" and capable of embodying any form. This suggests that Kronos, existing as it does in an impossible space the very nature of which defies and confounds physical existence, is completely Other – an almost Lovecraftian idea. So we have three simultaneous philosophical concepts existing – Buddhist enlightenment, Platonic Form, and the existence of this gap outside of time in which the incomprehensible Other resides.

But wait, what exactly is the difference between the eternal Platonic forms and something like Kronos? If, in fact, there is one at all. Kronos and the TARDISes both exist outside of time. So the implication is that these eternal, fixed objects are wholly beyond comprehension and understanding, containing within them concepts that are contradictory and unintelligible. The ideal form of things and the incomprehensible Other may well be two sides of the same coin.

Where this really becomes interesting, though, is in the fact that the TARDISes are also demonstrably linked to their pilots, with this story playing off the old sentient TARDIS/telepathic circuits ideas from *The Edge of Destruction*. Which suggests strongly that the Doctor and the Master themselves possess at least some measure of eternal and Platonic nature.

The story actually supports this in another way – via the fact that King Dalios and Queen Galleia each side with either the Doctor and the Master. Galleia notably declares that the Master "has the bearing of the Gods." What, exactly, does this mean? Here it is perhaps useful to acknowledge the fact that Robert Sloman had in mind at this point a climactic battle between the Doctor and the Master in which it is revealed that they are different parts of one psyche, with the Master being the Id and the Doctor the Ego (notably not the Superego).

But layering Freudian concepts onto this just seems a bridge too far. Still, let's take the basic idea – that the Master and the Doctor are themselves individual reflections of some larger form. Plato, after all, declares that the appropriate rulers of society are philosopher-kings. And in this story, the Doctor is declared a philosopher while the Master is viewed by Queen Galleia as the ideal king. In other words, they are here split parts of the same concept. The Master is a pure will to power without understanding, whereas the Doctor (too scared here to stop the Master, leaving it for Jo to take the crucial step of time ramming his TARDIS) has understanding without the will to use it decisively.

But if the Doctor and the Master are inherently linked concepts, this brings us back to one of the most fundamental questions of the Pertwee era: what, exactly, do the Time Lords intend the Doctor to be doing about the Master? It's worth noting that the Time Lords take a puzzlingly hands-off approach to him, after all. On the one hand, they know he's on Earth, since they tell the Doctor that in *Terror of the Autons*. But when the Doctor's location was known they arrested him. Here, despite knowing exactly where the Master was, they just tipped the Doctor off to him. Given that one is a homicidal maniac and the other is just a bit rude, this seems like a questionable reaction.

The most obvious explanation in terms of what the writers intended is probably that the Master, being a part of the Doctor as opposed to an individual in his own right, isn't the Time Lords' to deal with. The Doctor is the only one who can fix this problem. This will not, of course, remain a satisfying explanation through the end of the Pertwee era, since Sloman's plans never came to fruition – a result that, given the uneven quality of his scripts, would have to be considered a win were it not for the fact that what derailed them was not an outbreak of good sense but rather the tragic death of Roger Delgado. But it remains the best explanation for what happens in this story.

Let's back up to the big picture, since this is also the last story before the Time Lords restore the Doctor's TARDIS. The bulk of Season Nine has been stuck in an odd limbo between the earthbound format of Seasons Seven and Eight and the restoration of the traditional format that is going to come in Seasons Ten and Eleven. The easiest way to conceptualize this, as I've argued throughout the season, is that these stories form the evolving case for ending the Doctor's exile. Which means, given the seeming necessity that the Doctor be the one to confront the Master, that the easiest way to understand him is as one of the tests the Doctor must pass in order to be deemed worthy of traveling again.

Specifically, the Master can be read as an exaggerated parody of those parts of the Doctor that caused his exile in the first place. The Master, after all, is a character who engages with people only to use them. He is every bit as adventurous as the Doctor, but his adventures feature a complete disregard for any human interactions or social investment. And so in defeating the Master the Doctor is also tacitly struggling against the instincts which led to his exile.

In which case the most significant moment of this story comes when the two TARDISes are suspended in the void between Kronos's world and reality, and the Doctor, against all reason, insists that Kronos set the Master free instead of tormenting him for all eternity. In effect, then, the Doctor – after spending all story trying to reason with the Master and get him to stop trying to destroy the universe – still opts to save the Master from hell for the simple reason that he wouldn't condemn anyone to it. This is actually a landmark moment in Doctor Who – the first moment where the Doctor has insisted on a greater level of mercy than makes sense.

This is also where the Buddhism seems to come back to the story. The Doctor, being more enlightened, is able to overcome the desire for revenge in favor of a greater mercy, and is able to forgive his greatest foe. But more to the point, he is able to forgive himself to make peace with the instincts that caused his exile without excising them or surrendering to them. This is exactly what was demanded at the end of *The War Games* – that he find a deeper level on which to engage situations than "ooh, let's fight some monsters." And the final demonstration of this is that he is able to apply that deeper engagement to himself, as represented by the Master.

But before his exile is lifted there is, of course, one more matter – a more literal engagement with himself, if you will.

How Does the TARDIS Work?

Regular readers of this series may have noticed a certain formula to these essays in which, in the opening paragraph, I note that the question is fundamentally silly. In this case, however, it is particularly apropos. No possible answer to this question can fit with every Doctor Who story. For instance, picking just one oddball one from the Pertwee era, an attempt to reconcile the fact that the TARDIS apparently gets its air supply through the doors in *Planet of the Daleks* with anything else is almost surely doomed.

There are two ways to approach this problem, then. The first is to attempt to get general trends in how the TARDIS works to fit together, preferably using details from some of the odder moments to account for them. The second is historical, attempting to discern specific threads of thought about how the TARDIS works from over the history of the series.

I lean rather more towards the latter approach, though we can pay some attention to the former as we go. There are, after all, essentially only four stories to date that are substantively about how the TARDIS works, so we can just figure out the metaphors in them and go from there. These are: *The Edge of Destruction* (covered in the Hartnell Volume), *The Time Monster*, *Logopolis* and *Castrovalva* (to be covered in future volumes, though the blog has posts on them already), and *The Doctor's Wife* (coming some time from now in both the blog and book versions). There's also the TV movie, but that, like *Planet of the Daleks*, is more or less impossible to reconcile with anything else ever. So let's work out the TARDIS in each of them and go from there.

The Edge of Destruction demonstrates two things about the TARDIS. The first is a terribly important bit of series lore: it's alive and sentient. The second is more idiosyncratic: it's completely mad, engaging in the most ludicrously over-elaborate demonstration of a technical fault imaginable. The end result is that we get the sense of the TARDIS as a fundamentally metaphorical space. Or, more accurately, as something that understands its world through metaphoric terms.

This fits in well with David Whitaker's general tendency towards alchemy – note that in *The Wheel in Space* he has mercury as the substance that mediates between the police box exterior and the bigger interior. The removal of the Time Vector Generator causes the exterior of the TARDIS to have the dimensions of a normal police box. Noticeably, it does not appear to impact the interior as such: by all appearances everything is still there. Rather, it seems that some vital connection between the exterior and the interior is severed: whatever it is that keeps the bigger-on-the-inside interior space inside the police box. Mercury, in other words, connects two disparate realms, a deeply alchemic function of it. Given that one of the fundamental tenets of alchemy is the equivalence of symbols and reality, the TARDIS's behavior in *The Edge of Destruction* appears sensible as well.

So for Whitaker, it seems, the TARDIS is an agent of mercury – something that can mediate and translate between two worlds. In this regard what is most interesting about the TARDIS is its status as a threshold. The ship's interior doors allow the linking of two disparate spaces. Note that it's also from Whitaker's work as script editor in *Planet of Giants* and writer in *The Enemy of the World* that the idea that opening the TARDIS doors at inappropriate moments is dangerous – and how the ship opening its doors in *The Edge of Destruction* was taken as a particularly portentous sign.

The Time Monster seems to posit an almost completely opposite sense, however. The biggest problem with it is the moment in which the Doctor and the Master's TARDISes materialize inside one another. This requires us to think of the TARDIS less as a threshold between two spaces than as a discrete but dimensionally complex entity. This isn't irreconcilable with Whitaker – perhaps that's what the mercury in the Time Vector Generator accomplishes. But equally, we're told that the interior portion of the TARDIS exists outside of time in a manner similar to the Chronovores.

As we saw in the preceding essay, *The Time Monster* links this vision of the TARDIS to Platonic concepts such that the interior of the TARDIS appears to be the part of it that exists in the realm of the Platonic Forms. Various implications seem to stem from this, like that the Doctor, who is clearly inherently linked to the TARDIS, may possess an eternal, Platonic nature that manifests in individual and imperfect copies, an idea that links well with the idea in *Power of the Daleks* that the TARDIS is somehow essential to regeneration.

This is actually possible to make work with anything save for the TV movie. But nowhere does it work best than in *Logopolis*, where we have, for no obvious reason, a projection of the Doctor's future regeneration walking around at the same time that the TARDIS is being reconstructed. *Logopolis* and *Castrovalva* also mediate satisfyingly between the Platonic and alchemic conceptions of the TARDIS by grounding it in mathematics. On the one hand mathematics are routinely explained in Platonic terms, with numbers being transcendent and perfect objects. On the other, the relationship between mathematics and the physical world is alchemically flavored to say the least.

Castrovalva makes much of the ship's interior, including establishing it as reconfigurable, but all of this feels sensible. The interior and exterior of the TARDIS exist as a sort of living mathematics, and are thus subject to being rewritten or transposed. The mercury of the Time Vector Generator, in this view, is the physical manifestation of what connects the mathematics of the interior and exterior spaces. This links satisfyingly with the Platonic material of *The Time Monster* as well: mathematics is capable of describing impossible phenomena that correspond to real ones. For instance, it is possible to calculate the exterior angles of a regular polygon with negative seven sides (they are each about 231.43 degrees, as it happens) despite the fact that such a shape is a meaningless concept in physical space. The idea that the TARDIS's eccentric and impossible spaces exist within these conceptually valid but not physically valid aspects of mathematics is thematically compelling.

We could just about leave it there, only the new series has added one more major wrinkle, albeit one that comports well with some details from the Pertwee era. The issue is *The Doctor's Wife*, which reveals an awful lot about the precise nature of the TARDIS's consciousness, specifically that it is integral to the functioning of the TARDIS. House can make the TARDIS work, but the Doctor's ramshackle TARDIS requires Idris to function, suggesting that there must be some consciousness in the system for it to do anything. That is to say, the TARDIS not only is a conscious individual, individual subjectivity is necessary for it to function.

But *The Doctor's Wife* also establishes that all that is technically required for a TARDIS to travel is the console, although traveling that way is clearly ludicrously dangerous. This isn't a huge problem – if you note we've spent the preceding pages dealing entirely with the question of how the TARDIS is put together. The idea that the bit that makes it travel through time is the console is in no way contradictory to anything so far discussed. It suggests that the mathematically eccentric stuff accretes around the console, but that's not at all troublesome.

So, if we were to assemble this, we would get something along the lines of this: a TARDIS is formed when a consciousness is put inside of a TARDIS console. The consciousness-plus-console can travel through space and time, but typically creates a structure of a larger ship and exterior out of pure mathematics prior to doing so. This larger system employs higher dimensions and Platonic forms. And all of this, from the consciousness to the pure mathematics, is based on the relationships of individual subjectivity and symbols.

This also allows us to better understand the nature of the Doctor's exile. It's repeated several times that the problem with the TARDIS is with its ability to dematerialize, though it switches back and forth whether the TARDIS's "dematerialization circuit" is out, or whether the Doctor's knowledge of the "dematerialization codes" is blocked. But there is no particular reason these two things should be separate given the sentient and psychic nature of the TARDIS.

What's more interesting is the question of "dematerialization." Several things suggest that this is the process by which the TARDIS exits normal space-time and enters "the time vortex." Certainly this is the easiest way to explain the new series' love of having the TARDIS literally flying around – it's doing what it normally does, but in real space instead of the time vortex, having not "dematerialized." But let's think for at least a moment about the word "materialize." It means to become matter. If we take the TARDIS as in part a complex interaction between the theoretical/conceptual and the material then the block on dematerialization makes perfect thematic sense: the Doctor isn't allowed to leave the material realm.

But this meta-explanation is papering over the genuinely interesting gaps among the four distinct interpretations. Gaiman and Bidmead, for instance, are in practice coming at the problem from two wildly different perspectives. Bidmead's mathematical vision of the TARDIS fundamentally extends from a model of the TARDIS as absolute, while Gaiman revels in its idiosyncratic subjectivity. The eternal and transcendent nature of the TARDIS in *The Time Monster* is at odds with the avant-garde theatrical madness of *The Edge of Destruction*. And while they all end up in similar places, there is a real shift in this over the course of the series, with the original conception of the TARDIS as primarily a magical, symbolic, and literary object giving way to a more rigidly scientific conception, and then moving back towards the subjective and symbolic in later years. This divide is never inviolate – the alchemical thought of the 1960s is not hostile to science, and Bidmead's science-based approach is some of the most fantastic and magical Doctor Who ever to air. But the fact that a general theory of the TARDIS can be cobbled together does not erase the fact that there are two distinct trains of thought within the series.

On the other hand, maybe the TARDIS really is designed to be operated by humans and can be hermetically sealed by evil plants.

Pop Between Realities, Home in Time for Tea: *The Rise and Fall of Ziggy Stardust and the Spiders from Mars*

With thankful apologies to Chris O'Leary of Pushing Ahead of the Dame.

0. "Space Oddity"

In ancient days, men looked at the stars and saw their heroes in the constellations. In modern times, we do much the same, but our heroes are epic men of flesh and blood. – Undelivered speech in the event that Neil Armstrong and Buzz Aldrin were stranded on the moon.

As Chris O'Leary points out in an essay that will be showing up in the next volume, one is spoiled for choice when linking bits of David Bowie to Doctor Who. This is not surprising – the two great British chameleons of their era were always going to look alike. Add to this the fact that Bowie found his first real success with a timely bit of space folk in 1969 and you have an inevitable series of intersections.

When Bowie hit it big again in 1973 it was on a not entirely unrelated trick. "Space Oddity," you see, was about the crushing isolation of space. In this regard it was impressively prescient. Released, in a typical bit of Bowie publicity seeking, days before the Apollo 11 landing, the song impressively foreshadowed the disconnect between the moon landing and the Space-Age future that had been dreamt of throughout the 1960s. The moon wasn't our first step to the stars but our last one – the furthest point we reached before retreating back to Earth. And "Space Oddity," far from being a triumphant bit of space exploration, was a song about the crushing, bleak isolation of space.

But for *The Rise and Fall of Ziggy Stardust and the Spiders from Mars* the approach is turned slightly. Where "Space Oddity" is about the horrific emptiness of the cosmos, the Ziggy Stardust era is about all of the lost dreams of space showing up in the aftermath of their abandonment, in all their glorious, gaudy splendor, looking for a good party and maybe an opportunity to score.

1. "Five Years"

Some say the end is near
Some say we'll see Armageddon soon
I certainly hope we will. – Tool, "Aenema"

The smart money, you have to realize, was not on reaching 1978. The question was just which of the myriad of ways we might kill ourselves would pull it off. Nuclear war? Ecological disaster? Social collapse into anarchy? *Doomwatch*, after all, got three seasons out of cataloging the myriad of ways humanity might slaughter itself through the miracle of science.

So it's no particular surprise that Bowie starts the album with a song of apocalypse. And a remarkably concrete song of apocalypse at that – wandering through the streets and observing the people responding to the news that the Earth has five years to live. But notably absent is any explanation of how this happened – of which disaster will befall us. All of them. None of them. In a world in which the end is an absolute certainty, the means are beside the point.

The result, as Bowie exposes, is the fetishization of disaster. *The Atrocity Exhibition* writ large. The news isn't that we have five years to live. It's that we have only "five years left of crying." The end is a welcome thing. This has always been the logic of Doctor Who – the appeal of looking at the monsters, of seeing the threat. The money shot of *Inferno* is that we finally get to see the world end in fire instead of just being teased. At last, Armageddon stops blue balling us and gives us our payoff. The end of this growing agony and the cathartic release of knowing there is a genuine resolution. Finally, the finale. At its endpoint, Bowie's song explodes from its initial yearning sorrow into a soaring football terrace song. A rousing sing-along chorus of "five years," the end turned into the anthem it always was. "You'll Never Die Alone." "You're going home in a nuclear fireball." "Come on you Daleks."

2. "Soul Love"

The spectacle is not a collection of images; it is a social relation between people that is mediated by images. – Guy Debord, Society of the Spectacle

In a world defined by its imminent apocalyptic finale, the blinding flash of the nuclear inferno becomes the light of a film projector, pressing nuclear shadows to the screen for us to stare slack-jawed upon. There is nothing but appearances in a pre-apocalyptic world. Bowie's song begins with a mother kneeling before the grave of a heroic son "who gave his life to save the slogans that hover between the headstone and her eyes, for they penetrate her grieving." War, death, and even bereavement cannot exist without pop.

When the ultimate disaster porn spectacle has become the teleology of the world, there is nothing outside the gaudy glory of slogans. Love is nothing but an ideology, a product, another slogan. There is only idiot love, the love of love. But here again, there is a countermeasure to the bleak cynicism offered by this. The fact that love is empty and cold; a rote formal process. Our contact with each other is nothing but the empty, hollow execution of hormones and rhetoric.

And yet there is some faint remaining value. "Love descends on those defenseless" is a cynical sentiment, but still a variation of the sloganistic "love conquers all." The priest kneeling, experiencing "soul love" in the final verse, still experiences and is involved in some transformation. The singer's loneliness evolves.

The spectacle is not the end of love, but merely its reconfiguration. A love that exists in shallow images, and finds its truth in them, the nuclear shadows burnt into the walls begin, tentatively, to kiss and fumble at each other's clothing.

3. "Moonage Daydream"
Oh, I'm getting it wrong again, aren't I? I'm always doing that. So many mouths. – Prisoner Zero, The Eleventh Hour

Détournement, the great technique of Guy Debord, provides the crucial through line from the revolutionary ethos of '68 to the savage glory of punk and post-punk. Doctor Who rarely loses contact with this arc of history. Détournement devours the debris of images scattered across the culture and spits them back in a vehement parody, parroting the culture back. As he puts it, "in a world that is really upside down, the true is a moment of the false."

There is a roar of power chords as Bowie's vocal track spits braggadocio. "I'm an ALLIGATOR!" Another power chord. "I'm a Mamapapa comin' for YOOOOU."

The whole song – the whole album in fact – continues in this vein. The clichés of rock delivered wrong, and incoherently, with images that are as alluring as they are wrong. "You're squawking like a pink monkey bird," Bowie intones, straight-faced, as if unaware of his own absurdities. And yet out of this we get the soaring, anthemic chorus.

Watching the Ziggy Stardust concert documentary, the most interesting moment that D.A. Pennebaker manages is when he turns the camera on a single fan during this song. In religious ecstasy, she sways and dances, cradling her head in her own hands, pressing her space face close to the music, freaking out in glorious rapture.

This is the central power of Ziggy, of Bowie, of glam, and, yes, of Doctor Who – that in amidst the mad collage of spectacles it is possible to build a genuine moment of drama. This is love in the age of apocalypse. But what is crucial is that it is genuine. We do not need to take this on faith. We do not need to qualify. Stare into the electric eye of this moonage girl and the truth is clear.

4. "Starman"

Unknown gods who visited the primeval Earth in manned spaceships – Erich von Däniken, Chariots of the Gods?

The week after *The Time Monster* takes its final bow, David Bowie charts with *The Rise and Fall of Ziggy Stardust and the Spiders from Mars.* In many ways glam's high-water act, this album kicks off a phase in which David Bowie effectively has five albums out within a year. Between "Space Oddity" and this he was largely anonymous, even though he was making quite good albums. Then he suddenly hit it big. In a twelve-month period his three prior albums, Ziggy, and his follow-up album *Aladdin Sane* all chart. But it's Ziggy that is the spark – the album that suddenly explodes David Bowie out into the world.

More specifically, the spark is "Starman," the lead single, which first crept into the charts with the last episode of *The Time Monster*. More than any other song on the album, this is the one that nods at David Bowie's past. The thing about Ziggy is that, on paper, it is in no way Bowie's best album of the early '70s. That would be *Hunky Dory*, the album that has "Changes," "Oh! You Pretty Things," "Life on Mars?," and "Kooks" on it. But *Hunky Dory* initially died on the charts. Its only hit single, "Life on Mars?," charted in the wake of Ziggy Stardust.

It wasn't until Bowie returned to the themes of his until then one-hit wonder, "Space Oddity," that he took off. But as we've seen, "Starman" is no sequel. Rather, it's a complete inversion. The moment of Doctor Who that tracks most straightforwardly to "Space Oddity" is *The Ambassadors of Death*, with its bleak and scary portrayal of space and the Doctor sitting in his tin can. This is something else: a Starman, waiting in the sky, fearful that his splendor will blow our minds.

This is one of the songs where the supposed concept of the album actually distinctly makes sense. An alien love messiah cum rock star, striding from the sky to offer us salvation, an alternative to the eschatological spectacle surrounding us. Youth culture's rebellion gets stashed in plain sight, the children losing it, using it, boogying their way to a newfound nirvana, a secret midnight rebellion providing the sparkling landing lights for our freaky Space Age savior.

If it is not too obvious a point to make, this is where Doctor Who and Ziggy come closest to intersection, with Pertwee cast as the transcendent Starman, the great cosmic protector of Earth, the coolest damn thing ever to wear a velvet jacket.

It is worth looking up Bowie's *Top of the Pops* performance of this song – the performance that really broke him out. Watch as at first the camera creeps around him, treating the singer not as a beloved pop star but as an object of fear to be crept around – a Doctor Who monster. And then a minute in, Bowie's phenomenal guitarist, Mick Ronson, is suddenly wrapped up in a hug from Bowie, pulled towards the microphone, alien sex god and rock star arm in arm, the cosmos itself giving us leave to boogie.

5. "It Ain't Easy"
Is the enlightened man subject to the law of causation? – Question in a thirteenth-century Zen koan.

In the aforementioned concert movie, perhaps the strangest inclusion on Bowie's part is "Wild Eyed Boy from Freecloud," the overtly Buddhist B-side to "Space Oddity." This song is, in many ways, its counterpart on the album. Its inclusion is utterly given that in hindsight the better-known options like "Velvet Goldmine" thrashed about on the cutting room floor.

"Wild Eyed Boy from Freecloud" is a parable of a boy on the margins of his own village, a haunting piece that describes the marginalized prophet being put to death by his village and watching in horror as the Himalayan mountain takes the revenge he never sought on his behalf. The imagery of the mountain is present in "It Ain't Easy" as well, starting with a young man looking out upon the world and seeing the places he could be. But then he returns to the world, the strange materialism of the town and the hoochie coochie women. Enlightenment runs aground in the world. The singer of this song does not have the enlightenment of the wild-eyed boy, but instead claws desperately for it as it slips endlessly away from him.

Or at least that's perhaps the point. The song is a weak spot all the same, a puzzling side-ender that mostly seems to encourage flipping the record over early. The "concept album" status of Ziggy Stardust – of all of Bowie's four great "character" records, actually – is easily overstated, and the easiest explanation for this song may well just be that it's a piece of crappy filler. But the idea of crappy filler parallels Doctor Who at least as well as Buddhist parables and Starmen do. A well-meaning misstep, a piece that, not for lack of trying, never quite makes sense and never quite works. The only question is which of the many options within the Pertwee era we take as the analogue to this song.

6. "Lady Stardust"
Yates's fingers shifted position over his mouth, just this side of a threat to clamp down if he said another word. Benton swallowed and stayed still. He felt himself getting hard against his better judgment. – "Keeping Secrets" by platoapproved, from A Teaspoon and an Open Mind

The faint, tentative cabaret piano that introduces Ziggy's second side moves us to a strange new place. For the first time in the album, we are invited to view the alien externally. A sad beauty, mocked and laughed at even as he pours beautiful music out, singing "songs of darkness and dismay." Lady Stardust, in this song, is Marc Bolan, lead singer of T. Rex, yes. But perhaps the more interesting fact is that Lady Stardust is a male in the first place, referred to with the male pronoun throughout the song. The obvious analogy is the drag queen.

The main thing to recognize about drag queens is that there is next to no relationship between that concept and the concept of transgender people. Drag queens are men dressing as women – playing at femininity. They are not people gendered as male at birth who are in fact women. They are people who identify as men but enjoy playing the role of a woman. And crucially, the drag queen gets it slightly wrong, playing the part with too much gaudy excess. This is why there is the modern concept of the female drag queen. Drag sits on the line between idolatry and parody, between the sentimental embrace of camp and the cynical mockery of détournement.

Put another way, drag is weaponized camp – a loving attack. Drag is marginalized by design. It transgresses, but is willfully blind to its own failure to "pass" such that its transgression is always obvious. But through its blindness, it manages an eagerness, an honesty, a, dare I say it, authenticity. Just as the girl rapturously presses her space face close to Ziggy's, drag is another moonage daydream, a collage taken seriously. Drag, like glam, is a secret handshake, a shibboleth to the world of the outsider. "He's faking it, so he must be one of us fakers." The closet becomes as much a source of pride as of shame.

(The original drag queen, of course, is Beau Brummel. The dandy is drag to begin with, doubly so when embraced as a slight misunderstanding of the decadent cool of the James Bond-era action hero. This is why Doctor Who became an iconic show within gay culture – because for five years in the '70s, its leading man was a drag action hero.)

7. "Star"
I cross the void beyond the mind, the empty space that circles time. – Jon Pertwee, "Who Is the Doctor?"

In all of this, there is an unasked question. If the purpose of the exercise is to build a new form of love and meaning out of the discarded scraps of apocalyptic spectacle, can the figure of the rock star ever manage this? There is much to doubt here. The basic idea of a revolutionary cult of personality jars.

But more broadly, much of the underlying theory of this performance is overtly Marxist. This *Ziggy Pertwee and the Spiders from Metabelis Three* concept works for the era, and I maintain that it is by far the interpretation that throws up the most fascinating wonders, but we have to accept the Doctor as an actively Marxist figure. Which is fine – the era came straight out of psychedelic revolution, and one of the architects of the Pertwee era was Malcolm Hulke. Doctor Who is always allied, on one level, with Marxism.

But here we run into a problem. The rock and roll star is a capitalist phenomenon – a creature of consumption. Here Bowie sings of a longing to be a rock star, but what he really wants are the trappings: the money, the fame, the glory. Once those are obtained, perhaps, he can sleep at night and fall in love. The song begins with friends trying to change the world – fight in Belfast, or go on hunger strikes. But Bowie wants to be a rock star.

This is not a superficial refusal to join the fight. Rather, it is the realization that the revolutionary figure, the great celebrity who can change the world, is still an invention of the very system being fought. In his introduction to *The Society of the Spectacle*, Martin Jenkins describes celebrity as a capitalist lottery, a system by which just enough people are given the spectacular rewards of capitalism, and because it could be anyone, we all play along.

This is the sad truth underneath the song. The one thing that Bowie cannot do as a rock star is attack the system that creates the rock and roll star. The one freedom the Starman cannot grant us is the freedom not to have to look to the stars.

8. "Hang On to Yourself"
They're great favourites with the children, you know, with their gnashing and snapping and tearing at each other. – Vorg, Carnival of Monsters

The companion piece, in most regards, to "It Ain't Easy," "Hang On to Yourself" is an overdone pastiche of rock, a whirlwind tour of snippets from other rock stars. It's the sting in the trap, if you will . . . the song where the stitched together fakery of Ziggy Stardust stands revealed as the cheap fraud it is. The first verse sings of a cheap groupie "praying to the light machine," and seems like nothing so much as a slap in the face to the space faced girl dancing to "Moonage Daydream," a mockery of her for being thick enough to embrace something as stupid and plastic as the crazy space freak.

And the worst part is, the song knows full well that it's full of it. "You're the blessed," Bowie sings, "we're the Spiders from Mars." The song has the gall to dispense rock star ministry even as it laughs at the congregation. The singer has no such illusions, does not for a moment pretend this is anything other than a cheap act; "If you think we're gonna make it, you better hang on to yourself." Not only can't the Starman provide any relief from celebrity, he doesn't even want to.

9. "Ziggy Stardust"
This was exactly you. All this, all of it. – River Song, A Good Man Goes to War

What does a rock song written in the aftermath of the end of rock and roll sound like? Moments after admitting to the savage vacancy of the part, Bowie unleashes one of the great guitar riffs in rock history. The result is a riff that mourns its own passing, fitting for the song that introduces us to Ziggy himself by killing him. Consumed by his own fans, torn to pieces, eaten alive by the very spectacle he feeds upon, Ziggy nevertheless is here safely enmeshed in a knowingly iconic song, a glorious creature of guitar riffs and earworms.

Even after his critique of the rock star, in other words, Bowie is acknowledging its allure. The rock star is in many ways the ultimate alien – always in a fundamental sense distant from the fans whose lives he supposedly chronicles and speaks the truth of. The bliss, which the young girl sways to during "Moonage Daydream," exists not because of the accuracy of the description but precisely because of its source – the girl can only truly be understood by an alien who can never be a part of her world.

Ziggy and Pertwee are effectively indistinguishable. Space messiahs in drag, they stand astride the world with growing awareness of the fact that the salvation they offer requires their own death to realize. This song is that growing realization – the sense that even now as we understand the Pertwee era, as we reach his finest hour (and Season Ten is, without question, his finest hour) – that there is something unsustainable here. That the whole thing will, in time, come crashing down.

This song, then, is its tombstone. Here, suspended in that moment, shuddering in the post-coital bliss of Mick Ronson's reverb, we mourn the end with the very excess that brought it around. How glum. How glam.

10. "Suffragette City"
A woman without a man is like a fish without a bicycle. – Irina Dunn

Oh, all right, let's talk about Jo Grant – the one thing in Doctor Who more glam than Pertwee's Doctor, more glam than Axos, more glam, perhaps, than glam rock itself. The thing about Jo Grant is that in the course of trying to create a dumb broad who exists only to get captured, Terrance Dicks inadvertently created one of the great feminist icons of Doctor Who.

The decadent virility of the rock star is necessarily uncomfortable with the feminine. Bowie can wear its trappings, make it fall in love with him, use it, and abuse it. And yet still this song exists, telling of a harsh city of women who can use him better than he can use them. Wham bam thank you ma'am indeed, "Suffragette City" is the remainder of Ziggy's fall, and, at that, what killed him.

But this is no panicked ball of castration anxiety cursing the vagina dentata. This is an anthem of self-consumption, a man happy to have his spine put out of place by this girl who's total blam-blam. The final form of the elusive lunar goddess in the audience for "Moonage Daydream," we see the power she had at last, the capacity to draw pleasure from the rubble of the spectacle. Even as Ziggy consumes himself for her, she readies her raygun for the next head.

Loved too much to ever be hurt, knowing she can get away with anything, well aware of our gaze, Jo smiles and goes about her business. The Doctor grasps her hand, stares adoringly at his companion, and they run off from whatever monster is chasing them this week, she having the time of her life, he deludedly thinking he's actually in charge here and that he exists for something other than her pleasure.

(Still, there is something irksome here. An object that deforms the narrative is not the same as a subject.)

11. "Rock and Roll Suicide"
Don't cry. Where there's life, there's . . . – The Third Doctor, Planet of the Spiders

A mournful eulogy to the burnt out rockstar that gives way to his own garish resurrection, his cheapest spectacle proving to be his apotheosis. Torn apart by the very absurdity of a revolutionary rock star, killed by the basic impossibility of being a messianic commodity, Ziggy somehow lives on.

This is no surprise. Created to counter eschatology, to turn the fetishized spectacle of death into a mad celebration, this comeback is not his final move but his first. Of course death is no particular obstacle or stress for Ziggy. How could it be? Built out of the wasted salvage of death to begin with, Ziggy can make himself out of his own death as easily as anyone else's. Consume and burn out a rock star and another will take its place. The role survives its actor, and exists independently from him.

The ironic thing, of course, is that Bowie went on to literalize this final move, nearly flaming out in a staggering feat of recreational pharmacology, reduced to a pathetic shell of a man. This was always a possibility, and Ziggy Stardust is as much a reflection of Bowie's own fears about his family's history of mental illness and how it might impact him as it is a prediction or a diagnosis. But as if to prove his final point, Bowie's own course was to burn out and then move on, to come back, reinventing himself again, and again, and again, as immortal as Ziggy's doppelgänger.

∞. Ashes to Ashes
Time might change me
But I can't trace time – David Bowie, "Changes"

Put another way, the ending of the story is inscribed in the beginning. This is the curious condition of the 1970s. Suspended as they are between the youth counterculture of the 1960s and the conservative monolith of the 1980s, they seem to exist mostly to transform one into the other. They are not, crucially, the hand-off between two visions. Rather they are the crucible in which one turned to the other.

But this is a foolish view of both ends of the 1970s. It is not as though the 1960s did not have a powerful reactionary movement. Indeed, that reactionary movement ultimately won. Similarly, it is not as though the 1980s lacked a vibrant counterculture. The counterculture never did so well as when it had Thatcher to fight against. The 1970s are not some transition between two states. They're the cyclic period as we circle back around to the same status quo.

The ecstatic highs of Bowie's Starman star turn are bounded on either side by his Major Tom songs, the first chronicling the emptiness of space, the second revealing Major Tom to be a burnt-out junkie. The highs of raw ecstasy and the lows of oblivion become, in the course of this cycle, indistinguishable. This is the real truth of the 1970s: nothing changed in the least.

Time Can Be Rewritten (*Verdigris*)

The year 2000 is eschatological for anyone, but for a generation of Britain it very specifically marked the end of the future. A fluke of naming committed in 1977 inadvertently left the most important comics magazine in the UK with a name demarcating a clear and unavoidable sell-by date. It's tough to blame anyone – nobody starting a grubby comics rag ostensibly edited by a fictional galactic conqueror and featuring a barely coherent revamp of '50s icon Dan Dare would have taken seriously the question "but what are we going to do in twenty-three years?" The answer was clear – be working on something else, this magazine having gone under twenty years earlier. But come 2000, there we were, staring awkwardly at one of the most iconic mastheads in science fiction and going "well, that's underwhelming, isn't it?"

2000, then, is the perfect date to revisit early '70s science fiction. In 1972, nobody believed there would be a year 2000. And come the year 2000, it turned out they'd been right all along. There really was no future. Enter Paul Magrs and *Verdigris*. In previous volumes we have discussed the fact that the decision to replace the Virgin Books line with the BBC Books line in the wake of the 1996 TV Movie was a mixed blessing at best, and that the seven years since the series came back have by and large validated that by favoring writers and innovations from the Virgin line while ignoring most of the new blood brought in at BBC Books. All of this is true. But this is partially because unlike the New Adventures, BBC Books only really introduced two major Doctor Who writers. The first is Lawrence Miles, who, while he wrote a Virgin book, is most associated with the BBC line having written four key books for them and spun off his own Faction Paradox series from them. We will deal with him at the tail end of this volume. The second is Paul Magrs.

More than almost any other Doctor Who writer, Magrs visibly has a preferred approach to writing Doctor Who and little desire to deviate from it. Specifically, he has a signature character, Iris Wildthyme, who features in many (though by no means all) of his works, including *Verdigris*. And how one approaches the book depends almost entirely on how one approaches the character of Iris Wildthyme.

Central to any assessment of Magrs's work, after all, is the initial decision of whether or not an utterly barmy and frequently inebriated middle aged woman who travels around space and time in a double decker bus that is slightly smaller on the inside than it is on the outside is a brilliant idea or the worst thing ever. Unsurprisingly, if disappointingly, the latter view is not at all uncommon, which poses some insurmountable barriers to enjoying Magrs's work.

The real problem, though, is that Iris is just the tip of the iceberg. One of the usual lines of criticism about Paul Magrs is the accusation that he doesn't actually like Doctor Who. This is complete nonsense, but it's not entirely inexplicable why people would say it. Certainly *Verdigris* contains no shortage of things that, on the surface, appear to be jokes at Doctor Who's expense. The literal transformation of Mike Yates into a two-dimensional cardboard cutout, for instance, is admittedly hard to read as anything other than a comment on the fact that Yates is . . . well . . . a two-dimensional cardboard cutout of a character. Likewise, when a character suggests that Jo "think about every alien artifact or creature you have ever seen. Weren't they always surrounded by a crackling nimbus of blue light? . . . Didn't they sometimes look a little . . . unconvincing?" it is only an act of willful blindness not to read this as an explicit commentary on the visual artifacts left by the CSO process that was integral to the special effects of 1970s Doctor Who. Though for my money, the funniest swipe at the series comes at the end of Chapter Fourteen, when the main villain reveals himself and the chapter ends "'I am Verdigris,' the figure said, and didn't elaborate."

The thing is, arguing that someone who has written, at present, twenty-nine full length Doctor Who stories hates Doctor Who, or even has "contempt" for it, as the more mild phrasing seems to go, is patently ridiculous. Obviously Paul

Magrs doesn't hate Doctor Who, and saying he does is, frankly ludicrous. All the same, there's clearly something to square away about what he's doing with this book and, more specifically, about why he's opted to do it with the Pertwee era.

The answer hinges on what we've just seen about David Bowie and glam rock, and about two parts of that in particular: the focus on incongruent spectacle and the linking of the glam aesthetic to gay culture. We'll deal with the former first. Broadly speaking – and really, broadly is the only way to speak about the topic – what we're talking about when we talk about the incongruent spectacle of glam rock is postmodernism. Attempts to define postmodernism are usually comically doomed, but generally speaking it involves taking signifiers out of their context while trusting them to function anyway. So, for instance, David Bowie takes the signifiers of '50s rock and roll and of space aliens, puts them together when they don't actually go together, and then creates something new because two incongruent images are cut off from their normal contexts and forced to do something new. This is the basic logic behind the "Yeti-in-the-loo" theory of what makes good Doctor Who. What ostensibly makes that image is that the Yeti doesn't belong in the loo – they're two wildly different contexts functioning simultaneously and interestingly.

Which brings us to the second issue – gay culture. This is a somewhat trickier issue, in no small part because, as with most issues regarding minority groups, I'm not a member of the group in question and always wary of speaking for them. All of which said . . . imagine, if you will, that you were part of a group of people who were largely and systematically oppressed, to the point where the very fact that you belonged to that group meant you were a criminal. Now imagine that you had a pressing desire to identify other members of your group and identify yourself to other members of this group while keeping your membership a secret from the larger world. What you are looking for, in other words, is a way of hiding in plain sight – a set of traits that look innocuous to anyone who doesn't know what to look for, but that identifies you to those that do.

This process is the basic substance of the closet, and it is essential to understanding gay culture as a historical phenomenon. (These days increased, though clearly not total, acceptance of homosexuality in the US and UK make things more complex, but this is a very recent development.) I talked in the Bowie entry about the way in which ostentatious performance is a marker of gay culture – this is why. Because gay culture is designed to work around the closet. But the issue goes far deeper. The entire link between the arts and gay culture comes down to the fact that the arts, particularly in the UK, were somewhere homosexuals could work semi-openly. Even today it's one of the easiest places to be out of the closet – hence Derek Jacobi, Ian McKellen, and Simon Callow. Likewise, the knowing embrace of the over the top performativity that we usually describe as "camp" worked very effectively as a shibboleth in gay culture, because the act of embracing the obviously ludicrous is in a fundamental sense similar to the act of creating a public persona that simultaneously preserves your secret to the general public and reveals it to the right people. (Likewise, the embrace of over the top hedonism within gay spaces amounts to little more than casting off the bits of the performance that are "normal" – i.e. abandoning the closeted bits. Or, more pointedly, it amounts to throwing the performance back in the face of the people who make it necessary.)

So there are two things to note here. One is fairly obvious – postmodernism and gay culture are natural allies, because the act of making a symbol work in the wrong context is exactly how what I just described works. The second is less obvious to anyone without a passing familiarity with gay culture. One aspect of how the closet works is a careful relationship with the effeminate. I don't want to digress into a massive tangent about drag within a post that's not actually about drag in any direct or meaningful way, but it shouldn't be a terribly controversial observation that within gay culture, women who look like drag queens have obvious social utility. Being a fan of Cher or Bette Midler or, to reference a more old-fashioned icon, Carmen

Miranda is yet another way of covertly signaling your identity. So there's a band of women who serve as gay icons. One result of that is the social institution of (and for anyone who has never heard this term before, I should offer the reassurance that it is, in fact, the standard term) fag hags – women who largely hang around with gay men and are accepted as part of gay male culture. (This is also where it is necessary to make a brief tangent and note that while lesbian culture is not a completely different kettle of fish, the last few paragraphs have referred to gay male culture, and cannot just be applied blindly to lesbian culture.)

So, tacking back to *Verdigris*, there are two things we should say. The first is that the willingness to remove standard tropes of Pertwee-era Doctor Who from their narrative context and comment on them directly is straight-up postmodernism. The second is that the key to understanding Iris Wildthyme and why anyone thinks she's funny is that she is an archetypal fag hag. And the entire book works because of these two facts.

The many moments in the book in which it pokes fun at Doctor Who have one basic thing in common: all of them are jokes in which the fact that Doctor Who is just a TV show is acknowledged. And the book does this even when it's having fun in ways that don't involve poking fun at the show. For instance, Iris at one point comments that "without me here, [the Doctor] might perhaps be having a quiet week; a restful, forgettable week of holiday." In other words, Iris explicitly remarks on the fact that the book is "giving him extra interesting times" by filling in the week gap between two episodes. She is, in other words, clearly aware that she's interacting with something that works like a television show.

Other jokes are more subtle. At another point, the Master (or, rather, Verdigris pretending to be the Master, though we don't know this yet, since the book maintains the illusion even in its third-person narration) is described as having "stood by the gleaming chrome mirror beside the teleportation tubes and gazed into his own eyes, telling himself that he was the Master, he was the Master and he must bow down before his own magnificent will." But even this isn't just a joke about how rubbish the Master is. Rather, it's a joke about the basic absurdity of showing the morning ritual of a character that is built only to leer, hypnotize people, and create absurd schemes. The joke is that the Master doesn't make sense in such a mundane and real-world setting as getting out of bed in the morning.

So the central concept of the book is that none of the characters (save, partially, for Iris) understand that they're actually just characters in a television program as opposed to real people. Indeed, at one point, in what seems to be the most misunderstood bit in the book, the alien invaders admit that they made a mistake and confused fictional characters for real ones, and further admit that they invented postmodernism in the first place to try to cover up their mistake and successfully infiltrate the planet anyway. And both the Doctor and Iris proceed to criticize postmodernism, the Doctor describing it as "an epistemological quandary that will leave them stymied and perplexed for a century or more," while Iris accuses them of having "turned Earth into a vapid, smugly self-referential abortion of a world."

But this cannot be reasonably taken as Magrs criticizing postmodernism. Indeed, the Doctor calls Iris out for hypocrisy and notes that she's postmodern herself in the very next line. ("I'd rather have a culture with integrity . . . one that had nice, unreconstructed grand narratives," she says. "No you wouldn't," the Doctor replies, "You like everything to be as fickle and trivial as you are.") Again, to view this as just a critique of the concept misses the actual joke, which is that the Doctor doesn't like postmodernism even though he's stuck in a postmodern novel at the moment. The Doctor, in other words, doesn't understand his own situation. But equally crucially, Iris – being a character who is intimately familiar with postmodernism by definition – understands the real nature of the world she inhabits, or, more accurately, the unreal nature of it.

Once this is understood, we can finally turn to the actual plot of *Verdigris*, in which, in a bid to end the Doctor's exile (i.e. change the format of the show), Verdigris attacks the Doctor with thinly veiled parodies of *Star Trek* and *The Tomorrow People*. (*The Tomorrow People* actually post-dates the 1972 setting of this book, but it's what ITV tried to compete against Doctor Who with after abandoning *Ace of Wands*.) So the Doctor is overtly under attack from Doctor Who's nearest television rivals. The central tension, then, is establishing why Doctor Who is better than its rivals.

The answer, which is tacitly given by Iris, amounts to the fact that even when you treat Doctor Who as just a cheap sci-fi series with unconvincing monsters, cardboard cutout characters, and a really silly set of villains, there is still some essential genius in the premise that cannot quite be reduced out. The show, in other words, is still fun, just as the book is. The book demonstrates that you can still have fun with the tropes of the Pertwee era even while systematically acknowledging how silly they all are. And that's enormously compelling on its own merits. To go back and celebrate the Pertwee era not despite its faults but because of them, and more importantly, to do so in 2000, a year that posed a fundamental challenge to the entire idea of science fiction, is a big deal and a genuine endorsement of the era.

But on top of that, we have the implications of Iris: the fact that the specific way in which the Pertwee era is enjoyed is explicitly one that comes from gay culture. Something we've talked about in passing a few times is that UK Doctor Who fandom has, historically, had a disproportionate number of gay men in it. More importantly, this isn't just trivia about fans. It's something that's had massive impact on the series itself, most obviously in the fact that it was brought back in 2005 by someone who was previously best known as the creator of *Queer as Folk*. And in a lot of ways the Pertwee era is the point where the seeds of that fandom are planted, because the glam aesthetic that is so influential on the show under Barry Letts is also fundamentally intertwined with gay culture.

And so as much as *Verdigris* is a celebration of the show's quality, it is also unmistakably a book about laying claim to the show. It's a great show, but it's great in part because it's so compatible with the aesthetics of gay culture. This obviously doesn't mean the show is just for gay people, but it is a claim that it is for gay people in a real, unique, and special way. And there's really no point in the show's history from Season Ten onwards where the show's specific and unique intersections with gay culture stop being relevant.

Finally, a stray moment of squaring away continuity. Apparently the consensus on this book is that it takes place between *The Time Monster* and *The Three Doctors*. And while I agree that the ending does lead into *The Three Doctors*, there's also a clear time jump between the rest of the narrative and the ending. More to the point, however, every chronology that places it after *The Time Monster* ends up inventing an excuse about why the book acknowledges *The Sea Devils* as having happened, but explicitly says that *The Curse of Peladon* hasn't.

The obvious answer, given the book's overt metatextuality, is that the tangle is a reference to the fact that *The Sea Devils* and *The Curse of Peladon* are the first two Doctor Who stories transmitted out of order. In fact *Verdigris* takes place in the production gap between the two stories, i.e. after *The Sea Devils* and prior to *The Curse of Peladon*. Which also explains why Iris is filling a week with adventures instead of six months (the gap between the transmission of *The Time Monster* and *The Three Doctors*).

What that doesn't explain is why I put this chapter between *The Time Monster* and *The Three Doctors*. That's because that actually is a continuity error. So there.

This Point of Singularity (*The Three Doctors*)

It's 1807. Major hit songs of the year include Ludwig van Beethoven's Mass in C, the ballet *Hélène and Paris*, the operas *Joseph* and *La Vestale*, and Thomas Moore's publication of *Irish Melodies*. While in non-musical news, Napoleon makes an attack on Russia, Aaron Burr is acquitted of conspiracy, the England/Argentina soccer rivalry has a pre-season friendly as Britain mounts a disastrous attack on Buenos Aires, and Robert Fulton launches his first American steamboat.

While in London, William Blake abandons *The Four Zoas*, his masterpiece, or at least, what should have been it. Intended as the culmination to a lengthy series of what are now described as his "mythological works," the piece was never finished to Blake's satisfaction, although parts of it were recycled into *Jerusalem*, one of his two last great mythological pieces (the other being *Milton, A Poem*, whose introduction contains the other "Jerusalem," i.e. the popular Anglican hymn beginning "And did those feet in ancient times").

Fingers stained with ink and the caustic acids of his relief etchings, Blake stares with an unfathomable eye at angels, gods, and demons. A visionary in every sense of the word, he sees within the festering wounds of industry the promise of salvation. In every blade of grass within a pastoral landscape he can see the arc of man's fall. This unbound, incommensurable vision defies all efforts to capture its totality. Let us take a single corner of it – a tiny sliver. The mad king Nebuchadnezzar, bestial ruler of Babylon, cast down into insanity for his hubris, speaks:

> Without me, there would be no time travel. You and our fellow Time Lords would still be locked in your own time, as puny as those creatures you now so graciously protect. Many thousands of years ago, when I left our planet, all this was then a star until I arranged its detonation. It was an honour, or so I thought then. I was to be the

> one to find and create the power source that would give us mastery over time itself. I was sacrificed to that supernova. I generated those forces, and for what? To be blown out of existence into this black hole of antimatter? My brothers became Time Lords, but I was abandoned and forgotten!

While in his universe of antimatter, dark Urizen prepares. A lost shard of holy Albion, fallen and abject, Urizen spins law . . . gives shape and form to the universe. A solar engineer, Urizen collapses a sun into a cosmological abscess, a crack in the skin of the world. He does not create law so much as extrude it from his being, forming his net of continuity and myth purely by being. Because he exists, so too must certainty. His gravity is inescapable. Here begins the long history of Rassilon and the Other, of secret centuries-old plots to destroy Skaro and Looms. Here is the line between question and answer, between mystery and revelation.

He is called a fallen Time Lord, but this is wrong, implying as it does that there is some unified concept of "Time Lords" prior to his fall. Rather it is his fall, the schism of some primordial entity, that creates these categories in the first place. Time Lords and Urizen are both fragmentations of some greater being – each the emanation of the other. Urizen is that which is not Time Lord, that which can never be Time Lord. Time Lords are that which is not Urizen, and that which can never be Urizen.

Aware of this gulf, aware of that space his laws cannot encircle, Urizen casts out his emanation as he cast out Ahania, leaves them to wither, draining their very energy, unmaking them. This is not unification, not the reclamation of Edenic totality, but something else, a further splitting and division towards mere corpuscles suspended in ether, a world of single objects in static, known forms.

> Dire shriek'd his invisible Lust

> Deep groan'd Urizen! stretching his awful hand
> Ahania (so name his parted soul)
> He siez'd on his mountains of jealousy.
> He groand anguishd & called her Sin,
> Kissing her and weeping over her;
> Then hid her in darkness in silence;
> Jealous tho' she was invisible.

If we are to understand the Time Lords as the protectors of the arc of history, then we must understand them first as agents of change. When the Doctor declares that being without becoming is an ontological absurdity, he is firmly within the intellectual tradition of existentialism. To be said to exist, a thing must exist within time; it must be subject to change. Central to the idea of a "thing" is the prospect of its encounter and interaction with other things, the prospect of it shaping and being shaped.

Are the Time Lords themselves subject to this process? They must be – to exist they must be changed, must alter continuously. Nothing can exist as a constant, as a defined thing. The Time Lords must constantly change and adapt. Unless we take the corollary of the Doctor's maxim. Being without becoming is an absurdity. But what of becoming without being? A truly unceasing change, so rapid and complete that it never settles, never takes form. The raw power of transformation. This constant change is the shape of eternity. A unity comprised not of form but of chaos. Time becomes not the ordered progression of causal events but a cascade, a tide eroding away the very foundations of being.

At once, Albion casts out its emanation Jerusalem as feet walk among England's mountains green. Omega's black hole drains Ahania's energy, not consuming his emanation but denying it, rejecting it as Sin. While at the same time, in a junkyard on Totters Lane, an old man and his granddaughter hide within their magical box. In her garden, Amy Pond spends twelve years waiting five minutes, as Edward Young scrawls his thoughts on death and immortality in the margins of Blake's great, unfinished epic. Giles Deleuze and his closest working colleague, Félix Guattari, write on the rhizome:

> At the same time, something else entirely is going on: not imitation at all but a capture of code, surplus value of code, an increase in valence, a veritable becoming, a becoming-wasp of the orchid and a becoming-orchid of the wasp. Each of these becomings bring about the deterritorialization of one term and the reterritorialization of the other; the two becomings interlink and form relays in a circulation of intensities pushing the deterritorialization ever further. There is neither imitation nor resemblance, only an exploding of two heterogeneous series on the line of flight composed by a common rhizome that can no longer be attributed or subjugated by anything signifying.

The first episode of *The Three Doctors* is one of the great first episodes of Doctor Who's history. With alarming and methodical speed the episode transforms itself, performing the act of becoming that proves so central to its larger existence. It starts as a near mirror for *Spearhead from Space*, with a comedy yokel affected by objects falling from the sky. Then, as its twenty-five minutes unfold, the fixed tropes that provide the framework of the Pertwee era begin to be torn away. The enemy pre-empts UNIT's investigations, making a beeline for UNIT HQ until it is under siege from strange and bulbous horrors. The Doctor is given no time to investigate, is in fact given only a few clues before he becomes the very target of the threat. This threat is unlike any other. It breaks the rules. In a panic, he calls the Time Lords, begging them for help.

But they too are victims of this Urizenic siege, driven to a desperation the likes of which we had thought impossible. Their power almost vanished into Omega's abscess, drained by singularity, they are forced to abandon the First Law of Time itself, to allow the Doctor to cross his own time stream.

Let us reflect briefly upon the implications of this law. On the surface, it is a strange thing to have as the first law of time – more important, it seems, even than their long-standing opposition to meddling. The only thing it seems remotely commensurable with is the Doctor's old admonition that you can't rewrite history, not one line. The adamance of this plea to Barbara is the only other thing that seems anything like a sacred law of time, and even it, we now learn, is not the first. The first is that you cannot meet yourself. Why might this be?

The obvious answer is that it is a special and even worse case of rewriting history. So what is wrong with rewriting history? Let us quote David Whitaker, who did, after all, oversee that law:

> The basis of time traveling is that all things that happen are fixed and unalterable, otherwise of course the whole structure of existence would be thrown into unutterable confusion and the purpose of life itself would be destroyed. Doctor Who is an observer. What we are concerned with is that history, like justice, is not only done but can be seen to be done.

But as we know, time can be rewritten. Why can time be rewritten where history cannot? The standard answer given in the series – that there are fixed points in time – is strange for a series that has previously declared that a fixed point in time – a fact, if you will – is anathema to the Time Lords. Let us attempt a different explanation – one offered by William Whyte: the fundamental bound on changing history has little to do with the stability of the universe and everything to do with the stability of the self. One cannot alter the components of one's self – the stories and memories that create the unity of "I."

The reasoning is clear: in a world defined as formless chaos, the stability of the I, the observer, the visionary, is the only source of being available. The I, by dint of seeing, creates being out of becoming, literally altering the world into vision. To change it is to change the entire universe.

> And to allay his freezing age
> The poor man takes her in his arms:
> The cottage fades before his sight,
> The garden and its lovely charms;
> The guests are scattered through the land
> (For the eye altering, alters all);
> The senses roll themselves in fear,
> And the flat earth becomes a ball,

The First Law of Time thus abandoned, the Doctor, himself an I altering, is brought forward to meet himselves. But he is trapped in a time eddy. This is a strange concept – a point in which time moves counter to its own arrow, becomes circular, a whirlpool in time. This is fitting. It is, after all, not the first time in which we have seen Hartnell's Doctor in these circumstances. In Totters Lane, before Ian and Barbara fell out of the world and into his now, he existed separate from both past and future, a man without history who has not yet become.

But this is not the first strange hole we have seen. Urizen himself dwells within a whirlpool in space, a point where space itself swirls in on itself. The Doctor's time eddy and Urizen's black hole are inexorably linked, two sides of the same coin, at once equivalent and separate. Thus we must conclude that the Doctor and Urizen are also linked – that the Doctor is, just as much as Urizen, a cast off emanation of some greater eternity. (In an earlier draft this was explicit, with Urizen reduced to his first three letters: OHM, which, when read upside-down and backwards, spells LOS.)

These are not fixed oppositions, not simple points of defined balance. The Time Lords are not the opposite of Urizen, Urizen is not the opposite of the Doctor, the Doctor is not opposite himself. They are divisions, a fragmentation of a larger concept, each complete reflections of the whole, fractal consciousnesses within the radiant whole. As Donald Ault says of Blake:

> The spectator's desire to complete the drawing behind the text in these examples parallels the reader's urge to find an ur-narrative behind the poem. On the physical page, of course, there is literally nothing behind the verbal text, for the rectangular space and the inscribed words constitute their own complete visual field. Likewise there is literally no primordial story behind the surface details of the poem's narrative. The presumption of such a story dissolves under close scrutiny of particulars.

Without the possibility of fixed eternity, with no prospect of single vision to encompass the whole of *The Three Doctors*, we are forced to a new approach. Our understanding of the story must become polymorphic, incommensurable, perhaps even a bit mad. The entry must be allowed to shift beneath us. The figure of Omega, his mask a seeming reflection of Blake's vision of Nebuchadnezzar, must also become Urizen, one of Blake's *Four Zoas*, the aspects of eternal Albion. Urizen is reason itself, accompanied by Tharmas, instinct and strength, Luvah, passion and love, and Urthona, inspiration and imagination. The Time Lords must also be Ahania, the emanation of Urizen. And thus Omega must be Ahania, and the Time Lords Urizen, trapped in their laws, bound helplessly by singular vision.

The essay will not cohere. It will not make sense as such. It will make something else – vision, perhaps, or understanding. Or perhaps more accurately, it will make too many senses. It will be a textual labyrinth – one to get lost in and to puzzle over. The essay must be an act of becoming. But what shall it become?

> The Emanation is the visible and spatial aspect of a four-fold division of the individual into Humanity, Spectre, Emanation, and Shadow (see Albion and Eternal(s)). The emanations create the space in which Eternals meet, making their union possible, and the emanation is the visible embodiment of the Eternal, making it possible for the Eternal to interact with others. The Emanation is usually the feminine aspect of the androgynous Eternal. The separation of the Emanation from the individual marks a stage in the fall and means that the individual can no longer meet with others in Eternity. Thus when Enitharmon separates from Los and takes on a separate female form, the individual is divided internally and also divided from Eternity, being no longer able to meet other Eternals. The failure of the parts to recognize their divided state indicates their fallen nature.

At the center of things, Los, fallen form of Urthona, hammers forth the heartbeat of the world. Not the arc of change but its engine, he is the force that creates; that first great magick trick, the creation of something from nothing. The throbbing mass of ideas, churning wildly, seems to reverberate endlessly. In Lambeth, William Blake sees each strike as flashes of the world of angels and gods that lives behind his eyes. In London it is David Whitaker tracing the path of a bead of mercury across a sheet of glass seven years long. In Bristol, Bob Baker and David Martin swat desperately at the hydra of ideas the hammer beat brings forth. In Newtown, I nurse a cup of tea and work to tame this impossible tangle of ideas, or perhaps to be tamed by it. In Florida, my editor curses me for dumping this mess on her lap.

Who is this figure at the center of things? Peer through the raging fire and he is as invisible and impossible as the rest. One moment he seems an old man in a strange chair peering awkwardly at cue cards, the next a dashing dandy, Beau Brummel as action hero. Blink and through the smoke you can just make out some strange hobo, a pied piper clad in innumerable secrets. And in the shadows cast flicker countless other forms – a trailing scarf, a Cricketeer, an umbrella, a bow tie, and others that you know with eyes that have not yet seen, but someday will. Try to even see how many forms he has and you will fail, inevitably losing count at thirteen. Instead, pick one:

> When you're a character actor you're having to make decisions all the time, and that's a question of gaining confidence in the part you play, and that takes the time, really. Whereas with Doctor Who, the three years of it, you weren't learning lines, really, you were learning thoughts.

Patrick Troughton, whose acting I have praised before, is of course amazing. The most mercurial of actors, he, as ever, works his way through the narrative like a magic spell. His first scene is awkward. Troughton is impeccably gracious as an actor – a trait Pertwee, if we're being honest, never displayed. The two of them got on poorly at first, due to Troughton's tendency to improvise his lines during rehearsal, playing his way through the tone of a scene and learning that, then wrapping his dialogue around his already selected tone. Pertwee was put off by this, and a bit of a tiff ensued. Troughton, with astonishing deference, played it Pertwee's way, to the detriment of his performance (as, perhaps, intended – see also Pertwee's flagrant attempt to make sure Richard Franklin knew who the star is in his first appearance. For all that Pertwee was a gracious and fun colleague to many of his co-stars, he could also be depressingly catty).

But in the handful of scenes in the second episode of this story where he's with Nicholas Courtney and John Levene, both of whom he's worked with before, he visibly relaxes, playing, for that episode, the Doctor again instead of the "Second Doctor," the goofy comedy sidekick he invented for reunions. (Everyone gets shuffled around a bit for the reunion. Courtney, in an inspired turn, gets to play the Brigadier finally snapping, unable to believe what is going on around him, while Benton gets to be the utterly unflappable one, explaining to everyone how the "multiple Doctors" thing works.) But this moment to show himself as the Doctor allows him to assert genuine power over the narrative.

> (A moment tragically denied to Hartnell, who looks distressingly unwell on the monitor, and is visibly pausing between sentences to peer at cue cards, barely able to get through the lines, little yet add any character to them. It is of course still incredibly moving to see him and to have that connection to the very dawn of the program, but it is moving in the sense of managing to make it to the bedside of an ailing relative before they pass. Hartnell passed away just over two years after this aired of the same condition that was robbing him of his abilities in his final months on the show.)

He sneaks several moments to shine, and is central to figuring out how to defeat Omega. Pertwee's Doctor gets to figure out how to build a gizmo that will destroy Omega, but Troughton's is the one who works out how to trick Omega, and is the one to do the deed, thus providing the moral weight of the Doctors' judgment that death is the only freedom Omega can ever have. In tricking Omega, when he makes contact with himself, Troughton's Doctor turns and makes eye contact with the camera, repeating his frequent trick from his time on the series of peering out of television monitors. This trick suggests that the Doctor controls the medium of television itself – a suggestion we have probed the implications of before. (This is fitting, given that one of the monsters in this story is visually processed so that, despite being made with a physical prop, it looks like a video effect instead of like a physical object.) Here, then, the Master of the Land of Fiction himself returns – Los in his most powerful form.

> I loved Patrick Troughton, he was smashing to be with, and the whole thing was a real kick. Mind you, concerning the mini-skirt I wore in that story, there's a scene where you can see my knickers! Most improper for children's viewing time, don't you think?

Enitharmon, the emanation of Los, deserves to be talked about more, and this is in many ways the place to do it, because once she's paired with Patrick Troughton we finally get to see how her character works. Enitharmon may have originated in the mould of wholly consistent characters stuck in absurd worlds – beings without becoming stuck in situations of pure becoming, if you will – but she has steadily progressed. All of this is consistent – think back to the moment where she is caught by Urizen in *Terror of the Autons*. The way she rises up with a sheepish look on her face while being captured by someone she knows to be terrifying and evil is sheer brilliance. Enitharmon simply refuses to play by the rules of the narrative, and does so not out of rebelliousness but out of a sort of sheer plucky creativity.

Since then she has developed the process to an art, cheating the narrative regularly without ever seeming aware of it. In this regard, she is most like Los's Troughton, who was also not so much a character as a force of nature within the narrative. This is an essential realization. Los's Pertwee is in many ways the least whimsical of his forms. Or, to be blunter, he lacks mercury. Paired with Enitharmon, who is as steeped in mercury as Troughton, there is a completion. It is very hard to argue that Pertwee is a superior actor to Troughton – in fact, I'd go so far as to say that it is very easy to argue that Troughton is much superior to Pertwee. His tonal readings make the blows of his hammer echo through the entire scene, shaking the very foundations of the story. Pertwee is exciting and charming, but he never inhabits the story itself like Troughton does. Troughton controls the entire story with nothing so much as mad anarchy. Pertwee tries to anchor the entire story with the power of his charm and watches helplessly as bits of it always float away.

But on the other hand, it is equally hard to argue that the Pertwee/Enitharmon team is anything less than head and shoulders beyond any Los/Companion pairing to date. Even Los's Hartnell paired with Ian and Barbara did not quite sparkle like the two of them. Los's Pertwee and Enitharmon are perfect compliments to one another – the very model of the double act. She is the junior partner, and from that low position turns out to have more control over the narrative than anyone else.

Enitharmon, of course, is a complex and libidinous creature. She is on the one hand the Emanation of Los. But her name contains within it the name of another Zoa, Tharmas, who represents sensation. His emanation, in turn, is Enion, who represents sexual urges. It is their successful union which produces Enitharmon, who is herself the sexual counterpart for Los as well as, as mentioned, his Emanation. (Such multiplicities are common in Blake, and central to this essay.)

Fitting, then, that Enitharmon should be the one to pose nude with the Doctors' Shadow. This figure is the darkest part of Blake's fourfold division of man, the ashes left by dead desire festering away. Ahania, originally Urizen's emanation, becomes a shadow when she is cast out and denied by him, just as Omega becomes a shadow as he separates irrevocably from the Time Lords.

From Enitharmon and Los's union comes Orc: the spirit of revolution. At first he is embodied by Blake, but in time, as Blake grew skeptical of the possibility of charismatic revolutionary leaders, and so Orc pulled within, made an aspect of the soul.

> The terror answerd: I am Orc, wreath'd round
>   the accursed tree:
> The times are ended; shadows pass the morning
>   gins to break;
> The fiery joy, that Urizen perverted to ten
>   commands,
> What night he led the starry hosts thro' the wide
>   wilderness:
> That stony law I stamp to dust: and scatter
>   religion abroad
> To the four winds as a torn book, & none shall
>   gather the leaves;
> But they shall rot on desart sands, & consume
>   in bottomless deeps;
> To make the desarts blossom, & the deeps
>   shrink to their fountains,
> And to renew the fiery joy, and burst the stony
>   roof.
> That pale religious letchery, seeking Virginity,
> May find it in a harlot, and in coarse-clad
>   honesty
> The undefil'd tho' ravish'd in her cradle night
>   and morn:
> For every thing that lives is holy, life delights in
>   life;
> Because the soul of sweet delight can never be
>   defil'd.
> Fires inwrap the earthly globe, yet man is not
>   consumd;
> Amidst the lustful fires he walks: his feet
>   become like brass,
> His knees and thighs like silver, & his breast and
>   head like gold.

What, then, do we make of the ending, particularly the somewhat strained, long scene in which every single supporting character, whether we care about them or not, gets a farewell before stepping through the singularity to be restored to the world? The first thing to notice in this scene is that although the characters enter the singularity one by one, they seem to reappear on Earth simultaneously. Clearly, then, the singularity is not simply functioning as a portal.

We also know that the singularity is at the center of Omega's constructed reality – the tool by which he turns his will into things. (Just as Enitharmon is both Tharmas's daughter and Urthona's emanation, Urizen is also here the Doctor's Shadow.) We also know that the Master of the Land of Fiction is standing right by the singularity, and is moments from asserting his control over the story via his signature gesture of looking out of the television.

So into the singularity are put the elements of Doctor Who. Even the Doctor himself is symbolically there, since the singularity and the time eddy are aspects of the same thing. And then, by consuming their own shadow, Los turns Urizen's necrotic tangle of Law into Eternity.

For one moment, Jerusalem stands within Albion again. And from this moment Los builds Golgonooza, while the Doctors rebuild Doctor Who, or perhaps build it for the first time. In one moment, all of what the show was and ever has been coexists, overlapped, chaotic, contradictory, but there.

> Where is the Covenant of Priam, the Moral Virtues of the Heathen
> Where is the Tree of Good & Evil that rooted beneath the cruel heel
> Of Albions Spectre the Patriarch Druid! where are all his Human Sacrifices
> For Sin in War & in the Druid Temples of the Accuser of Sin: beneath
> The Oak Groves of Albion that coverd the whole Earth beneath his Spectre
> Where are the Kingdoms of the World & all their glory that grew on Desolation

> The Fruit of Albions Poverty Tree when the
> Triple Headed Gog-Magog Giant
> Of Albion Taxed the Nations into Desolation &
> then gave the Spectrous Oath
> Such is the Cry from all the Earth from the
> Living Creatures of the Earth
> And from the great City of Golgonooza in the
> Shadowy Generation
> And from the Thirty-two Nations of the Earth
> among the Living Creatures
> All Human Forms identified even Tree Metal
> Earth & Stone. all
> Human Forms identified, living going forth &
> returning wearied
> Into the Planetary lives of Years Months Days
> & Hours reposing
> And then Awaking into his Bosom in the Life
> of Immortality.
> And I heard the Name of their Emanations they
> are named Jerusalem

Patrick Troughton oozes like mercury around alchemic diagrams, while Roger Delgado leers maniacally. In Totters Lane, William Hartnell bundles Dodo through the doors of the TARDIS. Vicki and Jo skip arm in arm down the streets of Skaro looking at shopwindow dummies while fireworks mixed up by Liz Shaw and Ian Chesterton explode across the sky where Steven Taylor draws a Blue Peter Badge in contrails from the Planet Mondas. Jon Pertwee captains the HMS *Bessie*, reminiscing about Polly with fellow sailor Ben Jackson. For her part, Polly is slipping through the UNIT tearoom planting retcon as part of her new gig with *Torchwood*. Staying carefully on the other side of the room for fear of offending her ex-husband, Sara Kingdom chats with a familiar looking Brigadier like they're brothers, while Barbara cradles Katarina sapphically. Victoria has odd dreams of Sergeant Benton chasing her through the London Underground, while Mike Yates and Jamie

McCrimmon make like Izlyr and Sorg. And in the sky the *Wheel in Space* spins like a circle of destiny, as Zoe Heriot calculates the precise arcs of history.

There is no understanding this moment. No comprehension. Singularity itself is destroyed in favor of eternity. An unfinished show, an eternal cliffhanger, an act of eternal becoming. Never perfect, but in turn never done, Los's hammer driving forward in its heart.

And then she rises, Eternity herself in brilliant blue, at last restored to us, ready to take us anywhere. All of space and time. (But where does Eternity draw her name from?) Everything that ever happened or ever will. The hammer strikes. The Doctor fiddles the coordinates. There is a wheezing, groaning sound. Turn on the scanner, see where we are.

> And yet someone is absent. Some fundamental loss, a problem at the heart of the narrative, the sting in the trap that necessitates fall and separation. A fact of the series creation that is at once central to its existence but incommensurable with it, unspeakable within it. Doctor Who's own emanation: the problem of Catherine.

Between *The Time Monster* and *The Three Doctors*, Jane Fonda famously made her trip to North Vietnam, earning the moniker Hanoi Jain. Bloody Friday erupted in Northern Ireland as the IRA killed nine and seriously injures a hundred and thirty more in a series of twenty-two bombings in Belfast. Then came Bloody Monday, with three car bombs. In Munich, terrorists murdered eleven Israeli athletes at the Olympic Games, while Bobby Fischer became the first American world-chess champion. A race riot broke out on the USS *Kitty Hawk*. Richard Nixon stormed his way to re-election, and the first version of Pong was released. The last Apollo mission flew to the moon.

While during the story, the UK finally properly joins the ECC, and *Last of the Summer Wine*, the world's longest running comedy series, begins. As the final episode airs, Richard Nixon is inaugurated for his second term.

While in music, Jimmy Osmond's "Long Haired Lover From Liverpool" is at number one, and remains so for all four weeks of the story. This has the tragic result of blocking David Bowie's "Jean Genie" from the number one slot, as well as the even more tragic result of having millions of innocent people hearing a nine-year-old boy promising to be their long-haired lover from Liverpool and to do anything they say. Less openly pedophiliac songs in the top ten include T. Rex's "Solid Gold Easy Action," The Sweet's "Blockbuster," Carly Simon's song about me, Elvis Presley's "Always On My Mind," John Lennon's "Happy Xmas/War is Over," and Elton John's "Crocodile Rock."

It's December 30, 1972.

The Secret of Alchemy ("This Point of Singularity [*The Three Doctors*]")

Guest essay kindly provided by Anna Wiggins.

When Phil asked me to write a guest essay explaining his essay about The Three Doctors, I said yes. I have neither read Blake nor seen The Three Doctors, so I am the obvious choice. Bad jokes aside, I do have one thing on my side - I know a bit about magic.

"This Point of Singularity" is, of course, a magical working, and it should be understood in that context. That Phil is an alchemist comes as no surprise to the readers of these books. This, though, is the first actual spell that Phil works into the text (except for the lost introduction, about which more later, and the entire project, which is a spell on much larger terms, also about which more later). It will not be the last.

So what is the purpose of this spell? But that's the wrong question. Or, at least, not the first question. This is better: What is the purpose of TARDIS Eruditorum? We're only three books in, but thanks to an altogether different kind of magic, we can already see a lot further ahead than the printed word can show. So here, as a bonus, I am going to reveal the purpose of the project. The magic behind the text. The secret of alchemy.

Of course, we already know the secret of alchemy. From our place in the future, we can recite it like a litany: the secret of alchemy is material social progress. But that is not the only secret that alchemy holds. Here is another: words can change the world. Words can be magic.

TARDIS Eruditorum is an attempt to change the world. This is the definition of a work of magic. 'Magic' is something of a loaded term, so let's clarify: we're talking about magic as practiced in the Western Occult tradition, a term sometimes used synonymously with alchemy (although I think alchemy is best understood as one particular sort of magic). A decent working definition of magic might be 'an attempt to change the world through the exertion of will'.

The observant reader may have noticed that this definition includes a large amount of things that no one in the modern world really thinks of as 'magic', such as starting a business or publishing a book. This is not an accident, and these actions are considered magic in the occult tradition right alongside the alchemical working of manipulating symbols in order to sympathetically manipulate the things they signify. Of course, occultism does have a strong focus on symbol and signification, so words (which are, after all, just symbols that can be manipulated) are more likely to be described in terms of magic than, say, trading on the stock market (although see Neal Stephenson's Baroque Cycle for a discussion of the magical undercurrents in the latter, and its ability to turn lead into gold).

So our next question must be: what is TARDIS Eruditorum trying to change? Which brings us back around to "This Point of Singularity."

Pataphor, as a rhetorical technique, treats two things that possess some connection as functionally interchangeable. This is the central trick of "This Point of Singularity": at various points in the essay, typically at the block quotes, Phil switches around the names he uses to refer to things, drawing new parallels between concepts from Doctor Who and ones from Blake. For instance, at one point Jo Grant and the Blakean character of Enitharmon are treated as the same thing.

More broadly, of course, Phil is blurring Doctor Who and Blake's prophetic works at large. This suggests that there is some inherent link between them, and, of course, there is: they are both mythologies. More definitions are required. A mythology is a framework for truth that is based around iconic signifiers. The ageless wanderer in a blue box who travels time and space, companion(s) at his side. Albion divided. By the principle of pataphor, these can be the same mythology. But pataphor blurs the lines, making the parallels numerous and contradictory. Collapsing the ideaspaces into a mythological singularity.

The process is deliberate. The two endpoints of the essay are Blake and Doctor Who, and each one is coherent, straightforward - as you approach the midpoint from either direction, the two blend together and the concepts lose coherence and distinction. As you work outward from the center, the mythological potential coheres into something stable.

Why Blake? What is special about the man or his work that makes Blake and The Four Zoas the best choice for this spell? Even with just the glimpses of Blake we have here, we can find an answer. Blake's characters are complex, interconnected in seemingly contradictory ways. Change the angle, the context, the metaphor, and you have a new set of interrelations, variations on a theme. A new story. Each of Blake's prophetic figures split into various emanations and shadows, splintering further into new mythological characters, each of whom have new relationships with each other and with the preceding characters. So, for instance, Albion splits into four emanations, the Zoas, one of whom, Urthona, has the fallen form of Los, whose own emanation Enitharmon is also his lover, and with whom he fathers Orc. But Orc is also the fallen form of Luvah, one of the other Zoas, and Enitharmon is the child of Tharmas, a third of the Zoas, and his fallen form of Enion. Every character, in other words, has vast interior spaces. They are, if you will, bigger on the inside. And by virtue of being bigger on the inside they lend themselves to pataphor.

Doctor Who possesses a similar structure. The same characters are dropped into different stories, new contexts. And the TARDIS, of course, is a pataphor for television and for the vast inner spaces created by stories. And in both cases, these new worlds are grounded in an iconic imagery that is fundamentally British - the direct invocation of Albion on the one hand, and the ubiquitous blue police box on the other. Both works are fractal, full of interior worlds to explore.

So this spell is attempting to forge a connection between Blake's Mythology and Doctor Who, using the commonality of their inner dimensions. To turn them into the same thing, viewed from different angles. Two instances of the same abstract form. But why do this? What purpose is served?

The answer to that, and to the purpose of TARDIS Eruditorum as a whole, lies in the original introduction to the project, lost to these books but preserved by light and fire:

And so as long as there are stories, there are Doctor Who stories. When the stars go out and the universe freezes, around the last fire on the last world, there will still be Doctor Who stories to tell. And when we are done telling them, at long and final last, in the distance will be a strange wheezing, groaning sound. And out will step an impossible man, and he will save the day.

I believe this. I believe this because to disbelieve this is to disbelieve that stories have power. To disbelieve this is to disbelieve that there is hope. To disbelieve this is to believe that there is such a thing as being alone. I believe this because disbelieving it is too awful to imagine.

On the surface, this project is posited as a chronicle of the story of Doctor Who, its impact on the world, and the world's impact on it. Beneath that, though, is the magic. To ensure the immortality of Doctor Who by ensuring its status as mythology. By making every story into a Doctor Who story, every mythology isomorphic to the mythology of the TARDIS. If every story is Doctor Who, Doctor Who must, by definition, survive as long as there are people to tell stories.

And by simply putting these ideas out there, the success of the spell is essentially guaranteed. Because the easiest part of reality to manipulate with magic is ideaspace. Which is ironic, perhaps, because ideaspace is where the most durable truths exist. Our model of physics has changed repeatedly, coming closer to the truth but probably still not reaching it. The death of Hamlet, however, the iconic and mythic truths of narrative, are immutable. Even if alternate continuities are proposed, these things always happened. Ideaspace never forgets.

And so once the connection is suggested, it becomes inevitable. This is the power of words, and the reason they are rightly called magic. TARDIS Eruditorum is using that magic to transform Doctor Who from a set of stories with mythological properties to a mythology of stories. And "This Point of Singularity (The Three Doctors)," is simply the most overt part of that process.

This isn't all the magic woven by TARDIS Eruditorum, of course. But that is enough Spoilers for now.

The Outside Universe is Breaking Through (*Carnival of Monsters*)

It's January 27, 1973. The Sweet's "Blockbuster" has mercifully brought an end to this unfortunate Jimmy Osmond business, and holds number one for four weeks, marking a pleasant restoration of glam rock order. Gary Glitter, Elton John, David Bowie, and ELO all also chart. In non-musical news, Roe v. Wade is decided in the US, the US ends its involvement in Vietnam by signing the Paris Peace Accords, while in the UK *The Sunday Times* wins a court case allowing it to publish articles on thalidomide, making public what far too many people knew and were trying to cover up, which is that in addition to reducing morning sickness it led to debilitating birth defects.

While on television we have *Carnival of Monsters*. It ought go without saying that *Carnival of Monsters* is the best Pertwee story to date, is probably the best Pertwee story outright, and, perhaps more to the point, is flat-out one of the best Doctor Who stories ever. And yet somehow it does not go without saying. In fact, on the big *Doctor Who Magazine* poll, *Carnival of Monsters* inexplicably finishes behind *Inferno*, *The Daemons*, *The Silurians* and *The Sea Devils* – and those are just the stories it's completely bewildering why anyone would prefer to this as opposed to the ones where I can at least squint and pretend that there's some logic to. It's all told the tenth highest ranked Pertwee story, which, out of twenty-four stories, suggests that it is well-liked but not extraordinarily so.

And yet this was the story used for the Pertwee era in the *Five Faces of Doctor Who* repeat season. It was among the earlier DVD releases, has been rerun on television several times, and has generally acquired a reputation as the go-to Pertwee story for the general public. It's a rare case of a story that seems better regarded by non-fans than by fans. Which, given that the Pertwee era was long before Doctor Who's audience could ever be called a "fandom," is compelling in its own right.

It's worth taking a step backwards here and looking at Season Ten as a whole. Like almost all the Pertwee seasons, it consists of five stories. Unlike any of the other Pertwee seasons, fully four of these can be described as "event" stories in fannish terms. It opens with the anniversary special, closes with Jo Grant's departure, and spends two stories on an epic Dalek adventure co-starring the Master. The only other Pertwee season to have anything like this sort of focus on high concept stories that pay off the series' larger mythology is Season Eight, and that requires us to badly misread the role of the Master in that season.

More broadly, the Pertwee era is actually strangely short on primarily self-contained stories. If we take a broad view and count stories that are "events" for historical reasons – things like *The Silurians* or *The Time Warrior* that introduce recurring villains – Pertwee ends up with only four stories in his entire tenure that are definitively not event stories: *The Ambassadors of Death*, *Inferno*, *The Mutants*, and this. And save *Inferno*, that list consists entirely of stories I've claimed are underrated. Which tells us something about the taste of fans.

The non-event status of *Carnival of Monsters*, however, is more than just a reason why it's oddly overlooked by fans. It's the entire point of the story. This is the only Pertwee story to actively pursue a small scale instead of a large one. For the most part only a handful of people are ever in any peril. The bulk of this story is an old carnie arguing with some bureaucrats while the Doctor runs around inside a television. In a series that was doing threats to the entire universe last week and will be doing galactic war next story, this is astonishingly and willfully low rent. Even by the standards of the earthbound era that this story marks the first official break from this is small potatoes. There, at least, the entire planet is endangered on a regular basis. Or at least the country. Here there's a brief abstract threat to a planet, but that's about it.

But to call this a flaw in the story is to commit yourself to a deeply strange view of Doctor Who whereby its purpose is to do vast and sweeping epics. This isn't a criticism of vast and sweeping epics, which can be marvelous. But the pattern of the show in its early years mixed vast epics in with other stories. *The Aztecs* and *The Sensorites* were not huge stories about planet and universe-threatening menaces. Even into the Troughton era, stories like *Fury from the Deep*, *The Krotons*, or *The Macra Terror* are considerably smaller scale than anything in Seasons Nine or Ten other than this.

The value of these small-scale stories cannot be overstated. One thing that is frustrating about the Pertwee era has been the way in which Pertwee's Doctor is so patrician compared to many of the others, including the ones on either side of him. And part of that is because he's so often removed from humanity. This is a real problem, especially given that the challenge laid down at the start of the Pertwee era was to connect with humanity better than the psychedelic irresponsibility of Troughton's Doctor did. The fact that Pertwee's Doctor spends almost all of his time rushing around offices full of important and powerful men while the only way that working-class supporting characters are ever portrayed is as comedy yokels is genuinely troubling. Things are often better off-planet, with *Colony in Space* involving heavy engagement with a more working-class band of people and *The Mutants* interacting heavily with oppressed populations, but *The Curse of Peladon* was again about kings and ambassadors, and the remainder of Pertwee's space stories after this one are pretty far from everyday concerns. More than any other version, Pertwee's Doctor is one who spends the overwhelming majority of his time interacting with people in power.

And so for this story, the first since the basic premise of the show was restored, it's particularly important to break this cycle and show the Doctor interacting with ordinary people, if only to make sure that ordinary people remain firmly embedded in the premise of the show. In this regard, *Carnival of Monsters* is an odd inversion of the last time the TARDIS went on its first trip. After establishing its premise in *An Unearthly Child* and *100,000 BC*, the next thing the show did was go to a strange alien world and show us a truly brilliant science fiction concept in the form of the Daleks. More broadly, it introduced the basic idea of monsters. This makes sense. Having introduced two ordinary characters – Ian and Barbara – the first thing it needs to do is take them somewhere truly extraordinary. But here the show has the opposite issue – having spent fifteen stories doing huge, epic, planet-threatening stories in which the Doctor dashes around in the halls of power, the first thing the show needs to do once it has the ability to do absolutely anything is, ironically, to go for the ordinary.

What's a bit sad about all of this, as we said, is that the whole Yeti-in-the-loo premise was supposed to avoid this problem. The whole point of the earthbound format was that it was supposed to show monsters in ordinary places. Instead, it was largely, and even from its earliest moments, about showing monsters in iconic British, and more specifically English, places – Post Office Tower, Gatwick Airport, the Underground, or St. Paul's, for instance. What it has, up to now, basically never been used for is making the stores relevant to the viewer's life. Broad social relevance, sure – we've got plenty of that. But relevant in that intimate, personal way? No. That we've basically avoided, with the exception, basically, of Holmes's last story, which at least had everyday objects that were familiar to the viewer turned into homicidal plastic horrors.

This engagement with the small scale is, of course, a trademark of Robert Holmes. And so with *Carnival of Monsters* we actually get a story that thoroughly engages the viewer's life and world. Because *Carnival of Monsters* is fundamentally about the act of watching television. The entire story is a commentary on the act of passively watching spectacles and what that means. In this regard its high point has to be taken as the moment in which Jo responds in horror at the idea that anyone would be so cruel as to want to watch her get chased around by monsters, and says that anyone who does must be evil and horrible. And although Vorg gives a line about how the purpose of his entertainment is "merely to amuse," as opposed to do something serious or political, the story undercuts this actively by making the very act of watching it into an ethical issue to be commented on.

Speaking of Vorg, there's an emotional realness to the secondary characters that is truly extraordinary. Vorg is a penniless drifter trying to keep his head above water and barely managing. He doesn't know what he's doing – quite literally, as it eventually turns out he's lost the manual to his Miniscope. His major opponents are not horrible monsters but generic bureaucrats – an altogether familiar enemy. He is, in other words, a very literal working-class hero – someone trying to survive in a hostile system that is designed to benefit people other than him. That he's visually still firmly in the glitzy, glam aesthetic of Doctor Who makes the disjunct all the more intriguing.

On top of that, we have a proper, classic case of Doctor Who embracing constraints and playing with them. The entire reason this story was made was that, seeing that the rest of the season was going to be really expensive, the show needed a cheap one. And specifically, Barry Letts, who had converted Doctor Who's production method from doing one episode a week to doing two episodes simultaneously in a two-week block, wanted to try a specific method of making the show cheaper: have two sets and two groups of actors who would never actually interact with each other. Hence Ian Marter and company are on the SS *Bernice* while Vorg and the rest are on Inter Minor; Letts could shoot one set of actors in the first two week block, then the other in the second and, in the process, get away with paying all the actors save Pertwee and Manning for two weeks' work instead of four.

But what's interesting is, having come up with a cost-saver, Letts took on the directing himself and gave the script to one of the series' best writers. In other words, the production team came up with a cost-saving approach, but didn't make the cost-saving episode a throwaway. They put their best people on the task of doing an episode for cheaper. This is actually a bit funny – after the ridiculous laziness of stories that were supposed to be big such as the almost Dalek-free *Day of the Daleks* and the almost taste-free *The Time Monster*, the production team finally pulls out all the stops and goes for glory on their cheap story.

But another way to look at this is something we don't really see often at all in the Pertwee era: the production team trying to challenge themselves instead of playing it safe. Even the Pertwee era's most avant-garde episodes – *The Claws of Axos*, for instance – have a strange conservativeness to them. They have lots of crowd-pleasing moments, but they know what is expected of them and as a result can (and do) function on autopilot to an extent, trusting that the design department is going to compare to *Carnival of Monsters*. The visual effects are dodgy – so much so that Holmes made the monster names anagrams of "dishrag," where the monsters look like crap (as Robert Holmes expected, hence him making their names an anagram of dishrags, which he predicted would be what they were made of), but where the script is technically ambitious and the producer is taking an active hand to make sure it all comes off. It's refreshing, especially in an era that was often far too willing to decide that all that was required to enliven a flaccid script was a bit of Roger Delgado.

This is, in many ways, the one Pertwee story that's trying for something technically ambitious. Often the Pertwee era strove for a baseline of technical competence, which it generally hit. But after the awkwardness of the early part of the era in which the series figured out what it was again, Letts didn't do much that could be described as bold and experimental. He was never one for the bold artistic statement. Except here, the one story that feels like it's being made for the production team in order to test themselves. It's the one story that feels like it's trying for a more esoteric sort of greatness instead of trying to be well-liked television. And in the process it managed to be the best-liked bit of the Pertwee era. The fact of the matter is, the worst thing one can say about this story is it really shows how much better the rest of the Pertwee era could have been had the production team gone for "interesting" more often than it went for "big."

Instead we're left with an unfortunate fact: the Pertwee era is at its best when it most resembles the era immediately after it. A lot of what makes this story good is that it displays the traits that Robert Holmes eventually becomes known for. And the fact of the matter is, once he takes over as script editor and most of the stories show at least some of these traits, the show jumps to a whole new level of brilliance. We've brought much of the production team in for criticism at one time or another in the Pertwee era, and here it's time to admit it. The very skills that make Terrance Dicks the best person to go to for a functional novelization – his capacity to efficiently craft extremely competent, exciting plots – are at times a liability for him as a script editor. He can do exciting and thrilling like nobody else, but Dicks is first and foremost an entertainer.

Holmes, on the other hand, is certainly a capable entertainer, but that is in some ways almost incidental. Holmes has always had more of a willingness to risk upsetting his audience. He's always been prone to writing shockingly bitter scripts, even from *The Space Pirates*, a story that is most easily read as Holmes trying to show Derrick Sherwin how dumb an idea asking for a "realistic" space story was in the first place. Holmes is often prone to the absurdist trick of giving the audience exactly what they ask for, but in a form that isn't what they want anymore. Here, for instance, Holmes slyly suggests that the audience is morally bankrupt for watching the show in the first place. Towards the end of his period with the program he becomes even more hostile towards it.

And this in many ways captures the grim little pearl that is at the heart of Robert Holmes as a writer. He's often described as a cynic, which is true enough, but there's something altogether more complex about his cynicism. Holmes is, at the end of the day, a brilliant entertainer who is ambivalent at best about entertainment. And he's self-aware about it. There's an aggressive contradiction in play with everything Holmes writes, and that manifests in an ambivalence within many of his characters. This, in and of itself, makes his characters more lively and vibrant than almost anyone else's because, well, find me a person who isn't ambivalent.

For all that Hulke, Baker and Martin, and even Sloman have been brilliant over the course of the Pertwee era, it's difficult to argue that Holmes is not the most compelling voice in Doctor Who right now. And while this story fits smoothly into a truly great season of Doctor Who, it's impossible not to look forward a bit and know that in less than two years Holmes will be the script editor and the entire series will reflect his talent and vision. This is, in other words, at once the best Pertwee story and the one that most clearly shows why the Pertwee era's end might be a good thing.

The Sound of Empires Toppling (*Frontier in Space*)

It's February 24, 1973. The Sweet continue to be at number one with "Blockbuster," but are unseated after one week by Slade's "Cum On Feel The Noize," a more emphatic anthem to say the least. It lasts four weeks before Donny Osmond unleashes "The Twelfth of Never." Roberta Flack's "Killing Me Softly With His Song," T. Rex's "Twentieth Century Boy," Alice Cooper's "Hello Hooray," and the Jackson 5's (consisting at this point of Jackie, Tito, Michael, Jermaine, and Marlon) cover of Browne's "Doctor My Eyes" all also chart. Also during the course of this story, Pink Floyd's *The Dark Side of the Moon* is released.

The day before Pink Floyd's release, on the other hand, came Thomas Pynchon's release of *Gravity's Rainbow*. Other non-musical events of the six weeks included voters in Northern Ireland voting to remain part of the UK (Irish nationalists supported a boycott of the referendum), while IRA bombs go off in London. The Governor of Bermuda is assassinated by a small, Bermudan Black Nationalist group. The Watergate scandal begins to blossom in the news, while in the UK is the Lofthouse Colliery disaster, a mining accident in which seven coal workers died in West Yorkshire.

On television we have *Frontier in Space*, the annual Malcolm Hulke Lizard People Extravaganza. As with all of Season Ten, there's more going on here than in similar stories from past seasons. Which is good. One could be forgiven for thinking that we've been here before, after all we've got the Master manipulating two parties into a conflict for his own benefit, and misunderstandings between humans and lizard people and pig-headed military figures. Every Hulke story to date has included at least two of those tropes, and his Season Eleven story will break from tradition only by swapping out the lizard people for actual lizards. This time, as with *The Sea Devils*, there's even the explicit sense of this being a remake. Two years ago we had a colony in space. This time it's a frontier. One could be forgiven for thinking that Hulke has no ideas besides lizards and space imperialism. And yet it works, and, more to the point, works better than any other Hulke story.

The thing about the Pertwee era is that in a real sense, it builds logically and inexorably towards a peak in Season Ten. To give a sort of map of the era, at least for our purposes here, it spends its first three years working out a bundle of anxieties and contradictions. Then its last two seasons each end up embodying one half of that split, with Season Ten as the brilliant glam monument and Season Eleven basically flopping around like a dead fish. This is a strange split. It's not that Season Ten is doing something massively different from the seasons on either side of it. There are no writers in Season Ten that aren't used in at least one of Seasons Nine and Eleven, and only one director: David Maloney, who, while easily the era's most inventive director, is put on the most glaringly old-fashioned story in the season.

But for some odd, ineffable reason, perhaps down to nothing more than the lingering energy of the madcap singularity that was *The Three Doctors*, perhaps down to Doctor Who just being in the exact right place to catch a social wave, or perhaps down to good old-fashioned luck, the show is on fire in 1973. The next two stories – a throwback Terry Nation Dalek romp and the annual Sloman/Letts curate's egg – work better here than they have any right to. So here we get the Hulke story where every part somehow works out in the show's favor.

Part of this is that Hulke, who was always chomping at the bit for the earthbound format's demise, is clearly giddy to have a TARDIS to play with again. The appeal of the TARDIS has always been more than just its ability to go anywhere. Equally important is its ability to leave anywhere – to keep the show from being trapped in one premise for too long. Instead it gets to come up with a neat idea, explore the major consequences and highlights of the idea, and get out before things get too boring. And now he doesn't even have to shoehorn in some explanation of why the Time Lords want this mission. The

Doctor is free to get involved in any sort of story and setting Hulke wants.

Just as last time we talked about the comparative ordinariness of situations the TARDIS landed in during its early days, this time we should remind ourselves of the sort of genre romps that characterized the early days of the show. This is most obvious in things like *The Gunfighters* or *The Smugglers*, but also things like *The Web Planet* or the slightly later *The Enemy of the World*. What these stories have in common is that they all take a familiar high concept setting, explore the high points of dropping the Doctor into that setting, and then end and allow the show to move on to something else. This is one of the basic modes of operation for Doctor Who: drop the Doctor into X, where X is something well known and pre-existing, then pull him out when you've used up your best ideas on that. And as long as the broader popular culture doesn't run out of ideas there's not really any risk of running out of ways to do this.

This time the genre is "space opera," a genre that, surprisingly, Doctor Who hasn't really done all that often (the last straight-up execution of it is probably *The Ark*). And it's delightful. Both Pertwee and Manning give the sense of having fun in this story to a degree that they haven't really before, and it carries over to the characters. At one point, upon realizing that an unknown agent is using the Ogrons to try to spark a galactic war between the Human and Draconian empires and that this unknown agent has stolen the TARDIS, the Doctor and Jo seem to be kind of chuffed about it, as if they're glad to be having some fun. Likewise, while the Doctor is emphatic and furious as the leaders of Earth and Draconia ignore his warnings, he clearly takes a real joy in repeatedly breaking their mind probes. The restoration of a sense of vast anarchic possibility in the series' premise has, in other words, seemingly manifested in the characters themselves.

On top of that you've got the basic thrill in the scope of the story. One of the highlights of this story is the way in which its stakes steadily increase. At first it's a seemingly tiny story about

Ogrons raiding ships and a diplomatic crisis, but as it unfolds it becomes a story about trying to prevent an all-out war instigated by the Daleks and the Master. But equally impressive is the degree to which this story moves around among multiple space-ships, several Earth locations, the homeworld of the Draconians, and the homeworld of the Ogrons, giving this story a sort of giddy sense of scope and wonder.

Yes, the Draconians are just the Japanese in lizard costumes, but again, that curious tendency of Season Ten to just get on with it and make it work is on full display. For all that they are not a particularly creative alien species in absolute terms, they are the beneficiaries both of Hulke's insistence of making alien species actually have multiple characters with distinct personalities and perspectives instead of a hive mind, and from costume designers who managed to give them the ability to still have facial expressions. The masks are as much a high point of the Pertwee era's effects as the CSO in *Carnival of Monsters* is a low point. Legend, used here in the sense of "the stories Jon Pertwee told over and over again in every interview and convention appearance," claims that Pertwee, during lunch, got to talking to one of the Draconian actors and forgot he was talking to a man in a costume. Regardless of whether that's actually true, Pertwee repeatedly cited the Draconians as his favorite aliens, and they are one of those Doctor Who aliens whose popularity among professional fans far outstrips the actual size of their role in the series' history.

And yes, two empires on the brink of war is not a particularly original concept so much as it's the most generic pulp sci-fi imaginable. But Doctor Who has never relied entirely or even primarily on original concepts. Yes, it uses them, and when it does, as in the last story, it's usually wonderful. But just as many classic Doctor Who stories are about juxtaposing existing concepts or throwing them into chaos via the introduction of the Doctor as are based on novel and original ideas. And perhaps more to the point, just as many of the lows of Doctor Who are based on novel and original ideas as are based on recycling existing ones. So while warring space empires are nothing new, they're also not something we've see the Doctor running around in the middle of, and they're certainly not something we've seen Pertwee's drag action hero running around in.

Which is to say that this is a story that is much more than the sum of its parts, and another sadly overlooked gem of Season Ten. On paper it's filler – a five-and-a-half episode runaround before the Daleks show up and we get a ten-minute trailer for the next story that doesn't actually end up resolving this one. But in execution it's a masterful slow build that lets the dramatic tension reach its breaking point before finally exploding in a genuinely unexpected direction.

We should talk here, then, about the Master. This is actually the first time his presence in a story is used as a surprise reveal to spice up the plot midway through. In the 1980s this will become a tiresome cliché, but here it's wonderfully fresh. The situation is already bad when the Master shows up, and his arrival works because it's both shocking and one of the few ways the situation could actually get any worse. Every subsequent surprise appearance by the Master is just a feeble attempt to top this one.

The thing is, if we're being honest, it's a bit of a move of desperation. That doesn't make it any less brilliant or effective – it's definitely both. But on the other hand, in less than two and a half years, Roger Delgado appears in thirty-nine episodes of Doctor Who. In comparison, Vicki only appears in thirty-eight episodes total, and in the twenty-five months after their first appearances the Daleks and Cybermen appeared in thirty-two and twenty-six episodes respectively. Even allowing that Delgado's Master is an absolutely delightful character, this is an astonishingly high number of appearances by one villain and one actor in a short period of time.

One result of this is that, inevitably, and with no particular story being at fault, the Master has gone from being a character who transgresses against the narrative and throws it into chaos to being virtually the most predictable character on the show. Where Jo has found more and more outlandish and remarkable ways to break the rules of the narrative, the Master, because he always needs to be defeated, has been trapped in an increasingly small set of schemes. As we feared when it happened, there was nowhere to go but down once he summoned the Devil.

And so introducing him as a surprise twist has to be taken as a survival mechanism – a clever but desperate attempt to find a way to get the character to be unexpected and threatening again instead of a chump who will be defeated when his ambitious goes too far and his scheme backfires. Which is how he's been defeated in every prior story save for *The Claws of Axos*, whether because his allies betray him (*Terror of the Autons*, *The Sea Devils*), because some all-powerful being he sought to control tells him to piss off (*Colony in Space*, *The Daemons*, *The Time Monster*), or because the Doctor successfully turns his own plan against him (*The Mind of Evil*, and, ultimately, here). With the scope of what can be done with the character being, in the first place, so constricted, it's not a huge surprise that Hulke has to resort to a bit of a stunt to get him to be interesting.

This leads us to something that is a little bit unfortunate, which is that there is a degree to which it is lucky for the character that this is Delgado's last appearance in the role. I should hedge this, because there a number of ways in which that statement could be taken as shockingly offensive. The only reason this is Delgado's last story, after all, is that he was killed in a car accident about six months after *Frontier in Space* was filmed. This is unequivocally tragic. Delgado's contributions to the show were uniformly fantastic, and even in a problematic story like *The Time Monster*, Delgado does an incredible amount with what can charitably be called difficult writing to work with. In terms of Delgado and his legacy it's gutting that his last appearance should be a poorly edited scene with a bunch of grunting monkey aliens as opposed to a proper, grand farewell.

Unfortunately, we have some knowledge of what his grand farewell would have been, and the fact that we were spared it is unabashedly a good thing. What was planned was a Sloman epic in which we were to learn that the Master is literally the

Doctor's dark side and where the Doctor would fail to save him and be haunted by the guilt. This sounds hackneyed enough reading about it. Imagining it written with the staggering haphazardness of the Sloman/Letts team is simply excruciating. It is impossible to watch *The Time Monster*, or even a story that at least partially worked like *The Daemons* and imagine that this team could have made a story like that work, simply because they completely botched the dramatic beats and tension of both previous Doctor/Master stories they attempted. Indeed, given that much of the thematic material was reworked into *Planet of the Spiders* we can see how well it worked, and it's merciful that Delgado was spared that swansong. More to the point, the fact that Delgado never got a "proper" ending is what allowed the character to survive his playing it, and while there are more bad Master stories than good ones after 1973, this is, on balance, probably a good thing.

But more to the point, the Master was increasingly starting to fail as a character. As I said, he'd been overexposed without enough variety or new ideas, and ever since *The Sea Devils*, where he ended up badly dumbing down the moral complexity of what could have otherwise been an extremely successful updating and streamlining of the brilliant but flawed *The Silurians*, his appearances have been a mixed blessing at best. Delgado is great, but his character hasn't actually helped a story in some time.

Hulke, to his credit, actually seems aware of that. Certainly he recognizes that the Master and Jo, introduced in the same story, have expanded in different directions. The Master has progressively become a limited character while Jo has become more transgressive and capable of contorting the narrative. And so in this story the Master attempts to recycle his first trick with Jo and hypnotize her. And she casually kicks his ass, shrugging off his efforts and saying that she's far past falling for silly stunts like that. Even when he later tries to reassert his dominance over her by granting her a fake escape to trap the Doctor, it's rubbish on his part. Yes, Jo led the Doctor to an

Ogron ambush, but the fact of the matter is, the Doctor would have gone to rescue Jo even if he had known about the ambush. He was looking for the base and Jo told him where it was. Had she not escaped, he'd have found the base and still been ambushed by the Ogrons. The Master's "tricking" of Jo has zero effect. In every way that matters Jo has the upper hand on him in the narrative.

But more importantly, Hulke ends up executing a hilarious and brilliant snub on the overused character. Three episodes after his surprise unveiling as the story's real villain he gets upstaged by another surprise reveal in which it turns out that the real villain is actually the Daleks. And then he gets shoved offstage unceremoniously so we can have the real star attraction: six episodes of Dalek fighting! It's a bit of cynicism worthy of Robert Holmes, but it's spot on. If nothing else, the reverse reveal – the Daleks are secretly working for the Master – would have been a crushing anti-climax. Hulke is right: as arch-nemeses go, the Master is small potatoes compared to Daleks. So while it's an awful ending for a great actor, for a character that, largely due to the mistakes of Sloman and Letts, has passed his peak and begun to become a liability, there's a delightful justice in shoving him offstage in favor of a better foe for the Doctor. This is a story that proves that the Master has reached the end of his creative life.

But even beyond that, there's a sense that in that moment the show is making a real and meaningful decision about what it is. The Master, as a character, existed in part because by trapping the Doctor on Earth the show lost one of its major engines to bring strange and unusual things into the plot. So it created a character who would engage in bewildering schemes that make the stories more exciting. But now that the show is back in space, the Master is a crutch: a way of padding out a story that's run out of steam. Hulke makes it work here, but it works because it's the first time it's happened. The entire Ainley era of the character is a sobering reminder of what happens when this approach becomes the norm.

So instead the show turns away from that approach and towards a belief that the TARDIS means that you don't need gimmick characters to jumpstart the plot. Instead we turn to the first great monster of Doctor Who and prepare for the encounter that we were teased by and denied last time they appeared. It's time for a big ol' Dalek story the likes of which we haven't seen since 1966.

Because that's the other thing about this story. The Dalek reveal is, in fact, absolutely brilliant. For one thing, given a need to upstage the Master, the Daleks were outright the only things that could do that. For another, it's just the right thing to do. Especially since their last appearance was such a tease, suggesting as it did that the series didn't deserve the Daleks quite yet. Now, having restored the Doctor and the premise of the show, one of the things the show needed to do as a part of showing that it has fully reclaimed its own mantle was to show that it could still do the Daleks and do them right.

It is, after all, they who upstage the Master and take over the story. They are, in this regard, the last true threat the show has – characters that can plow in and completely unhinge and distort the narrative. Their appearance is a delicious throwing down of the gauntlet – a case of the show saying, "Bah, this situation is too easy for the Doctor to get out of. Let's see him get out of this!" Which brings us straightforwardly into the next story where we see him do just that.

A Thousand Years from a Disintegrated Home (*Planet of the Daleks*)

It's April 7, 1973. Gilbert O'Sullivan is at number one with "Get Down." David Cassidy, Donny Osmond, and Little Jimmy Osmond are also in the top ten. A situation along these lines persists for three weeks before Dawn reaches number one with "Tie a Yellow Ribbon Round the Ole Oak Tree," which ends up being the number one song for the year. David Bowie, Sweet, and Gary Glitter also chart in the other three weeks of this story.

In real news, the Labour Party takes over the Greater London Council, prefiguring their general election win ten months later. Also, the House of Commons declines to reinstitute the death penalty, and a one-day strike in opposition to government policy on inflation takes place among 1,600,000 workers. Elsewhere in Europe, the GSG 9, Germany's counter-terrorism force, is formed in response to the murder of Israeli athletes during the 1972 Olympics. In the US, a large swath of Nixon aides resign in an attempt to draw a line under the Watergate scandal, which I'm sure is going to work. A seventy-one day standoff with the American Indian Movement at Wounded Knee ends with the surrender of the Native Americans. Also the Sears Tower is built, and I shall never call it the Willis Tower.

While on television, it's pretty much 1965/'66 all over again. Actually, no. Not quite. 1965/'66 is *The Daleks' Masterplan*, which the stretch of twelve episodes we're tying up here was an explicit attempt to redo. That may be the goal, but it isn't at all what this story is like. On television, it's pretty much 1963/'64, as Terry Nation suddenly reappears and writes a story that is basically just a remake of *The Daleks* with an episode trimmed off.

For all that it is easy to criticize this, we should probably offer at least some defense of this decision. 1973 is a profoundly different time to 2013, in terms of television especially. Doctor Who was an extraordinary program in the fact that it was still going strong in its tenth season. But equally, it had evolved tremendously from its first season. More than that, not only didn't the VCR exist yet, neither did reruns of old material, and if they had, the BBC wasn't going to rerun an old black-and-white serial in the age of colour. What this meant was that the great Dalek epics of years past were wholly inaccessible. In April of 1973 there wasn't even the reprint of David Whitaker's novelization of *The Daleks* to fall back on. So the act of bringing back the Daleks and Terry Nation meant something fundamentally different. There was absolutely no mandate whatsoever to update the concept for 1973. Terry Nation was being hired to turn out a story just like all the other Dalek stories he wrote so that a new generation could experience one of the great styles of Doctor Who while an older generation experienced a nice nostalgia trip. In later stories his failure to do anything new with the Daleks will be fair grounds for criticism. Here, on the other hand, an excess of creativity would have been.

But why was the series doing this in the first place? There are a lot of reasons. First and foremost, Letts, having gotten the Daleks back in his toolbox, was understandably eager to use them. A feature of the deal to bring them back, however, was that Terry Nation got first refusal on the right to write a Dalek story. He'd been too busy to exercise it in 1972, hence Louis Marks incorporating them into an existing story, but was keen to now. So that meant that they had to use a Nation script if they were to do Daleks. Given that, a throwback was almost inevitable, so may as well be accepted.

But also attached with all of this was a more curious motivation. It was the tenth anniversary, and even before *The Three Doctors* had even been planned out there was a desire to do something nostalgic for it. Accordingly, the production team leafed through past "big stories," saw *The Daleks' Master Plan*, and said "Ooh, a twelve-week Dalek epic, that sounds fun." So they called Douglas Camfield, who had directed *The Daleks' Master Plan*, and asked him for advice. His advice was "don't do that." So they dropped to Plan B – let Nation write six weeks of retro Dalek adventure, then have a different six-parter that dovetails into it. Given that Nation was expected to write exactly the story he did, they went with Hulke for the other half, since he was reliably mature and, perhaps more to the point, not doing anything else for Season Ten. (Having lost Don Houghton to displeasure over how *The Mind of Evil* went, the only other active writers were Louis Marks and Brian Hayles, who were also throwbacks to the Hartnell era.)

That said, given that I don't even think *The Daleks' Master Plan* is one story, I'm certainly not inclined to treat all twelve weeks of this as one story. The fact of the matter is *Frontier in Space* ends decisively with the Master's defeat. In the course of his defeat, however, a new threat appears: Daleks. The two stories are certainly related, but so are *The Crusade* and *The Space Museum*, and nobody seriously claims those are one story. The one place where the connection between the two stories does matter, however, is in what we talked about last time: before this return to the original format of the series can be cemented completely, the Doctor has to face the Daleks. Especially given the deferral of that exact confrontation in *Day of the Daleks*.

Because effectively, everything that goes on in this story that is particularly interesting (and if we're being honest, that's a tiny fraction of what goes on in this story) comes down to the question of how Doctor Who in 1973 relates to Doctor Who in 1963. Because from a script perspective, this really is 1963 Doctor Who with a leading man who can do running scenes better. Nation has made zero effort whatsoever to update the format of the series.

To be fair, this is not the disaster that some people act like it is. Terry Nation has a raft of foibles as a writer, but his basic sense is solid. It's worth noting, since we haven't gotten to talk about him since the Hartnell era, that he is, from a writing perspective, second only to David Whitaker in terms of the depth of his influence on the shape of the show from the start. After all, within Doctor Who it was Nation who really started the idea of jumping around among divergent settings. It was Nation who invented monsters. Heck, it was Nation who invented invading Earth. Even beyond that, Nation was the first one to do space adventures, and remains enormously good at packing action into a story. The only problem with Nation is that his sense of what science fiction is more or less begins and ends with Dan Dare. In 1963, at least, that was old-fashioned, but still cool to see on television. In 1973, it's, if we're being charitable, retro. By 1979, when his association with the series ends, it becomes hopelessly out of touch.

The practical effect of this is twofold. On the one hand, *Planet of the Daleks* is a well-made action thriller in a sort of classic Dan Dare mould. On the other hand, that's not necessarily a great thing to be as Doctor Who in 1973. After three successful stories in a row with interesting complexities to them and after coming off a far longer run of stories with interesting goals (even if they aren't always met), suddenly ending up in 1963 is jarring, and not in an entirely satisfying way. And among the people who appear jarred by and not entirely happy with it are Jon Pertwee, Katy Manning, and director David Maloney. This could be a recipe for outright disaster. But instead, Season Ten's odd magic saves the day again, transmuting the story into an odd triumph of postmodernism.

Remember that postmodernism is about separating symbols from their contexts while still relying on them to function. To some extent, of course, that means Doctor Who has been postmodern since it shoved a Victorian inventor, a star child, and two school teachers in the same frame as a bunch of cavemen. But this is more thorough, in that you have two distinct elements each of which are extremely well developed. On one hand you have the logic of a classic Dalek story (of which, even if Nation only really did about three, there are so many in the comics as to be a very well-established genre). On the other you have the logic of the Pertwee era. These logics are not quite allied, nor are they quite opposed, which means that when bits of the story start pulling in different directions, which happens frequently given that prominent people involved with it clearly don't want to be, the tension is visible enough to be fascinating.

The bulk of this tension takes place in and around Jon Pertwee. Tat Wood observes that Nation really doesn't quite get Pertwee's Doctor, writing him primarily as a sage lawgiver. This is close enough to right that it's not jarring, but it fundamentally misses the central conceit of Pertwee's Doctor, which is that he's playing a patrician action hero and getting it slightly wrong. So Pertwee doesn't get to run around and be ostentatiously imperious, as he prefers. Nor does he get to be ignored and occasionally tortured, as he's best at. Instead he stands around and gives speeches about the meaning of courage. Pertwee certainly isn't bad at this, but it's neither in his wheelhouse nor something he visibly enjoys.

The solution he settles on, however, is perfect: he plays the story with a sort of cool detachment. The result is a perfect and postmodern commentary on the episode – as if the Doctor recognizes that he's in an unusually easy adventure of far less complexity than he deals with routinely, and that it doesn't actually require his full attention. The tendency to make speeches about fear instead of doing what are now the core elements of "Doctory" behavior becomes not a mischaracterization but a case of the Doctor taking it easy and figuring he doesn't have to work, he can just sit back and encourage everybody else.

The result ends up answering the basic question of the story: now that *Doctor Who* is back to being *Doctor Who*, how does this Doctor deal with the types of adventures people remember him having? And the answer given – they're a piece of cake to him and good for nothing so much as a nostalgia trip – is, for the show, an excellent one that speaks to a tremendous confidence in itself. The only downside is that the audience has to sit through six episodes of nostalgia trip, but for an audience with any fondness for the old Dalek stories – and presumably anyone watching Pertwee stories in 2011 is the sort of person who does have a fondness for the whole history of the show, since their diversion from modern taste is significant – two and a half hours of well-acted, well-directed, classic Daleks are still, frankly, a bit of a treat. There are obvious problems with doing it for six weeks with an audience primarily comprised of people who are too young to remember Season One, but this is a rare case where history is kind to the show – the story frankly works better in 2011 than it probably did in 1973.

As for Manning and Maloney, there's a lot to say. Manning is brutally served by the script, including going fully eighty percent of an episode without getting a line of dialogue. But she does magnificently with what she gets. In particular, saddled with an absolutely wretchedly built romantic subplot, she manages to sell it by just completely refusing to play that plot line with any seriousness, letting it turn into "the Thal who inexplicably falls for Jo" instead of "the pointless love story." It's a great call on Manning's part.

Maloney, on the other hand, shoots the hell out of this thing, using camera angles and editing to brilliant effect. He's back on Doctor Who for the first time since *The War Games*, and is obviously in the mood to see what color and the Daleks, both things he'd never gotten to use before, let him do. Unfortunately he has a script with little interest in letting him do anything new. But he keeps things moving.

Beyond that, however, there's a peculiar interaction between Maloney and Manning. I've been praising Manning for several essays now, but in this story she finally gets a director who seems to understand how it is her character works. Back on the blog version of this material I explained this with a video blog (still online at youtu.be/PSkL7PL3FMk), and it's certainly easier with examples. But in effect, Maloney comes up with a grammar for how Daleks and people are shot, with people shot with fixed camera angles that keep them in medium shots and Daleks filmed in close-up with the camera moving with them to keep them in the same place in the frame. Then, in the sequence where Jo infiltrates the Dalek base, Maloney progressively flips the visual grammar around. At first Jo is shot in the style of the Daleks, tacitly stressing how she's an intruder in their space. But eventually the rules reverse, with

Jo first sneaking around in the background of Dalek-style shots, and subsequently getting to where scenes are shot human-style despite the fact that Daleks are typically given visual priority over the humans, thus tacitly showing Jo to be narratively more important than the Daleks by breaking the very rules of the storytelling.

The result is that, despite being a largely unambitious throwback of a story, *Planet of the Daleks* gets away with it and manages to be far more compelling than it frankly deserves to be. The oddly triumphant train of Season Ten rumbles on towards its conclusion.

Time Can Be Rewritten Extra: *Find and Replace*

One of the figures this volume is most consistently deferential to is Katy Manning and her portrayal of Jo Grant. This is not, of course, a terribly controversial perspective; she's one of the absolute classic companions. But it is. Given my openly leftist leanings throughout this, there's an obvious problem, which is that at the core of Jo as a character is a tremendous sexism. The decision was taken — and Terrance Dicks has generally been all too willing to take credit for it — that Liz Shaw was too capable a companion and needed to be replaced by someone who would do the proper companion job of getting kidnapped and having the plot explained to her.

This is, of course, appalling and cynical. And it is a lucky thing that the companion worked out so well. But even still, the praise of Jo Grant issued throughout this book is problematic. Essentially we've just praised Katy Manning for playing what is these days called the Manic Pixie Dream Girl, only several decades early. In praising the way in which she can flit around the edges of the narrative and demonstrate plucky detachment from them we're really just putting her on a pedestal to be admired, and admired in a way that is deeply sexualized. Put another way, all we're really doing is praising her for handling her marginalization as a silly little girl in a particularly artful way. It's lipstick on a pig at best.

This is the starting point for Paul Magrs's audio *Find and Replace*. In it, Jo Grant and Iris Wildthyme fall temporary victim to a Narrator from Verbatim Six, who attempts to retcon the Doctor out of their lives and to instead assert that they had adventures with each other in the 1970s. Initially it appears that this is part of some nefarious plot on the part of Huxley, the aforementioned Narrator. But towards the end of the story it turns out that the plot is actually the Doctor's, who decided, without asking Jo, to have her memories of him wiped for her own safety.

There is a much larger critique implicit in this. Pertwee's Doctor is often described as a paternal figure, and here we get that taken to its pejorative form, whereby he becomes a paternalistic one. And that's implicit in the feminist critique of Jo Grant. No matter how fun and subversive a character she is, her default position is always as the helpless sidekick protected by the far more capable man. Jo Grant was conceived of, from day one, as a character who needed a man to look after her.

Given this, the psycho-sexual dynamics of her relationship with the Doctor are disturbing in the extreme. The Doctor is ostensibly a paternal figure. And yet his relationship with Jo has an odd element of the romantic to it. Jo is visibly sexual and sexualized (there are a downright sickening number of compilations of the points in the series where her underwear are inadvertently displayed), and it's impossible to read the tendency for her to hold hands with the Doctor when they run as anything other than a kind of sweet bit of romance. (In practice, of course, it was the opposite. Manning was profoundly near-sighted, and Pertwee held her hand so she didn't injure herself in those scenes. Far from being sexual, it's a moment of genuine and endearing paternal care.) And, of course, when she departs in *The Green Death* her romantic partner is overtly set up as a counterpart and rival to the Doctor, and Pertwee plays the Doctor's slinking out of the wedding party as a jilted lover. These two elements are, in other words, hopelessly intertwined in the series.

It is on the one hand perhaps over-egging the pudding, and on the other necessary to point out the systemic horror of this elision between paternal care and sexuality. It is increasingly clear that the 1970s were the heyday of Jimmy Savile's systematic sexual abuse of young women, and that Savile and other entertainers used their status as BBC icons to gain access to their victims and avoid scrutiny for what they did. Savile's status as a kindly man who helped children was, in other words, how he got away with raping them. At the same time, Doctor Who was busily teaching the youth of Britain that girls needed a kind father figure to protect them, and that this figure was interchangeable with their husband. No, of course I'm not blaming Doctor Who for Jimmy Savile. That would be stupid. But I am pointing out that the same culture contained both.

So *Find and Replace* is tacitly a critique of that logic, though by any measure a softer one than the preceding paragraph offers. It merely observes the way in which Jo is treated paternalistically by the Doctor and grumps about it. Except that there's one other key thing going on in it that elevates it from a critique to something of a redemption, and that's the presence of Iris Wildthyme.

On a basic level, as discussed back in the *Verdigris* entry, Iris Wildthyme is a mirror of the Doctor. Specifically, she's a highly postmodern alternative whose narrative willfully contradicts everything and who, in her first major appearance, openly claims to be a feminist reinterpretation of Doctor Who's basic mythology. *Find and Replace* handles her cleverly, positioning her at first as an undesirable and frankly absurd alternative to the Doctor who mostly just annoys everybody. But there's bits of venom in the joking. She scandalizes both Jo and the Doctor with the claim that she'd been the Doctor's lover, a claim that is scandalous only in the context of the enforced chastity that attempts to stave off the sexualized portion of the paternal/marital complex.

At the end, however, there's a more thorough subversion. After the Doctor's tacit betrayal of Jo's trust is discovered, Jo and Iris return to Iris's bus to go from the 1970s back to the present day, where the story started. But, of course, it goes awry, and instead Jo and Iris land in an unknown place, clearly setting up an indefinite period of Jo and Iris having the very adventures the story briefly played at giving them. And in the wake of the Doctor's betrayal it seems a redemption – a case of Manning getting to be the companion of a hero she doesn't have to be babied by.

All of this ignores the other salient point about Iris Wildthyme, which is that on audio she is played by Katy Manning. This predates *Find and Replace* by several years – Big Finish didn't even have any audio series that could cover the Third Doctor era when she started playing Iris. Instead it was a case of Big Finish casting someone who was a familiar figure in Doctor Who but whose Doctor Who character wasn't covered by any of their existing lines. But the later creation of the Companion Chronicles line, which allowed for companions of Doctors other than those Big Finish could do audios for to have stories, opened the door for Manning to play both parts in one audio, and *Find and Replace* is the one that finally did it.

So while Iris is a mirror of the Doctor, she also serves, in this story at least, as a mirror for Jo – a version of her that gets to be the starring role and doesn't have to play second fiddle to a domineering male character. The end isn't just the liberation of Jo from the Doctor, it's tacitly Jo stepping up to become equivalent to Iris in the narrative.

But it's telling that this takes place outside the context of Doctor Who. *Find and Replace* may set up the promise of Iris and Jo having wild adventures, but it doesn't give us that. It ends right at the cusp of that, because that story isn't doable within Doctor Who. Doctor Who can take us to the doorstep of Jo being liberated from all patriarchal authority, but it can't go through it. Of course it can't, because fifty years after its creation every single Doctor Who story is still, to this day, about the white British man who fixes things.

And much as we might stamp our feet and say that it doesn't have to be – that a racial minority could play the Doctor or that there could be a female Doctor – that's now how it works. Back towards the end of 2008 when there were rumors that Patterson Joseph was going to be the Eleventh Doctor – Patterson Joseph, who had basically played the part and been quite good at it in *Neverwhere* – people were already grumbling that the Doctor isn't black. Never mind that he can change his face and that nobody complained when Patrick Troughton took over that the Doctor isn't brunette. Because the fact of the matter is that the world is still racist and sexist and Doctor Who is, as a result, a white man's show. And while I hope thoroughly that changes and we get a Pakistani female Doctor for the Twelfth, in reality we're probably going to get yet another white British guy.

I don't for a moment think that Magrs isn't making that exact point when he cuts off the story just as Jo and Iris set off on their own. I also don't for a moment think this is meant as some general case condemnation of Doctor Who. But it's there, and it's real, and it's a perfectly valid and sensible critique of the series. And much as I love Jo Grant – and she remains one of my favorite companions – the fact of the matter is that she's a character born of sexist motivations and a callous disdain for women. The character I love is the best that could be done under those unfortunate circumstances. It's good. At times it's great. And given that action-adventure television is a maddeningly male-dominated genre, it's substantive and significant and deserves praise for all its faults.

But the later career of Katy Manning, particularly as Iris Wildthyme, is proof that we could have had so much more.

Tamper with the Forces of Creation (*The Green Death*)

It's May 19, 1973. Wizzard is at number one with "See My Baby Jive," which stays at number one for four weeks until Suzi Quatro's "Can The Can" unseats it for a week, followed by 10cc's "Rubber Bullets." Also in the charts are The Sweet, Gary Glitter, David Bowie, T. Rex, Lou Reed, Alice Cooper, and, um . . . Perry Como. I'm exaggerating a little bit, as Stevie Wonder and Fleetwood Mac also chart. Since we haven't talked about the albums chart in a while and it's worth checking in occasionally, David Bowie's *Aladdin Sane* is at the top, with Alice Cooper's *Billion Dollar Babies* and Pink Floyd's *The Dark Side of the Moon* all charting. In their midst are two Beatles compilations and *40 Fantastic Hits From The 50's And 60's*. So a bit of a nostalgia trip creeping in there.

In real news, Skylab launches, followed immediately by Skylab 2, which whizzes off to the stars to fix the first one. Lord Lambton resigns from Parliament after *The News of the World* busts him on his fondness for prostitutes. The Greek military junta puts an end to the whole monarchy business, Secretariat wins the Triple Crown, and the Ezeiza massacre takes place in Argentina, with snipers shooting supporters of Perón. And finally, Peter Dinsdale commits his first fatal act of arson, killing a six-year-old boy in Kingston upon Hull.

While on television, it's the end of Season Ten of Doctor Who, which means it's time for Robert Sloman and Barry Letts to lay another curate's egg. But unlike certain other curate's eggs, this one hatches giant maggots that kill you by turning you bright green.

Readers may be noticing a certain pattern of disdain for the writing of Mr. Sloman, and to a lesser extent Mr. Letts. (Though I've not seen a clear account of what their process is, my assumption, especially given that Letts demonstrates skill in other aspects of the program, is that Letts comes up with some story ideas and leaves them for Sloman to turn into a script, with most of the resulting defects entering at that stage. But there's a whiff of dangerous revisionism here. Much of the appeal of that apportioning of blame comes down to the fact that Barry Letts is a decades-long friend of the series with numerous positive contributions, whereas Robert Sloman goes away after *Planet of the Spiders*. Leaving the blame with the guy who doesn't keep showing up is simply more emotionally satisfying.) And while *The Green Death* is without a doubt their best script by miles, and rightly deserves much of the praise heaped upon it, what all of this misses is that it is also by miles their worst script yet.

This may seem a contradiction in terms, but it's one that gets at the heart of the issues with the Sloman/Letts scripts. They are full of some of the best scenes and ideas in the Pertwee era, and also full of some of the most atrocious plotting, torturous dialogue, and, in the case of *The Green Death*, appalling politics of the Pertwee era. And unlike a flawed genius of a story like *The Tenth Planet* or *The Talons of Weng-Chiang* (to pick examples from before and after this), the Sloman/Letts scripts seem to be utterly haphazard, as if written by the Batman villain Two-Face, flipping a coin before every decision to see if it will be a good one or a bad one. And somehow, when Sloman is involved, this process infects every aspect of the series, including ones like effects and acting that have no direct relationship with the script. The results are tortured marvels that swap unexpectedly from being aesthetic triumphs to being barely watchable amateur productions.

To start in a microcosm, let's take this story's most remembered feature: the maggots. The maggots are a tour de force — recognizably and definitively the most remembered and frightening monster of the Pertwee era and arguably of the entire show. A casual viewer of the show in the Pertwee era, if asked about Doctor Who, will almost unfailingly and without being prompted mention the maggots as their most vivid memory. This is easily explained: the monster construction was amazing, with fox skulls being used for the mouths of the maggots to give a truly gruesome, visceral look to them. This, combined with the surprisingly clever decision to scatter the landscapes with inflated condoms to suggest the number of maggots around, makes for some very, very effective monsters.

The "on the other hand" that usually follows this is a staggeringly awful sequence in which a giant fly attacks the Doctor. This is, admittedly, an absolutely awful effect, but highlighting it as the story's real face-plant in the effects department ignores the one in which the maggots themselves become laughable. There is a truly wretched sequence of the Doctor and Benton driving Bessie through maggot-infested hills that are achieved by putting a Bessie prop in the studio and using CSO to paste in a scrolling backdrop of maggoty hills. It looks unbelievably awful, in no small part because the visible difference between film and video gives the series a clear visual distinction between interior and exterior shots, and so when you plaster together a filmed landscape with a video foreground, it not only looks wrong because of that contrast, it looks wrong because it's in the completely wrong visual style for exteriors in Doctor Who. The result is that the maggots go, between shots, from being the best monster of the Pertwee era to contending with the Drashigs in the massive failure sweepstakes. And while on the one hand this is just another example of the Letts era's tendency to dramatically overestimate the extent of what can be done with CSO, the immediate gap between good and bad here is truly staggering. The fact that such care is taken with the monsters in some cases while the quality of effects is blatantly disregarded in others is genuinely puzzling.

I bring up this example not because I'm massively fascinated by the special effects in Doctor Who, which generally strike me as interesting only insofar as they demonstrate that serious science fiction can function with poor special effects provided that they're at least of a consistent style and the actors still take them seriously (a point I'll expand upon when we get to *The Ark in Space* in the next volume). Rather, it's that I want to highlight the real difficulty of talking at length about *The Green Death*. Not to pull the curtain back too far on the elite secrets of Doctor Who criticism, but when I hit a story

I'm ambivalent about for some reason, from a writing perspective, there is usually nothing easier in the world. The "on the one hand, X, on the other hand Y" structure has powered a number of essays to date, and will power a ton more because it's as reliable a structure as "then the Doctor and his companion get separated, and one of them ends up captured by the villains while the other ends up helping the good guys." The only decision is whether to lead with the good and close with the bad, or lead with the bad and close with the good, and that usually comes down to where I want the overall narrative to be going. But with *The Green Death*, the good and the bad are so utterly intertwined that it's impossible to create a coherent description of one that doesn't dip constantly into the other. There's no way to separate what works from what doesn't here.

In a lot of ways, this is fitting, if only because it captures my feelings on the Pertwee era at large very well. While the Pertwee era introduced a ton of stuff that was brilliant, along a fair number of things that were rightly massively influential on the ensuing thirty-eight years of Doctor Who, it also made a number of very fundamental missteps. And more to the point, it's not possible to easily separate those into "good Pertwee" and "bad Pertwee." This is more than just the schizophrenia of the early seasons as the show tried to balance its desire to be an action show with a large military supporting cast and its commitment to the roaring glam aesthetic – an issue that really came down to two competing aesthetics with no particular reason why someone who liked one would also like the other. This is something deeper – an ambivalence within the core DNA of the Pertwee era that at times manifests between or within individual shots or lines in a scene.

So talking about *The Green Death* precludes an easy structure of plusses and minuses. So instead, let's just start somewhere. Actually, since we were just talking about the action/glam distinction, perhaps the first thing to comment on is that none of the preceding eighteen Pertwee stories managed to split the difference between the action and glam aesthetics quite so evenly as this. On the one hand, this story is a corporate conspiracy thriller about pollution that happens to feature giant maggots of death. On the other hand, it's a story in which the Doctor teams up with a bunch of hippies to use the power of crystals to overcome an evil psychic computer in a bewildering blur of psychedelic video effects.

It's tempting to say that both plots have good and bad points, but I think this is actually a bad misreading of how this story works. More accurately, both plots are screwed up royally and delivered with the barest modicum of competence, but the fact that the show has finally managed to split the difference and have a plot that's firmly working in both the glam and action aesthetics, both of which are by now familiar modes for the show, and the fact that it juxtaposes them confidently is enough to make the whole work despite the massive deficiencies of the individual parts.

Judged as a conspiracy thriller, *The Green Death* is hilariously ham-fisted. It's not just that the malevolent corporation is so farcically malevolent that even I, the sort of person who has a favorite revolutionary Marxist (Guy Debord, of course), found myself going "oh, that's a bit unfair." Though the fact that they contrive to have Stevens (played by the amazing Jerome Willis, best seen in the sublimely good late seventies spy series *The Sandbaggers*) evoke both Neville Chamberlain's "peace in our time" and the famed "what's good for General Motors is good for America" quotes is almost charming in its over-earnestness. Nor is it that UNIT, by now a series of party pieces relying entirely on how good Nicholas Courtney and John Levene are and how good the production team appears to think Richard Franklin is, is comprised of sub-par conspiracy thriller characters at best.

No, the real problem is that this story misunderstands the nature of the conspiracy thriller. The genre works via a series of unexpected twists and revelations coupled with severe differences in who knows what at any given moment. But this story lacks any of that: it's an utterly straightforward story in which the only thing that resembles a twist is that there's an evil computer. While this is good for one of the best cliffhanger lines ever, as John Dearth laconically gloats "I am the computer," it's no *Manchurian Candidate*. (On the other hand BOSS is fantastic as a character, doubly so for the hilariously weird revelation that BOSS became sentient and all-powerful because he realized that the secret to human creativity was inefficiency and thus made himself more inefficient. Though this bit of cleverness would perhaps have had more impact if he didn't then obsessively rant about how everything must be made more efficient.)

Whereas in terms of psychedelic swirls of color, the story runs into a problem that fandom seems inexplicably to have blinded itself to. See, the entire resolution of the story hinges on a moment in the fifth episode in which the Doctor pulls a blue crystal out of his pocket and uses it to deprogram a brainwashed Mike Yates. This is fine. The problem is that the blue crystal has been almost entirely absent from the story up to this point. The Doctor acquires it in the first episode when he nips off in the TARDIS on a pleasure cruise to Metebelis III, mentions it about twice in the next three episodes, and then suddenly pulls it out of his pocket and solves all the world's problems in the fifth episode. It's a blatant deus ex machina to anyone but the most obsessive of fans.

Said fans make much of the fact that there's an off-handed mention of Metebelis III in *Carnival of Monsters* (the Doctor thinks he's arrived there but is wrong – the planet is mentioned exactly twice in the whole story), and of the fact that the blue crystal is central to the plot of *Planet of the Spiders* next season. Accordingly, when it appears here, they just take it in the context of those, often describing this story with some comment about how the Doctor "finally" makes it to Metebelis III as if it were the resolution to something more than a throwaway line over three months ago, thus giving the impression that the ending here is set up or built to in any way. It's not – the psychedelia is shoehorned in with the sort of subtlety usually reserved for sending in idiotic bureaucrats in two-thirds of the way through a six-parter.

But despite the fact that *The Green Death* is both a lousy conspiracy thriller and a lousy piece of glam-era psychedelia, the fact that it switches back and forth between them constantly and with utter confidence ultimately renders the bulk of these faults moot. Incredibly and improbably, the story gets away with it, skating through on the last of Season Ten's strange luck. The twenty weeks of quite solid postmodern juxtaposition before this, combined with how quintessentially Doctor Who the two registers the story works in are, makes the inadequacies of the two plots disappear under the cheeky thrill of seeing them done together.

The story's politics are similarly strangely muddled. Inasmuch as this series has higher goals than just being a bunch of essays about a cult British sci-fi show for dedicated fans, it is about the way in which the last half-century of history can be seen through the lens of an idiosyncratically persistent television series. In that regard, this book can, hubristically, be described as a story about utopian ideology in the aftermath of the 1960s that happens to be structured around a television series. Which is to say that of the things I am inclined to be fond of about Barry Letts, the degree to which he tries to use Doctor Who as a vehicle for his own leftist politics, is one of the big ones.

And if you're the sort of person who is disappointed that the utopian revolutionary movements of the 1960s petered out – and obviously, not only am I that sort of person, I think the nature of the Troughton era firmly commits Doctor Who to being that sort of show – there's a lot to love here. Overdone as the anti-corporate politics of this story are, there's a sincere anger to this story that's compelling and still relevant. And the way in which those issues are approached is genuinely interesting. By entwining the *Doomwatch*-style conspiracy thriller with psychedelia, Letts and Sloman come up with a unique perspective on it, and one that's worth unpacking briefly.

The previous two Sloman/Letts scripts make it clear that Letts (and this does seem to mostly be Letts) has an investment in a worldview that shares much of the mysticism of David

Whitaker's alchemical worldview, although as we've seen there are profound differences between the two men. (Specifically, as we saw in the last story and will see again in the next, the fact that Letts is a committed Buddhist.) This story is no different. Crucial to this is the role of decay and death in magical thinking. Alchemically speaking, putrefaction is best understood not as decay but simply as transformation. The rotting of the old is a necessary process in the creation of the new. This is literalized in the way that life springs out of rot – such as, for instance, maggots. Or, for that matter, mushrooms. Putrefaction, although obviously scary and traumatic, is a necessary phase of development – a sort of purification in which the old and unnecessary melts away and is replaced by new life. In a real sense, of course, putrefaction is inherent in any discussion of petroleum, crude oil itself being the product of putrefaction.

The thing that it is easy to miss in *The Green Death* is that both sides of the debate – the hippies at Wholewheal and the corporate nasties at Global Chemicals – fundamentally believe that the world as it exists is doomed and that some new world is going to take its place. And each of them have their own magic form of putrefaction – petroleum and maggots for Global Chemicals, mushrooms and psychedelia for Wholewheal. The central battle of *The Green Death*, in other words, is over what form of life will emerge from the putrefaction of the world, with Global Chemicals putrefying into lethal poison while Wholewheal putrefies into enlightenment. And it's a really interesting, rich take on the idea of apocalyptic fervor and utopianism that was deeply enmeshed in the culture in the early '70s.

On top of that, the story earns scads of political points by being set in Wales. For British readers, the significance of the show giving recognition and cultural legitimacy to the Welsh portion of the audience is clear. For Americans, we may need an analogy. The closest equivalent to Wales in the US is probably the Appalachian region of Kentucky and West Virginia. Both regions had an economic boom from coal mining that eventually turned sour, leaving gutted industrialized wastelands mixed with crushing poverty and no meaningful infrastructure for self-improvement. Both regions found themselves ignored by both sides of the political spectrum – the right displaying its usual lack of concern for poverty, the left turning its nose up at the uneducated and often socially conservative populations in favor of more glamorous causes. So to set a story there is a really significant move in moving the concerns of an unfairly marginalized population into the mainstream.

Unfortunately, Sloman delivers a script in which every Welsh character save Cliff is a generic comedy yokel with no discernible traits to differentiate them from the other comedy yokels. Even the Brigadier and Jo get in moments of sniggering at the cute little rural Welshmen and their funny dialect. It's crass, ugly, condescending, and wrong. But worse than that, it's one of those moments in which the show steps in it in such a way that a fundamental flaw is revealed – by all appearances, the show genuinely believes that the people of Llanfairfach are in some sense complicit in their own misfortune, or at the very least are simply hapless props in a war between corporations and well-educated hippies. (Malcolm Hulke's novelization of the story – and remember that the novelizations for the Pertwee era are in many ways more influential than the stories themselves, having spent at times two decades as the only repeatable versions of the stories – addresses many of these problems and offers a far, far more nuanced and graceful portrayal of the people of Llanfairfach.)

This condescension is in many ways just the tip of the iceberg however. The problems in this story really come up when we spend more than about five seconds looking at Cliff. Here's a fun question for anybody watching this story: given that the reason BOSS is evil is that it wants to become an absolute dictator in a world in which free will has been done away with, what, exactly, distinguishes Professor Jones from BOSS?

Consider: he's an overtly charismatic leader who attracts female groupies and talks about how he wants to reshape the world. This doesn't seem to have been what Sloman and Letts were originally going for, but somewhere along the line the story loses track of whether Cliff is an eccentric professor running a commune in Wales, or whether he's a Utopian visionary looking to rework the world into his own preferred form. But on balance, he mostly ends up the latter – someone who just wants to force the world to suit his will. In absolutely any other story, a character who has the attitudes towards other people that Cliff has would be the villain.

To be clear, it's not that Cliff's view of what the world should be is a bad one. Rather, it's his vision of how to obtain it, which appears to be to leverage UN funding into "unlimited money" so as to provide food for the entire planet while forcing people to abandon their lifestyles in favor of ones he finds more optimal. In that regard it's difficult to come up with an account of how his plan differs from Salamander's back in *The Enemy of the World*.

Worse than the story's embrace of a would-be dictator, however, is the fact that the story hammers on the point that Cliff is a younger version of the Doctor. The immediate instinct is to recoil at this and insist that, no, Cliff is nothing like the Doctor. Two things prevent this. The first, which we've alluded to before, is that Cliff actually is, in many ways, a plausible younger version of Pertwee's Doctor. The patrician "I know best and you're a fool who must be stopped if you don't listen to me" view implicit in Cliff's attitude to the world is easily ascribed to Pertwee's Doctor as well. And what's really crushing here is how impossible to disentangle from the best of Pertwee this is. Pertwee's high points are often his strident and passionate speeches about evil. But that's also the exact "privileged outsider lecturing everyone on how they should be like him" attitude that is so troubling in Cliff. The curate's egg nature of the story ends up being reflected all too well in the hero.

In many ways this is a sort of original sin for the Pertwee era: a fundamental consequence of conceiving of the Doctor as a dashing, charismatic action hero. Because he's also a brilliant alien, having him be such a creature of privilege fundamentally makes him the condescending outsider. And the nature of the politics engaged in from 1970–1974 means that he is constantly coming upon situations in which the privileged outsider is a morally problematic role.

The second reason we can't really avoid the claim that Cliff is a younger Doctor, however, is by far the more troubling one: Jo says he is. In fact, Jo goes ahead and marries him. The degree to which this is poorly set up is striking even given what we've already discussed. Cliff simply seems to assume that Jo is going to marry him, and once she acquiesces, the wedding is apparently held immediately. On top of that, Cliff is basically horrible to Jo through the entire story, berating and insulting her to an extent that is genuinely shocking, especially in ostensible comparison with the Doctor. It's almost impossible to root for the couple, or it would be if Jo hadn't been so well developed over three seasons that the mere fact of the plotline carried dramatic weight.

And so as poorly set up as it is, it's still unmistakably one of the main points of the story. Part of this is that for all its flaws, it is at least set up from the start, unlike the departures of past characters who have been unexpectedly married off – most obviously Susan and Vicki. As soon as she spurns his offer to go to Metebelis III in favor of going to South Wales, leaving him to slink into the TARDIS like Puff the Magic Dragon to his cave, there's a sense of this. Jo's first scene with Cliff is deliberately constructed to parallel her first scene with the Doctor, with her inadvertently spoiling an experiment and being yelled at in both cases. It's clear that more thought has gone into Jo's departure than any past companion departure, including the previous best in this regard, Victoria. That this thought is barely coherent is a problem, but it's a problem that must be taken in context.

Again, however, there's a tendency among hyper-knowledgeable fandom to make more of this than the show actually supports. There are those who insist on taking the scene in which Jo resists the Master's hypnosis in *Frontier in Space* and her departure in this episode and attempting to claim that there is some lengthy three-year plotline of her learning from the Doctor and eventually growing up to go her own way. To call this a ludicrous exaggeration would be understatement, and only the even more farcical claim that there is some sort of coherent Metebelis III plot running through Season Ten makes this idea look good. But that doesn't mean that the resolution of this story is any less effective than is claimed. For all the absurdity necessary to get to this point, the final scene of the Doctor sadly ducking out of the party and driving off alone, with Jo looking stricken as he leaves even though she stays with her new life is brilliant.

But its power comes not from how it's built to, but rather from how it's played. Pertwee and Manning are both on fire for the scene. And there's just a lot of momentum behind the scene. Jo has been the companion for longer than any previous companion, and, for that matter, for about as long as Troughton was the Doctor. So her departure is a major moment on its own, and having the Doctor devastated by it is an enormously effective way to get the audience to feel it. And more to the point, it's a brave decision to show the charismatic hero of the show vulnerable and hurt like this – something we haven't really seen since the Doctor left Susan behind, and that was a very different Doctor who was not played as the charismatic leading man.

But there's a larger issue here. Over the course of the three years Jo was around, the series learned to work in a new way based on glam and postmodern aesthetics, and reinvented itself back into its classic format after the experiment of the earthbound setting. And Jo became a cornerstone of that approach via her plucky and wholesale embrace of ridiculous adventures and her tendency to flagrantly break the rules of whatever type of story she's put into, deleting all manner of narrative logics to replace them with her own innocent charm. She was the perfect foil to the Doctor's patrician ways – a way of throwing worlds into chaos without the condescending privilege of a rich white man.

Her departure feels like the end of an era, in other words. And the fact that her departure coincides with a story that finally offers a decisive merging of the Pertwee era's two competing aesthetics heightens this sense. The self-consciously valedictory *Planet of the Spiders* can't hope to match this story's ability to be the definitive statement of the Pertwee era's aesthetic goals. *The Green Death* feels like the point where the Pertwee era's cultural moment can finally be allowed to pass. And sure enough, it's about to. Unfortunately for it, the Pertwee era still has another year to go.

Is There Any Way to Reconcile This with *Torchwood*?

The simplest answer, and arguably the most reasonable, is "no." There is, in fact, no sensible way to reconcile a television show made in 1973 with one made in 2006. It cannot be done. Certainly not without doing egregious violence to the show made in 1973. Any interpretation of *The Green Death* that attempts to incorporate *Torchwood*, in other words, is by definition a misinterpretation of *The Green Death*, which patently does not include *Torchwood*.

But more to the point, reconciling them does violence to the show made in 2006. Simply put, Torchwood's introduction in *Army of Ghosts/Doomsday* is absolutely ridiculous from the perspective of Doctor Who's own history. It requires us to credit an organization with the explicit mandate of tracking the Doctor, which has existed since the nineteenth century, and which failed to do so at any point prior to 2006. But here, at least, we have the ability to argue that this is deliberate. It's not like the new series is shy about acknowledging UNIT, after all. So there's presumably some explanation intended about why Torchwood spent the whole of the 1970s unable to find a man who was involving himself in every alien invasion to happen.

Of course, there's generally speaking the hint that Torchwood has only recently gotten competent. It's telling that Yvonne Hartman is all buzzwords and corporate culture – she is every inch the sort of person you'd expect to see put in charge of a failing organization to get it on the right track. The knowledge that there was recently a Prime Minister who was elected in the wake of an alien invasion supports this – of course Harriet Jones would go look for any dormant alien protection schemes lying around. So after finding a deeply incompetent Torchwood she sacked the leadership and put someone new in charge with an explicit mandate to shape things up. And if she didn't, her replacement is an even more likely candidate to put an amoral psychopath in charge of Torchwood.

The problem is that this only explains the failures of Torchwood 1, the London office. When it comes to Torchwood 3, the Cardiff outfit, there's a larger problem, because we know that's been run or at least staffed by Jack Harkness. We can believe in an incompetent Torchwood 1 that somehow misses every time the Doctor saves London. Believing that Jack, an actually intelligent and competent man who spends a century on Earth looking for the Doctor, somehow misses the several years that the Doctor spends on Earth is a trickier proposition.

None of the obvious explanations work. Torchwood 3 clearly has a remit outside of Wales, as we know Tosh was involved in the events of *Aliens of London*. Even if they weren't, *The Green Death* ought to have involved them. Did they really just sleep through an insane computer and giant maggots in the Welsh countryside?

There are a wealth of explanations we can come up with here. The easiest is that Jack is intelligent enough to put together the Doctor's timeline and knows that meeting up with Pertwee's Doctor would cause problems, given that the Doctor didn't know him six regenerations later. This is at least plausible, doubly so if you want to imagine Jack slipping the Doctor retcon, an image that is probably too deliciously wrong to turn down.

But once you've opened the door to secret Torchwood crossovers with the Pertwee era it's hard to shut it again. In *The Green Death*, of course, the most compellingly entertaining theory would have to be that the Nut Hutch is actually a Torchwood front, a theory that suggests that Jo's departure at the end is less "going to marry Cliff" and more "going to join Torchwood." Really, it's a pity *The Sarah Jane Adventures* mucks that one up.

Other entertaining options exist, but I'll leave it as an exercise for the reader to produce them. I recommend *The Mind of Evil*, *The Sea Devils* and *The Claws of Axos* as particularly entertaining starting points, particularly in light of the theory that Yvonne Hartman was put in charge of Torchwood by the

Master. All of these efforts require Jack's deference to the Doctor to have become institutional policy at Torchwood 3, but we know he's senior enough to be one of those who negotiates with the 456 in 1965, so the idea that he's setting policy is believable enough.

Another interpretation might arise if one assumes that Torchwood is comprised of more scavengers than alien fighters. If we assume that Harriet Jones/Harold Saxon/whoever put Torchwood on something more of a warlike footing in the new series, one assumes their previous approach was based more on gathering information and alien technology. They don't show up or involve themselves while UNIT is there because they'd rather sneak in afterwards and loot the alien technology. Long-term, after all, their legacy is as the "Torchwood Archives." Yvonne Hartman and Captain Jack may, in other words, be the exceptions in an organization that wouldn't have had much cause to appear in '70s Doctor Who in the first place. You just have to assume incompetence on the London branch and sabotage in the Cardiff branch and you're basically able to patch it all together without doing any egregious damage to either 1970s Doctor Who or *Torchwood*.

But at the end of the day the most satisfying explanation remains the first one. This is, after all, the same *Torchwood* and Doctor Who where, when one series did a big plot about nobody on Earth dying for months and horrific martial law and economic breakdown resulting, and the other show never mentioned it or gave any indication that it had ever happened. Which is to say that anybody looking to reconcile *Torchwood* and Doctor Who into a coherent timeline has more immediate problems to deal with than reconciling them over the span of thirty-five to forty years.

Pop Between Realities, Home in Time for Tea (*Dad's Army*, the Three-Day Week)

The stereotype, of course, is "stiff upper lip." Or as joked to my sister one winter when she was baffled how a couple of inches of snow were something that took four days to clear from the Heathrow runways, "why would the British fix something that they could just stoically endure?" It's one of the classic national myths of self-identity in the world. Every nation has them. The Americans are ambitious cowboys, the French have better taste than everyone else, and the British have the ability to keep a level head through anything. "Keep Calm and Carry On," as the idiom goes these days.

The origin of that idiom, of course, is World War II. The famous image was an unused propaganda poster in case of a German invasion of Britain, putting it squarely in the mythology of the Battle of Britain. I use the word "myth" here not to suggest that the claims are untrue, but rather to suggest that they have an almost religious character to them. What matters about these claims isn't so much their verifiable or falsifiable truth as the fact that they are so widely believed that their truth is almost irrelevant to their impact. Indeed, if they are true it is because they are so widely believed as to make themselves come true. For example: the photo during the 2011 riots that depicted a crowd of people hosting brooms triumphantly as they took to the streets to clean them up. The photo was, of course, at least partially manufactured, depicting an event that never quite "happened" as such. But this is almost beside the point – the crowd of brooms is such a fundamental part of the mythology of the riots because it feels like the sort of thing that would happen in the wake of riots in London.

Which brings us around to *Dad's Army*, the other major show in the early '70s featuring a comedic version of the military. There is a very straightforward similarity between *Dad's Army* and UNIT. We've talked already about how the Brigadier was always conceived of as a character who worked more like a Monty Python sketch character than like a dramatic character in the traditional sense, and how understanding this and the implications it has on the narrative structure is essential to being able to see how something like *The Claws of Axos* works. But saying this presents UNIT as if they were figures of pure postmodernism. And while they obviously work very well as postmodern figures, that's not the only thing going on with them. And understanding the rest of what UNIT signifies requires *Dad's Army*.

Some history: in the World War II era the bulk of able-bodied British men were, for obvious reasons, busy in the army fighting abroad. And so the Local Defense Volunteers, or, as they were eventually savvily rebranded, the Home Guard, were formed. Consisting of men who were unfit for active duty, generally because of age (hence the nickname "Dad's Army"), the Home Guard was intended as a line of defense for when (and it was expected to be when, not if) the Germans invaded. *Dad's Army* was a sitcom about members of the Home Guard in a fictional seaside town (which is where the Home Guard tended to be stationed).

The central comedic tension of the show is straightforward. On the one hand you have the sheer absurdity of a bunch of inadequately trained and supplied men who were defined largely by the fact that they weren't suitable for the real army who are nevertheless prepared to fight off the Nazis if they should ever invade. On the other you have the basic nobility of the fact that these men were unflinchingly willing to do just that. Essential to the show was the fact that the characters, while on the one hand utterly and hilariously inept, are on one level aware of their ineptness. And the way in which they are aware of it is fundamentally noble, in that they continue to risk their lives despite having a fairly good idea of how disastrously a Nazi invasion would actually go for them.

And in a real sense, the silliness of UNIT, with Benton being noble but thick and the Brigadier being insanely unflappable, is a variation of this: nobility in the face of the absurd. And that's something I haven't talked about much that needs to be acknowledged, because it is part of what is beloved about the Pertwee era. *Dad's Army* was an enormously popular sitcom, but it's crucial to realize that the characters weren't entirely laughed at. The main character, Captain Mainwaring, isn't a comedic buffoon to be looked down on and pitied – he's a genuinely aspirational figure for a culture that prides itself on the levelheaded bravery of ordinary people.

And so the UNIT era, with its similar "plucky yet slightly inept" setup, was similarly poised to be a beloved bit of comfort viewing. This gets at the other important thing to understand about the Pertwee era: it was made during a period where comfort television was important. See, the Pertwee era and Edward Heath's tenure as prime minister coincide almost exactly, with only Season Seven (save the last episode of *Inferno*) and the tail end of Season Eleven airing outside of his leadership. To say that this was a tumultuous period in Britain would be an understatement.

In the course of the just under four years Heath was Prime Minister the UK declared a state of emergency five times. This fact is, in many ways, the single easiest way to characterize his tenure: a state of constant crisis. Unsurprisingly, then, the sort of comforting competence of the Brigadier and the Doctor and UNIT was a nice tonic to this. And this explains a lot of the popularity of the UNIT setup. Even today the Pertwee era serves as comfort food in a way no other era of Doctor Who, regardless of quality, quite does.

But there's a dark side to all of this, and we need to deal with it briefly to see where the next era of the show is going. And this means looking at the tail end of the Heath era. The '70s were not a great time. In fact, it was an outright lousy time for an awful lot of people. And the period of the show we're looking at is one of the really nasty and for a lot of people scary bits of the '70s. But perhaps more important is the way in which they set up the far more iconic and monolithic issue of Britain in the 1980s.

There's a view in history where people refer to "the long X," such as "the long eighteenth century" or "the long sixties."

Basically, what this means is that the decade is looked at in terms of the lifespans of the major forces within it, so that the arbitrary calendar lines don't cut off important bits of history. So the long eighteenth century includes bits of the seventeenth and nineteenth centuries where things were either setting up or still mostly determined by the eighteenth century. And "the long '60s" extends, in most accounts, to the early to mid '70s. And if people talked about the long '80s, which they don't yet, we'd be just coming up to the brief pause between those and the long '60s.

So we're really on the cusp of moving from one era of history to another. And fittingly, we're also on the cusp of moving from one era of Doctor Who to another. So while we're not up to the long '80s yet, we're at a point where it's useful to start orienting our sense of the culture in terms of them. By any definition the long '80s are in full swing by the end of 1978. For my part, in terms of Britain, I'd put them as starting in 1975 with the rise of Margaret Thatcher to the leadership of the Conservative Party in the wake of Heath's defeat in the 1974 General Election. Which, notably, we're coming up on rapidly. Thatcher is going to, by necessity, exert a lot of gravity on this story as she ascends. This is mostly because Thatcher was, from the leftist perspective that I continue to argue Doctor Who is necessarily allied with, basically the raw embodiment of all evil.

This is, of course, not terribly subtle of me. But to a real extent it's impossible to be very subtle when dealing with Thatcher from the perspective of Doctor Who. Thatcher was an astonishingly polarizing figure, and the sections of British culture that were opposed to her are ones with huge influences on the show. The titans of the '80s and '90s British comics scene – Alan Moore, Neil Gaiman, and Grant Morrison – come out of that anti-Thatcher tradition, as do Paul Cornell and Andrew Cartmel, the figures most responsible for introducing those influences to Doctor Who. The entire image of British music in the '80s and '90s stems entirely from that tradition. As do the Sylvester McCoy and New Adventures eras of Doctor

Who, which remain tremendously influential on the series today. In short, huge swaths of Doctor Who's influences are defined by the extent to which they absolutely and completely loathe Margaret Thatcher.

While we are still early to introduce Thatcherism and the long '80s, there is one key aspect of Thatcherism that needs to be squared away now. Then we can safely put the whole Thatcher thing to bed for a number of years and get on with a nice period of calm between the death spasms of the long '60s and the moment when the long '80s reach their critical mass – a period in which, for the most part, Doctor Who is at one of its absolute creative high points (albeit with the exception of the next season). And that's the manufactured crisis. One aspect of Thatcher, and of Heath, for that matter, is that they are in many ways textbook examples of what is generally called disaster capitalism or the shock doctrine.

The basic premise of disaster capitalism – a practice that is now wholly normal on both the left and right – is that occasions of large-scale crisis are useful tools to dramatically reshape the order of things. On the left, Chicago Mayor and Obama's former Chief of Staff Rahm Emanuel's admonition that one should never waste a crisis is emblematic. On the right . . . well, take your pick, really. Naomi Klein's book *The Shock Doctrine*, from whence the term originates, makes much of the events going on in Chile around the time we're talking about here, whereby a bunch of University of Chicago trained economists aided Augusto Pinochet's brutal rise to power over the democratically elected (but, to US interests, inconveniently socialist) government, resulting in the murder of thousands of people at the hands of Pinochet's government and the torture of tens of thousands.

The logic of the shock doctrine is simple: extraordinary circumstances require extraordinary measures. And once those measures have been taken, it's easy to go on to normalize them. In the US, for instance, the aftermath of the 9/11 attacks was the pretext for a number of extraordinary intrusions on civil liberties in the name fighting terrorism, all of which went on to be permanent fixtures of the American political scene. But while disaster capitalism can work wonders with a real crisis, it hardly needs one. A manufactured crisis will work just as well, if not better. And Thatcher was absolutely masterful at them.

There is a sense in which the British national myth of the stiff upper lip is uniquely suited to disaster capitalism. A population that makes a virtue out of muddling through adversity is one that is incredibly easy to force drastic action onto. This manifests in some specific anxieties within British culture: the focus on mind control and social conditioning that caused *The Prisoner* to be made just didn't have enough resonance in the US for a show like that ever to be made there. But in Britain, where duty to "queen and country" is a fundamental part of the cultural landscape, the possibility that this duty could be subverted was a real fear – one that can be seen not just in *The Prisoner* but in things like *Doomwatch*, a show based on the fear that the scientific projects backed by the government could turn out to be dangerous and disastrous.

Which brings us to Edward Heath's great misapplication of the shock doctrine, the Three-Day Week. Some context: one thing we haven't talked about in the blog much is the fact that several countries, including the United States, reached peak oil during the 1970s. This resulted in massive spikes in energy prices, which helped set off nasty recessions, among other things. In the UK, one of those other things was an increased reliance on coal. This increased demand, combined with massive inflation, meant that coal miners were routinely working overtime without the sort of corresponding pay raises appropriate for that.

And so, in 1973, for the second time in a few years, they struck. And in what was, depending on your perspective, either a feat of staggering political suicide or a badly botched attempt at disaster capitalism, Edward Heath imposed the Three-Day Week at the start of 1974. This mandated that businesses were only to be open for three consecutive days, with no overtime or extended hours allowed, thus saving energy.

This was, to say the least, a bad situation. There were lots of real monetary policy issues that were making it very hard to keep the working class afloat, but there was still a genuinely strong sense of working class and union spirit that kept Britain sympathetic to the unions. Heath made a political gamble and tried to break the union's back by taking decisive action to try to refuse the miners' demands, then call a snap election and hope that the British public would rally behind the government in hard times and support their crackdown on the miners who were just going to have to tighten their belts like the rest of us. It's an early version of the Thatcher/Reagan playbook, plain and simple.

It is not entirely clear how manufactured this crisis was. There are claims that the government's on-hand stock of coal was deliberately underreported to provide justification for the Three-Day Week. But that's irrelevant in the face of the larger issue: Heath opted for measures that would impact the entire country to try to gin up support for union busting. Another option was always on the table – give the miners' their overtime pay. And, crucially, that was what they ended up doing, because it was a perfectly viable option from the start. Thus the Three-Day Week was a purely manufactured crisis – an energy shortage that was not merely allowed to happen but consciously caused to happen – in order to justify a political attack on the National Union of Mineworkers. This was done on the logic that it could then be leveraged into a snap election that would expand the Conservative majority – a strategy Thatcher implemented almost verbatim a decade later when she parlayed an appallingly stupid war into a massive electoral victory.

Except Heath got it all wrong. The attempt to manufacture a crisis to break the back of the unions failed spectacularly, and turned into a political disaster. Popular sympathy stayed with the miners, and the Conservatives crashed to a defeat at the polls in February. They narrowly managed a majority of the popular vote, but they lost their Parliamentary majority, restoring Harold Wilson to Downing Street and, after a second election in October, giving Labour an outright majority.

As I said way back when the '60s peaked, the leftist torch did not burn out in Britain with quite the crashing brutality that it did elsewhere. And Britain has this nice moral flicker in which a desire to side with the working class miners plays up, and it kicks the Conservatives out for a few years. The US goes through an analogous process two years later when lingering anger over Watergate hands a very nice and well-meaning peanut farmer the presidency, who gave it a very nice try even though it all ended in tears. Both of these brief flickers of leftism run for about four years, but Britain's starts two years earlier.

And, permitting ourselves to look ahead for a moment, Doctor Who, as I said, goes into a very, very big creative renaissance in a year. One that it is very hard for even the most ardent defender of the Pertwee era to deny is a massive, massive uptick in quality for the show. The next volume of this series starts off with what is, by many standards, the most undisputedly brilliant run on Doctor Who there ever was. And so this period of deeply uneasy political calm that settles in for four years between eras ends up as a sort of second psychedelic '60s off in the recesses of a sleepy little children's show that ended up being a real and genuine highlight of television as a medium.

Essentially this is Doctor Who's victory lap coming up – the point where it goes from an incredibly successful and long-running program to one that garners enough accumulated good will to be able to, by all appearances, run forever and become one of those literary characters who survives for centuries like Odysseus or Faust or Satan or Sherlock Holmes. (It is worth making a side comment here. In terms of characters of this sort who debuted in English-language works, Britain had ruled the art in the Victorian era, spitting out *Sherlock Holmes*, *Alice in Wonderland* and *Peter Pan* while the US managed *The Wizard of Oz* as its one feeble attempt. Come the World War II era, however, the US kicked Britain's ass in this department, creating Batman, Superman, and also sci-fi franchises like *Star Trek* and *Star Wars*. Doctor Who is, in this extended and grotesquely over-generalized analogy, the UK's version of *The Wizard of Oz* – it's one prize-fighting contender in the "let's create myths and gods" sweepstakes. This, if you were wondering, is why you read an insane epic on William Blake a few chapters ago.)

But between now and that victory lap is the rude awakening presaged by *The Green Death*. Though the Three-Day Week may have brought down a Conservative government, it was still an exceedingly scary and unstable period. The gaudy opulence of glam, previously the dominant aesthetic in British youth culture and especially in Doctor Who, was wholly unsuited to the era. In music it crashed to a resounding slump. It's worth looking in particular at Bowie's last properly glam album, *Diamond Dogs*, which abandoned the star-dusted optimism of Ziggy Stardust for a dystopian concept featuring Halloween Jack from Hunger City where "the last few corpses lay rotting on the slimy thoroughfare." *Ziggy Stardust* was the joyful party before the end. *Diamond Dogs* is the bitter party in the ruins of civilization. "This ain't Rock 'n Roll," Bowie shouts, "this is genocide!" Five years, it seems, was a somewhat optimistic estimate.

But Doctor Who doesn't regenerate itself for another year yet. Instead we get one more year in the glam paradigm after glam is dead. The result is, as you might expect, unsatisfying. More than that, it is unsatisfying in a way that echoes back to the problems that always existed with the Pertwee era, showing the way in which the failures of the glam aesthetic were inevitable. The end of *The Green Death* was perfect: the Doctor slinking out of the party before he overstayed his welcome. Season Eleven is the opposite: the party that goes on too long, reveling grotesquely in its own decadence.

Why Not Make Some Coffee? (*The Time Warrior*)

It's December 15, 1973. Slade is at number one with "Merry Xmas Everybody," with Gary Glitter, Roxy Music, Wizzard, and Mott the Hoople also lurking in the charts. Slade holds number one through Christmas, and into a new year, in the last real flourishing of glam.

I'd do the usual new season politics roundup, but I feel like the last entry did most of it. You've got the Yom Kippur War, tons more bad stuff in Northern Ireland, Pinochet's coup d'état in Chile, Spiro Agnew's resignation, and the mounting hilarity of Watergate. While during this story, OPEC doubles the price of oil, and the Three-Day Week itself comes into force at the start of the New Year, right as glam gives up the ghost.

It's fitting that *The Time Warrior* sits at the transition between glam and the uncertain darkness that followed. In practice, *The Time Warrior* was made at the end of the Season Ten block, and is the last Pertwee story that has any sort of consensus in favor of the idea that it might be a classic. It's also very much a passing of the torch. It's Robert Holmes's last story before he becomes script editor, a position he unofficially adopts for part of Season Eleven, and adopts in full for Season Twelve. And it's the debut of Sarah Jane Smith, the iconic companion of the Holmes/Hinchcliffe era renaissance. So there's a lot to love here, and the idea that it shows a series in decline is a tough sell. And yet it's also the first story of Season Eleven. As I've said, there are some real problems with Season Eleven and, though *The Time Warrior* is by miles the best it has to offer, something of an ill wind blows through this entire story.

As with the last Holmes story we saw, the major highlight here is that Holmes is a wizard at creating epic stories out of low-rent characters. In this regard the story is timely, fitting in perfectly with the sense of decline implicit in the Three-Day Week and the cratering end of the Heath premiership. Here we get Irongron, whose name makes him sound like a strange reject from *The Krotons*. At the start of the story, Irongron is a pathetic loser of a warlord complaining about his bad food and bad wine. Yes, he talks a big game about how he's going to have to go do some conquest to get new stuff, but it's clear from the start that he's a pathetic loser who's all talk.

This is the essential Robert Holmes move – to make a villain out of a pathetic schlub instead of out of some terrifying and powerful figure. So Irongron is scary not because he's inherently powerful, but for the far more interesting reason that he's an easily manipulable loser who's come under the influence of a powerful alien warrior. What Holmes does with this character – and with many of his other characters – is make him scarier by making him a less overtly powerful character. Holmes is intensely aware of the vicious sadism that ordinary people are capable of, and knows that by putting Irongron in the influence of Linx he gets a villain who is more rawly nasty than anything we've seen in the program since Benik in *The Enemy of the World*.

Holmes also gives us a helpful reminder of how much of a good idea the Master was. Remember that Holmes was the one who wrote the Master's first appearance – and yet it's also the only time he wrote for Delgado's Master, and one of only three times he wrote for the character at all. (And the third time killed him.) In Holmes's original conception, the Master was solidly the evil counterpart to the Doctor. Not just an evil genius, but someone who gets to out-Doctor the Doctor in scenes they share. Once the Master became as familiar as the Doctor, as I've said, he steadily became toothless and impotent. The bitter irony of this, of course, is that filming on this story ended mere days before Delgado's death, an event that, understandably, smashed the wind out of the sails of many of the people who had been working on the program for some time, most obviously Jon Pertwee, who, by all accounts, became deeply apathetic about the program after this story.

But in the gap right before that happens Holmes goes back to the drawing board and creates Linx. I should stress, because this is one of those points where obsessive fans skew things a bit, he does not create the Sontarans here. Rather, he creates a character who is a member of a previously unseen and unknown alien race. But Linx is not a particular instance of a mildly tedious Doctor Who monster – he's a specifically designed counterpart to the Doctor. Just as the Doctor is still one of two (or, given that *The Final Game* was still on the menu at the time of writing, one of one) Time Lords we have met in detail, Linx is meant to be the one Sontaran we meet – a representative of a larger and more powerful people. And notably, Linx is built up in a way that we've never really seen prior to this story – he talks sneeringly of the Time Lords as if they're a lesser race.

In other words, Linx is basically Holmes going back to the actual original idea of the Master and doing that again. More properly, what he returns to is the idea of an evil version of the Doctor. Linx is an alien, stranded on Earth, serving as the "scientific advisor" to a military figure, but mostly just trying to get off the planet. The difference is that where the Doctor ultimately embraced the glam approach, Linx embraces the militaristic approach completely, providing a typically Holmesian satire. Linx is an alternate direction the program could have gone. By hiding it in a medieval romp he can make this a proper savaging of that approach to the Pertwee era.

What this means is that Holmes is once again engaging with what is simultaneously the most important story to the Pertwee era and the one that is, in many ways, the least fully engaged with: *The War Games*. Recall that *The War Games* implied that the Time Lords are some form of counterpart to the War Lords, with both being powerful entities that oversee their respective concepts. This, of course, was largely dropped in subsequent stories, but it was at least the idea there. With the Sontarans, Holmes is essentially dusting off that dead end and reworking it into something else, asking what might have happened if a War Lord had fallen to Earth in the same manner as the Doctor. But since the Time Lords have developed considerably since the first try at that, the equivalent of the War Lords changes as well.

I've talked several times about the way in which the Time Lords appear to be the guardians of some notion of historical progress. And in this story, Holmes gives the Doctor a couple of lines that seem to support this, most notably in how the Doctor appears to view technological progress and social development as fundamentally intertwined, objecting to what Linx is doing because speeding human technological progress would ruin their moral and ethical development. Linx, as a Sontaran, is viewed as representing a different model of progress – one based on military might and power. And so the basic conflict of this story is an argument between a moral/technological view of historical development and one based on power and the use of force.

But then, in characteristic Holmesian style, he makes the forces of military might into silly buffoons – though as we've already discussed, this in no way takes away from the fact that they are effective and truly menacing villains. He creates an entire chunk of the story to serve as a view of history and the world centered on military might, then makes that portion of the story into a truly dark bit of comedy. We've already talked about Irongron's pathetic incompetence, but it's also worth looking at Linx, who promises endlessly to supply Irongron with weapons, but endlessly fails to deliver, or, when he does deliver, delivers a useless silly robot. And then there's the sublime visual gag of Linx unmasking himself at the end of the first episode, revealing that underneath his helmet is . . . a potato head the exact shape of his helmet.

This is the thing that is so wonderful about Holmes – his ability to weaponize humor and use it to lay into things like military bravado that he finds preposterous and wrong-headed. Holmes is not the funniest writer to do Doctor Who – both Douglas Adams and Steven Moffat reside in leagues of their own. But his humor has the most savagery and bite to it. He is the writer most capable of using comedy to damn his enemies. But this also brings us around to Holmes's biggest weakness as a writer – the fact that his unrepentant cynicism, which fuels his greatest moments, is at other times simply too unrestrained and too nasty. And *The Time Warrior* is the first place where this fault really comes through. Because as wonderful as Sarah Jane becomes, and as amazing as Lis Sladen is, Holmes is truly awful to her in this story.

Let's circle back briefly and look at Jo. As we saw back with *Terror of the Autons*, Jo was introduced to a great extent because Terrance Dicks thought that Liz Shaw was too strong and competent a character, and wanted a dumber companion who would get captured and rescued a lot. And this marked a major shift in how female companions were treated on Doctor Who. I'm certainly not arguing that all or even most of the previous female companions were paragons of feminism. But for the most part they did better than people give them credit for. Anneke Wills famously used to complain about how sexist the treatment of Polly was, pointing heavily to the infamous sequence in *The Moonbase*, where the Doctor tells her that the most helpful thing she could do would be to go make coffee. But then she actually saw the episodes and realized that, in fact, Polly is enormously resourceful and clever in that story, and a much stronger and better character than she'd assumed or remembered. This is perhaps the most dramatic example, but it's hardly the only one.

What I'm getting at here is that Doctor Who, contrary to Dicks's claims in justifying swapping Liz for Jo, was generally ahead of the curve on feminism in the 1960s. In fact, it was under Dicks and Letts that a crasser and more superficial view of what the companion was really took root. Yes, there was precedent, but the overall weight of the 1960s cuts against the view of the companion as a brain-dead peril monkey. So contrary to how Sarah Jane is presented – as a liberated and more mature woman than the show has given us in the past – she's actually a return to a better state of affairs. The show only had a major feminism problem because it had traded up from a minor feminism problem three years earlier.

The problem is that even though it's an improvement the show is still, on the whole, behind the curve on feminism under Letts and Dicks. And when the show does overtly turn to feminism in this period it does so with appalling condescension. The most toe-curlingly awful moments of *The Time Monster* are where Ruth is made into a comically annoying character by being made a feminist. And, not to look ahead too far, but Sarah Jane will never have a moment as wincingly horrifying as her attempts to explain feminism to the Queen in *The Monster of Peladon*.

But that's nothing compared to this story, which contrives to have the Doctor be a sexist ass to Sarah just so she can complain about it. The problem here should be obvious: the show goes out of its way to make a major character sexist just so it can get in a line complaining about sexism. In other words, the show's reaction to feminism is actually to make its major characters more sexist. Which reflects the larger problem with Sarah: she's only a feminist because Letts and Dicks decided feminists were trendy and that they thus wanted to have one.

Even worse, though, is the extended sequence in the second episode in which Sarah's complaining about how Irongron and company are sexist is played for laughs. Here part of the joke is that Sarah hasn't figured out that she's gone back in time and so is complaining about sexism to people who cannot possibly understand what she means and genuinely don't care. In other words, feminism is played for laughs: ha ha, look at how the dumb feminist gets it wrong and complains that the medieval brutes are sexist. She's so dumb. It's cruel, it's nasty, it's cynical, and, unfortunately, it's pure Robert Holmes. And this is his real weak spot – his cynicism can readily get carried away and start attacking the good guys with the same brutal fervor he applies to more deserving targets. Ironically, despite being the writer best at skewering bullies, he can lapse into being one all too easily.

Which also serves as a decent lead-in to the rest of the season. If Season Ten was the year in which Doctor Who improbably made it work, Season Eleven is the year in which no matter how good a set of ideas they have, they somehow find a way of screwing something big up. And although this is quite a good story, it demonstrates that problem all too well. Sarah Jane Smith is one of the great characters of Doctor Who, but in her first story she's treated dreadfully, and in a manner that ends up being far worse than the ostensibly more sexist Jo Grant character ever was. And unfortunately, this sort of thing is going to be par for the course this season.

Books! The Best Weapons in the World! (*Invasion of the Dinosaurs*)

It's January 12, 1974. Improbably, despite the fact that it has been two weeks since Christmas, Slade continues to hold the number one single, though after only one more week of this they give way to The New Seekers' "You Won't Find Another Fool Like Me," which in turn gives way to Mud's "Tiger Feet," which has a four-week run and is the number one single of the year. Andy Williams, The Sweet, Lulu, Diana Ross, David Bowie, and The Wombles all also chart.

While in real news, Patty Hearst is kidnapped by the Symbionese Liberation Army, and Alexander Solzhenitsyn is exiled from the USSR. Really, that's about what I can scrape together here. Oh. On US television, both *The Six Million Dollar Man* and *Happy Days* debut. There. Major world events, those are.

While on good television . . . oh, wait, never mind, it's *Invasion of the Dinosaurs*: a story that is not so much in the territory of "good" as it is "infamous." There are even (likely spurious) rumors that Barry Letts requested its destruction because he was embarrassed by the effects. I've usually foregone criticizing the effects of Doctor Who, generally stressing when they are adequate instead of when they're not. But here we have a story whose single biggest claim to fame is its wretched special effects, and let's face it, it's not like we're going to be able to go nine books on Doctor Who without talking about bad effects at least once. It's part of Doctor Who's cultural legacy, after all.

Let's start with a brief typology of special effects. There are essentially two types, which we can call visible and invisible effects. An invisible effect is one that is meant to work in the background. When we see it, we are not meant to gawk at the effect, we're meant to sail right over it, accepting it within the narrative. Invisible effects merely have to be good enough to not announce themselves. The sets are usually an example of invisible effects in Doctor Who. Very rarely is the point of a story or scene in Doctor Who up to 1974 to gawk at the studio scenery. If the scenery is working well in a Doctor Who story we shouldn't even notice it consciously – it's only when the set is flagrantly underdressed or one of the walls wobbles when someone bumps into it that we notice them. If we want to get properly philosophical about it, the invisible effect works like the Heideggerian object, invisible as long as it is ready-to-hand, but becoming a pronounced and visible thing upon its malfunction. Case in point, the horrible scene in *The Green Death* in which the Doctor sits in an unmoving Bessie while a CSO landscape scrolls by. This is jarring because it's supposed to be a scene where we're not thinking about the effects, but because they're so obvious and tacky we are forced to think about them anyway. (We'll talk more about invisible effects when we get to *The Ark in Space*, which provides a fabulous limit case.)

Visible effects, on the other hand, are showpieces. My usual go-to example is the scene in *The Muppet Movie* in which Kermit rides a bicycle. Nothing about this scene is meant to be realistic or believable. The audience is not meant to believe that Kermit is a real frog who happens to also be a cyclist. The only reason that effect is interesting is because the audience is consciously aware that Kermit is a piece of felt that cannot possibly ride a bicycle, and thus stare at the scene trying to figure out how the effect was done. Where the invisible effect strives to disappear, the visible effect tries to call as much attention to itself as possible. And so where an invisible effect just has to be "not awful," a visible effect has to be impressive. Impressive, mind you, is not synonymous with realistic: much of the glam aesthetic of the Pertwee era has involved ostentatious displays of non-realistic video effects and splashes of color, which are clearly visible effects.

On the other hand, a lot of visible effects do try to work in a more or less realist mode. That is, they attempt to show something the audience knows cannot possibly be real, but attempt to show it as much like the audience imagines it would look if it were real as possible. The audience knows it's a special effect, but the pleasure comes in it not being transparent how the effect was carried off.

Which brings us to the scene of a Tyrannosaurus rex making out with a Brontosaurus. It is not the worst effect Doctor Who has had to date. But it is the most frustrating, because it's supposed to be a visible effect. You can tell, because it's in a story called *Invasion of the Dinosaurs*. That pretty much explicitly says that the dinosaurs are the focus of the story. When you commit to that, you are pretty much committing to delivering decent dinosaurs. Especially when you decide to use the Yeti-in-the-Loo approach and put the dinosaurs in central London. Because you're putting dinosaurs in a real place, as opposed to an imaginary place, and then selling the story on the basis of the dinosaurs, the show fundamentally commits itself to high quality, realist dinosaurs. Which is off the bat a dumb idea, because Letts has attempted a giant lizard of one sort or another in every season to date and he's never once had it come off well. This hasn't been a big problem because he's usually done it in stories that are about something other than the giant lizards, so the embarrassing effects have just been brief dissonant notes that don't detract from the overall story. This time, however, the story is about dinosaurs, and instead we get more puppet snogging than *Meet the Feebles*.

So for the first time, we're really left with nothing to do but admit that the effects are getting in the way of the story. But this in and of itself is worth remarking on. We got through a decade of Doctor Who where about the worst thing that needed to be said was that the visual choices of *The Dominators* were kind of rubbish. It's not until the glam era of the show, in which visual spectacle becomes one of its primary pleasures, that the question of inadequate effects really becomes a fundamental problem for the show. But even still, it's not until this story that bad effects become a major problem for a story as opposed to a single bum note. Because here the bad effect means that one of the basic justifications for the story falls through. There's not a clear point to doing *Invasion of the Dinosaurs* without decent dinosaurs.

More unfortunate, however, is that several of the other basic justifications for this story fall through. On one level, what's going on here is another conspiracy thriller. Aside from the wholly valid question of why another one of those is a good idea so soon after *The Green Death*, there's a larger problem here: every single character introduced within this story save for a few very minor UNIT personnel is in on the conspiracy. There's not a single supporting character in this story who isn't on the bad guys' side. Again, seemingly the entire production staff of Doctor Who fails to quite get what it is that makes conspiracy thrillers work, which is uncertainty. Once it becomes painfully obvious that anyone who is not a series regular is evil, this story switches to just running out the clock with car chases until it hits six episodes. This serves to make the effects problem even worse. If the story were taut and gripping we might just be able to overlook the bad effects. But it's absolutely tedious, leaving us with nothing better to do than stare at the terrible dinosaurs.

That's not to say there aren't good bits. There are. Lis Sladen is fabulous, and is given a particularly meaty subplot that often leaves her with more to do than the Doctor. The supporting actors are mostly very well chosen, with both Martin Jarvis and Peter Miles showing up – as nice a double bill as the series manages in the '70s. And of course there's the first episode, in a deserted London, in which Hulke realizes that the return of the TARDIS allows new ways of starting off otherwise traditional UNIT stories. Where the series previously had to have the Doctor involved in the action from the start, and thus never had a situation where the supporting cast knows more than he does, here he can arrive with things already in progress and have to figure out what's going on in the first place. This gives us, for the first time in the Pertwee era, a story that's a credible redo of *The Web of Fear*, the story that, in fan lore, is the model for the entire Pertwee era. He even manages to have the Doctor and the Brigadier in the Underground – a nice nod in what is the beginning of the end for UNIT.

But by and large, the fact of the matter is that this is a slow and phoned-in effort that feels like the production team putting together one last UNIT story for the sake of doing it. It's a bitterly disappointing way for Malcolm Hulke to end his time on Doctor Who.

Good thing, then, it's not actually the end. Because this is also the point where the Target line of novelizations begins, with the first two books – Hulke's adaptation of *The Silurians* and Dicks's of *Spearhead from Space* – coming out five days after the first episode airs. Hulke ends up deciding that he prefers writing the novels to writing for the actual series, and departs the series to write half a dozen more: *The Green Death*, where he largely repaired the story's unfortunate treatment of the Welsh, *The War Games*, and his other four Pertwee stories, this one included. (*The Faceless Ones*, the other story he worked on, was novelized by Terrance Dicks after Hulke's 1979 death.)

We've talked before about the novelizations, but it's worth repeating a key fact: in many ways, these books were more influential in the fan consensus about the Pertwee era than the actual episodes. In the years before VCRs allowed any story to be preserved there was no difference between a story that had been novelized and one that was important. As a result, a good novelization is enough to give a story a permanent legacy of being a classic even if the actual televised story is dodgy. Which is what happened to this story, because the novel is great. We've also talked before about the prose stylings of Terrance Dicks, who remains the most prolific Target writer. But we should also stress the importance of Hulke, who, though he only wrote seven Target books, was every bit as influential simply because he wrote so many early on. (Of the seven books released in the first year of the Target line three were by Hulke.)

Where Dicks is a master of ruthlessly functional prose, Hulke prefers a more tersely suspenseful style that at times evokes the noir thriller style of someone like Raymond Chandler or Dashiell Hammett. And where Dicks, especially in his later books, shoots for faithfully capturing everything that happens on screen, Hulke cuts ruthlessly and, generally, in the story's favor. The tedious chases and action sequences that make up much of the last few episodes are cut entirely, with the fifth episode being reduced to a single chapter consisting of a mere tenth of the book. The result is far tighter plotting and a story that, unlike its original version, doesn't overstay its welcome. On top of that it had one of the single best covers of the Target line: a gaudy collage of gorgeously lurid dinosaurs menacing the Doctor topped with a giant pop-art caption of "KKLAK!"

But what Hulke brings to the story in novelizing it is far more than just a tightening of the pace. He also brings a moral center to it. The biggest problem with the episodes as aired are that they make precious little effort to differentiate between the villains' motivations and their methods. Hulke is trying to write a story in which people do terrible things in pursuit of noble goals. The idea is a critique of the way in which idealism and utopianism can be subverted in the same way in which manufactured crises can be. (Indeed, it's worth noting that Operation Golden Age is just disaster capitalism used by a different ideology.) This is all great, but in the televised version it ends up stymied by the fact that everyone just plays their part as a standard Doctor Who villain. The two lines in which the Doctor expresses any sympathy for what they're doing are swallowed up, in one case because Pertwee is visibly bored with the scene despite the fact that it's what, on paper, should be a corker: the Doctor and Mike's confrontation. Instead Pertwee delivers all the lines with no inflection beyond smug paternalism. (Of course, the larger problem here is the decision to have Mike be the traitor given the relatively limited range displayed by Richard Franklin in the previous three seasons. Even a moment's thought and/or looking at how well John Levene does when he's given a scene with actual material would tell you which character should have a fall and redemption plot, and which one should just get conked on the head by the Doctor.) The result is that the story as aired repeatedly seems to suggest that the real danger is eco-terrorists. Especially because Hulke ends up writing a conspiracy story in which eco-terrorists manufacture a crisis to bring about their real goals. In the wake of Heath's Three-Day Week this becomes a rare moment of Hulke completely and utterly getting the politics of his story wrong.

In the novelization, Hulke takes advantage of the ability to describe character thoughts to reiterate more regularly the distinction between what the Operation Golden Age people are doing and why they're doing it. Sarah, a character that it's immediately clear Hulke would have loved to have written for earlier, benefits the most from this, constantly trotting out journalistic wisdom ostensibly handed down to her by the pros, all of which is really just Hulke providing a running commentary on the story. This is nowhere near subtle, but given that the alternative is a story in which the people warning of ecological disasters are bad guys creating a manufactured dinosaur crisis so they can forcibly reorder society – i.e. a story that adheres almost perfectly to the right wing talking points against environmentalism – it's tough to treat the more explicitly moralistic novel as a step down. Certainly Hulke seems to be enjoying himself in the novel, which is more than can be said for anyone besides Sladen in the TV story.

But what is most interesting about the novel is that it reveals the degree to which Hulke has become so cynical about the program by this point that even Robert Holmes looks like a sunny optimist. It's not just his casual cutting of entire scenes on the grounds that they'd be dull, or his dispensing of the Whomobile. No, the key clue comes when he describes the man from the Middle Ages as having "a strong Midlands accent," a swipe at bad Doctor Who acting worthy of Paul Magrs. (The problem, of course, being that nobody from the Middle Ages would speak in a way even remotely describable by twentieth-century accents, and it is only in the world of the BBC that the idea of using a regional accent to denote "from eight-hundred years ago" would come up.)

Once you begin to look for it, the number of points where Hulke appears to just be making fun of the story blossoms rapidly. First of all there's the one that shows through even in the televised version: the fact that the fake space ship is a clear jab at the naive and reflexive embrace of space stories. Hulke turns a space ship from something responsible for a jaw-dropping, cliffhanging reveal, in which the story appears to have jumped three months and taken Sarah into outer space, into a cheap fake stored under London. But there's also the Reminder Room, an Orwellian terror seemingly consisting of a droning documentary and nothing else, which in the book gets an entire chapter named after it despite being, in practice, terribly underwhelming.

The strong sense is that Hulke just doesn't care anymore, and has given up on the program. Certainly his decision not to write for it again suggests that. And it's not hard to see why. Hulke had always opposed the earthbound format even as he helped set it up. But Hulke was also one of the writers who laid down the basic challenge of the Pertwee era back in *The War Games*: involvement in more than just blowing up monsters. Instead he's been stuck writing for an era that prefers star turns, showboating, and visual spectacle to serious looks at society, even in the earthbound stories that were supposedly designed to allow for just that. Even when the show does take on real political issues, it's generally been with ham-handed disastrousness, as with *The Green Death*, another story Hulke fixed in novelizing. One gets the sense that Hulke, on some level, knew that the story he wanted to do – one about the foolish danger of blind nostalgia and the fact that progress is still a good thing – was going to be sold down the river before it hit the screen.

Because frankly, the entire plot of *Invasion of the Dinosaurs* seems like nothing so much as a rejection of Doctor Who. The central flaw of Operation Golden Age is that it just tries to blow up a problem instead of working to improve the world. That's what the Doctor half-heartedly tries to persuade Mike of, at least. And of course, at the end of things the Doctor blows up the problem and goes on to . . . run off to Florana with Sarah. He utterly fails to make a single move towards improving the world or presenting a more positive version of the agenda he's supposedly sympathetic to. And Hulke ends up exposing this hypocrisy directly by confronting him with a situation in which he has no choice but to expressly praise the exact sort of person he isn't being in this story – people who work meaningfully to improve the world.

This is staggeringly bitter of Hulke. He takes an utterly cynical decision to cast the Doctor as no better than the villains. (Indeed, it's flagrantly Sarah, not the Doctor, who Hulke views as the primary hero of this story.) And it's fitting that the Pertwee era's most moralistic writer finally turns the lens onto the Pertwee era in this regard. This isn't just Hulke quitting the show. It's him penning a demonstration of why, in his eyes, the show has failed miserably at everything he wants it to be.

Still, Hulke does leave us with one parting gift in the story: the final scene of the story is the first instance of something we now take for granted as a completely standard trope of the show. It's the first time the Doctor seduces a companion with descriptions of the wonders of the universe to get her to travel with him. Because even though we're ten episodes in, Sarah Jane has not actually joined up to travel with the Doctor yet – she accidentally got taken back in time in *The Time Warrior*, the Doctor returned her here, and there's no implication that they had intervening adventures. This is good – especially after how popular and (quite rightly) beloved Jo was, having her replacement earn her stripes before the Doctor invites her on board goes a long way towards softening the blow of the transition. But more importantly, we get that delightful scene of the Doctor praising the wonders of the universe to a reluctant companion to get her to travel with him. As final scenes go, it's a lovely farewell to Hulke's tenure writing for the television show. And while there are many things about this story that can be called good, it is in many ways the only thing about it that can be called nice or lovely.

Time Can Be Rewritten Extra: *The Paradise of Death*

Amidst the many strange creative figures in the Pertwee era none stands out more visibly than Barry Letts. Terrance Dicks, at least, has an extensive later career we can peek at to understand him as he lurks invisibly behind the Pertwee era. But Barry Letts, despite producing, writing, and directing in the era, is something of an enigma. On the one hand we know for basic fact that he's a strongly leftist Buddhist. On the other hand, he oversaw an era of Doctor Who that flirts with reactionary conservatism constantly and manages to make a hash out of its liberal intentions on a regular basis.

Using a radio play written nearly twenty years after the Pertwee era's end is, of course, tricky. The legacy of Doctor Who under Letts had, by 1993, necessarily comingled with his actual vision. What we get in 1993 is not Letts's vision of Doctor Who, but Letts's vision of what his Doctor Who was all about, a subtle but important distinction. On the other hand, in understanding Letts himself, as opposed to his Doctor Who, this is in many ways superior. Inevitably *The Paradise of Death* becomes Letts explaining and justifying himself.

That is not to say that the story is an apologia. There is no accusation or critique that Letts is responding to as such. But Letts is implicitly asked to summon up the essence of his era here, which requires him to conceive actively of what that means. The story necessarily serves as Letts making some claim about what his version of Doctor Who is. Which makes this the moment when we can most clearly evaluate Letts. (The other contender, of course, is *Planet of the Spiders*, which is written, directed, and produced by Letts, and is self-consciously a retrospective on the Pertwee era, but which has so much else going on that it's difficult to use as a lens on Letts.)

He does not come off well. That said, it could be worse. He actually did two of these radio plays, and if I really wanted to skewer him I could have gone for *The Ghosts of N-Space*, a legendary trainwreck. *The Paradise of Death* is a largely fairer option. But it still has a host of problems, from the technical on down. Its basic cast is solid – Pertwee, Courtney, and Sladen are old pros who can make virtually anything work. But with a completely solid cast like this Letts inexplicably opts to add the character of Jeremy, whose sole character trait is that he's an incompetent idiot who provides comic relief. He is, in effect, Doctor Who's attempt at Jar Jar Binks, and is exactly as awful as you'd expect.

The overall structure is also flaccid. Letts uses the familiar structure from *The Time Monster* and *Planet of the Spiders* where an initially domestic story gives way to an interstellar one, but in this case the domestic angle is poorly connected to the space one at best. The Parakon Corporation is a bunch of aliens negotiating with the UN, but nobody has touched the implications of this, and what eventually sends the story to Parakon is nothing more than Sarah Jane accidentally stowing away on a surprise spaceship. In the Pertwee era proper the switch from the earthly to the galactic involves a jump of scale, whereas here it seems wholly arbitrary.

Equally frustrating, the ideas are insipid at best: evil virtual reality, a *Soylent Green* rip-off, and the blandest evil dictatorship ever. The villains are equally recycled. Peter Miles is solid playing what is blatantly Nyder from *Genesis of the Daleks* with the name changed, but how good he is at playing the part only highlights the fact that it's the same part. Meanwhile, the quite solid Harold Innocent, in what appears to be the last performance of his life, is wasted imitating Kevin Stoney's performance of Tobias Vaughn. (Innocent died during the story's transmission.)

And this is before we get to the appalling ethical lapses. The evil space empire is this time a society where almost nobody has to work because they've managed to find a plant that can be easily used to provide for all of society's needs, allowing everyone to live a life of leisure. This is, of course, utterly evil.

Letts's alternative to the horrors of Parakon is a slightly Buddhist-flavored version of capitalist democracy. The central horror of *The Paradise of Death* is nothing more than an improper response to the problem of scarcity. The victims of war and refugees are killed and repurposed into fertilizer for the rapine plant. But it's revealing that, in all of this, the logic of scarcity is taken completely for granted.

Letts positions the rapine plant as unnatural and as a spiritual sickness – the fact that large swaths of the population do not need to work is evidence of the fact that something horrible is going on. In other words, the problem isn't just that mass killings to support the lifestyle of Parakon are wrong, it's that the very idea of a post-scarcity society is morally abhorrent (as opposed to a potentially interesting thing to explore via science fiction). Letts outright cannot envisage any alternative beyond the existence of a massive working class.

This would be one thing if Letts were relatively egalitarian in his instincts. But the Pertwee era works against him here. He's using the Brigadier, and so ends up with an authoritarian military hero being central to liberating Parakon. He's still got "special people," like the character of Onya, who are put in charge of things. Which is to say that this entire story simply takes for granted the necessity of a ruling class and a larger working class.

Yes, it also bemoans violent and sensationalistic media as a morally appalling way of anesthetizing the masses. But this is just another authoritarian viewpoint – a swipe at those in charge of making mass entertainment for falling down on their Reithian duties. The media must be more paternalistic and less sensationalistic. But more bizarre is the fact that this viewpoint is coming from the director of *Terror of the Autons*. Letts's entire time on Doctor Who is based on an aesthetic of sensationalism. He was unrepentantly making trashy teatime television thrillers. No, he never went full *Hunger Games*, but given that public execution game shows are also not an element of real life entertainment, it's difficult to see *The Paradise of Death* as something that doesn't implicate the very era of Doctor Who it's supposedly participating in.

In the end, there's just not a visible way past this sort of blindness. All of this represents nothing so much as a massive failure of imagination. Which is, let's be honest, kind of the perfect summation for Barry Letts. It's not that he made lousy Doctor Who. Quite the contrary, he made Doctor Who of thoroughly consistent quality, with only about three outright and unfathomable turkeys over his twenty-four stories in charge. What he didn't do is make particularly ambitious, imaginative, or creative Doctor Who, or Doctor Who that had very much to say.

When the earthbound format was first proposed, Malcolm Hulke objected that the only two stories it allowed were an alien invasion or a mad scientist. Taking the Master as little more than a special case of mad scientist, it's difficult to argue that Hulke was wrong. To be fair, the earthbound format was not Letts's invention, and he brought it to an end reasonably quickly. But it's telling that after *The Three Doctors*, when the earthbound format came to a full and proper end, the non-earthbound stories he did consisted of one with a properly clever premise (*Carnival of Monsters*), two that add up to a remake of a Hartnell story (*Frontier in Space* and *Planet of the Daleks*), one that's a remake of last season's remake (*Death to the Daleks*), and one that's just a story from two seasons earlier done slower and worse (*The Monster of Peladon*).

And in the earthbound stories it's telling how little and how badly Letts's innovations went. His first act upon arriving was to break the ending of *The Silurians*. This is a decision we've talked about frequently throughout this book, but let's look at it one more time. On one level Letts's instincts are solid – the conflict between what the Brigadier wants and what the Doctor wants is by far the most interesting part of the story, and is the one moment in the entire Pertwee era where it looks as if the show might actually try to explore the implications of the Doctor working for the military. But Letts has no ideas of what to do with it. It gets a brief mention at the top of *The Ambassadors of Death* and is dropped forever.

What is telling, when taken in the context of the rest of the Pertwee era, is that Letts largely starts as he means to go on in this regard. The botched ending of *The Silurians* is the blueprint for the entire Letts era. He has all the right ideas and interests, but he doesn't have the imagination to take them to their successful conclusions. He's a well-meaning leftist with his heart in the right place, but when he gets political it's mostly just obvious how much he supports the status quo. There's a frustrating superficiality to his entire approach. Even his biggest strength, as a director, is based primarily on his ability to be visually striking more than on his storytelling abilities as such.

Thankfully, in that regard, at least, he was running Doctor Who at the exact right moment. The early 1970s were, as we've seen, a period where superficiality and artifice were exactly where one looked to find the aesthetically avant-garde. Letts was running Doctor Who at the exact cultural moment where his weaknesses were minimized and his strengths were accentuated. The result was workable within the context of the early 1970s, and was rightly enormously popular then.

But more than any other fact, this is what makes the Pertwee era seem so strange in hindsight. It's not the ways in which the earthbound setting, UNIT, or Pertwee's relatively humorless Doctor make the show tangibly different from what it is the rest of the time and thus what's usually thought of as "what Doctor Who fans like." It's the fact that more than any other era of Doctor Who, this is one that is of its time and for its time. This explains why, while the Pertwee and early Baker eras were about equally popular among audiences at the time, the Hinchcliffe era remains terribly popular among later fans, whereas the Pertwee era is an increasingly contested curiosity. The Hinchcliffe era was a timeless sort of good. The Pertwee era was a very timely one.

I do not mean this as some sort of "the past is a foreign country" defense of Letts's tenure. Throughout the Season Eleven essays I highlight egregious political and ethical failures of Letts's work, and I do not consider "but it was 1974" to be a reasonable defense for any of them. Nor do I disagree as such about the aesthetic failures of the era. The problem is that from a perspective outside of the early 1970s these are all that is visible. They're visible from within the perspective of the early

1970s, but more to the point, so is the aesthetic that makes it all work anyway. But divorced from that, as a remake in the early '90s, the spark that made it work is gone, and we're left only with the uncomfortable ghosts of the era.

Pop Between Realities, Home in Time for Tea (*Moonbase 3*)

Sometimes the most valuable thing one can do to understand something is to take a step back from it. It should be no secret to anyone reading the blog that I am less fond of the Pertwee era than I am of many of the other eras of Doctor Who. (And it is firmly "less fond," as opposed to "not fond.") And much of the book thus far has been grappling with those problems. But it's really with *Moonbase 3* that the fundamental and unfixable flaws of the Pertwee era come into focus.

Moonbase 3 is interesting. It's not the first time Doctor Who people went on to try something else – that's basically *Adam Adamant Lives!* – nor is it the first spinoff of Doctor Who – that's *K-9 and Company*. But it is the first time major production staff of Doctor Who used Doctor Who as a springboard for a new show. Basically, *Moonbase 3* is six episodes of Barry Letts and Terrance Dicks trying desperately to quit Doctor Who for something else. It's consciously positioned as something from the people who make Doctor Who, but it's also consciously a break from Doctor Who as opposed to "more" Doctor Who.

In practical terms, it was a failure – low rated, and with a mixed critical consensus. Accounting for why is a tricky project. Terrance Dicks has largely suggested the show was too dark and lacked a sense of wonder. It certainly is serious-minded in the extreme, but no more so than *Doomwatch* (from which its first twenty minutes are stolen wholesale) nor than Terry Nation's soon to be successful *Survivors* (which will be covered in the next volume). And anyway, dark and cynical is a pretty good fit for when the show aired, at least plus or minus a couple of months.

Nor is it quite fair to say that the show failed because it was bad. It had serious flaws, certainly, but no more so than the first season of any number of successful shows. Occasionally the show manages to feel like *Babylon 5* done twenty years early, which, given that *Babylon 5* is, for all its many faults, one of the absolute landmark pieces of science fiction television, is a feat worthy of real respect. No, the best case for why it failed, to my mind, is that a show about realistic space exploration in late 1973 is already two years past its sell-by date. Interest in moonbases after the Apollo missions were over is a bit . . . well . . . low.

But ultimately, why it failed commercially isn't even the most interesting question. One can just as easily ask why Doctor Who succeeded, and in real terms the answer is going to be a diffuse set of arbitrary and often seemingly small decisions that happened to successfully navigate a given crisis where other sets of decisions probably wouldn't have. The question of industry success is not an uninteresting one, but the answer turns out to be arbitrary and beyond the reach of what can be controlled. Interesting or not, it doesn't have a lot of broader implications.

No. Far more interesting is the question of why the show failed aesthetically. And that it did. Again, plenty of cancelled-after-one-season shows have had real impact. Six low-rated episodes can be quite important. But these weren't, really. And that is a bit odd. On the surface, they're a lovely homage to the spirit of classic science fiction – the sort of Asimov/Heinlein/Clarke stuff that was still popular in the pre-*Star Wars* days of the early '70s. Even with their slight misfit with the spirit of 1973, there's still a core to this that is interesting and seems as if it at least theoretically could have been picked up as a cult show. As I said, its sense of human greatness on the frontier is at times marvelous and stirring in the same way that *Babylon 5* is, and the basic concept and tone of the final episode, "View of a Dead Planet," is an extraordinary piece of bleakness that at least conceptually seems worth being remembered.

But there's something downright nasty lurking under the surface here, and it's something that captures a fundamental failing of the Dicks/Letts/Pertwee era – one that I've talked about in passing before, but that becomes systemic here, and in one key moment becomes completely inexcusable. And to get at it, I'm going to have to talk about a truly appalling moment of television – one, in fact, from the aforementioned final episode.

The premise of "View of a Dead Planet" is that the entire crew of the moonbase comes to believe that the Earth has been destroyed due to an ill-advised scientific project, and that they are going to run out of food and all suffocate. And in the course of their despair about that, one crew member breaks into the quarters of the only female regular (having already groped the only other significant female character in the series) and attempts to rape her. She manages to call for help, and the base commander shows up, sends the rapist to his quarters, and the next morning declares that "nothing very serious happened," and says that the man has apologized so it's all OK. The victim is given no opportunity on screen to give any sort of comment on what has happened to her, and the commander's declaration that a rape attempt is not serious and can be cleared up via an apology is allowed to stand unchallenged. And, of course, the commander is the moral center of the narrative, as is typical of this sort of sci-fi, so that's pretty much the last word.

So, one of the things I try very hard to do with this project is to engage in redemptive readings of what I analyze. Even when I'm dealing with something that I find deeply problematic and upsetting within Doctor Who, I try to counterbalance it with at least some positive upside. I do. And I extend that to the creators whenever possible. And that sets up a real problem here, because this is a very bad scene that reflects very badly on both Terrance Dicks and Barry Letts, who are two terribly beloved figures in Doctor Who fandom. And deservedly so, because they did some truly wonderful stuff. And I really, really want to stress that I am a huge fan of them both on the whole. And I would love to find a way out of calling this scene what it is.

But I can't. There's absolutely nothing I can possibly find to redeem this scene. It's abhorrent. It's sickening. Terrance Dicks and Barry Letts should be ashamed that they let it make it to screen. There is nothing good whatsoever that can be said about it. It is unacceptable by the standards of today. It was unacceptable by the standards of 1973. It is morally bankrupt, and creates a prima facie case against the ethical positions of everyone involved in it. And this is the really annoying thing to have to admit – that case has merits that extend to Doctor Who as well.

Because it would be one thing if the scene were appalling in a way that was massively disconnected from business as usual for Dicks and Letts. But it's not. It's a vile and offensive piece of work for exactly the same reason that Letts and Dicks are often problematic, which is that they've got no commitment whatsoever to the personal scale of things. Politics for them amounts to nothing more than broad moral statements unconnected to any actual material commitment to the world or to people. To overstate the case – though, actually, for the *Moonbase 3* scene, it's completely fair – their writing strays at times into overt sociopathy.

This is occasionally hard to see, because they have unflinching commitments to two things that are almost, but not quite, an interest in humanity. The first is, as I suggested, moral statements. Dicks and Letts love a good moral. They develop patrician characters just so they can have people to say morals for them. The second is drama. And so you'll get something like a character believing he is imminently going to die drunkenly trying to rape people, because it's dramatic to watch that, and *Corrie* isn't on twenty-four/seven. And you'll get the square-jawed commander decking him, because rape is bad, albeit not, apparently, "serious."

The only thing you won't get is anything resembling a human concern with the survivor, because she is neither an easily digestible moral statement nor a case of high human drama. Instead she becomes entirely overlooked – a mere detail in the narrative existing only to allow the "proper" drama, which is, inevitably, focused on the travails of the man who rapes her and the men who ultimately turn a blind eye to that fact. This sickeningly parallels the way in which survivors become incidental details in mainstream discourse about rape, often with the implication that they are partially complicit in their own fate. Rapists deserve some punishment, but victims are ignored or marginalized in such a way as to provide tacit justification and partial exemption for their attackers: "She's just some slut who got raped." Which is essentially how the show treats her.

But this isn't just one bum note in an otherwise great series. It's systemic. In the first episode, there's a passing discussion between two characters about whether they want to visit Earth, in which both imply that the conditions on Earth are such that it's preferable to live on the Moon. Given that this episode also establishes that the Moon is a harsh and brutal place, this is really interesting. And, predictably, not at all developed because, well, developing that sort of thing wouldn't lend itself to moralistic bon mots.

Similarly, in "View of a Dead Planet," at one point the weekly guest star (Michael Gough in this case) expresses a view that nationalism is the root cause of human disasters. This is all well and good. But then as soon as the global catastrophe happens, save for one scene in which the European base checks with the American and Russian bases (there are also Chinese and Brazilian ones) to make sure they're getting the same readings, no effort is made to look at how the moonbases deal with this, or to mirror the moral point about nationalism on the Moon divided among the last survivors of humanity according to the lines of nations that seemingly don't exist anymore. To call this an oversight misses the point – this isn't sight at all. This is self-evidently what the story is about. It's pitched as a parable against nationalism. And yet it completely fails to do anything with the way in which nationalism affects the main characters directly.

Instead the episode just ends with Michael Gough intoning that a man can make a mistake, but mankind must never make one. Which is fairly typical – instead of looking at the material conditions of an ethical or political problem, Letts and Dicks would prefer to craft a slogan, give it to a good actor to say in a serious voice, and leave it at that. See, you can make a mistake like raping someone, just so long as you oppose pollution (won't Jimmy Savile be happy to hear?).

For a show like *Moonbase 3*, this is a catastrophic failure. The value of realist (and this is probably the time to link to the "Pop Between Realities" entries that dealt with realism in general and specifically with social realism), hard SF is that it explores real human issues. When all of those issues are systematically trimmed out in favor of broad platitudes, you lose the fundamental point of the genre. The whole reason *Moonbase 3* is interesting as a premise is because it can explore thoroughly the implications of its world. But Letts and Dicks have no visible interest in doing so.

This isn't as bad in Doctor Who. For one thing, it's a children's show, so Letts and Dicks manage to avoid rape apologism by virtue of avoiding rape. But more broadly, it's a show where the main character is defined in part by his ability (and inclination) to move on to other things. Even in the context of the Doctor's exile and the turning of this into a criticism of him as a character, an anthology show with a mandate to show the audience something radically different every few weeks is always going to avoid the long-term implications of a given setting. No matter how much the show responds to the challenge laid down by *The War Games*, this is always going to be part of its basic structure, and so the degree to which it can engage in the material realities of a given setting is always limited.

But the disinterest in actual human lives still accounts for many of the most frustrating aspects of the Pertwee era – namely the points where the show seems to raise an interesting situation or point only to ignore it in favor of giving Pertwee a chase scene, or where it decides to crusade against a social ill and in doing so perpetuates it. For instance, when it suddenly includes a lot of overt sexism against female characters just so that the female characters can complain about sexism. Or when it does a story that's in part about the way in which Welsh mining communities are marginalized and ignored, and then fills the story with the most superficial and stereotypical Welsh miners imaginable.

Because while Doctor Who can often get away without dealing with humanity in a meaningful fashion, it can't always, as we've seen. And perhaps more to the point, it can shine when it takes a few tricks from social realism. And even in the Letts/Dicks era, both Malcolm Hulke and Robert Holmes were doing better jobs of this. Hulke did it by making sure to include gestures at the question of how to build a society instead of just how to blow up monsters. We discussed his final act of cynicism in this regard last time, but even more important is *Colony in Space*, where he packs in just as many anti-corporate bromides as a Letts/Dicks effort would demand, but also manages to put in numerous compelling accounts of what alternatives might be: positioning the Doctor in the role I described as "science vicar," or even just having Bernard Kay's character visibly and pointedly reject one way of life in favor of another.

But the thing that *Moonbase 3* really just cries out for is Robert Holmes, who is the obvious pick to write about a run-down and underfunded moonbase. Because, as I've said in past entries, what Holmes really excels at is the personal and the grubby. He is capable of effectively sketching a vivid character, and having characters who are driven by individual foibles and emotions. Where Dicks and Letts write, basically, good guys, bad guys, and immature guys who are learning to be good guys, Holmes writes cowards, gluttons, reluctant heroes, and a whole spectrum of humanity. And it's not that Holmes's characters are realistic – they're usually caricatures in the extreme. But Holmes draws on a broad spectrum of humanity to make his caricatures, and ends up with deeper characters than the more serious "realism" of characters that spring from a world as banal as Dicks and Letts's.

Either the Hulke or Holmes approach would have salvaged *Moonbase 3*. (Well, either approach coupled with not having a sickening rape apologist scene.) Just like either approach, throughout the Pertwee era, made for better Doctor Who than anyone else could manage on a regular basis. Holmes and Hulke were flat out the writing stars of the Pertwee era, to the same extent that Whitaker was the writing star of the Troughton era. The rest of the time, like *Moonbase 3*, the Pertwee era was variable – sometimes extraordinary, sometimes terrible, often quite good. But in the end, missing something very important: humanity.

Poor, Pathetic Creatures (*Death to the Daleks*)

It's February 23, 1974. Suzi Quatro is at number one with "Devil Gate Drive." A sort of post-glam piece of bubblegum, it holds the spot for two weeks before giving way to Alvin Stardust, another sort of sanitized glam cash-in. He lasts for one week before yielding the top spot to Paper Lace's "Billy, Don't Be a Hero," widely recognized as one of the worst songs ever recorded. David Bowie, Ringo Starr, The Hollies, Paul McCartney and Wings, and the Bay City Rollers all also chart.

The most obvious piece of news to cite here is the fact that the election that returns Harold Wilson as Prime Minister takes place. Charles de Gaulle Airport opens in Paris. And seven major Nixon aides are indicted in the Watergate break-in and cover-up.

Far from all of this, on television, is *Death to the Daleks*. There are many Doctor Who stories from the '70s that are well-remembered because they are classics. There are also, however, several Doctor Who stories from the '70s that are well-remembered because they came out on home video early. The 1980s VHS releases were focused almost entirely on classic monsters and highlights from the early Tom Baker years, which meant that both *Day of the Daleks* and this were among the stories that were widely and universally available on VHS. The logic on this was understandable, if crass: the early releases strongly favored four-parters, which were cheaper (in the UK, and six-parters got released as two tapes. The US generally condensed them to one, but the result was that in the early days, four-parters were strongly preferred). Within the era favored by the releases – Pertwee- and Hinchcliffe-era Baker – *Day of the Daleks* and *Death to the Daleks* were the only two four-part stories featuring the Daleks, and so they were shoo-ins for release. (This same logic is why *Revenge of the Cybermen* was improbably picked as the first release – it had the right Doctor, was four episodes long, and the series had just brought the Cybermen back in *Earthshock*.) For American fans, this release seemed particularly common, frequently ending up as the only

Doctor Who story that ended up at the local Blockbuster. So this is a very well-known story.

But the level of familiarity here is oddly incommensurate with the level of quality. It is not that *Death to the Daleks* is an especially bad story – although it's hard to argue with a straight face that it's a particularly good one. For the most part it feels like the embodiment of a standard issue Terry Nation Dalek story. Which, in many ways, it is. But the degree to which this story is familiar obscures the degree to which the story is also very, very weird. Watched on its own it feels like a standard Terry Nation story. Watched in sequence, after ten weeks of *The Time Warrior* and *Invasion of the Dinosaurs*, it sticks out like a sore thumb.

This is not necessarily a bad thing. It's just that for the past sixteen episodes and nine months, ever since we came back from the last Dalek story, Doctor Who has been, seemingly by choice, an earthbound show again. The stretch from the start of *The Green Death* to *Invasion of the Dinosaurs* is entirely stories that at least start in the UNIT format, and only the three episodes of *The Time Warrior* lacking the Brigadier interrupt this. Despite coming after the ostensible end of the earthbound format, this is actually the longest stretch without a story in which the adventure starts with the TARDIS actually traveling somewhere new since the stretch from *The War Games* to *Colony in Space*.

On top of that, there's a clear difference in style at the start of this. Some of this is the fact that Terry Nation remains thoroughly uninterested in piddly questions like "what has the series been dong since I stopped writing for it in 1965." And so we get a wealth of things that are just odd. The TARDIS is far more of a mechanical object than it usually seems, requiring a hand crank to open the doors when the power is out. This is not quite as jarring as Nation's strange idea that the TARDIS pulls in its air supply through the doors in *Planet of the Daleks*, but it still feels off. Nation is also, as ever, utterly uninterested in these "women" things that are apparently running around the universe, contriving to have Sarah mute or absent from as

333

much of the story as possible while leaving the only other female character with basically nothing to do.

But there are other things going on here as well. The basic plot and setting – an H. Rider Haggard story in space – is bizarrely incongruous within the Pertwee era. Even stranger is the script's apparent confidence that the audience will care about vast living cities and strange aliens making sacrificial offerings simply because they're vast living cities and strange aliens. I've been complaining for several entries now about the failure of the series to take seriously any broader notion of humanity, but this story expands this to ludicrous new levels. There is no sense whatsoever that Exxilon is a world with any meaningful culture so much as a video game level full of very dull puzzles. (Apparently there is a game of "spot the moment where Jon Pertwee decides to quit the series" to be played with this story. My nominee is when he has to pretend that solving a maze is an interesting and dramatic event, in particular when he expresses that he thinks they've got it when there is no ambiguity whatsoever that they have a straight shot to the exit.)

Adding to this is Terry Nation's bizarre sense of scale. Previously, we had the idea that an army of ten thousand Daleks is massively terrifying on a galactic scale. That would be, roughly, the population of Woodbury, Connecticut, or, if you prefer a British reference point, just a bit smaller than Devizes in Wiltshire. (No, of course you haven't heard of them. That's the point.) Nation goes on here to establish the stakes of this story – ten million people across the galaxy might die. Although ten million people is indeed a lot, it's somewhat less significant when you consider the fact that it's roughly the population of Michigan, or, if you prefer, about three-quarters of the population of the London metropolitan area, which actually means this story has lower stakes than the last one. And since we never see any of these people, or hear anything about them besides as a potential death toll, it's tough to say this story does much to give a sense that anything is at stake here. There's a moral stake, but it's played wrong: either the story needs to go with "it doesn't matter how many people there care, this is the right thing to do" or it needs a number that's actually suitable to setting up a prima facie case for the magnitude of events. Instead it's trying to set up a big number and badly misjudging what "big" means.

To be fair to Nation – although I'm honestly not sure if this is a point for the prosecution or the defense – he at least gives no sense of scale or humanity for a different reason than usual for the Letts era. Normally the complaint is that Letts prefers broad moral messages to details. But Nation seems not to care about either. It's actually that the number of people dying isn't, to his eyes, what anyone cares about in this story. He appears to genuinely believe that the lure of Daleks and an ancient city is sufficient justification for this story. Everything else is just a MacGuffin. Ten million people dying is the new "core of the Time Destructor" or "hollow out the Earth's core and drive it around picking up girls." It's not supposed to matter, it's just supposed to get you Daleks.

And even there, Nation is clearly realizing that he's got a problem, because he has to go for the cheap stunt of the Daleks having their weapons disabled so they have to be wily and tricky. (In fact they just append regular guns in place of their laser guns and basically get on with enslaving all humans.) This is a very bad sign. We already had some clear signs that Nation had run out of ideas for Daleks beyond "put them on a hostile planet with a human(oid) expedition and have them fight it out." Which would be one thing if it weren't for the fact that the three Dalek stories prior to *Planet of the Dalek*s all attempted far more interesting things, with two of them being among the all-time classics of Doctor Who. So for Nation to, in successive stories, roll the format back to its earliest version and then visibly hit a wall with variations on it is disheartening. Especially when no effort is made beyond that to tie it into any larger narrative or context for the viewers.

So, to recap, the series goes from three stories in a row that are set on Earth, only one of which even has an alien in it or moves outside of present day, to a space story with no meaningful ties to Earth even on a metaphoric or thematic level. The only thing anyone cites as a real world context for this story — the power drain as an analogue to the rolling blackouts of the Three-Day Week — falls apart when you realize the story was in the can before the end of December, with the scripts finished even earlier. The departure represented by this story is absolutely massive.

And in addition to all of this, the story is something of a departure in terms of narrative technique as well, at least in its first two episodes. Up until the third episode, what stands out most about *Death to the Daleks* is how visual most of the storytelling is. There are numerous sections in which the plot is advanced by what we see on screen instead of what we're told. It's not until the third episode that the story even begins to explain the nature of Exxilon; prior to that the plot is mostly people doing things instead of saying things. This is an odd register for Doctor Who to be in. It's more cinematic than the series usually is.

All of this conspires to give *Death to the Daleks* an odd and almost dreamlike feel compared to the rest of the Pertwee era. In a way this oddly prefigures the dark science fantasy tone of the looming Hinchcliffe years, doubly so because Robert Holmes is the uncredited script editor on this story. This story isn't usually pointed to as a prototype of the Hinchcliffe era, but it absolutely is, every bit as much as *The Tenth Planet* was a prototype of the Troughton era, or *The Invasion* was of the Pertwee era.

The essential problem with it is, ultimately, the Daleks. As I suggested earlier, the fact that Nation has to reduce to gimmicks like depowering them in order to get a story to work suggests a writer badly out of ideas — as, if we're being honest, did his previous script. But *Planet of the Daleks* at least had a reason to be a retread, given that it was the "proper" return of the Daleks. Doing a type of story that hadn't been done in a decade makes sense even when that type of story is dated. Doing the exact same story you were doing the last time the TARDIS was moving freely in space and time, however, is unfortunate. Particularly when the main effect of the previous outing was to give a real sense that the show has moved on and that this type of story was a nice nostalgia trip, but not what the show really is anymore.

Frankly, since David Whitaker left the program, nobody involved has had a clue what to do with the Daleks. Whitaker made them work in his two stories by realizing that, done right, the Daleks are a truly mythic enemy, and then putting them into a story where only a mythic enemy will do. *The Power of the Daleks* requires the Daleks because the new Doctor has to have a baptism by fire. *The Evil of the Daleks* requires the Daleks because it needs an enemy that is the literal embodiment of pure evil. But *Death to the Daleks* doesn't require the Daleks. In fact, it would probably be a more interesting story if it skipped the Daleks and just told a story about Exxilon. The idea of a living city worshipped as a god is far more interesting than "Oh no! Daleks!"

None of this is helped by the fact that the Daleks are in tacky '60s costumes that were obviously not made to present any interesting color visuals. Apparently the Daleks made for *Planet of the Daleks* were deemed low quality and discarded. Which I assume, from a production standpoint, they were. But visually speaking, they were great, with the gunmetal finish providing a real visual flare that the lumbering bright silver things in this story can't possibly match. Nor is it helped by the fact that the Daleks are apparently neurotic, with several just having nervous breakdowns and exploding for no apparent reason beyond that something hurt their feelings. This is limited not just to the Dalek in the fourth episode that explicitly commits suicide, but also the one in the second episode that just charges unarmed at the Exxilons shouting "Exterminate" before gibbering incoherently and exploding. Not only does the story have no ideas beyond "Wow! Daleks!", it isn't even particularly invested in those.

But the root problem is just that Terry Nation, frankly, never had any ideas for the Daleks in the first place. He has a very Dan Dare-style genre he likes to write in. He came up with a monster for his first one and Raymond Cusick, completely independently of Terry Nation, hit it out of the park with the design. But because of how copyright and the BBC works Nation got all the credit and ownership of the Daleks even though the things that make them popular and memorable have almost nothing to do with him. He didn't design mythic threats to the Doctor. He designed generic baddies lurking in an abandoned city. Even when he did bring them back in a more mythic mode, as in *The Dalek Invasion of Earth*, it wasn't really what he did that rendered them mythic (other than the frankly obvious trick of a first episode cliffhanging reveal) so much as the combination of the show's first returning monsters, Susan's departure, the first alien invasion of Earth, and everyone else playing it for the mythic despite the script not really supporting that. Having never invested in the mythic nature of the Daleks in the first place, Nation is in many ways the writer least suited to bringing them back because he lacks any sense of how to structure them into an event. The only thing saving *Planet of the Daleks* was the fact that Malcolm Hulke wrote six episodes leading into it that served almost entirely to set that story up as a massive Dalek event. Without that lead-up, and forced to have the Daleks be interesting on their own, Nation draws a complete blank.

The result is a story that, even if it is interesting in hindsight for its odd look forward, feels like a deeply flawed aberration that serves mostly as a strong case for why the Daleks need to either be put back to bed or given an impressive reboot – whichever one most effectively means we never see such a lazy and cynical use of them again. Yes, there are some interesting bits of tone in this story, but based on the story alone, you'd never be able to figure out what the point of the exercise was in the first place. *Death to the Daleks* may have a dreamlike quality to it, but then again, falling asleep often does.

You Were Expecting Someone Else (*Countdown/TV Action*)

And once again, it's time for the once-per-book engagement with the wide world of ancillary merchandising. When last we left this story, back in the Patrick Troughton volume, we noted how the late '60s comics fit firmly in a specific tradition of British comics, and were as accurate a translation of Doctor Who to that medium as was meaningfully possible.

For both the beginning and end of the Pertwee years, the existing Doctor Who comic strip appeared in the same magazine it did in the Troughton years: *TV Comic*. At the onset, the comics were very much in the same mould as the late Troughton strips only with a grotesquely caricatured representation of Jon Pertwee instead of one of Patrick Troughton. They shared the same mind-wrenchingly odd sense of plotting, and the same belonging to a different tradition. At the end of the era they were something different: the manic energy of the Troughton years had faded, replaced with a much more taut sense of how to handle action and suspense.

But beyond that there is a profound change in the visual stylings of the strips on either end of the Pertwee era. The early strips used a very straightforward grid structure – the page consisted of three rows of two-to-three panels each. But the later pages had a considerably more interesting visual style, using oddly shaped panels and page layouts, and using the panel structure as part of the storytelling. For instance, in one strip the panel shape distorts and becomes more eccentric when dealing with panels featuring the aliens. In another a round panel is situated about a third of the way down the page, with the other panels forming a sort of starburst panel around it. The art also grows more sophisticated, using light, shadow, and perspective as tools of the storytelling where the earlier strips were much flatter and simpler. In other words, the comic had become considerably more visual in its storytelling.

To understand how and why that happened, we're going to have to pull back and look at the British comics industry in general again. We've already talked about how the British comics industry is historically based around the anthology magazine in a way that the American comics industry hasn't been since the 1940s or so. What's crucial to understand is that for the most part, this meant that people were following brands of comics more than individual stories. Major magazines would have flagships characters, certainly: *2000 AD* has Judge Dredd, *Eagle* had Dan Dare, etc. But more important than the specific, iconic character a magazine features is the magazine's general tone. A given magazine couldn't survive by having one good strip and a bunch of filler. Not every strip could be a classic, but any successful magazine had multiple good strips and a fairly consistent tone across all of them.

The two big British sci-fi comic magazines are, as I've said, *Eagle* and *2000 AD*. *Eagle*'s heyday came and went before Doctor Who, meaning that the deserved "Pop Between Realities, Home in Time for Tea" entry on Dan Dare never really quite had a place to go. *2000 AD*, on the other hand, doesn't start for another few years, and we'll cover it in the Tom Baker volume. But several other significant titles exist beyond those two, and one of them is *TV Century 21*, later named simply *TV 21*.

TV Century 21 was one of the fingers of the Gerry Anderson media empire – another topic that we'll cover in the Tom Baker volume. The short form is that Anderson was a television pioneer in the 1960s who invented a puppetry technique he artfully named Supermarionation, and parlayed it into making very popular children's action serials, the most famous of which was *Thunderbirds*. But the other thing is that Anderson was a wizard at was cross-promotion. He was one of the first people to really understand how to build children's media as a franchise in which the television show was only part of a larger brand. This approach eventually became standard practice in children's television, reaching its commercial and creative peak with the American cartoon series of the '80s such as *Transformers*, *Teenage Mutant Ninja Turtles*, and *Masters of the Universe*, all of which were designed as television series for the explicit goal of marketing the toy line, often introducing characters in the toys first and then creating episodes to explain who they were.

So *TV Century 21* was part of that – an anthology of comic strips based on the popular Gerry Anderson shows and one or two others, including, for a few years, the Daleks (which it had licensed from Terry Nation directly, and thus came without Doctor Who). And as one would expect, its branding was tight and innovative even for a British comics anthology, with the strips being presented in the context of a supposedly futuristic newspaper with news stories and clippings of puppet characters in amidst the strips, all of which had a shared universe so as to strengthen the unified brand. It was a work of art.

But the real big gun *TV Century 21* had was an artist named Frank Bellamy. Bellamy had come up through *Eagle* in its latter days, and was, quite simply, one of the best artists ever to grace British comics – a sort of British Neal Adams. Had he been twenty years younger, he would have undoubtedly been among the wave of great British comics artists who jumped to American work along with Dave Gibbons, Alan Davis, and Brian Bolland. Instead he died at only fifty-nine in 1976 having never really broken out beyond his native country.

There are two things that distinguished Bellamy's work over that of his contemporaries. The first was that he could execute the photorealistic art style of American comic strip artists like Alex Raymond and Stan Drake. When drawing Jon Pertwee for the *Radio Times* he made an effort to capture the actual contours of Pertwee's face, a stark contrast from the caricatured rendition of the early *TV Comic* strips. Bellamy's style was not straight photo-realism, but rather a slightly rougher and more expressionist take on it. This was a far more dynamic and rich approach than was normal for British comics of the time, and was understandably revelatory.

But Bellamy's debt to American comic strips extends well beyond photorealism. He also has a visible debt to the massive full-page comic strips of the early twentieth century such as *Little Nemo in Slumberland* and *Krazy Kat*. If you've never had the pleasure of reading either of these strips, both are in the public domain and easily found online. But to be brief, what's remarkable about these strips is the degree to which they use the large canvas of the full page to create complex visual structures. Instead of the default grid model of comics in which comics amount to little more than stills from a television show (or, in the older tradition, stills from a theatrical production), these comics created a dynamic look for the page, functioning both as a single image and as an assemblage of individual image. Bellamy used similar techniques in *TV Century 21* when drawing *Thunderbirds*, using the space given to him by double-page spreads to draw elaborate page layouts. For instance, one strip had a half-page spread that included a train pulling into station, and the panel jutted out into the adjacent page, a narrow spire of train cutting across the entire spread and anchoring everything going on in the two pages around that one oversized panel. It's stellar comics art; Bellamy was far and away the best in the business.

One might ask why I'm making so much of Bellamy given that he never actually illustrated a Doctor Who comic. Here's the thing: in the early '70s, in part due to the fading popularity of the Anderson shows anchoring the magazine, *TV 21* folded. Polystyle, who published the competing *TV Comic*, swept in, grabbed the Anderson licenses, and attempted to launch *Countdown*, a glossy, high-quality publication. And since they had the quite nice Doctor Who license they added it to their magazine as well. They poached the art director from *TV 21*, and he proceeded to impose a house style of Bellamy clones and protégés. And so while Bellamy himself wasn't involved in the magazine, his general style, albeit watered down a bit, was all over *Countdown*, and, when it proved too expensive, all over the not-quite-as-nice but still very pretty *TV Action*.

The *Countdown* strips were the creative high point of Doctor Who comics prior to *Doctor Who Weekly*, and stand up mightily to much of the Marvel UK/Panini output too. As Tat Wood points out, although the Pertwee era Doctor Who was in color, it wasn't until 1976 that color sets became more common than black-and-white ones. In other words, for all that we've been talking about the glam era of Doctor Who, most of the audience wasn't actually seeing it in color or getting that aspect of the program (this is perhaps part of why the Pertwee era's reputation lies in its realism, a genre often associated with the "grit" of black-and-white – see also how the lack of color in *The Mind of Evil* is typically taken to have enhanced its reputation). But *Countdown* was color for everybody, and the sheer gloss of the strips alone makes them important.

They also, in a real sense, understood Doctor Who better than the people making it. In 1972, right as the transition from *Countdown* to *TV Action* was happening, they ran a story called *The Planet of the Daleks*. Not only was it a considerably better Dalek romp than the (unrelated) television story that shares its name, but it includes, in glorious (albeit by that point monochrome) detail, Daleks fighting dinosaurs. This image single-handedly encapsulates the visual style of the Pertwee era even better than the era itself. Barry Letts would have killed to be able to put that on screen, little yet to have it look good, which it did.

But more to the point, the adherence to a consistent visual style (and the comparative ease of doing so in comics compared to television) meant that even though the comic's writers weren't nearly as good as the best (or even the average) of what was on television, the comic managed a consistency of vision that the television series didn't really see until Russell T Davies started focusing on that with the implementation of tone meetings and conscious decision to make sure every department working on Doctor Who was actively working to tell the same story. The Bellamy-esque visuals gave the comics a real sense of tone, combining photorealist drawing techniques with a scratchy line and lurid color palate that was tremendously effective.

Particularly key is the way in which Bellamy-style color worked. The *Countdown* comics used color as if it were just another form of shading. Faces were often shaded with a single color, often a non-realistic one like an orange or blue. Sections of scenes were often demarcated with color so that, for instance, the Doctor and a set of rocks he's hiding behind might be pink while the rest of a panel was done in greens. The effect is like that of detailed shading in more photorealistic art, but in a sensationalist glam aesthetic instead. Like the combination of photorealism and chaotic page layouts, it adds a sense of real excitement to the comics. They seem very visceral and real, but simultaneously very stylized, which is an excellent combination to go for when crafting an action comic.

If the *TV Comic* era preceding it was Doctor Who comics that felt exactly like what they were – Doctor Who adapted into a low-rent action comic magazine – then the *Countdown* era is also exactly what it seems like: high-production-value action comics featuring Doctor Who. And in this regard, they're an important part of the Pertwee era in the same way that the old Dalek annuals are an important part of what the Daleks are. The Pertwee era often tried to be a fast-paced, thrilling action show. Sometimes it even succeeded. But *Countdown* and *TV Action*'s Doctor Who strips were fast-paced, thrilling action strips every week, always delivered with reliable quality and visual consistency. They are, in other words, the distilled essence of one aspect of the Pertwee era in a way that Polystyle's earlier comics, not just in the Pertwee era but in the Hartnell and Troughton eras, never were.

Unfortunately, *TV Action* folded a little more than a year after its launch and Doctor Who returned to *TV Comics*, losing much of its luster in the process. Even there the influence of the *Countdown* era remained, as evidenced by the more dynamic panel structures and composition. But though better than the earlier *TV Comics* strips it's impossible to argue that they're anywhere near the quality of the *Countdown* material. Much as Frank Bellamy was an island of artistic importance between the *Eagle* era and the *2000 AD* era of British action/sci-fi comics, the *Countdown* comics were a brief island of real importance in

Doctor Who comics, and it won't be until the *2000 AD* era that they really flare into being interesting again.

Too Narrow, Too Crippled (*The Monster of Peladon*)

It's March 23, 1974. Paper Lace continues to hold the number one spot with the legendarily execrable "Billy Don't Be a Hero," a song imploring a lover going off to war to "not be a hero" and, in particular, to "keep your pretty head low." It is basically one of the worst things ever, in that sense of the word "worst" that occasionally means "best." After two weeks it finally goes away to be replaced with "Seasons in the Sun," one of the most upbeat and cheery songs about dying ever recorded, and at only three minutes and twenty-four seconds, not so long that the listener actually wants to. Also in the charts are Paul McCartney and Wings, Ringo Starr, Gary Glitter, The Hollies, and Queen.

In real news, the OPEC oil embargo largely ends, bringing some stability to markets that had been lacking during the energy crisis. A major Palestinian terrorist attack in Israel – the Kiryat Shmona massacre – kills eighteen. And the Carnation Revolution takes place in Portugal, managing the amusing historical feat of being a military coup organized in part by using the Eurovision Song Contest as a pre-arranged signal to take action.

While on television, and speaking of the legendarily execrable, it's *The Monster of Peladon*. Along with *The Time Monster*, this is generally considered to be the worst story of the Pertwee era (although, inexplicably, *The Mutants* slots in between them on the *Doctor Who Magazine* poll, while *Death to the Daleks* is somehow at 128, just ahead of *The Claws of Axos*). And while there are cases where I will defend a hated story to the bitter end, or where I will opt to look at a story's virtues in lieu of its flaws . . . this is not one of them.

The last few entries have involved a lot of pointing out some fundamental failings of the Pertwee era. Actually, most of the entries on the Pertwee era have dealt with this, due largely to my not liking the Pertwee era very much. But I've at least generally hedged those with appreciation of the good sides and of what the era was trying to do. Here, then, is where the good will runs out. I have next to nothing positive to say about this story. It is an ugly train wreck at virtually every level.

To start, let's think about its source material. In particular, let's consider what it was that made *The Curse of Peladon* interesting and striking. By and large, it was that the story was so strikingly weird. Peladon was not like what we were used to seeing in Doctor Who in 1972. More to the point, *The Curse of Peladon* is one of only three stories not to rely on a concept from a previous story in order to generate or justify the plot. (Admittedly the majority of the others just use either UNIT or the Master, but it's still the case that only *The Curse of Peladon*, *The Mutants*, and *Carnival of Monsters* actually involve the Doctor, on his own, encountering a completely new situation.) So in that regard, the entire idea of a sequel to *The Curse of Peladon* is moronic.

Even worse is the fact that not only did they decide to remake the story (and with virtually the same plot), they decided to make it at two-thirds speed by turning it into a six-parter this time around. It is difficult to imagine how this is a decision that could possibly emerge out of a process that was focused on any level on creating quality television. By this point nobody working on Doctor Who could possibly have failed to notice the fact that six-parters are, generally speaking, train wrecks from a writing perspective. There is next to no way to accomplish them with at least one, if not two episodes that consist of running in place. There's a reason that Robert Holmes's first innovation as script editor is an attempt to do away with them by splitting them into a four-parter and a two-parter, and that he ultimately settles on seasons consisting of five four-parters and a six-parter instead of two four-parters and three six-parters, as was the norm for the Pertwee era. So dreadful were the six-parters that Holmes and Hinchcliffe make this switch, which was more expensive, despite having had to take extreme measures to get their first season in on budget, including planning entire stories around the fact that sets could be recycled. They were willing to commission and prepare an additional story every season under already tight conditions just to get rid of two of the three six-parters. So to remake the story as a six-parter is difficult to credit.

Admittedly, little attention has been paid throughout the Pertwee era to how many episodes a story needs, with the bewildering end of *The Daemons* being only the most obvious example. Stories were picked to be six episodes for little reason other than that three stories every year had to be that length. But even by the meager standards by which pacing was thought about by the production team, the decision to do a remake of a two-year-old story only slower has to be viewed as one made with a shocking lack of thought about whether anyone would actually enjoy the result.

From there we expand to other issues like how the effort to adapt and retool the story were handled. In the original version, there's a clever feint whereby we know one of the villains – the King's advisor – from the start, but don't know the other, and are misled to assume it must be the Ice Warriors, since they are traditionally evil monsters. This time we're misled to think that it's the Queen's advisor who's evil, when in fact it's the mining engineer Eckersley who's the villain. Now, to be fair, this is actually rather clever. If nothing else, it manages to be a far more interesting and elaborate conspiracy plot than *Invasion of the Dinosaurs*, in that "characters introduced for this story" is not simply a subset of "bad guys."

Less fortunate, then, is when the Ice Warriors are trotted out at the halfway mark in a cack-handed effort to keep the plot going, and are immediately established as evil. Again, this demonstrates a complete lack of understanding of what made *The Curse of Peladon* work so well. The Ice Warriors worked as decoy villains because we were well trained by their previous appearances to recognize them as villains. More to the point, the Doctor assumed they were evil, so even if you were unfamiliar with them (and their previous appearance in *The Seeds of Doom* was three years old in 1972) you had a very solid reason to suspect them. Given that, the twist that they weren't actually the bad guys meant something.

Again the problem appears to be little more than that nobody even thought about this. Dicks, whose script this mostly was, clearly looked at *The Curse of Peladon* and observed that there were two groups of characters in it – the royal court of Peladon and the aliens. Among the aliens there was a clear villain who turned out not to be evil, whereas among the Peladonians there was a clear villain who we recognized from the start. So Dicks, in a straightforward attempt to keep it fresh, flips it: he relies on the precedent of the high priest being evil from *The Curse of Peladon* to put the decoy villain in the royal court and the obvious one among the aliens. (The point where it becomes obvious that Dicks has just swapped the two groups of characters comes with the death of a minor character in the first episode to start off the mystery, which in *The Curse of Peladon* goes to the spare Peladon noble, whereas *The Monster of Peladon* kills off the spare alien.) He tinkers it up a bit by adding the new wrinkle of Eckersley as a human villain, but for the most part it's a straight swap of two groups of characters where each one plays the role the other did last time around.

Except it's rubbish. The new advisor isn't nearly as good a decoy villain as the Ice Warriors because, unlike the Ice Warriors, he doesn't have a lengthy history as a suspicious character: he's a completely new character we've never seen before. The only thing that casts major suspicion on him is the fact that last time they did this story the character most similar to him was evil. So while it's cleverer than *Invasion of the Dinosaurs*, it's still not exactly what you'd call a rock-solid red herring, and it certainly lacks the cleverness and the substance of having an old monster turn good.

Which is, of course, where the real problem is: in the decision to flip the Ice Warriors back to evil. The Ice Warriors, after all, are one of a kind. They're the only species originally introduced as a straightforward "monster" that has ever redeemed itself. And this is a significant thing, especially given the problems that the show had during the era they originally hail from whereby character traits often amounted to nothing more than "who can fight the monsters best." Redeeming a monster from the Troughton era into a peaceful species wasn't just a really good idea, it was something that was a genuinely important step for the Pertwee era to take. And so collapsing them back to generic baddies with nothing more than a quick explanation about how they're a splinter faction who wanted to return to the old ways is unfortunate. Especially because it makes the story look for all the world like a parable about how bad guys never change and will always betray you. This is all the worse given that *The Curse of Peladon* was a metaphor in part about the EEC and euroskepticism, which makes "your enemies might reform but they'll go back to being evil again" a point that it's difficult not to cast as a comment about, say, the Germans.

Which gets at another large problem with this story: its politics. First of all, this story manages to somewhat embarrassingly miss the boat. It's clearly a story about the miners' strike, but it aired after all the major events of that had come and gone and the issue was settled, making it a political story that fails to actually find any politics to talk about. Which is maybe for the best.

I'm not even going to pick up particularly on Tat Wood's suggestion that Ettis is intended as an analogue for Arthur Scargill, then effectively the second in command in the miners' union. We'll talk about Scargill in more detail in the Peter Davison/Colin Baker volume, but suffice it to say that he was a very controversial and fairly Marxist figure. In any case, if Wood is correct about this equivalence, the decision to have Ettis go mad and try to blow everyone up has to be ranked as the crassest political moment in Doctor Who since *The Dominators* decided that pacifists should all wear dresses.

Because frankly, just knowing that this story is overtly about the miners' strike is enough to condemn it. In this story, the miners are striking primarily because they believe that Aggedor, their deity, is angry at the Federation's mining practices and is killing them in protest. Of course, in reality Aggedor is just a killer statue controlled by Eckersley and the Ice Warriors. So in other words, the entire miners' strike appears to, in Terrance Dicks's eyes, be because of the insidious manipulation of the miners by enemy agents.

There have been a lot of frustrating moments in the politics of Doctor Who, especially during the Pertwee era. And there are many frustrating moments in this story, most teeth-gratingly the absolutely awful moment where Sarah Jane lectures the Queen of Peladon about Women's Lib, a scene that seems to have written on the logic that the viewing public needed a stirring motivational speech about how girls are just as good as boys to imagine a woman on the throne, which is strange in a country that had had a queen for the past twenty-two years. But for my money, this has to take the cake as the single most horrifically offensive political decision of the Pertwee era.

The problem is just how bluntly crass this is. If the Federation is the EEC, and *The Curse of Peladon* obliges us to read it that way, then the only people it makes sense for them to be at war with would be Eastern Europe. Which means that the claim is that the striking miners are just being manipulated by Communists. Given that this is a clear commentary on real political issues in Britain at the time, this is just horrifying. Especially coming as it does after a wealth of previous moments under Letts and Dicks where the show has been condescending about the working class.

We discussed the basic form of this back in *The Green Death*, but it's particularly overt here. Active effort is made to make the miners seem more marginal. They're denied individuality by the decision to give them all identical hairstyles. Their dialogue is delivered in the "working class" accents normally reserved for comedy yokels and other characters who aren't like the Doctor and his companion. They even get a subtle but noticeable difference in their names. The noble Peladonians – Thalia and Ortron – get names that are full of softer consonants and long vowel sounds (Ortron's name, as pronounced, sounds more like Autron). The miners get names like Ettis, Gebek, and Blor – full of harsh consonants and clipped vowels that are less aesthetically pleasing and quietly reinforce the message that the miners just aren't as good as everyone else.

So to recap, the miners are an underclass of comedy yokels with funny names who are all being duped by enemy agents, and that's the real reason they're striking. If Doctor Who were actually trying to write a pro-Thatcher allegory for the 1984–'85 miners' strike a decade early this would be one thing. But perhaps the most galling thing about *The Monster of Peladon* is that its writers appear to genuinely believe that, in spite of all of this, they're on the miners' side. Except even that's not accurate, because that would imply awareness of these problems. No, they appear to believe that casting the miners as stooges of foreign Communists is what being on their side means in the first place.

After all, they give the Doctor a bunch of lines about how the miners' concerns are justified, and they end by having Gebek replace Ortron as Queen Thalia's right hand man (a move justified with a callback to the horrid Women's Lib bit to help ensure it falls flat on its face). The miners are good people! Their concerns are valid! It's just that they should have pleasant and polite conversations with their noble benefactors instead of being fooled by those wily enemy agents!

I mean, gag me. Seriously. I don't even have words for the sheer crassness of this. Were it simply a right-wing hit job – and the script would need only a handful of changes to make it unambiguously into one – I could at least just give it the same vicious drubbing I gave to *The Dominators* or *The Celestial Toymaker* in previous volumes. It's one thing when at least the stories have overtly and unambiguously bad intentions. But no. This manages to be worse, because its good intentions only reveal the utter moral bankruptcy of the supposedly leftist politics of the Letts era. And it is Letts, not Dicks, who is actively leftist, and so it's him that I'll lay the fault with. Dicks prefers what he views as a sort of moderate neutrality that is, in practice, usually a bit reactionary, but Letts is ostensibly a leftist who used the show to reflect his vies.

Were I to, in a fit of Lettsian sloganeering, attempt to reduce my view of left-wing politics to a single principle, I would be hard pressed to come up with a better one than Carol Hanisch's classic observation that the personal is political. What I mean by this is that, to my mind, the fundamental moral principle of progressive politics is the belief that politics must be primarily understood on the level of the individual. And furthermore, it must be understood in terms of the real experiences and material conditions of actual people, not in terms of some theoretical image of what people are like. In other words, the basis of left-wing politics is actually going and talking to people, especially those who are marginalized or oppressed, and then engaging with their own experiences of their marginalization.

Unfortunately, as we saw when looking at *Moonbase 3*, Letts is absolutely terrible about this. And in some ways this is even worse than the rape apologism of *Moonbase 3*. That, at least, was a case of stepping in it by missing an issue entirely by not thinking about individual people at all. This characterizes his mishandling of feminism in general, really. Remember, after all, that "the personal is political" was a feminist slogan first. But this is an issue of Letts paying attention to an issue and then getting his position on it catastrophically wrong anyway.

The entire reason the miners' strikes mattered was the refusal of the working class to be exploited. The strike that caused the Three-Day Week was about the basic nature of what a fair wage is. Typically speaking, jobs that pay the most are ones requiring an education and ones that involve supervising other people and management. Pit crews were neither. But mining work is dangerous. People die every year in mines, often in truly horrible ways. You can flip through any number of mining disasters in any number of countries and see immediately that it is a dangerous and unpleasant job. And the root issue of the 1973–'74 strike was that the miners believed that danger meant that when they were called on to work extra shifts in the face of OPEC's oil embargo they should get generous overtime pay.

So they struck, because they knew full well that they were being used. And, on a larger level, they struck because they were tired of being marginalized and treated as though they were less important or valuable people because of their class. Britain was and remains an extremely classist society, and the working class is not unaware of this fact. Inherent in any issue like this is the fact that the working class knows that the upper class enjoys far better conditions than they do. The miners knew full well that they were risking their lives and doing work that much of the upper class neither could nor would deign to do, and that the upper class was reaping the benefits. When you're already getting screwed, the call for "shared sacrifice" (as it is called these days) is a bitter pill. People with little left to give are understandably reluctant to give up everything so that they can share the burden with those who have it all.

And that's a lot of what that strike was about. It wasn't about being listened to. It wasn't about getting a token position in the halls of power for the portion of your leadership that preached calm and got everyone to unite behind the government. It was about being respected. And Letts and Dicks miss that completely. They miss it with every single decision they take about the miners: in making them an identical caste so uniform they may as well be Ice Warriors, in giving them accents that mark them as unlike the main characters, in giving them the ugly names, in making them the hapless dupes of foreign powers, and, frankly, in phoning in such a crap story about them in the first place. They have zero respect for the actual people this story is ostensibly about, and it's sickening to see them blunder with such asinine and blinkered moral conviction and then pat themselves on the back for being so clever as to write a story that explains to everyone how the miners and the government can just compromise long after both parties had already worked it out just fine for themselves.

And the problem is that this immediately becomes an indictment of the entire Pertwee era. It's smug and superior and about a brilliant aristocrat from the stars who will come down and fix everything for the silly little people. It's a story about the viewer's world in which the viewer doesn't matter. They're not even there except as an object to terrorize. They have nothing to contribute, nothing to say, and no relevance to anything that is going on in the world of the story. Which is one thing when the story is about a part of the world that just isn't near the part the viewer is in. Given that an overwhelming majority of the viewers are not military officers, it's not a problem when UNIT doesn't reflect their actual experience. But for an era of the show that was so consciously "about" things – one that did a pollution episode, an EEC episode, a nuclear weapons episode and, yes, a miners' strike episode – to fail so spectacularly in every single case to do a story that is about anything other than the smug people in charge is appalling.

The Troughton era merely didn't go far enough and, like the Hartnell era before it, it needed a drastic change to push it to the next level. The Pertwee era, however, stands revealed as an era that has just gone completely off the rails. It's not that the Pertwee era isn't going far enough. It's that it's going wrong. It's trying to deal with human issues and human politics – just like the Troughton era demanded it did – but it's doing it in a way that is offensive and frankly abhorrent. And this is inseparable from the glam aesthetic that animates the best moments of the Pertwee era. Fundamentally the glam aesthetic is still about the pleasure of watching stars and important people, and there's a fundamental limit to what that aesthetic can say about the day-to-day sludge of everyday life.

Quite frankly, this isn't just an era of the show that's at its natural end and needs to evolve. This is an era of the show that deserves to die. It is not enough that Pertwee's Doctor change and regenerate. He needs to be struck down for his hubris.

Time Can Be Rewritten (*Interference*)

It's August, 1999. Doctor Who is as dead as dead can be. These are the heady early days of New Labour, two years after Tony Blair managed to end an eighteen-year stretch of Conservative rule. In the main stretch of the blog, we are a few years from the dawn of the long 1980s. Here we are a few years past that, in a murky transition into an era that it's not quite clear we've seen the end of yet – something alarmingly resembling the present. The clock ticks closer towards a millennial change stained deep with eschatology. Musically we are in a wasteland of Ricky Martin, Westlife, and Geri Halliwell doing Latin-inspired numbers. These are not days that anyone claims as the glory days of anything, least of all Doctor Who, which is off the air and seemingly never coming back.

In these transitional moments it is sometimes helpful to mine the past for ideas and directions. The shift between historical eras is a vague phenomenon existing more in the realm of ideas than in the realm of material objects after all – one reason that it is easier to track through psychochronography, which allows us the ability to walk and tour the realm of ideas. These dead spaces between eras mark the periods where old ideologies begin to stagger under their own weight and break down, and where new ideologies find themselves pulled in from the fringes. In these moments, one turns to the past, looking at approaches that have run aground and sizing up the repair job needed to get them running again.

Enter *Interference*. On one level, as we'll talk about when we come back around to it in several books' time, this is a desperate (and failed) throw of the dice – a last attempt to get the unmitigated catastrophe that was the Paul McGann era to act like a functional era of Doctor Who instead of a graveyard. And it's a clever one. The Past Doctor Adventures line took the month of August off, and instead the Eighth Doctor Adventures line released a two-volume novel featuring interconnected Eighth and Third Doctor stories. Furthermore, the novel was by Lawrence Miles, the hot shot of the BBC

Books line who was widely considered, at that point, to be the most ambitious and interesting person working on Doctor Who books. It was a big event – one that was clearly poised to launch a new era of Doctor Who. (It failed, as it happens, but that's a story for many books from now.)

Interference, to be clear, is not a multiple doctor story in the sense of *The Three Doctors*. It is two distinct stories, one featuring each Doctor, held together by a framing story in which the Eighth Doctor and I.M. Foreman each relate a story to one another. The stories share characters and events, and briefly intersect at one point, but are distinct, with each story occupying roughly half of each book. (Actually the two Eighth Doctor segments are both a bit longer than the two Third Doctor segments.) Since the Eighth Doctor material in no way belongs to this era, I'm focusing in this essay entirely on the Third Doctor segments of *Interference*.

In interviews, when asked why in both this book and his previous (and highly acclaimed) *Alien Bodies*, he made use of the Third Doctor, Miles's answer has been that Pertwee's Doctor is the one that most embodies the mythic and legendary portions of Doctor Who's history. But for all that Pertwee's Doctor is the "classic" Doctor (it is either him or Tom Baker, and a fair case can be made that Season Ten was in fact the zenith of the series' popularity), the Pertwee era was also one of considerable upheaval and uncertainty, much as the Eighth Doctor era was shaping up to be.

So in a period when Doctor Who's future is profoundly insecure, Miles turns back to engage with the series' past, and specifically with a point in the past where the series was at the time uncertain and in hindsight at its most mythic. More than that, he does something that, for obvious reasons, the series rarely does: he allows a future era of Doctor Who to actively invade the past of the series. In this case, he opens literally – an unfortunate accident involving temporal equations from the Eighth Doctor portion of the story causes an apparition of the Eighth Doctor to travel backwards along Sarah Jane's timeline and appear in the TARDIS to the Third Doctor. Or, rather, the

Eighth Doctor, in prison, beaten and abused, appears to him. Shortly thereafter, the TARDIS begins bleeding, and the Third Doctor is derailed from the adventure he should be having and taken to a very different one on a backwater planet called Dust.

It's worth stressing, because this is key to any understanding of what the blazes is going on in this book, exactly why the adventure he ends up having is so off-base. Miles admits openly that the basic idea of a bleeding TARDIS is not conceptually out of line with the Pertwee era: it's an idea that firmly belongs in the same conceptual tradition as, for instance, Exxilon. And yet there is something profoundly disturbing about the walls of the TARDIS bleeding out. And more to the point, there's something disturbing about this happening in the Pertwee era specifically. There is something profoundly wrong with the aesthetics here: Pertwee's Doctor encountered science fantasy, but never science fantasy of this flavor.

The question, then, is why? What, exactly, is wrong with the adventure the Doctor ends up having on Dust? Again, Miles – who has mastered the technique of late '80s and early '90s genre writers like Alan Moore and Neil Gaiman (though he is no fan of the latter) whereby thematic judgments and comments are slipped into the exposition and narration – makes this relatively explicit. The central difference is that Third Doctor expects romantic adventures among the machinations of history, whereas the adventure he's cast into is one of "pure brutality."

There is a broader significance to this point – one that crops up in a wealth of Magrsian postmodern side comments about things like how space food makes things too easy, or comments about how there might be unusual narrative devices in play within the story. And it's one that features massively in the Eighth Doctor portions of the narrative as well: the way in which politics and aesthetics are inevitably intertwined. The essential problem the Doctor has on Dust is that the world is brutal and unpleasant and unromantic in a way he is ill-equipped to handle. He was only ever designed to deal with politics in the noble and aristocratic sense, as opposed to the ugly realities of the subaltern.

But it's also worth looking at one of the most interesting scenes in the novel, where the Doctor interacts with Magdelana, who is basically the only native of Dust we ever see much of. In this scene he attempts to cheerily diagnose and explain her nature to her, which she responds to by calmly throwing a cup of scalding hot coffee in his face. Implicit in this scene is the point I made a few essays ago – that the Pertwee era did an excruciatingly bad job of dealing with the human dimension of issues. Pertwee's Doctor is accused of being condescending and insensitive in exactly the way that, in practice, he was throughout his era. The difference isn't in how the character acts, but in the fact that he's been put in a world with no patience for his pretensions.

Many commenters, however, in a thoroughly wrong-headed manner, have accused the book of being a hit job on the Pertwee era. First of all, this assumes that the critique of the politics of Doctor Who is limited to the Third Doctor segments, which is clearly not the case. But second of all, there is, fundamental to the Third Doctor segments of the book, an embrace of something that has been a fundamental and recurring concept within the Pertwee era, although we haven't really brought it up since *The Green Death*: magic.

The concept of magic is central to what Miles is doing. This includes the entire idea of the villains, Faction Paradox, and the rogue bunch of Gallifreyans who freely alter history, including their own, and who make their home in the Eleven-Day Empire, the period of time skipped by the realignment of the English calendar in 1752. As Miles says of Faction Paradox, in one of those sentences that reminds you just why he is such a landmark writer, "what would have been a metaphor to anybody else was solid reality to them." The entire concept of Faction Paradox, in short, is that they are just like the Time Lords, except they explicitly work according to the logic of fantasy, whereas the Time Lords ostensibly work under the logic of science fiction.

And so if the Third Doctor is fundamentally unsuited to the sort of brutal and harsh encounters involved in portraying society in a more socially realist manner, the flip side is that the Eighth Doctor's era lacks some sense of wonder. One of Miles's great hobby horses is that Doctor Who is not, in fact, a science fiction series but a fantasy series that uses science fiction iconography. He is adamant, in both interviews and in his own work, that Doctor Who simply does not belong in the same category as things like *Star Trek*. And during the Eighth Doctor era he even speculated that if and when Doctor Who next came back it would surely be as a cult sci-fi show in the mould of *Babylon 5* and flame out within a season or two. What's key to realize is that for all of Miles's acclaim, he was in the minority on this: the consensus thought on Doctor Who was that it's a science fiction show in the cult model, and the circumstances that led to Miles being wrong were genuinely extraordinary. And so the harkening back to the Third Doctor's era is, in part, Miles returning to a mythic lost era of Doctor Who in which the series could function unambiguously as a science fantasy series. Simply put, there was no cult fandom of the Pertwee era: that's a phenomenon that doesn't begin to emerge until the latter parts of the Tom Baker era.

And so it is in the Third Doctor's section of the book that Miles introduces the concept of IM Foreman's traveling circus, in which all thirteen regenerations of a single Time Lord travel together out from Gallifrey. Foreman, in each incarnation, becomes progressively more of a bizarre extremity of the concept of life, until in his eleventh incarnation he is the If, a creature that breathes raw time energy, and in his thirteenth he is simply a raw and all-consuming force of nature. It is also the Third Doctor who manages to, through a clever bit of jiggery-pokery, successfully persuade the thirteenth incarnation of IM Foreman to terraform Dust and make it a lush and beautiful planet instead of a decaying wasteland. This is, by any measure, an act of magic. The entire idea of Foreman's circus – a traveling show of human extremity – is magical, as is the basic idea of reversing death into life (an invocation of the putrefaction concept from *The Green Death* in many regards). And this is fitting as well. For all that I've been hard on Letts for the past few essays, he deserves some real credit that he rarely gets for making some truly interesting contributions to the magical aspects of the series.

It's not that Pertwee is the most magical Doctor – nothing can really pry that title away from Troughton. Rather, it's that he's the last Doctor to really follow primarily from Hartnell's patrician wizard model. He and Hartnell have a unique status as the "old men" Doctors: they're the last two to seem elderly. And that gives them each a particular function. There is an iconic and mythic moment in which the wizened and powerful old man makes his sacrificial last stand. Gandalf facing down the Balrog and Obi-Wan Kenobi getting cut down by Darth Vader are probably the two most obvious pop culture examples, though if you want to be particular about it you probably want to go back to Odin and Ragnarok as the most fundamental form of this myth. (Odin is a good analogue for the Doctor in several instances.)

And Pertwee can provide that moment. In fact, he does, which is the next essay. But Miles, in one of the most brazenly cheeky moves in Doctor Who's history, steals that last stand from *Planet of the Spiders* and uses it for himself. *Interference* retcons *Planet of the Spiders* out of existence by having the Doctor gunned down by Magdelana for endangering Dust in the first place, leaving him to die in a grim parody of his actual regeneration scene and, for good measure, be infected by a Faction Paradox virus that will eventually cause him problems in the Eighth Doctor Adventures line.

This, unsurprisingly, was largely the most controversial part of the book when it came out. In a way this is unfortunate. The accusation, of course, is that Miles somehow ruined or destroyed *Planet of the Spiders*, which is a bizarre claim. Miles did not break into anyone's house and deface their VHS tapes, after all. This book does no damage to the Pertwee era itself. One can watch the standard regeneration and standard sequence of episodes, and nothing Miles is capable of alters that.

Complaining about the story on those grounds is, in other words, profoundly foolish. And the obsession with that is exactly what Miles is objecting to when he says that the series is based on a logic of magic, not of science fiction. The sorts of fans who object to this are the ones Miles is mocking when he talks about the original sense of the word geek (one who bites the heads off of live chickens).

But there is still a sense of shock and wrongness to it – one Miles is clearly aware of and relishes in. To some extent this is the point – the ugly consequence of throwing Pertwee's Doctor into a situation that his character was never well-suited for or designed for. Of course the situation kills him. How could it not? That's what it means to be in a brutal and ugly world. There is a critique of the Pertwee era here mixed in with the appeal to its mythic power. He is not, after all, arguing for the reversion to an early '70s model for Doctor Who. He's pilfering the past to improve the future, and that involves figuring out what should be left in the past as well.

This is, in other words, an invocation of the Pertwee era's power, not a return to it. Because *Planet of the Spiders* is its own form of the powerful wizard's last stand, Miles takes that story and that sacrifice and uses it for its own purposes. But this is not theft. Rather, it is a trade. The Eighth Doctor era has given something of equal value to the Pertwee era here. Because it's not like the Pertwee era is in good shape at this moment in its history. I just got finished saying that the shabbiness of its politics were such that this Doctor's era deserved to die for them. And here it does, and for that exact reason. Pertwee's Doctor is killed because he's rubbish at a situation like this where there is real human suffering. His death is, in a perverse way, more faithful to the Pertwee era than the Pertwee era was actually capable of being.

In this regard, Miles's corruption of the Pertwee era is in fact a needed and cathartic addition. Pertwee still has his other departure, as I said. And that departure clears up its own issues, including many related to the inadequate politics of the Pertwee era. But still, the cruelty and directness of this is, in a real sense, exactly what the era needs: one story that properly calls it out for its most upsetting failings. This is a story that fills the most glaring and upsetting hole in the Pertwee era, and in doing so redeems the whole thing. In light of this confrontation, and of the fact that the Pertwee era now calls itself to task for its failures, we can move on and allow ourselves to enjoy the good parts of the era more freely.

But in doing so *Interference* opens an odd and magical gap in the Pertwee era: a tiny fissure into which the future intrudes. This intrusion alters the whole thing, making Pertwee's regeneration into a larger symbolic event for Doctor Who. And if Miles can play with that gap, perhaps we can as well.

Be Childish Sometimes (*Planet of the Spiders*)

It's mid-September, 1992. The Shamen are at number one with "Ebeneezer Goode." At least, in the UK. In the US, somewhat less fortunately, "End of the Road" by Boyz II Men is at number one, as it was for three months that year. Perhaps more importantly, at least for our purposes, in a small town in Western Connecticut, a newly minted ten-year-old flips through a book he just got from a family friend a week or so after his birthday. By a man he's never heard of called John Nathan-Turner, about a television show he's vaguely heard of called Doctor Who; the book is called *The Companions*. After said family friend leaves, and it is no longer rude to do so, he asks his mother what this Doctor Who thing is. She looks around in a drawer, and hands him a VHS tape, which he goes to the basement to watch. The Delia Derbyshire theme, familiar to so many people, plays, and something called *Planet of the Spiders* comes on. And so, in the wrong country, in the wrong decade, but every inch at the right time, I became a Doctor Who fan.

So yes. Hi. I mean, not that I haven't been obviously skulking about the blog entries and these books for some time now, though I've tried not to make a nuisance of myself. But at this point I am forced to make a somewhat more formal and more permanent entrance. I have talked before about moments in Doctor Who that fans can't quite see past: the introduction of the Time Lords in *The War Games*, for instance, or the tremendously vexed reputation of *The Gunfighters*. But past that, there's another horizon that it's impossible for anyone steeped in Doctor Who to quite see past, and that's our own growing up with the show. As the slogan emblazoned on countless different t-shirts goes, you never forget your first Doctor.

And mine was Pertwee. Specifically, Pertwee in *Planet of the Spiders*. And so it is impossible for me to talk or think about this story without my own childhood memories of it bleeding into the mix. I cannot possibly see past that. Even if I could, I wouldn't want to. I can't both be the sort of person who writes a nine volume critical history of Doctor Who and the sort of person who can just turn off his own personal history with Doctor Who. So my only choice is to allow myself to be a part of the narrative. This story and the start of the next volume are the stretch of Doctor Who I grew up with – the stretch I watched from in front of the sofa. (No, really – there was a hideous yellow floral print sofa in the basement where I watched, but I hated it and sat in a dilapidated black armchair in front of it.) This is in no way going to become a series of personal reflections and reviews. But it does mean that, along with utopian politics, alchemical mysticism, the evolution of television as a medium, and everything else, there's one more strand to this braid of narrative.

It's not that I don't have childhood memories of Troughton or Hartnell – I do. But those Doctors were all ones I encountered in a larger context of knowing about Doctor Who. I had at least some idea of what to expect, and had read descriptions of the stories I watched in books like *Doctor Who: A Celebration*. Almost all of the Hartnell and Troughton stories I saw in childhood were watched on tapes imported from the UK and watched on a multi-region VCR, a process that by its nature indicates a fairly established level of obsession.

In terms of watching Doctor Who for me, there were three basic phases of the operation. The third is the one I just talked about – my mother would buy tapes as they came out in the UK, and I would watch them on a multi-region VCR. The second is when I was watching primarily American VHS tapes – a more limited selection primarily focused on Hinchcliffe-era Tom Baker stories, which I'll talk more about in the next volume.

But the first was when I was watching old tapes my parents made of the show from their local PBS station. Recorded in gloriously lo-fi SLP with three or four stories per VHS tape, my parents' collection consisted of the two Peter Cushing movies, ten Pertwee stories, two Tom Baker stories, eleven Peter Davison stories, and *The Two Doctors*. So while *Planet of the Spiders* is the Pertwee story I have the most important formative memory of, the case could be made that I've been lurking around all book.

Many of my parents' old tapes were either unlabeled or incompletely labeled, and so watching their Doctor Who collection often meant putting in random tapes to discover what was on them. Often, as the above list shows, the answer was that a Pertwee story was. This inevitably involved a bit of disappointment, as of the options I was familiar with (Pertwee, Tom Baker, and Davison), Pertwee was firmly my least favorite. Even going through the era again to write all of this didn't entirely replace this feeling of childhood disappointment: the constant sense that this was a substitute for the good stuff I'd rather be watching.

But more than anything, this disdain for Pertwee was motivated by that first tape. Because that one started with *Planet of the Spiders*, and continued on to *Robot* and *The Ark in Space*, which were, naturally, my next two stories. And like much of the viewing public, I fell in love with Tom Baker. And so really every discovered tape – even from the Davison era – was criticized and dinged for the fact that it wasn't Tom Baker, as the extent of his stories were on that one first tape.

I knew going into *Planet of the Spiders* that it was Pertwee's last story, although I didn't entirely grasp what the concept meant beyond the basic idea that this wasn't business as usual and the Doctor was going to lose. This was actually part of why I picked this tape – I was confused over how the lead actor changes my mother described worked, and asked for an example.

This means that the story has an odd pair of resonances for me. On the one hand it is impossible for it to be anything other than the lead-in to the Tom Baker era. I watched all three stories on the tape in one day, and the Tom Baker stories left such an impression that *Planet of the Spiders* became little more than "that one where Tom Baker shows up at the end."

On the other hand, one of the commenters on the original blog version of this essay remarked upon the lost version of *Planet of the Spiders* where instead of regenerating into Tom

Baker Pertwee just regenerates into some brown-haired man with curly hair. Few people get to watch that version anymore, given how well known and iconic Baker's portrayal of the Doctor still is. But I didn't know that in 1992, and so I got to see the original version. The problem is that I also didn't know anything about Pertwee. So my experience of this story is an odd one. No matter how you approach it, it's a beginning, whether of Doctor Who in its entirety or of the Tom Baker era. And as it turns out, this is wholly fitting for this story.

First, some broader perspective. For the sake of formality and completeness, *Planet of the Spiders* aired over six weeks starting on May 4, 1974. ABBA was at number one with "Waterloo," their Eurovision winning hit. After two weeks this gives way to the Rubettes, who play out the Pertwee era with "Sugar Baby Love." Other artists making the top ten include various things I have seriously never heard of: Mud, the Chi-Lites, Peters and Lee, and Showaddywaddy. So hopefully all of that means something to someone, because I have virtually no idea what I just said. (I mean, I know the ABBA song . . .) While in real news, the Ulster Volunteer Force causes the most single-day casualties of the Troubles with bombings in Dublin and Monaghan, reminding everybody that the IRA aren't the only jerks with bombs. And India completes a successful nuclear test under the alarmingly inappropriate codename "Smiling Buddha."

But Raja Ramanna was not the only person in charge of a project with inappropriate invocations of Buddhism that week, because off on television, Barry Letts co-wrote and directed his last hurrah of a Pertwee story, *Planet of the Spiders*.

It is, of course, a Sloman script, with all the problems that this implies. And he and Letts find bold new ways of being rubbish this time around, including half an episode of thumb-twiddling with the Doctor unconscious to make sure that the plot doesn't get uppity and try to advance, an entire planet constructed out of bad CSO, and a twelve-minute-long car chase purely for the sake of having a car chase, and, furthermore, that also involves bad CSO. All of this is true, as is the fact that the story is horrible in its treatment of people with mental disabilities, as bewilderingly sociopathic as ever in its attitudes, and features the other appearance of the bloody Whomobile. And they, for good measure, after two episodes that are padded absurdly, idiotically shoehorn the entire K'Anpo plot into the sixth episode when it should have been the centerpiece of the whole thing, given that the introduction of the Doctor's mentor is pretty clearly the biggest deal in the story. All of this is true, and it makes watching the story as excruciating and frustrating as you would expect it to.

But all the same, I can't pummel this story. We've summoned up the d(a)emons of the Pertwee era in quite enough detail. The particulars of this story's failings are new, but the general pattern isn't. And look, if nothing else . . . this is my first Doctor Who story. It is not my favorite. Far from it. But I just don't want to be the one to do an extended critique of it, especially because those are so easy to find. So let's allow for Lawrence Miles's *Interference* with the Pertwee era whereby he injects a reckoning with its faults into it. Where does that leave *Planet of the Spiders* beyond "retconned out of existence?" What is this story if we accept *Interference* as a part of Doctor Who? The answer, I think, is something powerful: something that does not so much relegate *Planet of the Spiders* to non-canonical status as it does elevate it to being the story that redeems and sustains the entire Pertwee era.

There are two usual lines about this story. First, that it's a greatest hits reel of the Pertwee era. Second, that it's a Buddhist parable. Neither is quite right, though both come very close. The logic of it being a Buddhist parable is straightforward: in the first episode, Cho-Je gives a monologue about how "the old man must die and the new man will discover to his inexpressible joy that he has never existed," and then in the sixth episode the Doctor accepts that his greed for knowledge caused all of this and thus that he must face his worst fear in resolving all of it.

Of course, there's an obvious problem there, which is that the Doctor's "greed for knowledge" hasn't really featured in a remotely explicit manner since *The Silurians*. And it's tough to call his run through the studio sets of Metebelis 3 in *The Green Death* a case of him searching for knowledge, at least in any direct sense. If nothing else, he demonstrates considerable familiarity with the planet prior to arriving. In terms of knowledge, he seems to have many (though clearly not all) of the basics of the planet down prior to arriving.

It is tempting to suggest that he went to Metebelis 3 out of wanderlust, but generally speaking, it's tough to create a compelling argument that Pertwee feels much wanderlust. Since getting the TARDIS back he has gone on exactly two jaunts through time and space, each seemingly lasting two destinations before he heads home. Mostly he seems to still be based on Earth, and like a character who wants the freedom to leave more than he actually wants to leave as such.

All of this makes it very difficult to thread the needle and figure out what the Doctor is talking about when he says that his "greed for knowledge" had caused all of this. Which makes it, in turn, difficult to quite pin down what the Buddhist message at the core of all of this might be. It largely seems as though Barry Letts is just doing his usual high-concept moralizing, and that this time the moral is Buddhism. Just as *The Monster of Peladon* fails to deliver on its own ostensible moral, this story may proclaim that it's a Buddhist parable, but it doesn't act the part.

But it is just about possible, if you squint, to make this claim work. The clue comes in what seems at first glance like a throwaway line that doesn't even involve the Doctor, in which the spiders refer to invading the Earth as their "great work." On the surface, there is nothing much to that, but it is an odd phrasing. More to the point, it's a phrasing reminiscent of something Letts has done before. *The Daemons* gave the strong sense that Letts is familiar with the ceremonial magickal tradition from which Aleister Crowley stemmed – a tradition that refers to magick as "the great work." Indeed, all four of the Sloman/Letts scripts have, to some extent, dealt with mysticism and magic. Pulling on this thread just a little bit reveals a possible second meaning of "knowledge" – one that requires us to go back to the alchemical logic of David Whitaker. What we need to look at, as it happens, is the Kabbalah.

This is, of course, a terribly vexed term encompassing several traditions. I do not for a moment pretend to be knowledgeable about the actual Jewish mystical tradition of the Kabbalah, nor, for that matter, about the weird cult thing Madonna is into. But there is a tradition of thought about the Kabbalah in Western mysticism associated with the Hermetic approaches of Crowley and Whitaker. We've discussed it a bit throughout this project, most notably back in the essay on *The Tenth Planet* at the end of the Hartnell Volume – my description of the Cybermen as "qlippothic" stems almost entirely from this. But here let's deal briefly with the most tortured, complex, and mind-wrenching concept of the Kabbalah: the Abyss.

Essentially, the Hermetic conception of the Kabbalistic Tree of Life is a map of the way in which the divine and the earthly relate. The divine is divided into ten emanations, called the Sephiroth, with various paths among them. The most important set of paths is what is called the "lightning path," named for the zig-zag shape it takes down the tree, linearly connecting the highest Sephira, Kether, to the lowest, Malkuth. Towards the top of this path, however, there is a problem – the bridge that should connect the third and fourth Sephiroth doesn't exist. Instead there is posited a gap – the Abyss – which represents the inevitable and necessary breakage and gap between the divine and the earthly. And so the three highest Sephiroth are, in one sense, fundamentally and necessary separate from the seven lower ones.

Another name for the Abyss is Da'ath, conceived as an eleventh Sephira that is said to have fallen and collapsed inward. Da'ath is where Crowley situates the demon Choronzon, the demon that destroys the ego utterly. The alternative to facing Choronzon and having your ego obliterated is, essentially, to be trapped in the Black Tower, where magicians who have gotten overly committed and bound up to a system of dogma search fruitlessly and endlessly for spiritual completeness. But for our purposes the most interesting fact is what the name Da'ath translates to: "Knowledge."

Let us, for the moment, accept that the spiders are consciously designed as analogues for Crowley. Given this, it makes sense to understand the Doctor's greed for knowledge in the same context. The result is a far more sensible interpretation of the apparent flaw that dooms the Doctor. Is it perhaps not that the Doctor is curious, but rather that he insists on holding on to his own ego as he attempts to cross the Abyss?

This makes several things easier and more sensible. First of all, there are numerous reasons to think this form of "greed for knowledge" is bad – unlike the previous version, where it wasn't quite clear what was wrong with the Doctor's curiosity. Those who want easy explanations of the world are generally the villains in Doctor Who, whereas those who are curious and inquisitive are generally treated as good guys. Most obviously, the mad Blakean excess of *The Three Doctors* is antithetical to this sort of greed. The Doctor, in essence, stands accused of wanting to fix the universe into Newtonian certainty. Single vision and Newton's sleep, as Blake puts it, is anathema to the Doctor, or at least it should be. It characterizes nothing so much as Urizen, the figure we associated with Omega and the Master.

But, of course, this story is inevitably haunted by the story it should have been. This is where *The Final Game* was supposed to slot – the story that revealed the Master as another aspect of the Doctor that the Doctor would have to face and acknowledge as the Master sacrificed himself to save the Doctor. Here, then, we get the exact same story only with the Master already subsumed into the Doctor. This works, even to the detail of McIntee's line about scientific curiosity being the Master's last "uncorrupted vice."

But there is something more to this. Remember, after all, that our bluntest critique of Letts and Dicks, and by extension of the Pertwee era, is the way in which they are more loyal to slogans than they are to people. What are the deeply flawed politics of the Letts era if not a commitment to broad and universalizing dogma over the actual lived reality of people? This is exactly what was so wretched about the last story, exactly why I already said the Doctor deserves to die. And so in this reading we can see *Planet of the Spiders* as the story in which the Pertwee era concedes the point and admits its own fatal flaw, having been violently confronted with it in Miles's doppelgänger of this story.

If so, the excesses of the greatest hits segment of the story make more sense. Much effort is made to shoehorn as much of the Pertwee era as can be managed into this story. Jo Grant is brought up again, and sends a letter to UNIT HQ. Mike Yates makes his utterly unanticipated return. The Metebelis crystal is back. On top of that is the determination to work in the major set pieces. Pertwee gets one last big vehicle scene, a last chance to shout Hai!, and even one last Pertwee death pose, held long after his last line has been delivered. The story is drenched in its own egotism.

But if we take the end of the story for what it now appears to be, all of this makes sense. The entire Pertwee era must be, in a sense, re-enacted before it can allow itself to die. The Doctor doesn't just visit the cave of the Great One, he brings all of the trappings of who he is and who he has been for the past five years to the cave – laying down all of himself. In order to face Choronzon and have his ego forever shattered he must first recognize and pick up all of the parts of his ego, claiming them as his own.

In this regard even the production infelicities seem to aid the story. As I said, *Planet of the Spiders* displays all of the Pertwee era's worst instincts at one point or another. But it has to, and Letts, on some level, gets that. This story is in one sense an exorcism – a last summoning of all of the ugly ghosts of the Pertwee era so that they can finally be done away with. It's a celebration of the Pertwee era, but a celebration with the explicit goal of killing the era off. Everything that is brought up advances the Doctor closer to the point where he confronts his fear. Everything that's brought up here is brought up in part to show that it can be given up.

And of course, this does touch the zeitgeist well. Bowie's last great glam album, Diamond Dogs, came out not two weeks before this story began. "Rebel Rebel," Bowie's farewell to the glam era, peaked in the charts during *Death to the Daleks*. The glam aesthetic that had defined the Pertwee era was passing by. Always ill-suited for a recession, the over the top gaudiness of glam turned bleak rapidly, the distant and detached starmen proving, as we always knew they would, to be egocentric narcissists. In one sense, Pertwee here carries out the course set out for him two seasons earlier – his very own Rock 'n Roll Suicide.

But this must also be taken in light of the parable from the first episode about the old man dying and the new man's joy. Yes, Pertwee serves as the old man who dies, bringing about the new man. That's a crashingly obvious metaphor. But what's equally important is the sense of joy in this. The joy is in the fact that the new man has never existed. Central to this is how Cho-Je describes the death: "A man must go inside and face his fears and hopes, his hates and his loves, and watch them wither away. Then he will find his true self, which is no self. He will see his true mind, which is no mind." This is clearly, again, a description of the Doctor going into the cave. But what is key is that everything that the Doctor was must wither away. Not just his fears and hates, but his hopes and loves.

And so the Doctor faces his fear, and goes to confront the Great One – a terrible monster who can bend his will – who can finally mentally dominate him and make him cry in agony as she forces his broken body to march like a puppet on a string. He stands before her and he dies, begging her to see the error of her ways and to stop her from killing herself. This is not the frantic manipulation of Troughton's Doctor, trying to cajole or trick an enemy into doing what he wants. This is simply a good man trying to prevent a needless death. For the first time, Pertwee's Doctor looks so very small, and somehow this makes him more of a giant than ever before. And so he dies. In agony, this time. More agony even than facing the Qlippothic tendrils of Mondas. His body torn apart by radiation sickness, lost in the time vortex for God knows how long, he dies.

And the new man is joyously born.

But wait a moment. His regeneration takes place outside of the cave. The Doctor, when he staggers into UNIT headquarters, says, "I got lost in the time vortex. The TARDIS brought me home." At face value this line indicates that the Doctor spent some unknown amount of time lost with the TARDIS in transit. But there is another reading. Remember that we are talking about ego destruction here. The Doctor did not merely wander the time vortex: he lost his identity within it. Within, to quote Lawrence Miles, the machinations of history.

In truth, then, the new man is born inside the cave – the one who is no self and no mind, as Cho-Je puts it. He falls out of the world, the oldest magic trick the Doctor ever knew, and becomes fluid mercury, capable of being anything at all. And so the TARDIS takes the Doctor home. In a sense, then, he dies as he was born – cast down to Earth. But the word has changed meanings. He is no longer exiled to "one primitive planet," but instead brought home. After he makes contact with enlightenment and eternity, recognizing himself as pure mercury, he also finally recognizes Earth not as the planet of his exile but as home – as the place where he belongs. It is not his regeneration into Tom Baker that creates the new man, but the obliteration of all of the trappings of the Pertwee era such that the Doctor can realize who he is and see that Earth is home.

Hartnell and Troughton both regenerate in moments of failure. Hartnell is unable to stand up to the Qlippothic horrors of the Cybermen. Troughton is unable to rise to the occasion required by the horrors of war. But Pertwee does not fail. Pertwee triumphs, becoming in his final moments the purest version of what he always was: the Doctor from Earth.

And so I am left unable to approach *Planet of the Spiders* as anything other than a beginning. A beginning of the Tom Baker era. A beginning of my own entanglement with Doctor Who. But perhaps most importantly and most thoroughly, a beginning of the Pertwee era – its purest and most succinct expression. Pertwee doesn't regenerate because his time is past. He regenerates because he's finally accomplished what his era set out to do in the first place. And having done that, he can move on to a new era in peace.

Now My Doctor: Jon Pertwee

The point of these final essays is to present the best case for a given Doctor. Not just the most sympathetic reading in general, but the one that presents the Doctor at their best. It's the case for a given Doctor's greatness. And while I've been upfront throughout the volume that Pertwee was my least favorite Doctor, that's not even the problem here. The problem is the one that's lurked around through this entire book: there are two distinct and mutually incompatible visions of Pertwee's greatness.

In one corner is the Pertwee era, the pinnacle of exciting adventure TV. Story after story of big, action-packed thrills, car chases, fight scenes, military derring-do, and other such things. Sure, it looks cheap now, but if you were ten in the early 1970s it was the best thing ever. In the other corner is the Pertwee era, a gaudy glam rock spectacle of gloriously poor taste. Filled with irony and bizarre juxtaposition, the entire era is a mind-wrenching spectacle of strangeness.

The problem is that these views are impossible to reconcile. The former relies on the implicit sincerity of the Pertwee era while the latter relies on the assumption of deep structures of irony within it. It is difficult, if not impossible, to hold to both views at once. Either the Pertwee era is good for what it sincerely attempts, or it is good for the mad interference pattern its schizophrenia produces. One devalues the other.

If we want to reduce this debate to its essence it would, in effect, come down to whether the Pertwee era is camp or not. It is worth briefly defining camp, then. On its simplest level, camp is the only partially ironic valuation of aesthetic excess and tastelessness. More specifically, it is what arises when something on the one hand plays it straight and goes for seriousness, and on the other makes a hash of it and ends up over-earnest and slightly embarrassing. This is sensible enough. What's more complex is why camp might be desirable.

At the heart of it is the way in which camp calls into question the rigidity of social normality. Camp objects are on the one hand earnest and serious, and on the other ludicrous. And, crucially, there's no separating the two. Without the earnestness the inappropriateness would not be tolerable, and without the excess the seriousness would be unremarkable and dull. In other words, camp by its nature undermines the idea of "appropriateness" and "normality," noting the basic silliness of the status quo. This is, you may recall, more or less where the book started.

This exposes something about the glam interpretation of the Pertwee era that is on the one hand obvious and on the other worth stating explicitly: it is in no way equivalent to reading the Pertwee era as a sendup of itself. The glam reading of the Pertwee era hinges on the fact that Pertwee plays his role with such consistent seriousness. In the late Tom Baker era we'll get an era with similar aesthetic missteps, but we'll also have a star who is consistently and consciously sending up the program, and the result is something very, very different. But the Pertwee era relies on the fact that it can, if you want, be read as an earnest and serious attempt at an action-adventure program.

Put another way, a key aspect of reading the Pertwee era as glam spectacle is that it rejects not only straightforward love of the Pertwee era but straightforward disdain of it. If on the one hand those who suggest that the Pertwee era is compelling action-adventure drama are clearly just ignoring *The Claws of Axos* in its entirety, similarly those who say that it's poorly made, a bit dull, and unlikable are missing the tremendous fun of something like, well, *The Claws of Axos*. Put another way, the glam approach jumps back and forth between shutting off one's brain to enjoy a kid's action series and laughing at the sheer ridiculousness of the series.

But there's one wrinkle that makes it difficult to straightforwardly enjoy the Pertwee era this way, and that's Jon Pertwee. There's no way to dice things such that we don't run into the fact that Pertwee appeared to take the role utterly seriously, and, more to the point, seriously in a way that seems hostile to being sent up. He would appear at conventions, throw back his cape, and proudly proclaim, "I am the Doctor!" He could be profoundly egotistical and vain, insisting on camera angles that he found flattering to his face and nose.

And, perhaps most troublingly, his Doctor was consciously modeled on himself. This was unlike his other roles. He was known as a character actor and the "man of a thousand voices." But for Doctor Who he largely played himself. To treat his Doctor as a big, camp bit of male drag is necessarily to treat him as one, and to do so in a way that there is no real evidence he thought of or would approve of.

But the alternative is to try to straightforwardly and unironically enjoy a show about a tremendously patrician man teaming up with the military to fight anything that is outside the norm of British life. Even if we could somehow handwave away the aesthetic eccentricities of the era, why would we want to in order to reach that point? The line of defense that requires us to do that is not a defense worth having.

But it is, in many ways, a bizarre fannish logic that would worry so much about fealty to Pertwee himself in the first place. Jon Pertwee has been dead for over fifteen years now, and his feelings are at this point unlikely to be hurt. Given the choice between personal loyalty to a man I have never met and to whom my approval would have meant little even while he was alive, and the ability to like and praise five years of Doctor Who, the choice is clear-cut.

What I am proposing, in other words, is that Pertwee's Doctor be loved not in spite of his sillinesses, nor even because of them, but through them. That the Pertwee era is a ludicrous stretch of television that looks strange and has deep flaws is obvious. But equally, more than any other era of Doctor Who, its flaws are an integral part of what it is. There is no way to repair or improve the Pertwee era without fundamentally making it into something other than the Pertwee era. It is an era of Doctor Who that could only have existed in the first half of the 1970s.

But if it is difficult to imagine the Pertwee era existing any time other than the early 1970s, it is perhaps even harder to imagine the early 1970s existing without the Pertwee era. For the glam rock era to lack its most intricate and thorough expression, to paraphrase the future, scarcely bears thinking about. The Pertwee era is part and parcel of its era, wholly integral to what it was. Yes, it's odd and a bit silly now.

But only some of that oddness is due to the intervening forty years. Some of it is simply that the early seventies were a good period for weirdness. And if it's hard to like the Pertwee era on its own terms then perhaps the problem is that our assumptions about its terms are simply too narrow. What we have is an era steeped in clever ironies and bewildering images that takes itself just seriously enough to still be fun.

But none of this explains Pertwee himself. If we take an irony-laden and camp approach as the frame in which Pertwee's Doctor exists, that's all well and good. But thus far we've only defended the Pertwee era, not Pertwee's Doctor as such. If anything he's receded to the background, becoming almost the least essential part of his own era. This is unsatisfying to say the least.

Let's look at Pertwee and his Doctor, then. Throughout this book I've suggested that Pertwee is at his best when his Doctor is put on the back foot. Dramatically speaking this makes sense: they're the occasions where Pertwee really has to act. And interestingly, they reveal a lot about Pertwee. His pre-Doctor Who status as the "Man of a Thousand Voices" pushes us towards understanding him as a character actor. But within Doctor Who the fact that he largely plays the Doctor as himself is interesting in terms of British acting, in that it suggests that he was, on Doctor Who, working largely as a method actor.

Boiled down to its simplest, the difference between method acting and the more presentationalist British style is that British acting traditionally focuses on acting as a means of communicating information to the audience, whereas the method (typically an American approach) starts from the internal mental state of the characters and on portraying them authentically. So Pertwee, in basing the Doctor largely on himself, is working in a fundamentally more method-like manner. Notably, this is very different from the style normally associated with the sort of character parts he did elsewhere.

And so the degree to which Pertwee can make his character work dramatically when he's put in a position of being scared or when events are spiraling out of his control is compelling. It speaks to Pertwee's deep skills as an actor that he can succeed at a task so radically different from what he's best known for.

And this gets at what is so important about Pertwee to the Pertwee era. For all that his Doctor is a dashing leading man of, at times, little nuance or irony, Pertwee is a genuinely impressive utility player. The steadfastness of his character works precisely because Pertwee, as an actor, is capable of so much. The solidity of his character provides a sturdy foundation on which the rest of the Pertwee era could be built. The era can make bold glam experiments and throw out visual spectaculars because it has a calm, competent, and wholly unflappable lead actor to ground it.

To suggest that the Pertwee era is a frame in which his Doctor exists is, in other words, exactly backwards. Rather it is that Pertwee's Doctor is the frame and platform upon which the extravagant weirdness of the Pertwee era can function. Pertwee may be the least zanily eccentric Doctor to date, but this enables one of the strangest and most spectacular eras of Doctor Who. Ironically, the actor who most thoroughly advanced the degree to which the Doctor is normatively the star of the show is the one who is most impressive in brightening everything around him.

TARDIS Eruditorum Volume 3: Jon Pertwee

About the Author

Philip Sandifer is the author of three volumes of *TARDIS Eruditorum* and counting. He lives in Connecticut and occasionally ventures outside, just to see what that's like.

He blogs at tardiseruditorum.blogspot.net, and is also the author of the forthcoming 33 1/3 volume on They Might Be Giants' *Flood* and a critical history of Wonder Woman.

Printed in Poland
by Amazon Fulfillment
Poland Sp. z o.o., Wrocław